CCNP Cisco Networking Academy Program: Remote Access Companion Guide

Cisco Systems, Inc.

Cisco Networking Academy Program

Mark McGregor

Cisco Press

201 West 103rd Street
Indianapolis, Indiana 46290 USA

**CCNP Cisco Networking Academy Program:
Remote Access Companion Guide**

Cisco Systems, Inc.

Cisco Networking Academy Program

Mark McGregor

Published by:
Cisco Press
201 West 103rd Street
Indianapolis, IN 46290 USA

Printed in the United States of America   2 3 4 5 6 7 8 9 0

Second Printing   July 2002

Library of Congress Cataloging-in-Publication Number: 2001087347

ISBN: 1-58713-028-9

Trademark Acknowledgments

All terms mentioned in this book that are known to be trademarks or service marks have been appropriately capitalized. Cisco Press or Cisco Systems, Inc. cannot attest to the accuracy of this information. Use of a term in this book should not be regarded as affecting the validity of any trademark or service mark.

Warning and Disclaimer

This book is designed to provide information about advanced Cisco router configuration skills. Every effort has been made to make this book as complete and as accurate as possible, but no warranty or fitness is implied.

The information is provided on an "as is" basis. The author, Cisco Press, and Cisco Systems, Inc. shall have neither liability nor responsibility to any person or entity with respect to any loss or damages arising from the information contained in this book or from the use of the discs or programs that may accompany it.

The opinions expressed in this book belong to the author and are not necessarily those of Cisco Systems, Inc.

Feedback Information

At Cisco Press, our goal is to create in-depth technical books of the highest quality and value. Each book is crafted with care and precision, undergoing rigorous development that involves the unique expertise of members from the professional technical community.

Readers' feedback is a natural continuation of this process. If you have any comments regarding how we could improve the quality of this book, or otherwise alter it to better suit your needs, you can contact us through e-mail at networkingacademy@ciscopress.com. Please make sure to include the book title and ISBN in your message.

We greatly appreciate your assistance.

Publisher	*John Wait*
Editor-in-Chief	*John Kane*
Executive Editor	*Carl Lindholm*
Cisco Systems Management	*Michael Hakkert*
	Tom Geitner
Acquisitions Editor	*Shannon Gross*
Production Manager	*Patrick Kanouse*
Development Editor	*Audrey Doyle*
Senior Project Editor	*Sheri Cain*
Copy Editor	*Cris Mattison*
Technical Editors	*Phil Benfield*
	Steven A. Crawford
	Rick Graziani
	Barbara Nolley
	Todd White
Editorial Assistant	*Sarah Kimberly*
Cover Designer	*Louisa Klucznik*
Compositor	*Scan Communications*
Indexer	*Larry Sweazy*

About the Author

Mark McGregor, CCNP, CCDP, CCAI, is the regional coordinator for the Cisco Networking Academy Program at Los Medanos College, in Pittsburg, California. He has taught in the Academy program since 1997, and he currently works for Cisco Systems World Wide Education on Academy-related projects. Mark holds a bachelor's degree in English from the University of California, Davis, and has authored several books for Cisco Press. As a public school instructor for more than eight years, he has enjoyed the opportunity to teach and learn from students of all ages and backgrounds. He lives in Antioch, California.

About the Technical Reviewers

Phil Benfield, CCNA, CCAI, has a bachelor of arts degree in human biology from Stanford University, and he studied network engineering at the University of California-Santa Cruz. He has been a Cisco Regional Academy instructor since 1998. Phil is currently a senior network engineer at the Santa Clara County Office of Education, where he is one of the people responsible for a WAN that provides Internet and business systems access to 33 school districts and 3 county offices, and for a LAN that provides network services to more than 500 users.

Steven A. Crawford has a BA from the University of New Brunswick, and has been certified as an MCP+I, MCSE, CCDA, CCNP, and A+ computer technician. Steven currently holds the position of certified subject expert in the Content Services department of the world's largest e-learning company, SmartForce.

Rick Graziani, CCAI CCNP, has worked in the networking and computer technology area for more than 16 years, and is currently a computer science/networking instructor at Cabrillo College in Aptos, California. He holds a BA degree from Loyola Marymount University and an MA degree in Computer Science and Systems Theory from California State University, Monterey Bay. He would like to thank his friends and colleagues Mark Boolootian, Dave Barnett, and Jim Warner for all their assistance over the years, and especially his wife Teri for all her support.

Barb Nolley is the president and principal consultant for BJ Consulting, Inc., a small consulting firm that specializes in networking education. Barb has developed training courses for Novell's Master CNE certification, as well as for Cisco Systems' Engineering Education group. Barb also likes to deliver high-energy presentations about networking technologies and recently started developing and teaching a CCNA track targeted at universities and colleges. Prior to starting her own company in 1993, Barb worked for Apple Computer, Tandem Computer, and Tymnet, where she held positions in everything from technical support to project management.

Todd White, CCIE #7072, taught for five years at Mainland High School in Daytona Beach, Florida. He also ran the Cisco Academy Training Center (CATC) for the southeast while there. In addition, he was the CCNP Development Lead for version 1 of the CCNP curriculum.

Dedication

For Jody

Acknowledgments

What you hold in your hands is the work of a talented team of professionals; I am truly fortunate to have worked on this book with such great people and friends.

First, I must thank my development editor, Audrey Doyle. With professionalism and care, she skillfully shepherded this project from the first page to the last. Thank you, Audrey.

This project's greatest reward, for me, was working with a first-rate technical review team. The best parts of the book came from this collection of experts, teachers, and friends: Phil Benfield, Steve Crawford, Rick Graziani, Barb Nolley, and Todd White. Todd deserves much of the credit for this book's existence, as he and Kevin Johnston laid the original groundwork for this effort.

The folks at Cisco Press continue to amaze me with their supportiveness and genuine hard work. In particular, I thank Shannon Gross for her faith, advice, and perpetual supply of patience. I owe thanks to the entire team at CP, the best in the business: Carl Lindholm, Sheri Cain, Patrick Kanouse, and Cris Mattison.

At Cisco Worldwide Education, the guidance and support lent by Vito Amato, Matthias Giessler, Kevin Johnston, Andrew Large, Joe Marti, and Dennis Frezzo made this project successful. We couldn't have done it without you. Of course, Wayne Lewis deserves special credit for amusing me with his back flips and unique perspective on everything.

I would also like to thank my colleagues closer to home. At Los Medanos College, Tim Forrester, Dave Behling, Lokesh Bali, and Al Schwartz tolerated my self-induced chaos, and helped a friend when it really mattered. Meanwhile, the LMC lab crew, led by Riz Minion and Cynthia Dugan, kept me afloat and reaffirmed that they run the best lab in the country.

Finally, I thank my friends and teammates at Cisco WWE: Eric Yu, Jody Mills, Nathan Slattengren, and Shane Grimes. You are the best.

Overview

Table of Contents

Introduction

CCNP Cisco Networking Academy Program: Remote Access Companion Guide is designed to supplement your study of remote access concepts in the Cisco Networking Academy Program. Through examples, technical notes, and review questions, this book seeks to provide intermediate-level students with the knowledge and skills needed to pass the CCNP remote access exam and to further their career opportunities in computer networking.

Concepts in this book include asynchronous dial-up, Integrated Services Digital Network (ISDN), dial-on-demand routing (DDR), dialer profiles, X.25, Frame Relay, on-demand routing (ODR), WAN backup, queuing, compression, Network Address Translation (NAT), and Authentication, Authorization, and Accounting (AAA).

As with all advanced networking topics, students will find that their studies are best complemented by hands-on lab exercises. To that end, Cisco Press offers the *CCNP Cisco Networking Academy Program: Remote Access Lab Companion,* which includes comprehensive lab exercises that can be completed individually or in small groups.

Who Should Read This Book

This book's primary audience is students who are seeking advanced Cisco router configuration skills and certification. In particular, this book is targeted toward students in the CCNP Cisco Networking Academy Program, which is offered in schools around the world. In the classroom, the book can serve as a supplement to the online curriculum.

A secondary audience for this book includes corporate training faculties and staff. For corporations and academic institutions to take advantage of the capabilities of networking, a large number of individuals must be trained in the design and operation of networks.

This Book's Organization

The book is organized into 12 chapters, 3 appendixes, and a glossary.

Chapter 1, "Remote Access," introduces you to common WAN and remote access technologies.

Chapter 2, "Modems and Asynchronous Connections," describes how to use plain old telephone service (POTS) to establish network connections and remotely manage Cisco routers.

Chapter 3, "PPP," provides an overview of Point-to-Point Protocol, including Link Control Protocol (LCP) options such as authentication, compression, and asynchronous callback.

Chapter 4, "ISDN and DDR," discusses ISDN standards, ISDN devices, and ISDN reference points. Configuring dial-on-demand routing is also explored in detail.

Chapter 5, "Dialer Profiles," compares legacy DDR configurations to newer configurations that use the dialer profile concept.

Chapter 6, " X.25," overviews packet switching and the X.25 protocols.

Chapter 7, "Frame Relay," describes Frame Relay operation and introduces Frame Relay topologies.

Chapter 8, "Shaping Frame Relay Traffic," examines advanced Frame Relay configurations, including traffic shaping and On-Demand Routing (ODR).

Chapter 9, "WAN Backup Connections," discusses ways to use POTS and ISDN to back up WAN lines.

Chapter 10, "Queuing and Compression," surveys Cisco IOS queuing and compression methods.

Chapter 11, "NAT," describes how to configure Network Address Translation (NAT) to conserve IP addresses for campus and remote connections.

Chapter 12, "AAA," introduces the Authentication, Authorization, and Accounting features in the Cisco IOS. These features are used to secure remote access connections.

Appendix A, "Answers to Review Questions," provides the answers to the review questions found at the end of each chapter.

Appendix B, "Emerging Remote Access Technologies," provides an overview of emerging remote access technologies such as digital subscriber line (DSL), cable modems, and wireless networking.

Appendix C, "Configuring Cisco 700 Series Routers," introduces the Cisco 700 Series ISDN routers and presents configuration guidelines for this series.

The glossary includes all the key terms used throughout the book.

This Book's Features

This book contains several elements that help you learn about advanced networking and Cisco IOS technologies:

- **Figures, examples, and tables**—This book contains figures, examples, and tables that help to explain concepts, commands, and procedural sequences. Figures illustrate network layouts and processes, and examples provide students with sample IOS configurations. In addition, tables provide command summaries and comparisons of features and characteristics.

- **Notes, warnings, and tech notes**—The margin notes highlight important information about a subject, and the warnings alert readers to configuration pitfalls. This book also includes tech notes, which offer background information on related topics and real-world implementation issues.

- **Chapter summaries**—At the end of each chapter is a summary of the concepts covered in the chapter, which provides a synopsis of the chapter and can serve as a study aid.

- **Review questions**—After the chapter summaries in each chapter are ten review questions that serve as an end-of-chapter assessment. The questions are designed to reinforce the concepts introduced in the chapter and to help students evaluate their understanding before moving on.

The conventions used to present command syntax in this book are the same conventions used in the *Cisco IOS Command Reference*, as follows:

- **Boldface** indicates commands and keywords that are entered literally as shown. In examples (not syntax), boldface indicates user input (for example, a **show** command).

- *Italics* indicates arguments for which you supply values.

- Square brackets ([ ]) indicate optional elements.

- Vertical bars (|) separate alternative, mutually exclusive elements.

- Braces and vertical bars within square brackets—for example, [x {y | z}]—indicate a required choice within an optional element. You do not need to enter what is in the brackets, but if you do, you have some required choices in the braces.

Objectives

After completing this chapter, you will be able to perform tasks related to the following:

- Remote access
- Deploying the appropriate WAN technology
- Identifying site requirements and solutions
- Selecting Cisco remote-access solutions

Chapter 1

Remote Access

Introduction

Over the last several years, Web-based applications, wireless devices, and virtual private networking have changed our expectations about computer networks. Today's corporate networks are accessible virtually anytime from anywhere—and many users expect some degree of access to their company's network while at home or on the road.

Corporate networks are typically built around one *central site* that houses key network resources. These resources include file servers, Web servers, and e-mail servers that deliver information and services to all users in a company. Such services are readily accessible to the central site's users through the local-area network (LAN). But how will users working remotely gain access to these resources?

As a networking professional, your job is to provide users with remote access to the network. Remote users might be working at *branch offices* or home offices, or they might even be on the road with a laptop or a handheld mobile device. Essentially, a remote user is any user who is not presently working at the company's central site.

Remote-access solutions come in all shapes and sizes. Each company's solution typically involves a combination of heterogeneous wide-area network (WAN) services. Most of these services are obtained from a service provider, such as a regional telecommunications company. Because the transmission facilities belong to a service provider, your role is primarily to select the appropriate service, not actually to design and maintain the WAN links themselves.

Types of available WAN services and their costs vary depending on geographical region and the provider. Unfortunately, real-world budgetary constraints and service availability are often the overriding selection criteria.

TECH NOTE: SERVICE PROVIDERS

The terms *service provider*, *telephone company*, and *carrier* are often used interchangeably when discussing remote access. These terms refer to the entities that own and operate telecommunications lines, switches, and other equipment. Because of the expense associated with building a comprehensive telecommunications infrastructure, customers almost always lease or purchase services from these entities rather than build the physical network themselves.

To better understand the role of the service provider, consider the task of building a telephone network. If you want to connect your telephone to five neighbors' telephones, you and your neighbors could run copper cables to each other's homes. In the end, you have five cables connected to your telephone, each leading to a different neighbor. But what would happen if you tried to scale that network to 5000 homes? Or 500,000 homes? Clearly, a more efficient system of cabling and connecting must be used.

In fact, the phone system uses a star configuration. Each telephone in an area connects to one single point, called the *central office* (CO). The line that connects a customer to the CO is called the *local loop*. The company that owns and operates the local loop connections and the CO is called the *local exchange carrier* (LEC). LECs serve a limited geographic area called a *local-access transport area* (LATA).

When you place a call to your next-door neighbor, the CO's switching equipment temporarily connects your local loop with your neighbor's local loop. This is the way calls are handled if both the caller and the called party are in the same LATA. Because it isn't feasible to connect everyone to a single CO, the telephone system has been designed as a hierarchy of switching systems. The COs are interconnected through long-distance carriers, or interexchange carriers (IXCs). Thus, telephone calls between different LATAs must go through an IXC. When a link between two sites crosses LATAs, even if the link covers only a short distance, the resulting charges can be much higher than the cost of leasing a link that covers a much greater distance, but stays within a single LATA.

Until recently, the telecommunications infrastructure in the United States was essentially owned and operated by a single monolithic company, AT&T (originally known as the Bell Telephone Company). But the 1984 breakup of AT&T and the subsequent 1996 Telecommunication Act have drastically changed the way telecommunications companies operate in the US. The 1984 breakup of AT&T resulted in the creation of regional Bell operating companies (RBOCs): Ameritech, BellSouth, Bell Atlantic, NYNEX, Pacific Telesis, Southwestern Bell, and US WEST. Since the breakup, several of these RBOCs merged together. As of this writing, SBC Communications now includes Ameritech, Pacific Telesis, and Southwestern Bell.

Initially, the RBOCs served as LECs, while other companies, such as AT&T, MCI, and Sprint, served as IXCs (long-distance carriers that linked the LECs together). The 1996 Telecommunication Act allowed AT&T to enter the LEC business, while LECs can now crossover and offer IXC-level service. In addition, new companies sprung up to compete with the already established local telephone business, providing their own network and switching. These companies are called *competitive local exchange carriers* (CLECs).

The result of these changes and growth is that many new players are in the US service provider business. You must thoroughly research the options available in your area before you select a service provider.

In order for you to implement the most appropriate solution, you must understand the advantages and disadvantages of the different types of WAN services. This chapter surveys the general types of WAN connections and provides criteria for you to use so that you can select the service—or blend of services—best suited to your organization's needs, budget, and geography. In addition, this chapter offers guidelines for selecting the best remote-access solution from the large number of available products.

WAN Connection Types

A WAN is a data communications network that covers a relatively broad geographic area, often using transmission facilities leased from service providers and telephone companies. As shown in Figure 1-1, WANs connect various sites at different geographic regions so users and devices at each site can exchange information.

Figure 1-1
A WAN allows a central site, branch office, telecommuters, and mobile users to connect across a broad geographic area.

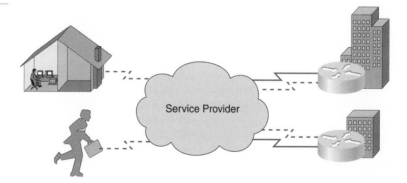

Service Provider

In this section, you examine synchronous and asynchronous communication and the three types of WAN services: dedicated lines, circuit-switched networks, and packet-switched networks.

Asynchronous Versus Synchronous Transmission

Before you look at the types of WAN services, you must review the two basic methods of data communications: *asynchronous transmission* and *synchronous transmission*. Typically, synchronous communications are more efficient, but dial-up asynchronous transmission is usually cheaper and more readily available.

Asynchronous means "without respect to time." In terms of data transmission, asynchronous means that no clock or timing source is needed to keep both the sender and the receiver synchronized. Without the benefit of a clock, the sender must signal the start and stop of each character so that the receiver knows when to expect data.

NOTE

ASCII uses a 7-bit value to represent a single character, allowing for 128 possibilities. An 8th bit is used in the extended ASCII character set, thus providing 256 characters.

Asynchronous transmission is often described as *character-framed* communication, because this method frames each character with a start and stop bit. Each character is typically a 7- or 8-bit value that can represent a number, a letter, a punctuation mark, and so on. Each character is preceded by a start bit and followed by a stop bit, or in some cases, two stop bits (see Figure 1-2). An additional bit can be added for parity error checking.

Figure 1-2
For asynchronous transmission, a 7-bit ASCII character is framed by a start bit and one or two stop bits.

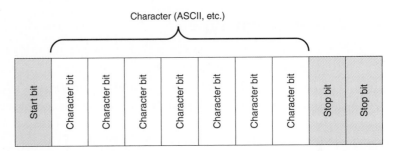

Synchronous means "with time." In terms of data transmission, synchronous means that a common timing signal is used between hosts. A clock signal is either embedded in the data stream or is sent separately to the interfaces.

If two hosts use a timing signal to synch up, start and stop bits for every 8-bit character value are not necessary. Instead, a large amount of data—hundreds or even thousands of bytes—can be preceded by synchronization bits. For example, in Ethernet, a field of synchronization bits precedes the data payload. This field of synchronization bits, called a *preamble*, forms a pattern of alternating 1s and 0s. The receiver uses this pattern to synchronize with the sender.

Service providers offer a variety of synchronous and asynchronous WAN services. These services can be grouped into three categories depending on their connection type. Each connection type offers distinct advantages and disadvantages. As shown in Figure 1-3, the three connection types are the following:

- Dedicated connectivity
- Circuit-switched networks
- Packet-switched networks

Figure 1-3
The three different types of WAN services are dedicated, circuit-switched, and packet-switched.

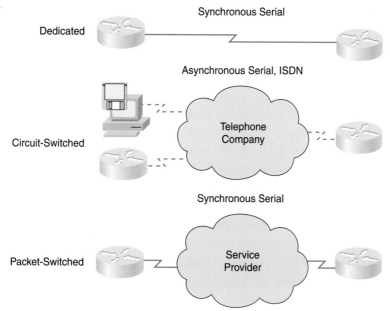

> **NOTE**
>
> Because service providers can maintain complex WAN infrastructures made up of various types of switching equipment and media, their networks are represented as a cloud in this book's figures. Assume that the traffic that enters the cloud will exit the cloud in a predictable fashion.

Dedicated Connections

A dedicated connection is a continuously available point-to-point link between two sites. Dedicated connections typically carry high-speed transmissions. Because of the expense associated with building and maintaining transmission facilities, dedicated connections are almost always leased from the telephone company or some other carrier network. Thus, a dedicated connection is often referred to as a *leased line*.

A point-to-point dedicated link provides a single, pre-established WAN path from the customer premises, through a carrier network, to a remote network. A dedicated line is not actually a line at all. Dedicated lines are switched circuits that establish a fixed path through the carrier network. Thus, leased lines are circuits that are reserved full-time by the carrier for the private use of the customer. The private nature of a dedicated line allows an organization to maximize its control over the WAN connection.

Leased lines also offer high speeds of up to 45 Mbps. Leased lines are ideal for high-volume environments with steady-rate traffic patterns. However, because the line is not shared, they tend to be more costly. You must pay for the line whether or not you are

> **NOTE**
>
> Today, virtually all leased lines are digital.

sending traffic over it. Some services, such as *T1*, include a fixed fee for local-loop access for both locations and a distance fee for linking those two locations.

If your organization's network must support a constant flow of mission-critical data, such as e-commerce or financial transactions, a high-speed leased line might best suit your needs.

Dedicated leased lines typically require synchronous serial connections. Each leased line connects to a synchronous serial port on the router through a *channel service unit/data service unit (CSU/DSU)*, as shown in Figure 1-4. Thus, each connection requires a router port and a CSU/DSU, in addition to the actual circuit from the service provider. As you can see, the cost of maintaining multiple leased lines can add up quickly. For this reason, most companies find a fully meshed WAN—a WAN in which every site maintains a connection to every other site—too costly to build using only dedicated lines.

Figure 1-4
Dedicated links are established by using the synchronous serial ports of the routers.

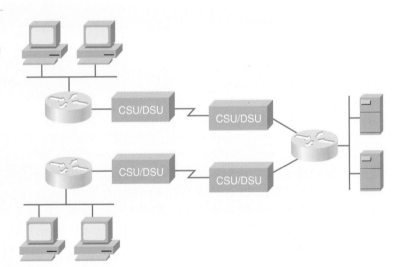

A CSU/DSU is classified as a *data communications equipment (DCE)* device. A DCE adapts the physical interface on a *data terminal equipment (DTE)* device to the signaling used by the carrier network. A router is an example of a DTE device.

The CSU/DSU provides signal timing for communication and is used for interfacing with the digital transmission facility. Essentially, the CSU/DSU is used by a router to connect to a digital line in much the same way that a PC uses a modem to connect to an analog line.

Typical connections on a dedicated network operate at the following speeds:

- 56 Kbps
- 64 Kbps

NOTE

The ITU expands the acronym DCE as data circuit-terminating equipment. Both data communications equipment and data circuit-terminating equipment refer to the same thing.

- T1 (1.544 Mbps) US standard
- E1 (2.048 Mbps) European standard
- E3 (34.064 Mbps) European standard
- T3 (44.736 Mbps) US standard

NOTE

CSU/DSUs, which
are sometimes
called DSU/CSUs,
can also be built
into a router as
internal modules.

Typically, a router's synchronous serial port connects to a DCE (such as a CSU/DSU) using one of the following standards:

- EIA/TIA-232 (RS-232)
- EIA/TIA-449
- V.35
- X.21
- EIA-530

Throughout this book, I focus on the EIA/TIA-232 and V.35 standards. When connecting a DTE (such as a router) to an analog modem, you will typically use EIA/TIA-232 compliant cabling and interfaces. First released over 30 years ago as RS-232, the EIA/TIA-232 standard is common. However, it provides relatively low transmission speeds (typically less than 64 Kbps), and is not appropriate for high-capacity dedicated lines.

When connecting a Cisco router to a T1/E1 or fractional T1/E1 via a CSU/DSU, you must use V.35 cabling and interfaces, which are capable of much higher throughput (over 2 Mbps).

Circuit-Switched Connections

In a circuit-switched network, a dedicated physical circuit is temporarily established for each communication session. Switched circuits are established by an initial setup signal. This call setup process determines the caller's ID, the destination's ID, and the connection type. A teardown signal brings the circuit down when transmission is complete.

Plain old telephone service (POTS) is the most common circuit-switched technology. With telephone service, the circuit doesn't exist until you place a call, but after the temporary circuit is built, it is fully dedicated to your call. Although circuit switching is not as efficient as other WAN services, it is extremely common and relatively reliable.

Circuit-switched connections provide mobile and home users with access to the central site or to an Internet service provider (ISP), as shown in Figure 1-5. Corporate networks typically use circuit-switched connections as backup links, or as primary links for branch offices that exchange low-volume or periodic traffic. In such cases, a router must route traffic over the switched circuit.

Figure 1-5
Low cost circuit-
switched connec-
tions are most com-
mon among home
and mobile users.

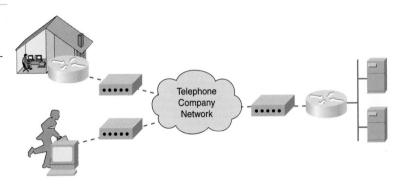

Anyone who pays a long-distance phone bill knows that circuit-switched connections can be costly if left continuously established. For this reason, routers connected to circuit-switched networks are configured to operate in a specialized way, called *dial-on-demand routing (DDR)*. A router configured for DDR only places a call when it detects traffic defined by a network administrator as "interesting." DDR and "interesting" traffic are discussed in Chapter 2, "Modems and Asynchronous Connections."

Typical circuit-switched connections include the following:

- Asynchronous serial (POTS)
- ISDN Basic Rate Interface (BRI)
- ISDN Primary Rate Interface (PRI)

Asynchronous Serial Connections

Asynchronous serial connections offer inexpensive WAN service through the existing telephone network. In order for digital devices, such as computers and routers, to use analog telephone lines, modems are required at each end of the connection. Modems convert digital data signals to analog signals that can be transported over the telephone company's local loops asynchronously. Although this is convenient, modems have one overwhelming drawback: They do not provide high throughput. Today's modems provide transmission speeds of only 56 Kbps or less.

Because modems can be used with virtually any phone line, mobile and home users often rely on asynchronous serial connections to connect to a corporate network or ISP. An end user can easily start and teardown a call by using software that controls the modem.

Routers can also use asynchronous serial connections to route traffic using DDR. Because modems do not support high transmission speeds, asynchronous serial connections are typically used as backup links or for load sharing.

Some routers are designed with dozens of asynchronous lines to support a large number of dial-in users. Routers that act as concentration points for dial-in and dial-out calls are called *access servers*. Throughout this book, the term access server refers to a router with at least one dial-up interface.

To place or receive an asynchronous serial call, a router must have at least one asynchronous serial interface, such as the auxiliary (AUX) port, which connects to a modem.

ISDN Connections

Integrated Services Digital Network (ISDN) connections are typically synchronous dial-up connections that provide WAN access when needed, rather than providing a permanent link. ISDN offers more bandwidth than asynchronous dial-up connections; it's intended to carry data, voice, and other traffic across a digital telephone network. ISDN is commonly used with DDR to provide remote access for small office/home office (SOHO) applications, backup links, and load sharing.

ISDN offers two levels of service: BRI and PRI. With BRI, two channels exist, called Bearer (B) channels, which are designed to carry data. A third channel, called the Delta (D) channel, sends call set-up and teardown signals. When both B channels are used together to send data, ISDN BRI yields 128 Kbps (more than twice the top speed of POTS).

With PRI, 23 B channels on T1 are used in North America and Japan. Thirty B channels on E1 are used in Europe and other parts of the world. PRI employs a single D channel as well.

Packet-Switched Networks

Unlike leased lines and circuit-switched connections, packet switching does not rely on a dedicated, point-to-point connection through the carrier network. Instead, data packets are routed across the carrier network based on addressing contained in the packet or frame header. This means that packet-switched WAN facilities can be shared (see Figure 1-6), which allows service providers to support multiple customers over the same physical lines and switches. Typically, customers connect to the packet-switched network through a leased line, such as a T1 or fractional T1.

In a packet-switched network, the provider configures its switching equipment to create *virtual circuits (VCs)* that supply end-to-end connectivity. Frame Relay is the most common packet-switched WAN service in the United States, although the older X.25 remains a prominent packet-switching technology worldwide.

NOTE

A detailed discussion of ISDN can be found in Chapter 4, "ISDN and DDR."

Figure 1-6
Packet-switched networks work by creating virtual circuits (VCs) within the provider's network, which is shared among customers.

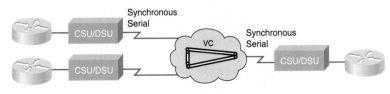

Packet-switched networks offer an administrator less control than a point-to-point connection. However, the cost of a packet-switched VC is generally less than that of a leased line because the WAN facilities are shared. VCs can be permanent, or they can be built on demand.

A Frame Relay VC offers speeds of up to T1, or even T3, making this packet-switched technology a high-speed, cost-effective alternative to leased lines. Moreover, a single synchronous serial connection can support several logical VCs in a point-to-multipoint configuration (see Figure 1-7). This process of combining multiple data conversations into a single physical line is called *multiplexing*. Multiplexing in a packet-switched network is made possible because a DTE (usually a router) encapsulates the packet with addressing information. The provider's switches use the addressing to determine how and where to deliver a specific packet. In the case of Frame Relay, these addresses are data-link connection identifiers (DLCIs). The ability to multiplex means that a single router port and CSU/DSU can support dozens of VCs, each leading to a different site. Thus, packet-switching makes a full- or partial-mesh topology relatively affordable.

Figure 1-7
Packet-switching technologies, such as Frame Relay, allow multiple logical connections (VCs) using a single physical interface.

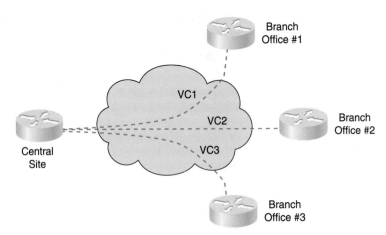

Frame Relay is a popular WAN service for providing high-speed WAN connections to branch offices and other remote sites. However, Frame Relay does not offer the degree of reliability, flexibility, and security afforded by dedicated lines. Despite Frame Relay's lower cost and multipoint capability, dedicated lines are the preferred WAN service for mission-critical traffic and continuous, high-volume exchanges.

Frame Relay is discussed thoroughly in Chapter 7, "Frame Relay," and Chapter 8, "Shaping Frame Relay Traffic."

Asynchronous Transfer Mode (ATM) is cell-switched technology that boasts incredibly high throughput. Cell switching is a kind of packet switching that transports data in fixed-length cells. All ATM cells are the same length, which is 53 bytes. An ATM device doesn't have to waste time and resources figuring out how long each individual frame is. Thus, fixed-length cells allow processing to occur in hardware, instead of software. Hardware-based processing results in more efficient and faster operation. ATM typically operates over Synchronous Optical Network (SONET), which includes the following:

- OC-3 (155 Mbps)
- OC-12 (622 Mbps)
- OC-48 (2.4 Gbps)

ATM's speed makes it the most attractive WAN technology that we have surveyed so far. ATM can also serve as a LAN technology. Many service providers rely on ATM at the core of their networks.

WAN Encapsulation Protocols

Routers encapsulate packets with a Layer 2 frame before sending them across a WAN link. Although several common WAN encapsulations exist, most have similar anatomies. This is because the most common WAN encapsulations are derived from High-Level Data Link Control (HDLC) and its antecedent, Synchronous Data Link Control (SDLC). Despite their similar structures, each data link protocol specifies its own specific type of frame, which is incompatible with other types. Figure 1-8 shows which common data link protocols are used with each of the three WAN connection types.

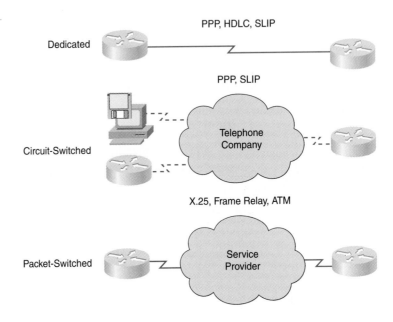

Figure 1-8
The data link protocol that's used depends in part on what type of WAN connection is deployed.

By default, serial interfaces on a Cisco router are set to encapsulate packets using HDLC. You must manually configure the interface for any other type of encapsulation. The choice of encapsulation protocol depends on the WAN technology and the communicating equipment that you are using. Common WAN protocols include the following:

- **Point-to-Point Protocol (PPP)**—PPP is a standards-based protocol for router-to-router and host-to-network connections over synchronous and asynchronous circuits.

- **Serial Line Internet Protocol (SLIP)**—SLIP is the forerunner to PPP, and is used for point-to-point serial connections using TCP/IP.

- **HDLC**—HDLC implementations are proprietary, so Cisco's HDLC is typically used only when connecting two Cisco devices. When connecting routers from different vendors, PPP (which is standards-based) is used instead.

- **X.25/LAPB**—X.25 is an ITU-T standard that defines the way connections between DTE and DCE devices are maintained for remote terminal access and computer communications in public data networks. X.25 provides extensive error-detection and windowing features because it was designed to operate over error-prone analog copper circuits.

- **Frame Relay**—Frame Relay is a high-performance, packet-switched WAN protocol that can be used over a variety of network interfaces. Frame Relay is streamlined to operate over highly reliable digital transmission facilities.
- **ATM**—ATM is an international standard for cell relay, in which multiple service types (such as voice, video, or data) are conveyed in fixed-length cells. ATM is designed to take advantage of high-speed transmission media such as SONET.

NOTE

PPP, X.25, and Frame Relay encapsulations are discussed in Chapter 3, "PPP," Chapter 6, "X.25," and Chapter 7, respectively.

Selecting Appropriate WAN Technologies

Each WAN connection type has advantages and disadvantages. For example, using a dial-up asynchronous connection offers only limited bandwidth, but a user can call into the office from anywhere over the existing telephone network. In this case, throughput is sacrificed for convenience. This section examines the factors that you must consider when you select a WAN service.

Selecting the Appropriate WAN Service

When selecting a WAN connection type, there are many factors to consider. Chief among them are availability, bandwidth, and cost. Obviously, if a particular service is not available in your geographical area, then you can't choose that service. Once you determine which services are available, then bandwidth and cost typically become the overriding factors. Table 1-1 compares applications for various types of WAN connections.

Table 1-1   WAN Connections Summary

Connection Type	Characteristics
Leased lines	High speed, high cost, dedicated connectivity. Appropriate for mission-critical applications and in situations where use is high and constant.
Asynchronous dial-up	Offers limited bandwidth over ordinary telephone lines, but is highly available. Appropriate for home users and mobile users who need temporary connectivity for low-bandwidth applications, such as e-mail.
ISDN	ISDN BRI offers a speed of 128 Kbps when both B channels are aggregated. Appropriate for telecommuters and small offices. Also used as a backup to other WAN connections.
X.25	An older packet-switched technology that features extensive reliability features that contribute to X.25's overhead. Typically appropriate only where more modern services, such as Frame Relay, are not available.

continues

Table 1-1   WAN Connections Summary (Continued)

Connection Type	Characteristics
Frame Relay	Generally offers speed at T1 (1.544 Mbps) or less over shared WAN facilities. Permanent Virtual Circuits (PVCs) make Frame Relay appropriate for remote offices that require constant connectivity for bursty, intermittent traffic.
ATM	High-cost cell-switching technology that offers exceptionally high throughput. As a WAN technology, appropriate for service providers and bandwidth-intensive applications.

Although every home user would like a T1 line run to their house, and every administrator would like to run an OC-12 to all their remote offices, the cost of deploying such services so liberally would be ridiculous. Clearly, as a networking professional, you must carefully gauge which connections require high-cost, high-throughput links, and then spend accordingly. WAN usage costs are typically 80 percent of a company's entire Information Services budget. When possible, shop around for WAN services. If more than one provider offers service in your area, you might be able to purchase services at competitive prices.

TECH NOTE: WIRELESS LOCAL LOOP

An emerging technology, wireless communications, promises to radically change the telecommunications industry. Today, wireless local loop (WWL) can be deployed in place of a traditional copper local loop. This allows a customer to connect to the PSTN using a high-frequency radio link.

In many parts of the world, running fiber-optic or copper cable is extremely problematic because it might require special drilling techniques or explicit "right-of-way" permissions from local governments. WLL, also called fixed-radio access (FRA), solves such problems. In fact, WLL might spur increased competition among service providers, who would no longer need an established network of landlines.

Check with your provider to see if wireless services are available in your area.

You must consider other important factors when choosing a WAN service, including ease of management, quality of service (QoS), and reliability. You will probably find that leased lines are easier to manage and configure than packet-switched connections. In terms of QoS, some applications, such as Voice over IP (VoIP), require guaranteed bandwidth, minimal delay, and high reliability, which can make anything short of a leased line problematic.

Identifying Site Requirements and Solutions

When selecting WAN services, a networking professional must evaluate the needs of each site within a company. Individual worksites within a company can be broadly categorized as one of the following: a central site, a branch office, or a *telecommuter site*.

The term *telecommuter site* applies to both mobile users and SOHO locations. In this section, these categorizations are applied to an example network (shown in Figure 1-9).

Figure 1-9
A worksite within a company can be categorized as a central site, branch office, or telecommuter site.

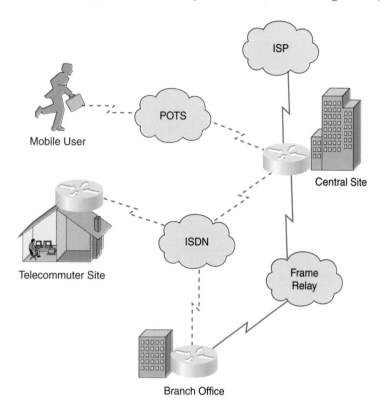

The central site is the focal point of a company's network. Typically, all remote sites and users must connect to the central site to access information, either intermittently or continuously. Because many users access this site in a variety of ways, a central site's routers should have a modular design so that interface modules can be added (or swapped out) as needed. The chassis of a modular router allows you to install the interfaces needed to support virtually any media type. Figure 1-10 illustrates the slots on a modular router, the Cisco 3660.

If you look at the example network (refer to Figure 1-9), the central site's router must accommodate circuit-switched connections, packet-switched connections, and at least one dedicated line to the ISP.

The technologies and features used to connect company campuses over a WAN are developed to optimize the WAN bandwidth, minimize the cost, and maximize the effective service to end users.

Figure 1-10
A modular router, the Cisco 3660 offers six slots that can accept over 70 different kinds of interface modules.

A branch office, commonly referred to as a remote site, typically maintains at least one WAN connection to the central site, and might have several links to other remote sites. Generally, branch-office networks support fewer users than the central site, and therefore, require less bandwidth.

Because remote-site traffic can be sporadic, or bursty, you must carefully determine whether it is more cost-effective to offer a permanent or dial-up solution. The example network employs both (refer to Figure 1-9): a Frame Relay connection as a primary link and an ISDN connection as a backup.

Telecommuters might also require access to the branch office through various connection types. Therefore, the branch-office routers need to have the capability to support a variety of WAN connections. Typical WAN solutions for connecting the remote site to the central site include the following:

- Leased lines
- Frame Relay
- X.25
- ISDN
- DSL (digital subscriber line)—DSL enables delivery of high-speed data, voice, and multimedia over conventional telephone wires. In order for a remote site to connect to the corporate network without traversing the public Internet, DSL typically requires ATM at the central site.
- Wireless
- Virtual Private Network (VPN)—See the sidebar, "Tech Note: Virtual Private Networks."

Over the past decade, the improvement of WAN technologies, notably DSL and cable modems, has allowed many employees to do their jobs remotely. As a result, the number of telecommuters and small offices has increased.

TECH NOTE: VIRTUAL PRIVATE NETWORKS

A *Virtual Private Network* (VPN) is a method of implementing a private data network over the public Internet. In effect, VPN presents an affordable alternative to companies that want to extend their corporate network to several remote sites and mobile users. Rather than lease private lines for each site, a company can deploy VPN so that users and sites connect to the public Internet to access the corporate network.

Privacy over the public backbone can be achieved by using a tunneling protocol, such as Point-to-Point Tunneling Protocol (PPTP) and encryption. Data is encrypted before traversing the VPN over the public network, and then decrypted at the receiving host. Typically, a router or firewall at each location handles the encryption. The Cisco IOS offers comprehensive VPN support.

VPN is a powerful solution for home and mobile users. With an ordinary analog dial-up connection and VPN client software, users can securely connect to their corporate network as a remote node, and access services as if they were in the office. The advent of residential broadband means that home users can enjoy a high-speed VPN connection using cable or DSL. Although it's possible to build a private DSL (or even cable) network, it's more cost-effective to let home users subscribe to a local ISP, and then use VPN over cable or DSL.

ISPs offer VPN services to their corporate customers as well. An ISP can build a private network for the customer over shared WAN facilities. This private network is created using a technology such as X.25, Frame Relay, ATM, or Multiprotocol Label Switching (MPLS). VPNs configured and managed by a service provider are sometimes called ISP-based private networks.

As with the corporate and branch offices, you must select the telecommuter site's WAN solution by weighing cost and bandwidth requirements.

An asynchronous dial-up solution using the existing telephone network and an analog modem is often the solution for telecommuters because it is easy to set up and the telephone facilities are already installed. As usage and bandwidth requirements increase, other remote-access technologies must be considered.

Because mobile users must connect from many different locations, an asynchronous dial-up connection might be the only remote-access solution that is consistently available. Employees on the road can use their PCs with modems and the existing telephone network to connect to the company.

Typical WAN connections employed at telecommuter sites include the following:

- Asynchronous dial-up
- ISDN BRI

- Cable modems
- DSL
- Wireless and satellite
- VPN

Implementing WAN Solutions

Cisco offers access servers, routers, and other equipment that allow connection to various WAN services. Table 1-2 lists the key features and WAN options for each series of Cisco router.

Table 1-2   Common Cisco Router Platforms

Platform	Remote Access Options
700 series	Designed for telecommuters, the Cisco 700 router is a multiprotocol ISDN router. It can connect to any network that supports ISDN and IP/IPX routing. This series router does not run the standard Cisco IOS.
800 series	Designed for small offices and corporate telecommuters. Models support ISDN, DSL, and serial connections. Unlike the 700 series, 800 series routers run the Cisco IOS.
1000 series	Intended for remote-office networking using the Cisco IOS. Models support ISDN and serial connections.
1600 series	Similar to the Cisco 1000 series routers, but they have a slot that accepts a WAN interface card (WIC).
1700 series	Desktop router for small- and medium-sized businesses, and for small branch offices that want to deploy Internet/intranet access or VPNs. The Cisco 1720 access router has two modular WAN slots and an autosensing 10/100-Mbps Fast Ethernet LAN port to provide flexibility for growth.
2500 series	Designed for branch-office and remote-site environments. These routers are typically of a fixed configuration, with at least two of the following interfaces: Ethernet, Token Ring, synchronous serial, asynchronous serial, and ISDN BRI.
2600 series	Replaces the 2500 series as Cisco's flagship access router and features single or dual fixed LAN interfaces (10/100 Mbps). A network module slot and two WIC slots are available for WAN connections.
3600 series	Replaces the 4000 series as Cisco's flagship distribution router, and offers a modular solution for dialup and permanent connectivity over asynchronous, synchronous, and ISDN lines. Up to six network module slots are available for LAN and WAN requirements.
4000 series	High-performance modular central-site routers with support for a wide range of LAN and WAN technologies. The Cisco 4500 and 4700 are intended for large regional offices that do not require the density of the Cisco 7200 series. Their modular design allows easy reconfiguration as needs change.

Table 1-2   Common Cisco Router Platforms (Continued)

Platform	Remote Access Options
AS5000 series access servers	Integrate the functions of standalone CSUs, channel banks, modems, communication servers, switches, and routers in a single chassis. The AS5000 series contains synchronous serial, digital ISDN, and asynchronous modem access server functionality, which are ideal for mixed-media requirements.
7200 series	High-performance, modular central-site routers that support a variety of LAN and WAN technologies. The Cisco 7200 is designed for large regional offices that require high-density solutions.

As you can see from Table 1-2, you can choose from many models of routers. The router that you select for your WAN connection must offer the interfaces that will support your WAN service, such as the following:

- **Asynchronous serial**—Supports asynchronous dial-up connections using a modem.

- **Synchronous serial**—Supports leased lines, Frame Relay, and X.25.

- **High-speed serial interface (HSSI)**—Supports high-speed serial lines, such as T3.

- **BRI**—Supports ISDN BRI connections.

- **T1 or E1**—Supports connections such as leased lines, dialup, ISDN PRI, and Frame Relay.

- **DSL**—Supports Asymmetric Digital Subscriber Line (ADSL), Symmetric DSL (SDSL), or ISDN DSL (IDSL) connections.

- **ATM**—Supports ATM connections.

Some routers, such as the 2501, offer fixed interface configurations. A fixed configuration is one that cannot be changed or upgraded. The advantage of a fixed interface configuration is that you do not have to buy and install WAN or LAN interface modules. The number and type of interfaces are predetermined for a specific model of router.

A fixed-configuration router might be appropriate for a small remote office or telecommuter. In such cases, the flexibility afforded by a modular design might not be worth the additional expense and complexity. Instead, a fixed-configuration router might offer the most affordable and simplest WAN solution for the small office.

Unlike a fixed configuration router, a modular router allows you to add, remove, and swap out interfaces to meet the needs of a growing network. Modular routers and access servers are built with one or more slots that allow you to customize the interface configuration.

If you have a modular router, you can choose some or all of the interfaces on the router by installing various feature cards, network modules, or WAN interfaces. Although modular routers require that you purchase each interface card separately, they are more scalable than their fixed-configuration counterparts. For that reason, modular routers are typically installed at large remote sites, and should always be used at the central site. In the long run, it's cheaper to add new interface modules rather than to replace an entire router.

Figure 1-11 presents three routers in a company's network: one at the central site, one at the branch office, and one at a telecommuter site. Each of these sites has different requirements in terms of bandwidth and availability. For example, the central site requires a permanent high-speed connection to the Internet, while the telecommuter site merely requires a switched connection for intermittent, low-speed access to the rest of the network.

Figure 1-11
The central site, branch office, and telecommuter site typically require different router solutions.

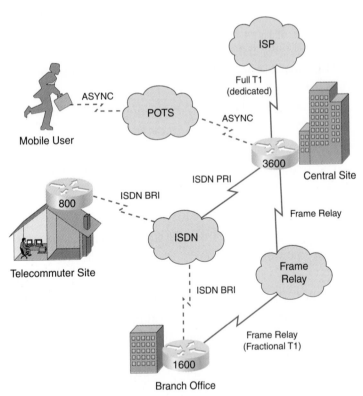

The following sections examine the specific requirements of each of the three sites in this example, and suggest solutions appropriate to each.

Central-Site Solutions

In this example network, the central-site router must have the following interfaces (refer to Figure 1-11):

- ISDN PRI interface
- Asynchronous serial interface and modem for asynchronous calls
- Serial interface for Frame Relay connections
- Serial interface for leased line to the ISP
- Ethernet interface to access resources on the central-site LAN (not shown in Figure 1-11)

To meet the requirements of a central site, select a modular router that allows for growth. Remember that a fixed-interface router will not allow the central site to grow easily. Depending on the amount of growth you are expecting, select a modular router from one of the following series:

- **Cisco 3600 series**—The Cisco 3600 series modular routers can provide dial access, routing, and LAN-to-LAN services and multiservice integration of voice, video, and data in the same device. The 3600 series replaces the legacy 4000 series routers. Like the newer 3600 series, Cisco 4000 series routers are modular and can support many variations of protocols, line speeds, and transmission media.

- **Cisco AS5x00 series**—The Cisco AS5x00 series access servers combine the functions of an access server, a router, and analog and digital modems in one chassis (see Figure 1-12). They provide a high level of scalability, and multiprotocol capabilities for both ISPs and enterprises.

- **Cisco 7200 series**—The Cisco 7200 series routers allow for maximum scalability and flexibility, by combining high-performance hardware and software with a modular design (see Figure 1-13). The 7200 series supports any combination of Ethernet, Fast Ethernet, Token Ring, Fiber Distributed Digital Interface (FDDI), ATM, serial, ISDN, and HSSI interfaces.

NOTE

You can obtain the latest product information at www.cisco.com.

For the central site in the example network, the 3600 series router makes the most sense. For now, you only need to support five interfaces. The 3600 series provides the necessary scalability and support of Frame Relay, ISDN, and asynchronous dial-up through specialized interface modules.

The AS5x00 series offers a high-density dial-up solution. But because the central site does not require a large number of dial-up interfaces, an AS5x00 solution is overkill

Figure 1-12
The Cisco AS 5800
series access server
provides a highly
scalable remote-
access solution.

Figure 1-13
The Cisco 7000,
7200, and 7500
series routers
deliver high-end,
scalable routing.

and not cost-effective. Likewise, a 7200 series router probably offers more expandability and horsepower than necessary for so few connections. The large chassis of this series provides more scalability than a 3600 series router, but unless the company is planning on significant short-term growth, the 7200 proves to be too costly a solution.

Of the three product series, the Cisco 3600 series offers the right combination of scalability and affordability (see Figure 1-14). With over 70 modular interface options, the

3600 series is often called the Swiss-Army knife of routers because of its versatility. The 3600 series includes the following models:

- **3660**—Has six network module slots
- **3640**—Has four network module slots
- **3620**—Has two slots

Figure 1-14
The 3600 series includes the 3620 (top), 3640 (middle), and 3660 (bottom).

An ideal solution for this example would be the 3640 router. The 3620 might not provide enough interfaces as the network grows, and, although the 3660 would provide maximum scalability, it will cost more. To serve the example network, the 3640 can be equipped with the following interface cards:

- **1-Ethernet 2-WAN card slot network module**—Supports a single Ethernet connection and two WAN connections.
- **1-port CT1/PRI-CSU network module**—Provides the PRI interface.
- **Digital modem network module**—Internal modem used in conjunction with the PRI for dial-in connections. One digital modem network module can support up to 30 MICA modems.

Optionally, you can include a 4-port serial WAN network module, which is used for Frame Relay and, if needed, to connect to an external modem. However, budgetary constraints might dictate the fourth slot remain open for future expansion.

Branch-Office Solutions

In contrast to the central-site solution, the branch-office router needs only one primary WAN connection and, in this case, a second WAN interface for dial backup. Thus, the branch router must have the following interfaces:

- Serial interface for Frame Relay connections
- BRI interface for ISDN BRI

To meet the requirements of a branch office, you can choose either a modular router or a fixed-configuration router. Unless you determine that the remote office will act as a WAN hub for smaller offices (in which case, a 3600 series router might be needed), you will probably select an access router from one of the following series:

- **Cisco 1600 Series**—The Cisco 1600 series routers are designed to connect small offices with Ethernet LANs to the public Internet, and to a company's internal intranet or corporate LAN through several WAN connections such as ISDN, asynchronous serial, and synchronous serial (see Figure 1-15). The Cisco 1601 R - 1604 R models have an Ethernet port, a built-in WAN port, and a slot for an optional second WAN port. The 1605 R router has two Ethernet ports and one WAN slot.

- **Cisco 1700 Series**—The Cisco 1700 router is a small, modular desktop router that links small- to medium-sized remote Ethernet and FastEthernet LANs over one to four WAN connections to regional and central offices.

- **Cisco 2500 Series**—The Cisco 2500 series routers provide a variety of models that are designed for branch-office and remote-site environments. These routers are typically fixed-configuration with at least two of the following interfaces: Ethernet, Token Ring, synchronous serial, and ISDN BRI.

- **Cisco 2600 Series**—The Cisco 2600 series of modular routers features single or dual fixed LAN interfaces, a network module slot, two Cisco WIC slots, and a new Advanced Integration Module (AIM) slot (see Figure 1-16). LAN support includes 10/100 Mbps autosensing Ethernet and Token Ring. The WICs support a variety of serial, ISDN BRI, and integrated CSU/DSU options for primary and backup WAN connectivity. The AIM slot supports the integration of advanced services, such as hardware-assisted data compression and data encryption for optimizing the 2600 series for VPNs.

A 1600 series router with the appropriate WAN interface card might meet the immediate WAN requirements of the branch office shown in Figure 1-11. However, a more flexible solution, such as the 1700 series or 2600 series router, might be needed if the company plans to implement VoIP, or allow telecommuters to dial in to the branch office. Also, the 1600 series routers do not come with a FastEthernet interface, while the 1700 and 2600 series routers do.

Figure 1-15
Branch-office routing solutions include the 1600 series router, which features a WIC slot.

NOTE

The Cisco 2600 series shares modular interfaces with the Cisco 1600, 1700, and 3600 series.

Figure 1-16
The modular design of the 2600 series router makes it a flexible branch-office solution.

If the company has no immediate plans to offer expanded service, and a FastEthernet connection is not necessary, a 1600 series router will make the most cost-effective solution. The 1600 series includes the following:

- The 1601 (one Ethernet, one serial, one WIC slot)
- The 1602 (one Ethernet, one serial with integrated 56-Kbps DSU/CSU, one WIC slot)
- The 1603 (one Ethernet, one ISDN BRI (S/T interface), one WIC slot)
- The 1604 (one Ethernet, one ISDN BRI with integrated NT1 (U interface), one S-bus port for ISDN phones, one WIC slot)
- The 1605 (two Ethernet slots, one WIC slot)

In this case, the 1603 or 1604 routers would meet the branch site's ISDN BRI requirement and have a WAN slot for a serial interface that can be used for Frame Relay.

Telecommuter-Site Solutions

Figure 1-11 also shows one telecommuter site and a mobile user. Mobile users do not require a router; they can dial up to the central site's access server (3640 router) and connect to the corporate network using a modem. But the telecommuter working in a home office should have an ISDN BRI connection to the branch office or central site. Thus, the telecommuter WAN solution must include the following interfaces:

- BRI interface for ISDN BRI
- Ethernet LAN interface

When selecting routers for a telecommuter site, cost is typically the primary concern, especially because only minimal flexibility and scalability are required. In this case, you can select a telecommuter-site solution from the following router families:

- **Cisco 700 series (760 or 770)**—The Cisco 700M family of products are low-cost, multiprotocol ISDN access routers. These devices provide small professional offices, home offices, and telecommuters with high-speed remote access to enterprise networks and to the Internet (see Figure 1-17). However, the 700 series does not support the Cisco IOS.

- **Cisco 800 series**—The Cisco 800 series router is the entry-level platform that, unlike the 700 series, uses Cisco IOS technology. The fixed-configuration 800 series is designed to connect a small Ethernet LAN to a corporate network or ISP. Various models include support for DSL, ISDN, and serial connections. (See Figure 1-18.)

- **Cisco 1000 series**—The Cisco 1000 series routers are easy-to-install, inexpensive, multiprotocol access products that are designed for small offices. This IOS-based series currently includes three models: the 1003 (1 Ethernet port, 1 ISDN BRI S/T interface), the 1004 (1 Ethernet port, 1 ISDN BRI U interface), and the 1005 (1 Ethernet port, 1 serial port).

Figure 1-17
The 700 series offers an ISDN BRI solution for SOHOs.

Figure 1-18
The 800 series router uses the Cisco IOS to provide ISDN, synchronous serial, or DSL connectivity.

Models from each of these router families can provide the ISDN connection required by the telecommuter site. The Cisco 800 series might make the best choice for this telecommuter site because it is the most affordable series that supports ISDN, and it runs the feature-rich Cisco IOS.

Summary

In this chapter, you learned about WAN connections and how to determine the requirements of a central site, a branch office, and a telecommuter site. You also learned how to select Cisco products to suit the specific needs of each site. In the rest of the book, you learn how to configure the Cisco IOS and cable a Cisco router to support the WAN technologies surveyed here.

Review Questions

Use the following review questions to test your understanding of the concepts covered in this chapter. In some cases, there is more than one correct answer, so choose all that apply. Answers are listed in Appendix A, "Answers to Review Questions."

1. Which type of transmission uses start and stop bits, and is sometimes called character-framed transmission?

   A. Asynchronous

   B. Synchronous

   C. Isosynchronous

   D. Ethernet framing

2. If you use a modem to connect to your ISP, which of the following WAN connection types are you using?

   A. Leased-line

   B. Circuit-switched

   C. Packet-switched

   D. Cell-switched

3. If you use Frame Relay to connect a remote site to the central site, which of the following WAN connection types are you using?

   A. Leased-line

   B. Circuit-switched

   C. Packet-switched

   D. Cell-switched

4. If you use HDLC encapsulation over a full T1 to connect a remote site to the central site, which of the following WAN connection types are you using?

   A. Leased-line

   B. Circuit-switched

   C. Packet-switched

   D. Cell-switched

5. ATM service is described as what type of connection?

   A. Leased-line

   B. Circuit-switched

   C. Dedicated line

   D. Cell-switched

6. Which of the following is true about CSU/DSUs?

   A. They are DCEs.

   B. They are DTEs.

   C. They provide a clock signal.

   D. They are used for asynchronous dialup.

7. Which of the following is true about HDLC?

   A. HDLC implementations are proprietary.

   B. On a Cisco router, HDLC is used only when connecting to another router.

   C. HDLC is a LAN encapsulation protocol.

   D. HDLC is used when connecting routers from different vendors.

8. Which of the following routers would be an appropriate choice for a central site that serves four remote sites over Frame Relay and ISDN?

   A. Cisco 2509 AS

   B. Cisco 2621

   C. Cisco 3640

   D. Cisco 7205

9. Which of the following router models would make an appropriate choice for a remote site that requires a single ISDN connection?

   A. Cisco 1601

   B. Cisco 1602

   C. Cisco 1603

   D. Cisco 1604

10. Which of the following router models would make an appropriate choice for a home office that requires an IOS-based router with an ISDN interface?

   A. Cisco 760

   B. Cisco 770

   C. Cisco 804

   D. Cisco 1720

Key Terms

Access server   A router configured to accept dial-in calls over an ISDN or asynchronous interface.

Asynchronous transmission   A method of data transmission in which each sent character is framed by start and stop bits. Because asynchronous transmissions use no clock or timing source to keep both the sender and the receiver synchronized, the sender must signal the start and stop of each character so that the receiver knows when to expect data.

Branch office   A remote office that typically maintains at least one WAN connection to the central site, and might have several links to other remote sites. Generally, branch-office networks support fewer users than the central site, and therefore require less bandwidth.

Central site   The focal point of a company's network that houses enterprise services. Typically, all remote sites and users must connect to the *central site* to access information, either intermittently or continuously.

CSU (channel service unit)   A digital interface device that connects end-user equipment to the local digital telephone loop. Often referred to together with DSU, as CSU/DSU. See also DSU.

DSU (data service unit)   A device used in digital transmission that adapts the physical interface on a DTE device to a transmission facility such as a T1 or E1. The DSU is also responsible for such functions as signal timing. Often referred to together with CSU, as CSU/DSU. See also CSU.

DCE (data communications equipment, EIA expansion) or *data circuit-terminating equipment (ITU-T expansion)*   The devices and connections of a communications network that comprise the network end of the user-to-network interface. The DCE provides a physical connection to the network, forwards traffic, and provides a clocking signal used to synchronize data transmission between DCE and DTE devices. Modems and CSU/DSUs are examples of DCE. Compare with DTE.

DDR (dial-on-demand routing)   A technique whereby a Cisco router can automatically start and close a circuit-switched session as transmitting stations demand. The router spoofs keepalives so that end stations treat the session as active. DDR permits routing over ISDN or telephone lines using an external ISDN terminal adapter or modem.

DTE (data terminal equipment)   A device at the user end of a user-network interface that serves as a data source, destination, or both. DTE connects to a data network through a DCE device (for example, a modem) and typically uses clocking signals generated by the DCE. DTE includes such devices as computers, protocol translators, and multiplexers. Compare with *DCE*.

Leased line   A transmission line reserved by a communications carrier for the private use of a customer. A leased line is a type of dedicated line. Also called a dedicated line.

Multiplexing   A scheme that allows multiple logical signals to be transmitted simultaneously across a single physical channel.

POTS (plain old telephone service)   A general term referring to the variety of analog telephone networks and services in place worldwide.

Synchronous transmission   A method of data transmission in which a common timing signal is used between hosts. A clock signal is either embedded in the data stream or is sent separately to the interfaces.

Telecommuter site   A home office that connects to the central site or branch office as needed.

Virtual circuit   A logical circuit created to ensure reliable communication between two network devices. A virtual circuit can be either permanent (a PVC) or switched (an SVC, covered further in Chapter 6). Virtual circuits are used in Frame Relay and in X.25. In ATM, a virtual circuit is called a virtual channel. Sometimes abbreviated VC.

VPN (Virtual Private Network)   The use of encryption and tunneling protocols to create a private data network over the public Internet.

Objectives

After completing this chapter, you will be able to perform tasks related to the following:

- Modem functions
- Configuring asynchronous interfaces and terminal lines
- Basic dial-on-demand routing
- Modem configuration
- Configuring a Windows PC dial-up connection

Chapter 2

Modems and Asynchronous Connections

Introduction

Asynchronous, analog dial-up connections are a cheap and readily available remote access solution. For this reason, virtually all organizations use modems and analog telephone lines to some extent. As a networking professional, you must understand how modems work. In addition, you must be able to cable and configure a dial-up connection.

Workstations, such as Windows PCs, can be configured for dial-up networking with modems. Cisco routers can be configured to use a modem as well.

This chapter introduces basic modem concepts and functions. It also covers modem configuration, Cisco IOS asynchronous connection commands, dial-up networking, and basic dial-on-demand routing (DDR).

TECH NOTE: CALL TYPES

When you are configuring a Cisco access server for dial access, there are essentially three types of calls:

- Circuit-switched digital calls
- Analog modem calls
- Asynchronous character stream calls

Circuit-switched digital calls are usually ISDN 56-kbps or 64-kbps data calls that use Point-to-Point Protocol (PPP). Such calls require ISDN network devices, ISDN switching equipment, and a digital local loop.

Analog modem calls travel through traditional telephone lines, and ISDN lines. Regardless of the media used, these calls are initiated by a modem and terminated on another modem at the remote end. For example, if one end is an analog modem connected to an analog local loop, and the other end is a Basic Rate Interface (BRI) connected to a digital leased line (Primary Rate Interface, or PRI), the digital end must terminate with a digital modem.

Asynchronous character stream calls enter the router or access server through virtual terminal (VTY) lines. These virtual lines terminate incoming character streams that use the following proto-cols: Telnet, local-area transport (LAT), V.120, TN3270, Link Access Procedure Balanced-terminal adapter (LAPB-TA), and packet assembler/disassembler (PAD) calls.

Modem Functions

When selecting a remote access solution for remote offices and home users, network designers often choose analog dial-up connections because they are supported over ordinary phone lines. Ordinary phones lines, also called *plain old telephone service* (POTS), were originally designed to carry voice using analog signaling.

You might recall from previous study that data transmissions are categorized as either analog or digital. Electronic analog transmissions manipulate the frequency, amplitude, and phase of a continuous electromagnetic waveform. At first, all broadcast and phone transmission relied on analog technology. Today, digital transmission is commonplace. Although most local loops to residences and small businesses remain analog, larger businesses and organizations lease digital local loops, as shown in Figure 2-1.

Figure 2-1
Most residential areas still access the public switched telephone network (PSTN) via conventional analog local loops, although many large organizations now lease digital local loops.

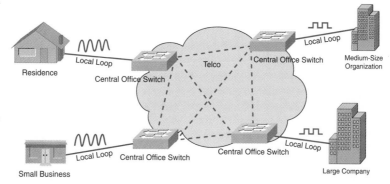

Digital communications represent information as binary 1s and 0s by using pulses of electricity, light, or some other method. Because computers represent and store data digitally, a digital transmission medium is ideal when networking computers.

To use analog phone lines for data transmission, a computer's digital signals must be converted to an analog tone that can be carried by POTS. Furthermore, analog signals must be converted back to digital signals so that the receiving computer can decode the information. A modem performs these two conversions.

A modem is both a modulator and a demodulator. The word *modem* comes from a combination of these two words. A *modulator* varies the amplitude, frequency, or phase of a carrier wave for the transmission of information. A *demodulator* converts an analog carrier wave into digital signaling. Modems modulate the analog waveform in various ways so that it can transmit what was once digital signaling over POTS. Modems can also receive analog waves and convert them to digital so that receiving computers can understand them.

Figure 2-1 illustrates how most residential areas and small offices access the *public switched telephone network* (*PSTN*) through analog local loops. However, virtually all telecommunications companies (telcos) use digital facilities within their own networks. By using digital transmission, telcos can transmit data efficiently between their switches and keep error rates to a minimum. Relaying analog signals is less efficient because analog signals require amplification, which in turn amplifies any noise in the signal and creates errors. On the other hand, digital signals are repeated by signal regenerators. This repeating method is a more reliable process; the "on" or "off" state of a signal is merely determined by the network device and then recreated.

A typical modem connection is depicted in Figure 2-2. In the figure, the modems connect digital computers to the digital telco network through analog local loops. When the telco switch receives the modem's analog signal, it must encode the signal so that it can traverse the digital network.

Figure 2-2
A modem converts a data terminal equipment's (DTE's) digital signal into analog for transmission over the local loop.

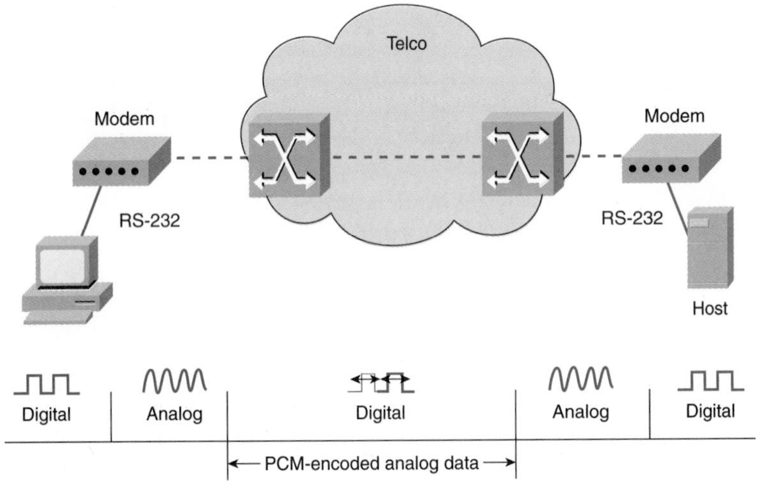

Telcos use a device called a *codec* to encode analog waveforms into digital pulses (analog-to-digital conversion), and vice versa. The name "codec" comes from the words "coder" and "decoder." The standard for encoding analog to digital is a technique called *Pulse Code Modulation* (*PCM*). PCM and its variants work by sampling an analog signal thousands of times per second. Each sample is then measured, or quantified, so that it can be encoded as a binary value (typically 8 bits). These approximate values can be used to reconstruct the waveform digitally. Today's telecommunications rely heavily on this kind of digital-to-analog and analog-to-digital conversion.

Each device depicted in Figure 2-2 plays a specific role in the communications process. To fully understand remote access solutions and cabling requirements, you need to be familiar with the terms *data terminal equipment* (*DTE*) and *data communications equipment* (*DCE*), which are used to describe the general function of a device.

The following sections describe the role of DTEs and DCEs, modem signaling (EIA/TIA 232), modem cabling, and modem modulation standards.

Modem Signaling

The end stations, or hosts, in Figure 2-2 are acting as DTEs. Examples of DTEs include end devices such as PCs, terminals, routers, and mainframe computers. A DTE is an end device that will be the source or destination of data communication. These end stations transmit signals to each other through DCEs, as shown in Figure 2-3. Examples of DCEs include modems and channel service units/data service units (CSU/DSUs). To communicate with remote DTEs, a DTE device typically must communicate with a directly connected DCE device.

Figure 2-3
DTEs, such as routers and PCs, access the carrier's network via DCEs, such as CSU/DSUs and modems.

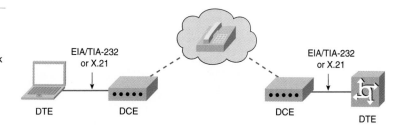

For example, a router's WAN interface (DTE) is usually directly connected to a CSU/DSU (DCE) so that the router can access a digital local loop. The CSU/DSU provides loopback and diagnostic functions, and "translates" between the router's signaling method and the signaling method of the carrier's local loop.

Several different standards define the signaling between a DTE and a DCE over a directly connected serial cable, some of which are listed in Figure 2-4. The standard you use depends on the type of DTE you have, the functionality of your DCE, and the type of connection you have obtained from your provider. In North America, you are most likely to encounter three DTE-to-DCE signaling standards when connecting Cisco routers to telco lines:

- RS-232 (*EIA/TIA-232*)
- *V.35*
- *HSSI* (*High-Speed Serial Interface*)

Figure 2-4
Several standards define the interface and signaling between a DTE and a DCE.

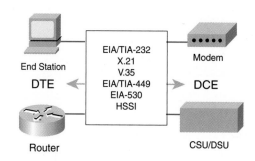

Asynchronous serial modems are connected to end stations (see Figure 2-5) and routers (see Figure 2-6) using EIA/TIA-232. EIA/TIA-232 is the most commonly used asynchronous interface for analog data communications in North America.

Figure 2-5
Typically, an external modem is connected to a PC via an RS-232 connection.

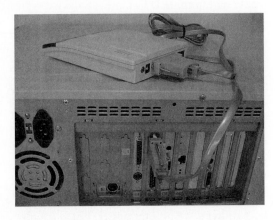

Figure 2-6
You can connect an external modem to a router using an RS-232 cable connected to the router's serial interface.

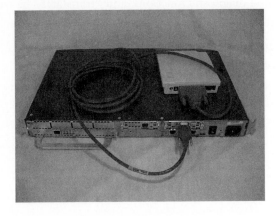

If you are connecting a router to a digital local loop using a CSU/DSU over a leased line, you are likely to use V.35 or HSSI. The V.35 standard is appropriate for T1/E1 leased lines (see Figure 2-7), although HSSI's 52-Mbps throughput makes it suitable for T3/E3 lines (see Figure 2-8).

Figure 2-7
A router typically connects to a CSU/DSU using V.35 cables and interfaces.

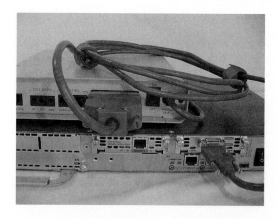

Figure 2-8
An HSSI interface is used to connect to T3 lines.

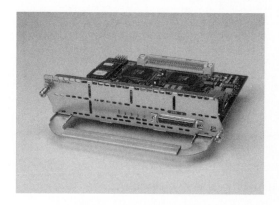

The EIA/TIA-232 Standard

The EIA/TIA-232 standard was first issued in 1962 as RS-232 (the RS stands for "requested standard"), and revised as RS-232-C in 1969. This pervasive signaling standard has been adopted by the EIA/TIA, and is now officially known as EIA/TIA-232-C.

The EIA/TIA-232 standard specifies a cable that uses a 25-pin connector (DB-25); yet only 8 pins of the DB-25 are actually used for connecting a DTE to a DCE. Thus, many RS-232 cables use a DB-9 or RJ-11/RJ-45 connector instead of a DB-25.

Table 2-1 shows EIA/TIA-232's pins and their definitions. As you read the table, note the direction of the signal and whether the DCE or DTE uses the pin.

Table 2-1   EIA/TIA-232 Pin Assignments

Pin Number	Designation	Definition	Description
2	TxD	Transmits data	DTE-to-DCE data transfer
3	RxD	Receives data	DCE-to-DTE data transfer
4	RTS	Request to send	DTE signal buffer available
5	CTS	Clear to send	DCE signal buffer available
6	DSR	Data set ready	DCE is ready
7	GRD	Signal ground	
8	CD	Carrier detect	DCE senses carrier
20	DTR	Data terminal ready	DTE is ready

The eight pins used in DTE-to-DCE signaling can be grouped into three categories by their functionality, as shown in Figure 2-9:

- Data transfer group
- Hardware flow control group
- Modem control group

Figure 2-9
The pins used by
EIA/TIA 232 are
grouped by their
function.

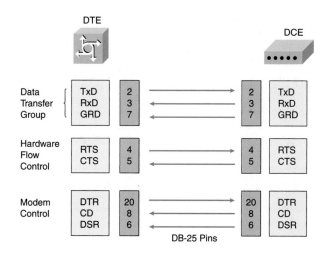

The following sections describe each category in detail.

Data Transfer

RS-232 uses pins 2, 3, and 7 for data transfer. Pin 2 (TxD) is used by the DTE to transmit data to the DCE (the modem), and Pin 3 (RxD) is used by the DCE to transmit data to the DTE. Pin 7 (GRD) provides both devices with the ground reference for voltage measurements.

Data Flow Control

Pins 4 and 5 are used to control the flow of signals between the DTE and the DCE. Pin 4 (RTS) is controlled by the DTE device. When the DTE raises the voltage on Pin 4, it is issuing a request to send. The DTE is telling the DCE that it has buffer space available to receive data. After a call is established by the modem, the DCE should raise the voltage on Pin 5 (CTS), which tells the DTE that it is clear to send and that it can begin transferring data on Pin 2. The modem can also lower voltage on Pin 5 to signal that its buffer space is full.

Modem Control

Both the DTE and DCE use pins 6, 8, and 20 to initiate, terminate, and monitor the status of the connection. Pin 6 (DSR) and Pin 20 (DTR) control how the modem operates. When the modem powers on, the voltage on the DSR pin is raised, informing the connected computer that the DCE is ready for use (thus, Data Set Ready).

Likewise, the DTE raises the voltage on Pin 20 to alert the DCE that the DTE is connected and available to send or receive data (thus, Data Terminal Ready). Usually, the DTE raises the voltage on the DTR pin on power up, but in some cases the DTR pin's voltage is controlled by software.

Pin 8 (CD) is controlled by the DCE. The modem raises the voltage on this pin to indicate that it has established an acceptable carrier signal with a remote DCE (thus, Carrier Detect). In other words, the CD pin tells the DTE that a DCE-to-DCE connection has been established.

A DTE, such as a computer or a router, can terminate the connection by dropping the DTR signal. By dropping this signal, the router (DTE) communicates that it is no longer connected and not available to receive data. The modem (DCE) should terminate its connection with the remote modem and revert back to its base settings.

When using a modem with a Cisco router, you might have to manually configure the modem to interpret the loss of DTR as a call-ending event. Depending on the modem, accepting the default configuration might allow it to function properly. But in some cases, you will have to access the modem's onboard software and program it to respond appropriately to the loss of DTR. This can be done manually for each call, or alternately, you can use the Cisco IOS to send the proper configuration commands to the modem using a *chat script*, which is a string of text that defines the login "conversation" that occurs between two systems. On asynchronous lines, Cisco routers support chat scripts used to send commands for modem dialing and logging on to remote systems.

If a remote modem drops the CD because the remote DTE has ended the transmission, the local modem should alert the local router (DTE) that the connection has been terminated. By default, most modems understand that a drop in the CD signal indicates that the call is to be terminated. But again, you might have to manually configure the modem to react appropriately to the CD signal loss.

When modem control is not configured properly, the following symptoms might occur:

- The modem does not hang up when you quit your session. This means the DTR is not dropped or recognized, so the modem is not aware that it should break the connection.

- You end up in someone else's session, which means that the CD drop is not recognized. This can happen when Caller A terminates its dial-up session, and the modem does not pass the true state of the CD to the DTE. The router (DTE) is not aware that Caller A terminated its session, so it maintains the line for Caller A. When a new caller, Caller B, comes in by the same line (interface), the router continues with the session previously initiated by Caller A, instead of starting a new one. Thus, Caller B ends up in Caller A's session without having to authenticate.

It is very important that the true state of CD is always passed back to the DTE, so the router can terminate sessions when callers hang up.

Modem Cabling Components

Exactly what kinds of cables, adapters, and interfaces you use to connect modems to your DTEs depends on the specific type and model of equipment you have, as shown in Table 2-2. When selecting the proper cables and adapters, you should be familiar with the following terms:

- **Straight-through cable**—If you hold the two ends of an RJ-45 cable side by side, you'll see eight colored strips, or pins, at each end. If the order of the colored pins is the same at each end, then the cable is straight
- **Rollover cable**—If the order of the colors is reversed at each end, then the cable is rolled.
- **DB-9 Terminal Adapter**—A DTE terminal adapter used to connect to a PC's serial port, or to 9-pin console ports on older routers.
- **DB-25 Terminal Adapter**—A DTE terminal adapter (rarely used) that connects to a PC's 25-pin serial port, or to a 25-pin console port on an older router model.
- **DB-25 Modem Adapter**—Also called the DCE modem adapter used to connect to a modem.

The three kinds of DB connectors are shown in Figures 2-10 and 2-11.

Figure 2-10
The serial interface of DB-9 Terminal, DB-25 Terminal, and DB-25 Modem adapters (from left to right), used to adapt serial ports to RJ-45.

Figure 2-11
The RJ-45 connector
on DB-9 Terminal,
DB-25 Terminal,
and DB-25 Modem
adapters (from left
to right).

Table 2-2   Modem Cabling Components

Router Port	Examples of Where Found	Cabling Required
DB-25 DTE	Male DB-25 AUX on the Cisco 4000, 7000, 7200, and 7500.	Straight-through DB-25F—DB25M RS-232 cable.
DB-25 DCE	Female DB-25 console port on the Cisco 4000 and 7000 series.	Null-modem DB-25M—DB25M RS-232 cable. A rolled RJ-45–RJ-45 with CAB-25AS-MMOD adapters on both ends will work.
DB-60	Sync/async interfaces. Cisco 1005, 1600s, and 2500s; network modules on the Cisco 2600, 3600, and 4000.	Cisco-specific cable, the CAB-232MT. This cable has a DB-60 connection on the router side, and a DB-25 connection on the modem side.
RJ-45	AUX or CON on the Cisco 2500s, 2600, 3600, AS5200, and AS5300.	Rolled RJ-45–RJ-45 cable with adapter marked MODEM (part number CAB-25AS-MMOD).
68-pin	Cisco 2509-2512; network modules on the Cisco 2600 and 3600.	Cisco parts CAB-OCTAL-ASYNC (with connectors marked MODEM) and CAB-OCTAL-MODEM.
"Smart Serial"	WAN interface card (WIC) on 1720 and 2600s.	Cisco part CAB-SS-232MT.

External modems are built with a female data communications equipment (DCE) DB-25 port for connection to a controlling device such as a PC or a router.

Table 2-2 also includes information on the required cabling and the types of physical ports on Cisco routers to which a modem can be connected. You can't mix and match these components randomly. Only the combinations shown in Table 2-3 work.

Table 2-3   Proper Cabling Combinations

Port	RJ-45 Cable	DB-25 Style	Attaches To
AUX/Console	Rolled	DTE	Terminal
AUX/Console	Straight	DCE non-modem	Terminal
AUX/Console	Rolled	DCE modem	Modem

The specific pinout to be used on an RJ-45 interface for EIA-232 is not defined by any standards. As such, Cisco defines the RJ-45 as a DTE pinout, as shown in Figure 2-12.

Figure 2-12
Cisco defines the
RJ-45's DTE pinout.

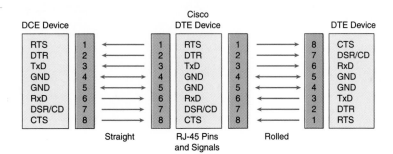

The following sections describe how to connect various types of DTEs to a DCE.

Connecting a Modem to a Router

How you connect a modem to a Cisco router depends on the specific model of router and modem you are using. External modems can be connected to several different kinds of router ports:

- AUX (Auxiliary)
- Console
- Serial interface (on some models)
- Async

Connecting to the AUX Port   Not all models of Cisco routers have an AUX port. The AUX port is typically used to connect a modem so that the router can be managed remotely out-of-band, or so that the router can send and receive data in-band (DDR). Most AUX ports are RJ-45, although older router models might use DB-9 or DB-25.

To connect a modem to a Cisco router's AUX port, you typically use a rollover cable and an RJ-45-to-DB-25 male DCE modem adapter. The DCE adapter is connected to the modem's EIA/TIA 232-interface, and the rollover cable connects to the adapter, as shown in Figure 2-13. The other end of the rollover cable plugs directly into the router's AUX port. (If the AUX port is not a RJ-45 cable, then the appropriate DTE female adapter is used.)

Figure 2-13
A rollover cable can be used with a DCE Modem adapter to connect an external modem to the router's RJ-45 AUX port.

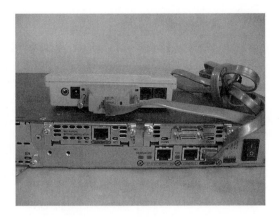

Connecting to the Console Port   All routers have console ports, but modems are rarely connected to them. This is because the console port does not support hardware flow control. The Ready To Send (RTS) and Clear To Send (CTS) pins are not supported as they are on an AUX port.

The console port's primary job is to allow a serially connected terminal to manage the router. To connect a PC to a Cisco router's console port, you use a rollover cable and a DB-9 or DB-25 adapter at either end of the connection, if necessary.

A modem can be connected to the console port using a rollover cable and an RJ-45-to-DB-25 male DCE adapter, which is attached to the modem. Because flow control is not supported by the console port, you should limit the connected modem's speed to 9600 bps. Also, be sure to configure the console port to require a login password, as this is not the default setting.

Connecting to a Serial Interface   Among the routers with serial interfaces, some have the ability to support low-speed asynchronous communications (if configured with the **physical-layer async** command). You should check your specific hardware's documentation to verify its capabilities.

To connect a modem to a router's serial interface, you will need to use an EIA/TIA-232 cable designed for your router's specific type of serial interface (Smart Serial, DB-60, etc.). Figure 2-14 shows a connection between a Cisco 2620 series router and an external modem using an EIA/TIA-232 Smart Serial cable.

Figure 2-14
Use an RS-232 Smart Serial cable to connect an external modem to a Cisco 2620 series router with a WIC 2A/S card.

Connecting a Modem to an Access Server—Async Lines

Any router configured to make and receive calls can be called an *access server*. In terms of product names, Cisco Systems applies the term "access server" only to devices built especially as concentration points for dial-in and dial-out calls. Some of these devices can feature hundreds of asynchronous interfaces.

Cabling an access server with high port densities can be complex. To simplify cabling, multiple asynchronous interfaces can be grouped together at a single physical port on the access server. Figures 2-15 and 2-16 show the Cisco 2509 and 2511 model routers, respectively, which are considered entry-level access servers. The 2511 features two 68-pin ports for asynchronous connections (see Figure 2-16). Up to eight modems or other devices can be connected to a single 68-pin port via an octal cable.

Figure 2-15
From top to bottom:
the AS2511-RJ, 2511,
AS2509-RJ, and
AS2509 model
routers.

Figure 2-16
The 2511 router sup-
ports 16 asynchro-
nous lines using two
68-pin ports.

This octal interface is common and is used to connect to modems, or even the console ports of other routers (for management purposes). Figure 2-17 shows a 2511 router using an octal cable to connect to multiple modems.

Figure 2-17
A 2511 router can connect to up to 16 external modems using two octal cables.

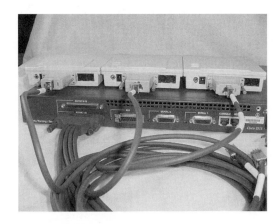

Connecting a Modem to a PC

Today's PC generally comes with an internal modem, either built in to the PC's motherboard or installed as an expansion card.

If you purchase an external modem, the vendor typically supplies you with an EIA/TIA-232 cable designed to connect the modem to your PC. You can also connect an external modem using a rollover cable and a RJ-45-to-DB-25 male DCE adapter, which is attached to the modem. One end of the rollover cable connects to the DB-25 adapter on the modem. The other end of the rollover cable connects to a 9-pin or 25-pin serial port on the PC (also called a COM port). Because a PC does not have a RJ-45 jack, you will have to use either a DB-9 or DB-25 female adapter to connect to the rollover cable.

Figure 2-5 shows an external modem connected via a rollover cable to a 9-pin serial port on a PC.

Directly Connecting a DTE to Another DTE—Null Modem

When two DTE devices (for example, an access server and a workstation) are near each other, it makes sense to connect them directly without going through a telephone network and two modems. An ordinary EIA/TIA-232 cable does not work in this case because both DTE devices transmit on the TxD lead (Pin 2), and both expect input on the RxD lead (Pin 3). A special cable, called a *null modem cable*, is required for the DTE-to-DTE connection.

Null modems crisscross DB-25 pins 2, 3, and other corresponding pins so that the two DTE devices can communicate, as shown in Figure 2-18. Some devices can be configured to operate either, such as a DTE or a DCE. Configuring a device as a DCE usually means that it receives data on Pin 2 and transmits data on Pin 3, instead of the reverse.

Figure 2-18
Directly connected
DTEs use a null
modem cable to
communicate.

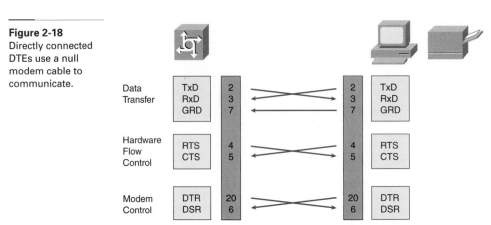

For example, many serial printers are configured as DCE devices so that they can be connected directly to a DTE (for example, a PC or a terminal server) with an ordinary EIA/TIA-232 cable, eliminating the need for a null modem connection. On a null modem cable, the CD signal is on the same pin as DSR.

Modem Modulation Standards

The function of a modem is to convert digital signals (DTE-to-DCE) into analog signals (DCE-to-DCE), and vice versa. Modulation techniques determine how modems convert digital data into analog signals. An analog waveform can be modulated in terms of its amplitude, its frequency, its phase (position of the sine waves), or a combination of these qualities.

Several modem manufacturers and standards organizations, including the Telecommunication Standardization Sector of the International Telecommunications Union (ITU-T), have released modulation standards. The ITU-T V Series Recommendations are the most commonly used modulation standards and enjoy international acceptance. Despite these international standards, proprietary techniques are not uncommon. Thus, interoperability among different types of modems is not always easily achieved.

Before the V Series Recommendations, AT&T offered its own standards, Bell 103, and Bell 212A. These standards supported the low transfer rate of 300 bps. By altering the height (amplitude), frequency, and phase (position) of analog waveforms, the V Series

Recommendations incrementally improved transfer rates. Table 2-4 lists the most common ITU-T standards and their maximum transfer speed. Some common international and proprietary modem standards are also shown in Figure 2-19.

Table 2-4   ITU-T Modulation Standards

Standard	Maximum Transfer Rate
V.22	1200 Bps
V.22bis	2400 Bps
V.32	9600 Bps
V.32bis	14,400 Bps
V.34	28,800 Bps
V.34bis	33,600 Bps
V.90	56,000 Bps

Figure 2-19
Common modem modulations standards include V.32 and V.90.

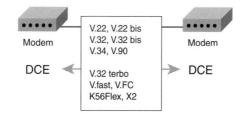

In general, when modems initially connect, they "handshake" and agree on the highest standard transfer rate that both can achieve.

Modems can achieve throughputs ranging from 300 bps up to 56 Kbps, depending on the modulation standard supported. Most modems will adapt their transmission rates to achieve the maximum supported speed given several factors, including the best speed supported by the remote modem and the best speed supported by the local loop.

To achieve 56 Kbps, both the local and remote modem must support the same 56 Kbps transmission standard (X2, K56Flex, V.90). Also, the signal must be converted from digital to analog to digital only once. Therefore, the PSTN must be completely digital (as is the case in the United States), and one end of the connection (usually the ISP) must use a digital local loop to the central office.

Even if the previous requirements are met, 56 Kbps modems cannot exceed 53.3 Kbps under current FCC rules that place a limit on amplitude (signal strength).

NOTE

Modulation standards typically go through at least one revision. When a second version of a standard is introduced, the Latin suffix *bis* is added to its name; *bis* means two. Thus, the second version of the V.32 standard is called V.32bis. The suffix *ter* is applied to the third release of a modulation standard; *ter* means three.

The access server is unaware of modulations because it is directly involved only with DTE-to-DCE communication. However, the access server-to-modem speed must account for modulation speed and compression ratio for optimal end-to-end performance.

TECH NOTE: UART

The transmission speed achieved by a computer using a modem can also be limited by the *Universal Asynchronous Receiver/Transmitter* (*UART*). A UART is a specialized microchip designed to control a computer's interface to its attached serial devices (such as an external modem or a mouse). More specifically, the UART provides the computer with an RS-232C DTE interface so that the computer can exchange data with modems and other serial devices.

Every computer contains a UART to manage serial ports, while internal modems have their own UART.

Controlled by a clock usually running at 1.84 Mega-Hertz (MHz), UARTs have a maximum throughput of 115 Kbps. UARTs also have a memory buffer to temporarily hold incoming data. This buffer varies by model, but it is usually quite small. The following is a list of the different types of UARTs:

- 8250
- 16450
- 16550 uses a 16-byte buffer
- 16550af
- 16750 uses a 64-byte transmit buffer and a 56-byte receive buffer

---

Error Control and Data Compression

Error-detection and error-correction methods were developed to ensure data integrity at any speed. Some widely used methods include Microcom Networking Protocol (MNP) and Link Access Procedure for Modems (LAPM).

Compression algorithms typically require error-correction algorithms. Common compression algorithms include V.42bis and MNP 5. These two types of compression typically operate in concert with the error-correction standards, LAPM and MNP 4.

How well the modem compression works depends on the kind of files being transferred. In general, you will be able to achieve twice the speed for transferring a standard text file. Decreasing by 50 percent means that you can double the throughput on the line so that a 9600-bps modem can effectively transmit 19200 bps. However, V.42bis and MNP 5 modems cannot compress a file that is already compressed by software. In some cases, the modem even tries to compress a precompressed file and actually expand it, thus slowing down the file transfer!

Although some application software supports data compression, it is usually better to let the modem compress data for transmission. Data-compression algorithms that run in modem hardware are faster than those performed by host software. If two modems have agreed on V.42bis compression, you need to turn off the compression capability of the application. This means transferring data at a higher speed on the interface between the DTE and the DCE.

Confusion often arises between the DCE-to-DCE modulation speed and DTE-to-DCE speed. DCE-to-DCE represents how fast the modems communicate with each other across the telephone network (56 Kbps or less). DTE-to-DCE represents how fast your computer communicates with the attached modem.

To gain full benefits from compression in an ideal situation, the DTE (for example, a PC) must send to the DCE (for example, a modem) at speeds matching the potential compression ratio (as shown in Figure 2-20). The DTE should be set to clock the modem at its fastest rate to take advantage of compression (usually 115,200 Kbps).

Figure 2-20
A PC should transmit to the modem as fast as possible to match the modems transmit speed and compression ratio.

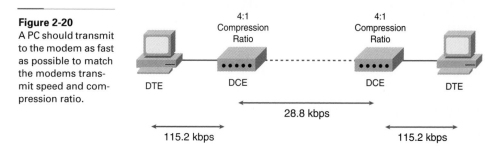

An improperly configured modem might automatically adjust DTE-DCE speeds to match the established DCE-DCE speeds. This is often called *speed mismatch*. To avoid speed mismatch, you must lock the DTE-DCE speed so that it remains constant, as originally configured.

Figure 2-21 shows the maximum theoretical speeds that are possible for selected modem-modulation standards. Also shown are the possible speeds if V.42bis compression is used with the same standards.

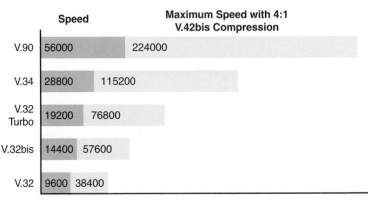

Figure 2-21
With V.42bis compression, the potential transmission speed is quadrupled.

Configuring Asynchronous Interfaces and Terminal Lines

After you physically connect a modem to your access server, you must configure the modem's software. Modems have a default software configuration, which is set by the vendor at the factory. In most cases, you need to modify this configuration to suit your needs. For example, you can configure the modem to answer calls on the second ring, or lock its speed, etc.

Some modems can be configured by using a panel on the unit; however, most modems don't have configuration panels. Instead, you must access the modem's software via another device, such as an access server. When using a Cisco access server, you have the option to manually configure the modem, or automatically configure the modem using a script. Manual configurations are accomplished using a technique called *reverse Telnet*.

The following sections describe how to configure reverse Telnet, asynchronous interfaces, and terminal lines. An example configuration is also provided.

Reverse Telnet

Access servers support both incoming and outgoing asynchronous line connections. As shown in Figure 2-22, incoming connections are *forward connections*. Outgoing connections are *reverse connections*. A remote terminal user who dials into the access server through an asynchronous line makes a forward connection. A user who connects through an access server to an attached modem makes a reverse connection. This reverse connection, called *reverse Telnet*, can be used to configure modems. You can make reverse Telnet connections to various types of attached devices, such as modems, routers, and terminals.

Figure 2-22
A router can establish a reverse Telnet session to a directly connected device, such as a modem.

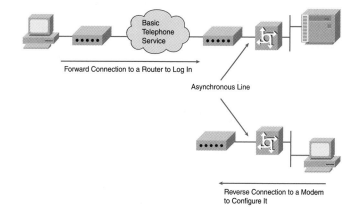

Forward Connection to a Router to Log In

Asynchronous Line

Reverse Connection to a Modem
to Configure It

As the name implies, reverse Telnet sessions are established using the Telnet protocol. Telnet daemons typically listen on TCP port 23 for connection requests. If you want to communicate with and configure a modem that is attached to a router, you would telnet to the router's IP address, but not to the default TCP port, 23. Instead, you would telnet to a TCP port that the router maps to the specific line connected to the modem. Figure 2-23 shows that to connect to a modem attached to asynchronous line 7, you would telnet to 10.10.10.1 on port 2007 (not 23).

When using reverse Telnet, you can use the **telnet** command to connect to any IP address configured on the router, as long as the interface associated with that IP address is up. Typically, you will configure the access server with a loopback IP address. Because a loopback interface is a logical interface, it is not susceptible to physical failures. In Figure 2-23, loopback 0 is assigned the address 10.10.10.1. This address can be used for all reverse Telnet sessions.

You must be able to identify line numbers on an access server (router) to determine the TCP port number needed to establish a reverse Telnet session with a device on a given line.

Cisco devices have the following four types of lines:

- **CON (Console line)**—Typically used to log in to the router for configuration purposes; this line is also referred to as CTY.
- **AUX (Auxiliary line)**—EIA/TIA-232 DTE port used as a backup asynchronous port (TTY).
- **TTY (Asynchronous line)**—Same as asynchronous interface; available on access server models only (Cisco 2509, 2510, 25511, 12, AS5x00, etc); used typically for remote dial-in sessions that use such protocols as Serial Line Internet Protocol (SLIP) and PPP.

- **VTY**—Used for incoming Telnet, LAT, X.25 PAD, and protocol-translation connections into synchronous ports (such as Ethernet and serial interfaces) on the router.

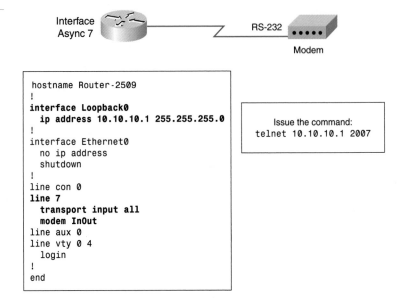

Figure 2-23
Reverse Telnet sessions are established by using specially reserved TCP port numbers.

```
hostname Router-2509
!
interface Loopback0
  ip address 10.10.10.1 255.255.255.0
!
interface Ethernet0
  no ip address
  shutdown
!
line con 0
line 7
  transport input all
  modem InOut
line aux 0
line vty 0 4
  login
!
end
```

Issue the command:
telnet 10.10.10.1 2007

Different router models assign different numbers to the line types, but all routers follow the same rules when assigning numbers. Figure 2-24 shows the Cisco line-numbering rules, where n represents the first physical line after the console line, and m refers to the number of the VTY line. For example, the VTY 4 line corresponds to line 14 on a router with 8 TTY ports. Because line 0 is for the console, lines 1 to 8 are the TTY lines, line 9 is for the auxiliary port, and lines 10 to 14 are for VTY 0 to 4.

Figure 2-24
All routers follow the same rules when assigning line numbers.

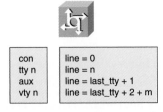

con	line = 0
tty n	line = n
aux	line = last_tty + 1
vty n	line = last_tty + 2 + m

TTY lines correspond to asynchronous interfaces on a one-to-one basis, and VTY lines are virtual lines that are dynamically assigned to the synchronous interfaces. Usually, you associate VTY lines with incoming Telnet sessions. You can enter the **interface line tty ?** command to view the maximum number of TTY lines supported by the router.

Reverse Telnet connections to an individual line can be used to communicate and configure an attached device. To connect to an individual line, the remote host or terminal must specify a particular TCP port on the access server. For reverse Telnet, that port is 2000 plus the line number. For example, to initiate a Telnet connection to line 1 (2000 + 1), use the following command:

```
Router#telnet 131.108.30.40 2001
```

If you want to reverse Telnet to a modem on line 14, you would use TCP port 2014.

Table 2-4 shows that ports in the range 2000–2999 are reserved for reverse Telnet sessions to individual lines. Additional ranges have been reserved for rotary groups and other services, such as raw TCP and XRemote.

Table 2-4   **Service and Port Numbers for Lines and Rotary Groups**

Services Provided	Base TCP Port for Individual Lines	Base TCP Port for Rotary Groups
Telnet protocol	2000	3000
Raw TCP protocol (no Telnet)	4000	5000
Telnet protocol, binary mode	6000	7000
XRemote protocol	9000	10000

Because line numbering varies among Cisco router models, you might want to rely on the **show line** command to display all types of lines and the status of each line, as exhibited in Example 2-1 (note that the AUX port is assigned line 17 in the example).

Example 2-1 Using the show line Command to Identify Assigned Line Numbers

```
RTA-2511#show line
  Tty Typ     Tx/Rx      A Modem  Roty AccO AccI  Uses   Noise   Overruns
*   0 CTY                -    -      -    -    -     0       0       0/0
    1 TTY    9600/9600   -    -      -    -    -     0       0       0/0
    2 TTY    9600/9600   -    -      -    -    -     0       0       0/0
    3 TTY    9600/9600   -    -      -    -    -     0       0       0/0
    4 TTY    9600/9600   -    -      -    -    -     0       0       0/0
    5 TTY    9600/9600   -    -      -    -    -     0       0       0/0
    6 TTY    9600/9600   -    -      -    -    -     0       0       0/0
    7 TTY    9600/9600   -    -      -    -    -     0       0       0/0
    8 TTY    9600/9600   -    -      -    -    -     0       0       0/0
```

continues

Example 2-1 Using the show line Command to Identify Assigned Line Numbers (Continued)

```
 9 TTY    9600/9600    -    -       -    -    -    0    0    0/0
10 TTY    9600/9600    -    -       -    -    -    0    0    0/0
11 TTY    9600/9600    -    -       -    -    -    0    0    0/0
12 TTY    9600/9600    -    -       -    -    -    0    0    0/0
13 TTY    9600/9600    -    -       -    -    -    0    0    0/0
14 TTY    9600/9600    -    -       -    -    -    0    0    0/0
15 TTY    9600/9600    -    -       -    -    -    0    0    0/0
16 TTY    9600/9600    -    -       -    -    -    0    0    0/0
17 AUX    9600/9600    -    -       -    -    -    0    0    0/0
18 VTY                 -    -       -    -    -    0    0    0/0
19 VTY                 -    -       -    -    -    0    0    0/0
20 VTY                 -    -       -    -    -    0    0    0/0
21 VTY                 -    -       -    -    -    0    0    0/0
22 VTY                 -    -       -    -    -    0    0    0/0
```

This command also provides useful information about modem control and asynchronous port configuration.

The **show line** *line-number* command displays more detailed information on the specified line, including some useful data such as baud rate, modem state (idle or ready), and modem hardware state (CTS, DSR, DTR, and RTS for hardware flow control and session control).

Some router models don't have AUX ports, and the Cisco 1600 series is one of them. Example 2-2 shows the way the relative and absolute line numbers are presented with the **show line** command.

Example 2-2 Using show line on a 1600 Series Router

```
RTB-1600#show line
Tty Typ Tx/Rx A Modem Roty AccO AccI Uses Noise Overruns
     *   0 CTY - - - - - 0 1 0/0
         2 vty - - - - - 0 0 0/0
         3 vty - - - - - 0 0 0/0
         4 vty - - - - - 0 0 0/0
         5 vty - - - - - 0 0 0/0
         6 vty - - - - - 0 0 0/0
Line(s) not in async mode -or- with no hardware support: 1
```

The CTY port is the console. As shown in Figure 2-24, the AUX port receives the number TTY + 1. Because this Cisco 1600 router has no Async interfaces (zero TTYs), the AUX port, if present, would have received line number 1. The VTY line numbers are derived using the following formula: last_TTY + 2, which in this case is 0 + 2, or just 2. Thus, the router's five virtual connections are numbered 2, 3, 4, 5, and 6.

In order for reverse Telnet to work, you must configure the access server's line with the **transport input** *protocol* and **modem inout** commands. Example 2-3 shows the commands to allow reverse Telnet via line 10.

Example 2-3 Configuring a Router for Reverse Telnet

```
RTA#configure terminal
RTA(config)#line 10
RTA(config-line)#transport input all
RTA(config-line)#modem inout
```

Use the **transport input** *protocol* command to specify which protocol to allow for incoming connections. Because reverse Telnet is a kind of incoming connection, you must allow at least the Telnet protocol. In Example 2-4, **transport input all** allows all the following protocols to be used for the connection: LAT, MOP, NASI, PAD, rlogin, Telnet, and v120. Each of these protocols can be specified individually as a command option, as shown in Table 2-5. If you don't specify Telnet or "all," you will receive the message "Connection Refused" when you try to establish a reverse Telnet connection. The **modem inout** command is required to permit both incoming and outgoing connections on a given line.

Table 2-5   transport input Command Syntax

Keyword	Description
all	Selects all protocols.
lat	Selects the Digital LAT protocol and specifies incoming reverse LAT and host-initiated connections.
mop	Selects Maintenance Operation Protocol (MOP).
nasi	Selects NetWare Asynchronous Services Interface as the input transport protocol.
none	Prevents any protocol selection on the line. This makes the port unusable by incoming connections.
pad	Selects X.3 PAD incoming connections.

TIP

You can get "hung" in a reverse Telnet session if you don't know the escape sequence. To leave a reverse Telnet session, press Ctrl-Shift-6, and then the letter x. This sequence, Ctrl-Shift-6-x, suspends any Telnet session and returns you to the router console.

continues

Table 2-5   **transport input Command Syntax (Continued)**

Keyword	Description
rlogin	Selects the UNIX rlogin protocol.
telnet	Specifies all types of incoming TCP/IP connections.
v120	Selects the V.120 protocol for incoming async over ISDN connections.

Asynchronous Interfaces and Line Configuration

Access servers have terminal lines (TTYs) that differentiate them from other routers. You have already seen that modems are typically connected to these terminal lines.

The Cisco IOS assigns a logical interface to each physical terminal line, or group of terminal lines. As shown by the shaded portions of Example 2-4, these logical interfaces are labeled *interface Async interface-number* (for individual lines) and *interface Group-Async group-number* (for grouped interfaces).

Example 2-4 Using show run to View Logical Interface Configurations

```
RTA#show run
<output omitted>
!
interface Ethernet0
 ip address 172.24.1.1 255.255.255.0
!
interface Serial0
 ip address 10.3.0.1 255.255.255.0
 no ip mroute-cache
!
interface Async1
 ip address 10.1.1.1 255.255.255.0
 encapsulation ppp
!
interface Async2
 ip address 10.1.2.1 255.255.255.0
 encapsulation ppp
!
interface Async3
 ip address 10.1.2.1 255.255.255.0
```

Example 2-4 Using show run to View Logical Interface Configurations (Continued)

```
 encapsulation ppp
!
interface Group-Async1
 ip unnumbered Ethernet0
encapsulation ppp
 peer default ip address pool DIAL-IN
 group-range 4 8


<output omitted>
```

Thus, asynchronous interfaces correspond to physical terminal (TTY) lines. This means that, for a connection using TTY 8, configuration commands can be applied to the logical interface (interface async 8) and the physical line (line 8). As shown in Example 2-5, commands entered in the asynchronous interface mode allow you to configure protocol-specific parameters for asynchronous interfaces; commands entered in line configuration mode permit you to configure the physical aspects of the line's port.

Example 2-5 Configuring an Asynchronous Interface and Corresponding Terminal Line

```
RTA(config)#interface async 8
RTA(config-if)#encapsulation ppp
RTA(config-if)#ppp authentication chap
RTA(config-if)#ip address 10.1.1.1 255.255.255.0
RTA(config-if)#exit
RTA(config)#line 8
RTA(config-line)#login local
RTA(config-line)#modem inout
RTA(config-line)#speed 115200
RTA(config-line)#flowcontrol hardware
RTA(config-line)#autoselect ppp
```

The interface commands can be thought of as the logical configuration; the line commands configure physical characteristics of the configuration. For example, you configure the basic modem-related parameters on an access server using line configuration mode, but you configure the protocol encapsulation and authentication schemes using interface configuration mode.

Asynchronous interfaces can be grouped as one logical interface (*interface Group-Async group-number*) to simplify configuration. To create a group, issue the **interface Group-Async** command in global configuration mode, as shown:

```
RTA(config)#interface Group-Async 1
```

Example 2-6 shows that you can use the **group-range** command to specify which individual interfaces are members of the group.

Example 2-6 Adding Asynchronous Interfaces to an Interface Group

```
RTA(config)#interface Group-Async 1
RTA(config-if)#group-range 1 7
```

Example 2-6 assigns asynchronous interfaces 1 through 7 under a single master interface (interface Group-Async 1). This one-to-many structure allows you to configure all associated member interfaces by entering one command on the group interface, rather than entering this command on each interface.

Basic Terminal Line Configuration

You must configure an access server's terminal line to asynchronously communicate with a modem. Example 2-7 shows some of the most common commands used to configure a TTY line. The commands are issued in line configuration mode and set the following parameters:

- Login
- Line speed
- Flow control on the line
- Number of stop-bits (default is 2)
- Enable the modem to initiate outgoing calls or to accept incoming calls

Example 2-7 Basic Line Configuration

```
RTA(config)#line 2
RTA(config-line)#login
RTA(config-line)#password letmein
RTA(config-line)#speed 115200
RTA(config-line)#flowcontrol hardware
RTA(config-line)#stopbits 1
RTA(config-line)#transport input all
RTA(config-line)#modem inout
```

The configuration shown in Example 2-7 assumes that the modem will be configured manually using reverse Telnet. Alternately, you can include line configuration commands that automatically configure your modem to communicate with the router. Automatic modem configuration is discussed later in this chapter.

The **login** command shown in Example 2-7 enables password checking at login on line 2, while the **password** command sets the password to **letmein**.

The **speed** command is used to set the speed of transmission (both transmit and receive) between the modem and the attached access server. Depending on the router hardware, TTY line speeds can be set from between 50 and 115,200 bits per second (bps). The default speed setting is 9600 bps. Typically, you should set this value to the maximum supported speed between both devices. Note also that you must lock the speed of your modem to match the router's line configuration.

The **flowcontrol** command sets the type of flow control to be used on the line. Options are **software, hardware,** and **none** (default). This example router is configured for hardware flow control (RTS/CTS flow control).

The **stopbits** command configures the number of stop bits to be used (1, 1.5, or 2). The default setting is 2. The modem and the router must use the same number of stop bits. Reducing the number of stop bits from 2 to 1 will improve throughput by reducing asynchronous framing overhead.

Recall from the explanation of reverse Telnet that the **transport input all** command allows all protocols to be passed to the access server through the configured line. The **modem inout** command allows both incoming and outgoing commands on the line.

Both of these commands can be used with more restrictive keywords, as shown in Example 2-8.

Example 2-8 Configuring a Line to Allow only Specific Types of Connections

```
RTA(config-line)#transport input telnet
RTA(config-line)#modem dialin
```

The **transport input telnet** command will allow the Telnet protocol inbound on a specific line, while the **modem dialin** command restricts the line to incoming calls only.

It is essential that the TTY line be configured *before* configuring/initializing the modem itself. Otherwise, you cannot reverse Telnet to the modem. Moreover, if you change the line speed after the modem has been initialized, the modem will no longer communicate with the router until it is again told at what speed to talk to the router.

Basic Auxiliary Port Configuration

The AUX port is typically configured as an asynchronous serial interface on routers without built-in terminal lines. Depending on the hardware, an AUX port might not perform as well as a built-in TTY. As shown in Table 2-6, most AUX ports are limited to 38,400 bps. Note that AUX ports on 2600 and 3600 series routers support speeds up to 115,200 bps.

Table 2-6   Bit Rates for Asynchronous Interfaces

Maximum Speed	Supporting Platforms and Interfaces
38,400 bps	Most AUX ports.
115,200 bps	Cisco 1005, 1600, and 2509 through 2512 AUX on Cisco 2600 and 3600. Modules and WICs that support external asynchronous modems (for example, NM-16A, WIC-2A/S).

To configure the AUX port as an asynchronous interface, configure it with line commands, as you would any TTY. Use the **line aux 0** command in global configuration mode (see Example 2-9).

Example 2-9   Configuring the AUX Port for Asynchronous Operation

```
RTA(config)#line aux 0
RTA(config-line)#login
RTA(config-line)#password letmein

RTA(config-line)#speed 115200
RTA(config-line)#flowcontrol hardware
RTA(config-line)#stopbits 1
RTA(config-line)#transport input all
RTA(config-line)#modem inout
```

It is interesting to note that you can configure an AUX port by its line number as well. For example, on a 2511, where the AUX port is assigned line 17, you can configure the port's physical parameters issuing either **line aux 0** or **line 17** in global config mode.

You might want to issue the **show line** command to determine what line number is assigned to your router's AUX port. Depending on your router's hardware, this might be line 1, line 17, line 65, or some other number. After you identify the line number, you will know which corresponding asynchronous interface to configure (interface async 1, interface async 17, interface async 65, etc.).

Configuring the Console Port to Use a Modem

There are several advantages to connecting a modem to the console port of a router instead of the AUX port; however, the disadvantages are significant.

Here are the advantages of connecting a modem on the console port:

- Passwords can be recovered remotely. You might still need someone on-site with the router to toggle the power, but aside from that, it's identical to being there with the router.

- It is a convenient method of attaching a second modem to a router without async ports. This is beneficial if you need to access the router for configuration or management while leaving the AUX port free for DDR.

- Some routers (for example, Cisco 1600s) do not have AUX ports. If you want to connect a modem to the router and leave the serial port(s) free for other connections, the console is the only option.

But there are disadvantages of connecting a modem on the console port:

- The console port does not support EIA/TIA-232 modem control (DSR/Data Carrier Detect (DCD)), data terminal ready (DTR). Therefore, when the EXEC session terminates (**logout**), the modem connection will not drop automatically; the user will need to manually disconnect the session.

- More seriously, if the modem connection drops, the EXEC session does not automatically reset. This can present a security hole, in that a subsequent call into that modem will be able to access the console without entering a password. The hole can be made smaller by setting a tight **exec-timeout** on the line. However, if security is important, it is recommended to use a modem that can provide a password prompt.

- Unlike other async lines, the console port does not support hardware (Clear to Send/Ready to Send (CTS/RTS) flow control. It is recommended to use no flow control. If data overruns are encountered, however, software (XON/XOFF) flow control might be enabled.

- The console ports on most systems only support speeds up to 9600 bps.

- The console port lacks reverse Telnet capability. If the modem loses its stored initialization string, the only remedy is to physically disconnect the modem from the router and attach it to another device (such as an AUX port or a PC) to reinitialize. If a modem on an AUX port loses its initialization string, you can use reverse Telnet remotely to correct the problem.

- A console port cannot be used for DDR; it has no corresponding async interface.

Configuring a Serial Interface to Use a Modem

Depending on your router's hardware, a serial interface can be configured as a low-speed asynchronous line. To configure a serial interface as asynchronous, issue the following command in interface configuration mode:

```
Router(config-if)#physical-layer async
```

Example 2-10 shows the output of the **show line** command after issuing the **physical-layer async** command on Serial 0/1. The line number assigned to this particular router's Serial 0/1 is 2 (Serial 0/0 would be line 1), and the type of line is TTY.

NOTE

If your router does not recognize the **physical-layer async** command, it does not support this configuration.

Example 2-10 Verifying a Serial Line's Physical-Layer Configuration

```
RTA(config)#interface s0/1
RTA(config-if)#physical-layer async
RTA(config-if)#^Z
RTA#show line
    Tty Typ     Tx/Rx      A Modem  Roty AccO AccI   Uses   Noise  Overruns    Int
*     0 CTY                 -    -     -    -    -       0      1     0/0        -
      2 TTY     9600/9600   -    -     -    -    -       0      0     0/0     Se0/1
     65 AUX     9600/9600   -    -     -    -    -       0      0     0/0        -
     66 VTY                 -    -     -    -    -       0      0     0/0        -
     67 VTY                 -    -     -    -    -       0      0     0/0        -
     68 VTY                 -    -     -    -    -       0      0     0/0        -
     69 VTY                 -    -     -    -    -       0      0     0/0        -
     70 VTY                 -    -     -    -    -       0      0     0/0        -
```

Line(s) not in async mode or with no hardware support: 1, 3-64

Configuring Asynchronous Interfaces

We have seen that modems attach to asynchronous lines (TTYs, AUX), which, in turn, map to asynchronous interfaces (interface async 1, interface async 2, and so on). Asynchronous interfaces receive logical configurations (Layer 2 encapsulation, Layer 3 address, and so on) that enable the access server to route traffic over the terminal lines. You might configure asynchronous interfaces on access servers to provide the following:

- Network protocol support, such as IP, IPX, or AppleTalk
- Encapsulation support, such as PPP
- IP client addressing options (default or dynamic)
- IPX networking addressing options
- PPP authentication

If you don't configure a line's corresponding asynchronous interface, you can only use the line to dial in to the router and establish an EXEC management session. Typically, however, async lines are used to provide users with remote access to network resources, which means the access server must be able to route traffic through the async interface.

Asynchronous Interface Configuration Example

Asynchronous interfaces can receive complex configurations. Table 2-7 describes some common commands used to configure asynchronous interfaces for PPP and IP.

Table 2-7   Asynchronous Interface Configuration Commands

Command	Purpose
interface async *interface-number*	Brings up a single asynchronous interface.
ip address *address mask*	Specifies an IP address.
encapsulation ppp	Enables PPP.
async mode *dedicated*	Places a line into dedicated asynchronous mode using Serial Line Internet Protocol (SLIP) or PPP encapsulation.
ppp authentication [*chap*| *pap*| *chap pap*]	Enables Challenge Handshake Authentication Protocol (CHAP) and Password Authentication Protocol (PAP) authentication on the interface.
dialer in-band	Specifies that dial-on-demand routing (DDR) is to be supported.
dialer map *protocol next-hop-address*	Configures a serial interface to call one or multiple sites, or to receive calls from multiple sites.
dialer-group	Controls access by configuring an interface to belong to a specific dialing group.

Examples 2-11 through 2-13 explore these commands in detail.

Example 2-11 Configuring an Asynchronous Interface with an IP Address

```
RTA(config)#interface async 10
RTA(config-if)#ip address 10.1.1.1 255.255.255.0
```

The **interface async 10** command puts the router in interface configuration mode for the asynchronous interface that corresponds to line 10. The **ip address** command assigns a Layer-3 address to the interface.

Example 2-12 Configuring an Asynchronous Interface for PPP

```
RTA(config-if)#encapsulation ppp
RTA(config-if)#ppp authentication chap
RTA(config-if)#async mode dedicated
```

The **encapsulation ppp** command shown in Example 2-12 sets the Layer-2 encapsulation to PPP, while the **ppp encapsulation chap** command configures CHAP authentication on the line. PPP and its features are discussed further in Chapter 3, "PPP."

When the **async mode dedicated** command is issued, the interface uses either SLIP or PPP encapsulation, depending on which encapsulation method is configured for the interface (in this case, PPP). This means that an EXEC prompt will not appear, and the router is not available for EXEC mode access. You should configure all lines with this command unless you want dial-in users to be able to access the router EXEC mode.

Example 2-13 Configuring an Asynchronous Interface for DDR

```
RTA(config-if)#dialer in-band
RTA(config-if)#dialer map ip 10.1.1.2 name RTB modem-script hayes56k broadcast
  5556002
RTA(config-if)#dialer-group 1
RTA(config)#dialer-list 1 protocol ip permit
```

The commands shown in Example 2-13 configure DDR. If you want an asynchronous line to support DDR, you must issue the **dialer in-band** command. The **dialer in-band** command is required on any dial-up interface that does not have an out-of-band control (such as an ISDN D channel). Also, if the router is to place an outgoing call, you must configure a **dialer map** or **dialer string** statement. In this example, the **dialer map** command is used to map the IP address 10.1.1.2 to the phone number 555-6002. Dialer maps are discussed further in Chapter 4, "ISDN and DDR."

TECH NOTE: IN-BAND AND OUT-OF-BAND SIGNALING

To build dial-up switched-circuit connections, switching equipment and network devices must exchange information to establish the circuit, maintain it, and eventually, tear it down. Such information can include phone numbers, both the number being called and the number of the caller.

Originally, all signaling was in-band. In-band signaling means that the signals travel over the same channel used for voice or data. For analog voice calls, in-band signaling works well. However, today's digital facilities use out-of-band signaling.

Out-of-band signaling occurs on a separate digital channel called a *signaling link*. The PSTN uses Signaling System 7 (SS7) as the out-of-band signaling protocol. This separate channel typically carries 56 or 64 Kbps, which is much more data than in-band signaling can send. Out-of-band signaling also allows for signaling at any time during the call; in-band signaling typically occurs only at the beginning of a call. Features such as caller-ID and call waiting are made possible by SS7.

In the Cisco IOS, the **dialer in-band** command specifies that chat scripts will be used on asynchronous interfaces and V.25*bis* will be used on synchronous interfaces. V.25bis is the ITU standard for in-band dialing.

Dialing on synchronous serial lines can be initiated using V.25bis dialing or DTR dialing. V.25bis is used with a variety of devices, including synchronous modems, ISDN terminal adapters (TAs), and Switched 56 DSU/CSUs.

With DTR dialing, the DTR signal on the physical interface is activated, which causes some devices to dial a number configured into that device. When using DTR dialing, the interface cannot receive calls. But using DTR dialing allows lower-cost devices to be used in cases where only a single number needs to be dialed. Enable DTR dialing with the command **dialer dtr**.

With ISDN BRI, call control messages are sent over the D channel, while the B channels send data and voice. Thus, you do not need to issue the **dialer in-band** command on a BRI.

Introduction to DDR

DDR allows you to use dial-up modems or ISDN devices to establish low-volume, periodic network connections over public circuit-switched networks.

When implementing DDR, you must configure the router with a *dialer list*. A dialer list defines what traffic is "interesting," that is, worthy of establishing a call. A router will only establish a call if it receives interesting traffic that needs to be routed. Because establishing a call generally results in a toll, it's important that you make sure your router's dialer list is configured correctly.

To configure a dialer list, you use the **dialer-list** command, as shown here:

```
Router(config)#dialer-list dialer-group protocol protocol-name {permit | deny | list
   access-list-number | access-group}
```

The **dialer-list** command can be used to permit an entire protocol, which defines any traffic using that protocol as "interesting." You can also use the **dialer-list** command to specifically permit (or deny) types of traffic, based on criteria you configure with an access list. Table 2-8 defines the syntax and keywords that can be used with the command.

Table 2-8   *dialer-list* Command Syntax

Syntax	Description
dialer-group	Number of a dialer access group identified in any **dialer-group** interface configuration command.
protocol-name	One of the following protocol keywords: **appletalk, bridge, clns, clns_es, clns_is, decnet, decnet_router-L1, decnet_router-L2, decnet_node, ip, ipx, vines,** or **xns.**
permit	Permits access to an entire protocol.
deny	Denies access to an entire protocol.
list	Specifies that an access list will be used for defining a granularity finer than an entire protocol.
access-list-number	Access list numbers specified in any DECnet, Banyan VINES, IP, Novell IPX, or XNS standard or extended access lists, including Novell IPX extended service advertisement protocol (SAP) access lists and bridging types.
access-group	Filter list name used in the **clns filter-set** and **clns access-group** commands.

The **dialer-list protocol** command also specifies a dialer group, represented by a number. If the router matches traffic to a dialer list, it will use only the interfaces that are members of the specified dialer group to make the call.

Example 2-13 configures a router for DDR triggered by any IP packet. The **dialer-list 1 protocol ip permit** command defines interesting traffic as any TCP/IP packet and links this definition to interfaces in dialer group 1. The interface, int async 10, is then placed in this dialer group with the **dialer-group 1** command. Several interfaces can belong to this group.

DDR is explained further in Chapter 4.

Modem Configuration

Earlier in this chapter, you saw how to access a modem for manual configuration using reverse Telnet. After you establish a reverse Telnet session to the modem, you can send specialized modem commands, called attention (AT) commands, to configure it.

Figure 2-25 shows that modems can also be configured automatically by an attached Cisco router. You can configure the router to automatically discover and configure the modem. Alternately, you might specify a preloaded string of modem configuration commands that the router sends to configure the modem. These preloaded configuration commands are stored in a database as part of the router software.

Figure 2-25
Modems can be configured manually or automatically.

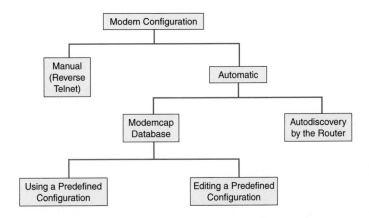

These three modem configuration methods—manual, automatic discovery, and automatic configuration using a database—are explored in greater detail in the following sections. We also look at chat scripts and an example configuration for asynchronous connections between remote routers.

Manual Modem Configuration

To manually configure your modem, you can connect to the modem using reverse Telnet and then type in modem commands (AT commands). It is highly unlikely that a modem's default configuration will suit your needs. You might find that you must configure your modem to do the following:

- Answer a call.
- Perform hardware flow control.

- Lock DTE speed to ensure that the modem will always communicate with the access server at the specified speed; as an example, when you use an async interface, you lock the speed to its theoretical maximum of 115.2 Kbps; the router speed command sets both transmit and receive speeds.
- Hang up when you quit a session.
- Have the CD signal truthfully reflect the carrier state.

Unfortunately, the AT commands used to make these and other configurations might vary among different types of modems. Essentially, each modem vendor has its own modem command set. However, the AT commands shown in Table 2-9 are common among most vendors.

Table 2-9   Common Modem AT Commands

Command	Description
AT&F	Loads the factory default settings.
ATS0=1	Sets the modem to automatically answer all incoming calls on the first ring.
AT&C1&D3	Sets up modem control (CD and DTR).
ATE0	When echo off is set, the modem will not echo keystrokes.
ATM0	Turns off the external audio output from the modem.

Table 2-9 show that the **ATS0=1** command configures the modem to answer calls on the first ring. Note that, because the Caller ID function activates on the second ring, hackers typically target modems that answer on the first ring. If a modem takes more than one ring to answer, many hackers don't pursue the matter. You are, therefore, advised to set your modem to at least **ATS0=2**, thus pretending that your line subscribes to Caller ID.

When working with modem commands (AT commands), you might notice the use of characters such as the ampersand (&), percentage sign (%), and dollar sign ($). These symbols are used to differentiate between command sets. A list of some of these command sets, and an example of each, follows:

- **Alphabetic command set**—Q0 enables output of result codes.
- **Caret command set**—^V displays the modem current Flash memory bootstrap revision.
- **Dollar command set**—$Bn sets the serial port rate to n bps, for example $B 115200.
- **Percent command set**—%Bn sets the modem port data rate, for example %B 33600.

- **Ampersand command set**—**&D3** sets the modem on-hook and resets when detecting an on-to-off transition of DTR.
- **Parenthesis command set**—**)M1** auto-adjusts the power level for cellular modems.
- **Asterisk command set**—*** I** displays the modem identifier.
- **Hyphen command set**— **-DL** redials the last number dialed.
- **Colon command set**—**:Dn** sets manual dial.
- **@ Character command set**—**@E** gives detailed modem call status.
- **Backslash command set**—**\F** displays stored phone numbers.
- **# Character command set**—**#E0** enables the escape code sequence in answer mode.

Many modem commands are not standardized, and vary from one vendor to another. The following modem configurations and commands are essential for modems that are attached to Cisco access servers:

- **Hardware flow control**—Uses CTS and RTS signaling.
- **Lock DTE speed**—Sets the serial port of the modem to a fixed data transfer rate. Locking the speed between the modem and DTE device prevents the speed from being negotiated downward during the initial call setup.
- **Error correction**—Sets error control.
- **Compression**—Uses the best compression algorithm that can be negotiated between the two communicating modems.
- **Show configuration**—Shows current modem settings.
- **Getting help**—Shows all the AT commands for your specific modem.
- **Saving the configuration**—Saves the configuration that you just entered in the nonvolatile RAM (NVRAM) of the modem.

Table 2-10 shows examples of the AT commands used by three vendors' modems. For nonstandard modem commands, refer to the vendor's manual that comes with the modem.

Table 2-10   Nonstandard Modem Commands

Command	Microcom	Hayes	USR
Hardware flow control	AT\Q3	AT&K3	AT&H1&R2
Lock DTE speed	AT\J0	AT&Q6	AT&B1
Error correction	AT\N6	AT&Q5	AT&M4
Compression	AT%C1	AT&Q9	AT&K1

continues

Table 2-10   Nonstandard Modem Commands (Continued)

Command	Microcom	Hayes	USR
Show configuration	AT\S1	AT&V	ATI4
Getting help	AT$H	AT$H	AT$
Saving the configuration	AT&W	AT&W	AT&W

Automatic Modem Configuration

Initialization strings are used to configure the modem to a known state. They are a series of parameter settings that are sent to your modem to configure it to interact with the access server in a specified way. For example, you can use initialization strings to configure the modem to accept calls or place them. Here's an example of a modem initialization string for a Hayes Optima modem:

AT&FS0=1&C1&D3&K3&Q9&W

Rather than using reverse Telnet to manually enter AT commands, you might prefer to take advantage of automatic modem configuration. When using automatic modem configuration, the Cisco IOS can issue initialization strings automatically for most types of modems. Remember that a modem initialization string is a series of parameter settings that are sent to your modem to configure it to interact with the access server in a specified way.

The Cisco IOS Software predefines several initialization strings that have been found to properly initialize most modems so that the modems function properly with Cisco access servers. These predefined initialization strings are stored in the modem capability database, or modemcap, which is discussed later in this chapter.

There are three approaches to automatic modem configuration:

- **Use modem autodiscovery**—Configure the router to initialize the modem by running through each of the strings stored in the modemcap until one appears to work.
- **Use modem autoconfiguration**—Configure the router to initialize the modem by explicitly specifying one of the several preloaded strings in the modemcap.
- **Use modem autoconfiguration after editing the modemcap database**—Configure the router to initialize the modem by using a user-defined string stored in the modemcap. You can create an entirely new modemcap entry or use an existing entry as a template.

The following sections introduce the modem capability database, and explain how it relates to the three approaches to automatic modem configuration.

Modem Capability Database

The modem capability database (modemcap) is a list of modems with a known set of AT configuration commands for setting the attributes for each modem type. For example, many modems use the string **AT&F** to reset the modem to its factory default attributes.

The specific modemcap entries found on a particular system are determined by the hardware and Cisco IOS Software version that is installed. As shown in Example 2-14, the **show modemcap** command displays the modems in the modemcap database. In addition, if you issue this command while specifying the modem type, it shows a complete list of the modemcap entries including command description, command abbreviation, and command string (see Example 2-15).

Example 2-14 Using the show modemcap Command to Display the Modem Capability Database

```
Router#show modemcap
default
codex_3260
usr_courier
usr_sportster
hayes_optima
global_village
viva
telebit_t3000
microcom_hdms
microcom_server
nec_v34
nec_v110
nec_piafs
cisco_v110
mica
```

Example 2-15 Using the show modemcap Command to Display a Specific Modemcap Entrance

```
Router#show modemcap codex_3260
Modemcap values for codex_3260
Factory Defaults (FD): &F
Autoanswer (AA): S0=1
Carrier detect (CD): &C1
```

continues

Example 2-15 Using the show modemcap Command to Display a Specific Modemcap Entrance (Continued)

```
Drop with DTR (DTR):  &D2

Hardware Flowcontrol (HFL):  *FL3

Lock DTE speed (SPD):  *SC1

DTE locking speed (DTE):  [not set]

Best Error Control (BER):  *SM3

Best Compression (BCP):  *DC1

No Error Control (NER):  *SM1

No Compression (NCP):  *DC0

No Echo (NEC):  E0

No Result Codes (NRS):  Q1

Software Flowcontrol (SFL):  [not set]

Caller ID (CID):  &S1

On-hook (ONH):  H0

Off-hook (OFH):  H1

Miscellaneous (MSC):  [not set]

Template entry (TPL):  default

Modem entry is built-in.
```

For example, if you issue the command **show modemcap codex_3260,** the router outputs the AT command string attributes and their values for the Codex 3260 modem, as shown in Example 2-15.

The first modem type listed in Example 2-14 is called "default." The default modem type has modemcap values for a few of the most common attributes. It does not contain strings for attributes that vary widely by modem type, such as locking speeds, setting hardware flow control, or dealing with compression and error correction.

As you see later in this section, you can also create custom modemcap entries to add new modems or to extend the functionality of a modem in the modemcap database. The preloaded modem strings included in the IOS modemcap cannot be edited or deleted.

Modem Autodiscovery

The easiest way to configure a modem is to use the router's automatic modem discovery feature, but this approach has substantial disadvantages. With modem autodiscovery, the router sends modem commands until it gets an expected response. From the responses it receives, the router attempts to classify the modem as one of the modems in its modemcap database. The Cisco IOS Software initially tries the first of the modemcap strings to see if the modem initializes properly. If not, the Cisco IOS Software cycles to the next string and repeats the process until the appropriate string is found. If none of the strings properly initializes the modem, you must manually configure the modem using reverse Telnet.

You can enable modem autodiscovery by issuing the following command in line configuration mode:

```
Router(config-line)#modem autoconfigure discovery
```

Although this approach is simple, modem autodiscovery must be avoided when possible for the following reasons:

- The router might fail to recognize a modem, even though it might be part of the modemcap database.
- The router might misidentify a modem, leading to unexpected results.
- Autodiscovery is slower than autoconfiguration.

In practice, you should use the autoconfiguration feature—not autodiscovery—whenever possible. Modem autoconfiguration is enabled with the **modem autoconfigure type** command. By specifying exactly which modem string to use out of the modemcap database, autoconfiguration is quicker and more predictable than autodiscovery.

Modem Autoconfiguration

The preferred way to configure an attached modem is to use modem autoconfiguration. Autoconfiguration requires that you determine which one of the modemcap strings works with your modem. If none of the included strings works, you can create your own string and still use the autoconfiguration feature.

Enable modem autoconfiguration by issuing the following command in line configuration mode:

```
Router(config-line)#modem autoconfigure type modem-string
```

This command requires you to specify which modem string to use out of the modemcap database. By specifically defining the string, you eliminate the overhead, delay, and unpredictability associated with autodiscovery. Table 2-11 compares autodiscovery methods with autoconfiguration when using a USR modem.

Table 2-11   Time Elapsed when Using Autodiscovery and Autoconfigure

Test Description	Time
Autodiscovery with no match found (therefore, default settings were applied), unknown discovery	Six seconds
Autodiscovery with a match found (USR Sportster), known discovery	Five seconds
Autoconfigure with modem type specified (type USR)	Two seconds

In Example 2-16, the access server (RTA) is configured to send an initialization string for a USR Sportster modem on line 1.

Example 2-16 Specifying a Modem for Autoconfiguration

```
RTA(config)#line 1
RTA(config-line)#modem autoconfigure type usr_sportster
```

With automatic modem configuration, each time a modem is reset, a chat script is processed that sends a string of modem configuration commands (AT commands) to the modem. This modem configuration command string is generated automatically whenever the modem is power cycled.

Fine-Tuning Modem Autoconfiguration

If none of the strings from the modemcap properly initializes the modem, you can either manually configure the modem or add an entry to the modemcap database.

To manually configure the modem, you can use reverse Telnet to connect to the modem and issue AT commands, as discussed previously.

Alternately, you can use the autoconfiguration feature by creating a modem-string in the modemcap database. To add to the modemcap database, use this command:

```
modemcap edit new_modem_name
```

Note that user-defined modemcap entries become part of the running-configuration file, and not a permanent part of the IOS database. Be sure to copy your running-config to NVRAM after making changes to the modemcap database.

Chat Scripts for Async Lines

A *chat script* is a string of text that includes commands that can be sent to a device when performing a specific task. For example, a router can use a chat script to send AT commands to a modem, instructing the modem to place a call. Because modem commands are not standard, you must write custom chat scripts to perform certain tasks, including:

- Instructing the modem to dial out (modem script)
- Logging in to a remote system (system script)

You have already seen how to initialize a modem manually using reverse Telnet, and automatically using modem strings in the modemcap database. Even after your modem is initialized, the router still has to pass commands to the modem to instruct it to dial out, or log in to a remote system.

The structure of a chat script is simple, although actual chat scripts look complex:

```
Router(config)#chat-script script-name expect-string send-string
```

Chat scripts are written in the form *expect-string send-string*. The expect-send pairs define both the string that the local system expects to see from the remote device and the reply that the local system should send.

Example 2-17 presents a typical **chat-script** command.

Example 2-17 A Typical chat-script Command

```
RTA(config)#chat-script Reno ABORT ERROR ABORT BUSY "" "ATZ" OK "ATDT \T" TIMEOUT
  30 CONNECT \c
```

Example 2-17 creates a chat script called Reno. The **ABORT** keyword designates a string whose presence in the input indicates that the chat script has failed. In this case, if the modem returns either **ERROR** or **BUSY**, the router will determine that the script has failed.

The first expect-send pair (**""** **"ATZ"**) tells the router to expect nothing and issue the ATZ command. The next pair, (**OK "ATDT \T"**) tells the router to expect the modem to return with **OK**. After the router sees **OK**, it will issue the next command (**ATDT \T**).

The **ATDT \T** command is critical when you are writing a chat script for placing a call (otherwise known as a modem script). The **ATDT** string instructs the modem to tone dial a number. The **D** stands for "dial," while the second **T** stands for "tone." The router replaces the \T (the third T in the string) with a pre-configured phone number before sending the string to the modem.

Where does the router get this phone number? Because this script is written to be a modem script, its name will probably be included in a **dialer map** statement, as shown here:

```
RTA(config-if)#dialer map ip 10.1.1.2 name RTB modem-script Reno 5556002
```

In this example, the chat script, Reno, is being used as a modem script. A modem script applies commands immediately to a line. Here, the example router should eventually send the **ATDT \T** command, where \T will be replaced by the phone number specified in the **dialer map** statement (555-6002). There are several different ways to invoke a chat script; the **dialer map** command is one of the most common, because a chat script is required for the modem to dial out.

Configuring Asynchronous Connections Between Remote Routers

Figure 2-26 presents a simple asynchronous dial-up scenario that applies the concepts covered in this chapter, including chat scripts and DDR. The branch router at the San Francisco site (a 2620) uses a Hayes modem to dial the central site router in San Jose, a 3640 router.

> **NOTE**
>
> Chat scripts can also be used to pass login information to a remote system. These scripts, not covered in this book, are referred to as *system scripts*.

Figure 2-26
The San Francisco
branch office uses
an asynchronous
dial-up connection
for DDR.

Because the AUX port on the San Francisco router is used for out-of-band management, the router's serial 0/1 interface is connected to the modem for DDR. Remember that for a router to use a serial interface as a TTY, the **physical-layer async** command must be issued in interface configuration mode.

The commands shown in Example 2-18 configure the logical interface for the AUX port on the San Jose router.

Example 2-18 San Jose Router Configuration Tasks

```
SJ(config)#interface async 129 (corresponds to AUX on a 3640 router)
SJ(config-if)#ip address 10.1.1.1 255.255.255.0
SJ(config-if)#encapsulation ppp
SJ(config-if)#ppp authentication chap
The following lines configure DDR:
SJ(config-if)#dialer in-band
SJ(config-if)#dialer map ip 10.1.1.2 name SF modem-script hayes56k 5551002
SJ(config-if)#dialer-group 1
SJ(config-if)#exit
SJ(config)#dialer-list 1 protocol ip permit
The following lines configure the physical terminal line:
SJ(config)#line aux 0
SJ(config-line)#login
SJ(config-line)#password cisco
SJ(config-line)#speed 115200
SJ(config-line)#flowcontrol hardware
SJ(config-line)#stopbits 1
SJ(config-line)#transport input all
SJ(config-line)#modem inout
SJ(config-line)#modem autoconfigure type hayes_optima
SJ(config-line)#exit
The following line configures a chat script so the modem can dial out:
SJ(config)#chat-script hayes56k ABORT ERROR ABORT BUSY "" "ATZ" OK "ATDT \T"
  TIMEOUT 30 CONNECT \c
SJ(config)#ip route 172.16.2.0 255.255.255.0 10.1.1.2
```

The last line of the example uses the **ip route** command to configure a static route (so DDR will work).

The commands shown in Example 2-19 configure interface serial 0/1 as async on the San Francisco router.

Example 2-19 San Francisco Branch Router Configuration Tasks

```
SF(config)#interface serial 0/1
SF(config-if)#physical-layer async
SF(config-if)#ip address 10.1.1.2 255.255.255.0
SF(config-if)#encapsulation ppp
SF(config-if)#ppp authentication chap
The following lines configure DDR:
SF(config-if)#dialer in-band
SF(config-if)#dialer map ip 10.1.1.1 name SJ modem-script hayes56k 5551001
SF(config-if)#dialer-group 1
SF(config-if)#exit
SF(config)#dialer-list 1 protocol ip permit
The following lines configure the physical terminal lines:
SF(config)#line 2 (corresponds to serial 0/1 tty on this model)
SF(config-line)#login
SF(config-line)#password cisco
SF(config-line)#speed 115200
SF(config-line)#flowcontrol hardware
SF(config-line)#stopbits 1
SF(config-line)#transport input all
SF(config-line)#modem inout
SF(config-line)#modem autoconfigure type hayes_optima
SF(config-line)#exit
The following line configures a chat script so the modem can dial out:
SF(config)#chat-script hayes56k ABORT ERROR ABORT BUSY "" "ATZ" OK "ATDT \T"
   TIMEOUT 30 CONNECT \c
SF(config)#ip route 0.0.0.0 0.0.0.0 10.1.1.1
```

The last line of this example uses the **ip route** command to configure a static route (so DDR will work).

Verifying and Troubleshooting Modem Configuration

The **debug confmodem** command displays the modem configuration process, and is a useful troubleshooting tool. Example 2-20 shows the output of the **debug confmodem** command when using modem autodiscovery. Example 2-21 shows debug output for an autoconfiguration process on the access server's line 2 with a Hayes Optima modem attached.

Example 2-20 Using the debug confmodem Command with Autodiscovery

```
RTA#debug confmodem
Modem Configuration Database debugging is on
RTA#config t
RTA(config)#line 2
RTA(config-line)#modem auto discovery
00:22:44: TTY2: detection speed (115200) response ---OK---
00:23:10: TTY2: Modem type is default
00:23:10: TTY2: Modem command:  --AT&F&C1&D2S0=1H0--
00:23:12: TTY2: Modem configuration succeeded
00:23:12: TTY2: Detected modem speed 115200
00:23:12: TTY2: Done with modem configuration
```

Example 2-21 Using the debug confmodem Command with Autoconfigure

```
RTA#debug confmodem
Modem Configuration Database debugging is on
RTA#config t
RTA(config)#line 2
RTA(config-line)#modem auto type hayes_optima
00:21:33: TTY2: detection speed (115200) response ---OK---
00:21:33: TTY2: Modem command:  --AT&F&C1&D2&K3&Q5&Q9&Q6S0=1H0--
00:21:36: TTY2: Modem configuration succeeded
00:21:41: TTY2: detection speed (115200) response ---OK---
00:21:41: TTY2: Done with modem configuration
```

You can also use the following commands to verify operations:

- The **show line** command shows the type of modem configured on a line.
- The **clear line** *line-number* command returns a line to its idle state. Normally, this command returns the line to its conventional function as a terminal line with the interface in a down state.

The **clear line** command is very useful, especially if you cannot reverse Telnet to the modem because the line did not reset properly.

To troubleshoot modem autoconfiguration, consider the following conditions and solutions: the modem is not responding, the modem is not recognized by autodiscovery, or there is a modemcap entry problem.

If the modem is not responding, check the following:

- Is the modem plugged in and turned on?
- Is the power-up configuration set to factory default?
- Can you connect to the modem through reverse Telnet?
- Do you have a dial tone at the phone jack?

If the modem is not recognized by the modem autodiscovery process:

- Use the **show line** command to verify the modem configuration that the line is using.
- Make sure that the Cisco access server recognizes the modem.
- Use the modem **autoconfigure type modem-name** command.
- Use the **show modemcap** command to verify modemcap support for this modem.

If there is an original modemcap entry problem:

- If you configured your own modemcap entry and reconfiguration appears to function, verify that the DTR attribute is not set to **&D3**.

As a last resort, don't forget that you can also check the modem manufacturer's manual.

Configuring a Windows PC Dial-Up Connection

Until now, this chapter focused on using modems with access servers. Typically, a networking professional must support remote end-users as well. To connect to the central site using POTS, mobile users will use a modem connected to their PC.

Today's PC modems are generally internal, and today's PC operating systems can automatically configure modems without requiring the user to enter confusing AT commands.

However, despite these simplicities in cabling and configuration, there is still configuration work to be done. An end-user PC must be configured with dial-up information such as phone numbers, passwords, and protocols.

This section focuses on configuring Microsoft Windows 95/98 PCs. The same configuration principles described here can be applied to PCs running Microsoft Windows ME, XP, NT, and 2000.

Windows 95/98 includes a specialized software component called Dial-Up Networking (DUN). This software allows you to configure dial-up connection parameters so that you can send to and receive data from remote systems. If DUN is not already installed on a PC, it can be easily added by using the Add/Remove Programs feature from the Windows Control Panel. (You must have access to the Windows *.cab* files to install this software. The *.cab* files can be found on a Windows System CD.)

When you install DUN, any Layer-3 protocols that are already installed on the computer are automatically enabled for dial-up use. Windows 95/98 includes support for TCP/IP, IPX/SPX, and NetBEUI network protocols.

After DUN is installed, you can create a connection using the Make New Connection wizard by following these steps:

Step 1   From the My Computer window, double-click the Dial-Up Networking folder, as shown in Figure 2-27.

Step 2   From the Dial-Up Networking window, double-click Make New Connection, as shown in Figure 2-28.

Step 3   Supply information that the Make New Connection wizard needs to define a connection, including a name for the computer you are dialing and your PC modem type, as shown in Figure 2-29.

Step 4   Provide the area code, telephone number, and country code of the system that you will call, as shown in Figure 2-30.

The new icon for your connection appears in the Dial-Up Networking window. You need to provide this information only once for each connection that you define. After the New Connection icon is created, you might want to make it a shortcut and place it on your desktop.

Figure 2-27
Windows 95/98
includes a Dial-Up
Networking folder in
the My Computer
window.

Figure 2-28
Use the Make New
Connection wizard to
create a Dial-Up Net-
working connection.

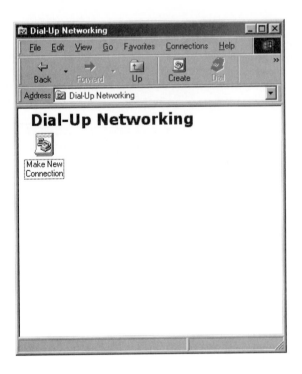

Figure 2-29
Use the Make New
Connection wizard to
define connection
parameters.

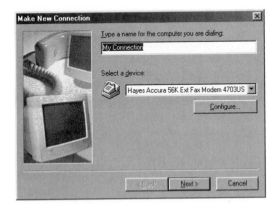

Figure 2-30
While using the
Make New Connec-
tion wizard, provide
the area code, tele-
phone number, and
country code of the
system that you
will call.

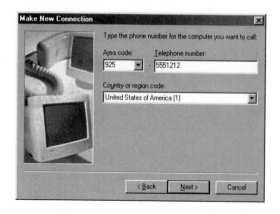

To configure the Windows 95/98 Dial-Up Client, complete the following steps:

Step 1   From the Dial-Up Networking window shown in Figure 2-31, click
Properties from the File menu (or right-click on a connection icon and
then click Properties).

Step 2   From the General tab of the dialog box, click Server Types, as shown in
Figure 2-32. Depending on your Windows 95 revision, the Server Types
function appears either as a button or a tab.

Step 3   From the Server Types dialog box, select the correct remote-access server
type, as seen in Figure 2-33.

Step 4   From the Server Types dialog box, you can optionally select the follow-
ing advanced options:
— Log on to network—NT domain only
— Enable software compression—Use Microsoft's compression feature
— Require encrypted password—Registration / Authorization / Status
(RAS) dial-in

Step 5   From the Server Types dialog box, select from the following allowed
network protocols:
— NetBEUI
— IPX/SPX compatible
— TCP/IP

Figure 2-31
To configure the properties of a DUN connection, right-click the connection and select Properties.

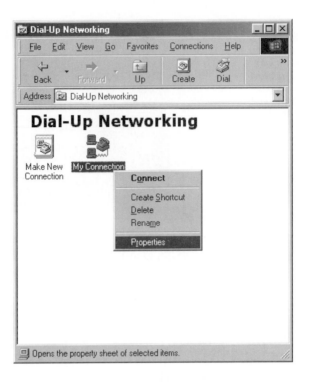

Figure 2-32
You can configure various connection options from the Server Types tab.

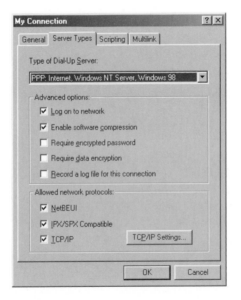

Figure 2-33
From the Server
Types tab, you can
select the type of
dial-up server.

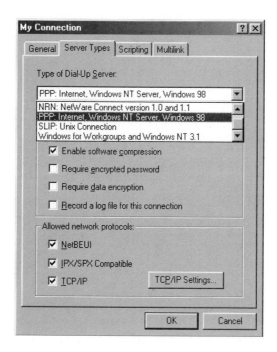

With Windows NT and locally defined usernames on a network access server, you
need to configure the username with the **DOMAIN\\username** command string in
order for direct network login to work with CHAP authentication.

After you define a remote connection with the Make New Connection wizard, you can
use the connection in two ways:

- Double-click the connection icon in the Dial-Up Networking window.
- Connect to a remote network resource when you work in an application other
  than DUN. If you cannot find the resource on the current network, Windows
  responds by automatically activating DUN.

After you establish or end a connection, you do not need to restart the computer
or Windows.

Windows automatically starts DUN when:

- You try to access a network resource and your computer is not connected to a
  network.
- Your application specifies a Universal Naming Convention (UNC) name (which
  uses the form \\servername\sharename) that cannot be accessed by using the LAN.

■ You double-click a link that points to a remote network object (for example, when an application attempts to connect to a file on a network server or when you reconnect to a remote OLE object).

To disable the DUN prompt in Dial-Up Networking, click the Connection menu and then click Settings. Select the Don't Prompt To Use Dial-Up Networking option.

Summary

In this chapter, you learned how to configure an access server for modem connectivity. To do this, you learned how to perform a reverse Telnet session to the modem, how to configure the modem and router for basic asynchronous operations, and how to use modem autoconfiguration. You also learned how to set up DUN on a Windows PC.

In the next chapter, you will learn how to establish a PPP session over the terminal lines you have configured for asynchronous connectivity.

Review Questions

Use the following review questions to test your understanding of the concepts covered in this chapter. In some cases, there is more than one correct answer, so choose all that apply. Answers are listed in Appendix A, "Answers to Review Questions."

1. Which of the following is not true about modems?

   A. Modems convert digital signals to analog waves

   B. Modems convert analog waves to digital signals

   C. Modems are DTEs

   D. Modems are DCEs

2. Which of the following are signaling standards used for DTE-to-DCE signaling?

   A. V.34

   B. V.35

   C. X.21

   D. X.25

3. Which of the following devices would you most likely use to connect your router to a leased T1 lines?

   A. Modem

   B. Access server

   C. HSSI

   D. CSU/DSU

4. Which of the following standards would you most likely use to connect an external modem to your router's AUX port?

   A. EIA/TIA-232

   B. V.35

   C. HSSI

   D. X.21

5. What types of connection use reverse Telnet?

   A. Secure, handshake-oriented connection from workstation to router

   B. Connection from router to attached modem

   C. Connection from Telnet server to Telnet client

   D. Secure, handshake-oriented connection from router to remote TCP/IP host

6. At which prompt would you issue the **transport input all** command?

   A. (config)#

   B. (config-router)#

   C. (config-line)#

   D. (config-if)#

7. What is the function of the **dialer-list** command?

   A. Specify "interesting" traffic

   B. Specify dial-out phone numbers

   C. Specify a group of modems or terminal lines

   D. Specify a list of allowed dial-in users

8. Which of the following configures modem autoconfiguration using an entry from the modemcap database?

   A. (config-if)#**modem autoconfigure type usr_sportster**

   B. (config-if)#**modem autoconfigure discovery**

   C. (config-line)#**modem autoconfigure usr_courier**

   D. (config-line)#**modem autoconfigure type mica**

9. What is a chat script used for?

   A. String of characters that can used to instruct a modem to dial out

   B. String of characters exchanged between a PC and a router for management purpose

   C. String of characters used for logging in to a remote system

   D. String of characters used to configure a router

10. Which Windows 95/98 component manages dial-out modem connections?

    A. DUN

    B. Network Neighborhood

    C. TCP/IP

    D. Modem control panel

Key Terms

Chat script   String of text that includes commands that can be sent to a device as an instruction to perform a specific task, such as dialing out, or logging in.

Codec   Device used by telecommunications companies to encode analog waveforms into digital pulses and vice versa.

EIA/TIA-232-C   Common physical layer interface standard, developed by EIA and TIA, that supports unbalanced circuits at signal speeds of up to 64 Kbps. Closely resembles the V.24 specification. Formerly known as RS-232.

HSSI (High-Speed Serial Interface)   Network standard for high-speed (up to 52 Mbps) serial connections over WAN links.

Null modem cable   Cable used to join DTE devices directly, rather than over a network.

PCM   pulse code modulation. Transmission of analog information in digital form through sampling and encoding the samples with a fixed number of bits.

PSTN   Public Switched Telephone Network. General term referring to the variety of telephone networks and services in place worldwide. Sometimes called plain old telephone service (POTS).

Reverse Telnet   Outgoing Telnet session that passes from the access server to an attached device over an asynchronous serial connection. Used to configure attached modems, routers, and terminals.

UART   Universal Asynchronous Receiver/Transmitter. A UART is a specialized microchip designed to control a computer's interface to its attached serial devices (such as an external modem or a mouse).

V.35   ITU-T standard describing a synchronous, physical layer protocol used for communications between a network access device and a packet network.

Objectives

After completing this chapter, you will be able to perform tasks related to the following:

- PPP fundamentals
- LCP configuration features
- PPP authentication
- PPP callback
- PPP compression
- Multilink PPP
- Verifying PPP configurations

Chapter 3

PPP

Introduction

Chapter 2, "Modems and Asynchronous Connections," explained how to configure an asynchronous line for a dial-up connection. In this chapter, you learn how to configure that dial-up connection to connect to the network using Point-to-Point Protocol (PPP) at the data link layer.

PPP is used extensively in today's networks. It is based on open standards and includes a variety of essential features, making it the de facto standard for dial-up and dedicated WAN connections. As a network professional, you need to be familiar with PPP's features, particularly the authentication protocols it supports: *Password Authentication Protocol* (*PAP*) and *Challenge Handshake Authentication Protocol* (*CHAP*).

This chapter provides you with an overview of PPP and surveys its link configuration options: authentication, callback, compression, and *Multilink PPP* (*MLP*). Finally, this chapter includes PPP verification, troubleshooting techniques, and a PPP configuration example.

PPP Fundamentals

In order for any Layer 3 protocol to traverse the WAN over a dial-up or dedicated link, it must be encapsulated by a data-link layer protocol. Figure 3-1 shows that remote nodes connecting to an access server can use TCP/IP or other protocols at the network layer (Layer 3). The figure also shows PPP, the *Serial Line Internet Protocol* (*SLIP*), and the *AppleTalk Remote Access Protocol* (*ARAP*) working at the data link layer (Layer 2) to encapsulate these routed protocols.

Figure 3-1
PPP supports multiple Layer 3 protocols, including TCP/IP, Novell IPX, and AppleTalk.

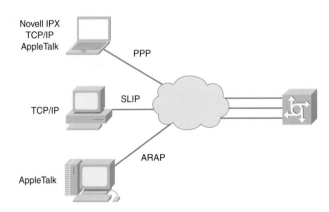

Although some organizations continue to provide remote access to hosts using Novell IPX and AppleTalk, TCP/IP is now the dominant protocol on corporate networks. For this reason, the rest of this chapter focuses only on encapsulating TCP/IP.

Today, essentially two data link layer protocols are used to encapsulate TCP/IP:

- **SLIP**—SLIP is a standard protocol for point-to-point serial connections, using TCP/IP. SLIP was a predecessor of PPP.
- **PPP**—PPP provides router-to-router and host-to-network connections over synchronous and asynchronous circuits, which can be either dial-up or leased lines.

PPP is a more recent standard than SLIP and is almost always the preferred data link layer encapsulation on dial-up asynchronous links. On a Cisco router, SLIP is the default encapsulation on an asynchronous dial-up interface, so you must manually configure the encapsulation in order to use PPP.

Although both SLIP and PPP were designed with Internet Protocol (IP) in mind, SLIP is essentially limited to use with IP, whereas PPP can be used for other network-layer protocols, such as IPX and AppleTalk. Moreover, PPP supports essential features such as dynamic address allocation, PAP authentication, CHAP authentication, and MLP. SLIP does not support these features. As legacy technologies, SLIP and ARAP are rarely implemented in new network designs, although both protocols remain in use. Neither protocol is covered in this book. For additional configuration information, refer to Cisco Connection Online (CCO) at www.cisco.com.

High-Level Data Link Control (HDLC) is the default encapsulation for ISDN and serial interfaces on a Cisco router. Although HDLC is the default encapsulation, Cisco's HDLC is not compatible with other vendors' HDLC implementations. PPP implementations follow open standards and are almost always compatible. PPP is the protocol of choice when configuring serial links in a multivendor environment.

PPP Architecture

PPP is a non-proprietary protocol that is defined by a series of open Internet standards called Requests for Comments (RFCs). For this reason, PPP is referred to as a standards-based protocol.

PPP can negotiate link options dynamically and can support multiple Layer 3 protocols (IP, IPX, AppleTalk, and so on). PPP accomplishes these two tasks by encapsulating Layer 3 datagrams with a specialized frame. PPP's frame format is based on the HDLC frame format put forth by the International Organization for Standardization (ISO). Unlike the ISO's HDLC frame, the PPP frame defines a Protocol field.

PPP defines the Link Control Protocol (LCP). The job of LCP is to establish, configure, and test the data-link connection. When hosts negotiate a PPP connection, they exchange LCP packets. These packets allow link partners to dynamically negotiate link options, including authentication, compression, and MLP.

After the LCP establishes the Layer 2 connection, the *Network Control Protocol* (*NCP*) takes over. Link partners exchange NCP packets to establish and configure different network-layer protocols, including IP, IPX, and AppleTalk. Each Layer 3 protocol has its own NCP, as shown in Table 3-1.

NOTE

PPP actually uses HDLC as a basis for encapsulating datagrams. However, PPP is more extensible than HDLC because it adds extensions (features) to the link layer. PPP's use of HDLC is discussed in the next section.

Table 3-1   Common PPP NCPs

Protocol	NCP
TCP/IP	IPCP
IPX	IPXCP
AppleTalk	ATALKCP
Cisco Discovery Protocol	CDPCP
DECnet	DECCP
XNS	XNSCP
Vines	VINESCP
CLNS (OSI)	OSICP

The NCP can build and tear down multiple Layer 3 protocol sessions over a single data link. This capability is called *protocol multiplexing*. When a host requests that the connection be terminated, the NCP tears down the Layer 3 sessions, and then the LCP tears down the data link.

Figure 3-2 shows that PPP is similar to an HDLC frame. The Protocol field contains the Layer 3 protocol ID. The LCP can negotiate modifications to the standard PPP frame structure. Figure 3-3 shows that PPP's components operate at Layer 2 of the OSI model.

Figure 3-2
The PPP frame is based on the HDLC frame, but it defines a Protocol field.

HDLC ISO Frame

Flag	Address	Control	Data (Payload)	FCS	Flag
1 byte	1 byte	1 or 2 bytes	1500 bytes	2 (or 4) bytes	1 byte

PPP Frame

Flag	Address	Control	Protocol	Data	FCS	Flag
1 byte	1 byte	1 byte	1 or 2 bytes	Up to 1500 bytes	2 (or 4) bytes	1 byte

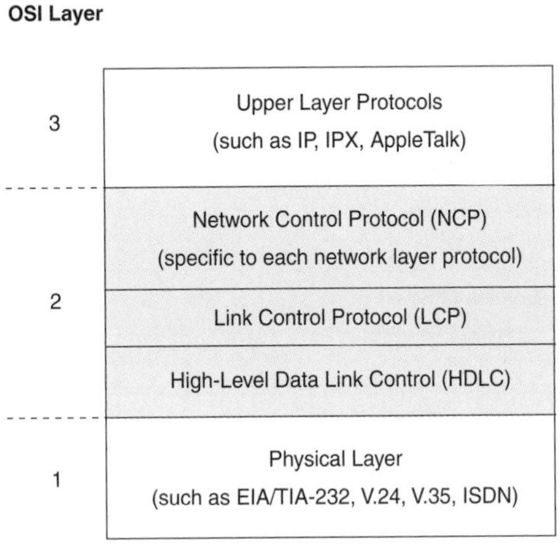

Figure 3-3
PPP works at Layer 2 of the OSI model.

OSI Layer

Layer	Protocol
3	Upper Layer Protocols (such as IP, IPX, AppleTalk)
2	Network Control Protocol (NCP) (specific to each network layer protocol)
2	Link Control Protocol (LCP)
2	High-Level Data Link Control (HDLC)
1	Physical Layer (such as EIA/TIA-232, V.24, V.35, ISDN)

Basic PPP Configuration

Enable PPP encapsulation on a WAN interface by using the following command:

```
Router(config-if)#encapsulation ppp
```

If you want dial-in hosts on terminal line 2 to use PPP, you must enter the commands shown in Example 3-1.

Example 3-1 Configuring an Interface for PPP

```
RTA(config)#interface async 2
RTA(config-if)#encapsulation ppp
```

When a remote host dials in to an access server's asynchronous interface, it can start an EXEC session with the router. This feature allows remote users to log in to the router and issue commands as if the user were connected to the console port. No IP addressing or PPP encapsulation is needed for this type of connection. Data is sent as asynchronous characters.

Alternately, a remote host can dial in to an access server and send a Layer 3 protocol packet encapsulated by PPP, SLIP, or ARAP. This type of connection allows the remote user to access network resources, such as file servers and mail servers. Figure 3-4 illustrates the difference between an EXEC session and a PPP session from the user's perspective.

NOTE

The **encapsulation** command is issued in interface configuration mode, not line configuration mode.

Figure 3-4
PPP sessions can be used to encapsulate Layer 3 protocols, such as IP, whereas an asynchronous call can also establish an EXEC session with the router.

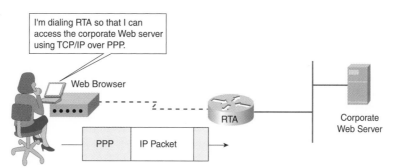

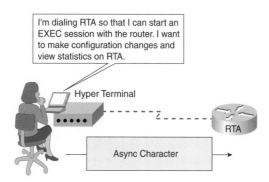

Although some organizations still provide dial-in EXEC access to their users, this practice is becoming increasingly rare. Typical end users do not require access to the router's command-line interface. Instead, they need a Layer 3 protocol (IP and so on) connection to the corporate network or the Internet. In most cases, you should force the asynchronous interface to use PPP and not allow an EXEC connection.

The following sections detail how to configure an access server to autoselect the type of session (PPP or EXEC), and how to force a dedicated PPP session over asynchronous dial-up connections.

Configuring Interactive PPP Sessions

With the PPP autoselect feature, you can configure an access server's terminal line to provide either a PPP session or an EXEC session based on input from the remote host. This feature allows the remote host to determine the session type. The access server automatically detects which type of session is being requested and responds accordingly.

Enabling this feature requires two steps. First, you must configure the asynchronous interface(s) with the **async mode interactive** command in interface configuration mode. This command configures the router so that it allows the remote host to choose either a PPP session or an EXEC session. The following commands show how to configure interface async 1:

```
RTA(config)#interface async 1
RTA(config-if)#encapsulation ppp
RTA(config-if)#async mode interactive
```

Second, you must configure the corresponding terminal line(s) with the **autoselect ppp** command in line configuration mode. To complete the example configuration, enter the following commands:

```
RTA(config)#line 1
RTA(config-line)#autoselect ppp during-login
```

NOTE

PPP frames always start with the same flag byte, 01111110 (7E in hexadecimal).

The **autoselect** command permits the access server to allow an appropriate process to start automatically when a starting character is received. If the start character is a return character, the access server starts an EXEC session. Users who want to begin an EXEC session typically press the Return key after establishing a dial-up connection. On the other hand, if the access server recognizes the start character as PPP, SLIP, or ARAP, it begins a session for whichever protocol it detects (see Figure 3-5). If an end user is using a program that sends a PPP frame, the access server automatically starts a PPP session.

Figure 3-6 illustrates that the access server detects either a return character, which is the start character for an EXEC session, or the start character for one of the protocols specified (in this case, PPP). PPP frames always start with a flag character having the value 7E in hexadecimal (or 01111110 in binary) format.

The **during-login** option of the **autoselect** command causes the username/password prompt to display in the remote host's terminal window without the user needing to press the Return key. The **during-login** keyword is not required.

Figure 3-5
PPP can be configured to autoselect between an EXEC session and a data session using PPP, SLIP, or ARAP encapsulation.

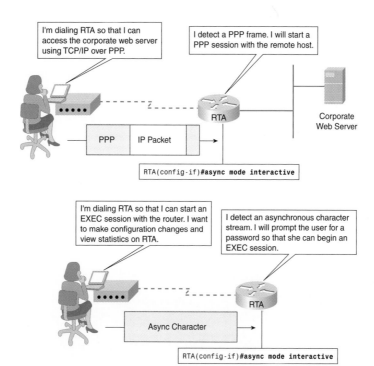

Figure 3-6
The router determines whether to start an EXEC session or data session using PPP, SLIP, or ARAP based on the type of frame received from the remote host.

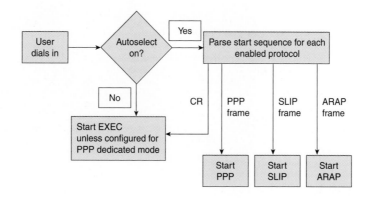

After a host establishes an EXEC session, the remote user can switch to a PPP session at any time by issuing the **ppp** command at the router prompt, as shown in the following code and in Figure 3-7:

```
Router>ppp
```

Configuring Dedicated PPP Sessions

In most cases, you need to configure your access server's asynchronous lines in dedicated mode so that users are forced to use PPP. In dedicated mode, an interface is automatically configured for PPP connections. There is no user prompt or EXEC level, and no end-user commands are required to initiate remote-node connections.

To ensure that the dial-in user must run PPP on the specified line, use the **async mode dedicated** command:

```
Router(config-if)#async mode dedicated
```

Configuring the Interface Addressing Method for Local Devices

Most dial-up PPP sessions are established for sending and receiving TCP/IP packets. Asynchronous PPP connections allow remote users to dial up and access the corporate IP network or the Internet.

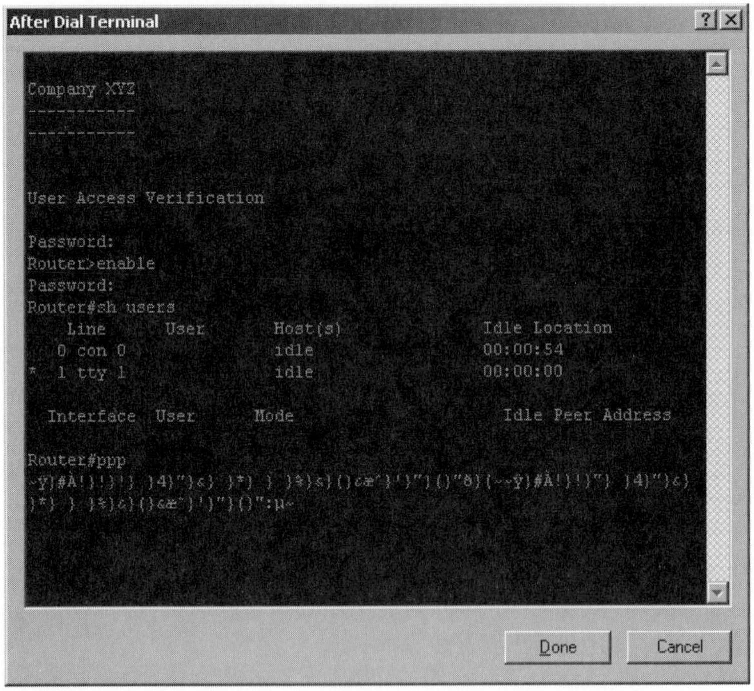

Figure 3-7
After logging in to a router through an asynchronous dial-up connection, a user can issue the ppp command to start a PPP session.

In order for remote nodes to participate in a TCP/IP network, they must have an IP address. This means that the remote node's link partner, the router's asynchronous interface, must also have an IP address.

To assign an IP address to an access server's asynchronous interface, use the **ip address** command (which is the same command that assigns addresses to Ethernet or Serial interfaces). Example 3-2 configures the IP address of interface async 1.

Example 3-2 Configuring a Dial-In Interface for TCP/IP

```
RTA(config)#interface async 1
RTA(config-if)#ip address 10.1.1.1 255.255.255.0
```

Because access servers can have literally hundreds of asynchronous interfaces, and because all of them are not likely to be in use at the same time, you might want to conserve IP addresses by using the IP unnumbered feature.

When a serial or asynchronous interface is configured with the **ip unnumbered** command, it does not have an IP address. Packets generated by that interface borrow the address of another interface and use that as the source address. The IP unnumbered feature can only be used with point-to-point configurations. The syntax for the **ip unnumbered** command is the following:

```
Router(config-if)#ip unnumbered type number
```

With this command, you must specify the type and number of the interface to borrow the IP address from (Ethernet 0, Loopback0, and so on). A *loopback interface* is a virtual interface that never goes down, and is therefore an ideal interface to use as the reference with the **ip unnumbered** command. Example 3-3 shows how to configure an asynchronous interface for IP unnumbered using a loopback interface.

> **NOTE**
>
> Multiple async interfaces on the same router can share the same IP address, including an address assigned by the IP unnumbered feature.

Example 3-3 Configuring IP Unnumbered

```
RTA(config)#interface loopback 0
RTA(config-if)#ip address 10.1.1.1 255.255.255.0
RTA(config-if)#exit
RTA(config)#interface async 1
RTA(config-if)#ip unnumbered loopback 0
```

Configuring the Interface Addressing Method for Remote Devices

Addressing the access server's asynchronous interface is only half of the IP address configuration equation. You must also implement a mechanism for assigning IP addresses to remote dial-in users. PPP allows for the automatic assignment of IP addresses using a specific address, a pool of addresses, or the Dynamic Host Configuration Protocol (DHCP). Alternately, you can configure the access server to allow the remote host to choose its own address.

> **NOTE**
>
> For more information on DHCP and DHCP configurations, see *CCNP Cisco Networking Academy Program: Advanced Routing Companion Guide.*

To assign a default (predefined) IP address to the remote dial-in host, use the **peer default ip address** command, as shown in Example 3-4.

Example 3-4 Assigning a Predefined IP Address to a Remote Dial-In Host

```
RTA(config)#interface async 1
RTA(config-if)#peer default ip address 10.1.1.2
```

Additionally, the **pool** and **dhcp** arguments allow address allocation from a local pool of addresses or from a DHCP server. Example 3-5 shows how to configure a group of asynchronous interfaces (rotary group) to assign IP addresses from a locally defined pool.

Example 3-5 Assigning IP Addresses from a Locally Defined Pool

```
RTA(config)#ip local pool DIAL-IN 10.1.1.2 10.1.1.254
RTA(config)#interface group-async 1
RTA(config-if)#ip peer default ip address pool DIAL-IN
```

The **pool** and **dhcp** options in the **peer default ip address** command require a global command to create the pool of addresses. This command follows the syntax, **ip local pool** *pool-name starting-address end-address*. In Example 3-5, the command **ip local pool DIAL-IN 10.1.1.2 10.1.1.254** creates a pool of 253 different addresses that can be assigned to dial-in hosts.

As an alternate remote addressing strategy, you can allow the remote host to choose its own IP address. If you configured an asynchronous interface for interactive mode, you have the option to allow the IP address to be assigned dynamically by the caller. After the remote user enters the **ppp** EXEC command, the access server prompts the user for an IP address or logical host name.

To enable this dynamic addressing feature, use the **async dynamic address** command in interface configuration mode:

```
Router(config-if)#async dynamic address
```

LCP Configuration Features

In Figure 3-8, PPP offers a rich set of features that are configured by LCP during link establishment. The configuration features negotiated through the LCP are the following:

- Authentication, with PAP or CHAP, is used as a security measure with PPP and PPP callback. Authentication allows the dial-up target to identify that any given dial-up client is a valid client with a preassigned username and password.

- *Callback* is a PPP option that provides call and dial-up billing consolidation. PPP callback was first supported in Cisco IOS Release 11.0(3).

- *Compression* improves throughput across existing lines. PPP compression was first supported in Cisco IOS Release 10.3. Cisco routers support *Stacker, Predictor,* and *Microsoft Point to Point Compression* (*MPPC*).

- MLP takes advantage of multiple ISDN B channels to improve throughput. Datagrams are split, sequenced, transmitted across multiple links, and then recombined at the destination. The multiple links together are called a *bundle.* Multilink is especially useful with ISDN BRI configurations, where both B channels can achieve 128-Kbps throughput. MLP also works with modems to provide additional bandwidth. This protocol was first supported in Cisco IOS Release 11.0(3).

Figure 3-8
LCP configures four key optional features: authentication, callback, compression, and MLP.

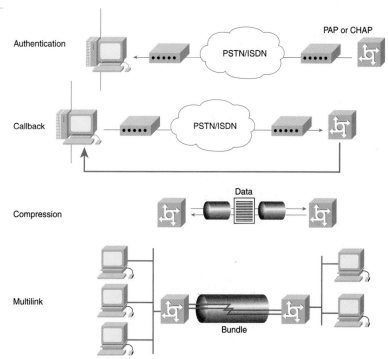

The following sections explain how to configure these PPP link options.

PPP Authentication

You should always configure asynchronous lines to require authentication. With PPP, you have the option to require that callers authenticate using one of two authentication protocols, PAP or CHAP. If you are using PPP over a point-to-point leased line, authentication is unnecessary and should not be configured.

Figure 3-9 shows the following PPP authentication process steps:

Step 1   When a user starts a PPP session, the system determines the type of authentication configured. If no authentication is configured, the PPP process starts immediately.

Step 2   Otherwise, the system determines the authentication method to be used and does one of the following:

— It checks the local database (established with the username password commands) to see whether the given username/password pair are a match (CHAP or PAP).

— It sends an authentication request to the security server (TACACS+ or RADIUS).

Step 3   The system checks the authentication response sent back from the security server or local database. If a positive response is received, the access server starts the PPP process. If the result is negative, the access server rejects the user immediately.

Figure 3-9
If PPP authentication is configured, users and passwords can be checked using a local database or a remote security server.

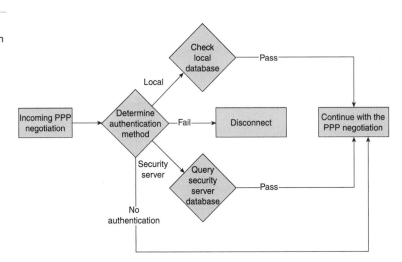

CHAP is considered a superior authentication protocol and should be used when possible. When is it appropriate to run PAP? You might find that hosts running legacy software do not support CHAP; in which case, PAP is your only authentication option.

When using PAP, the remote host is in control of the frequency and timing of login requests. This is undesirable, as the access server must respond to all login requests, even the repeated attempts of a hacker to guess, or brute force, a username/password combination. PAP also sends passwords as clear text over the media, which means a strategically placed packet sniffer could capture and easily decode the password.

On the other hand, access servers that are configured with CHAP are in control of login attempts. The server must send a challenge packet. The challenge packet consists of an ID, a random number, and the host name of the local router.

The required response consists of two parts:

- An encrypted version of the ID, secret password, and the random number
- Either the host name of the remote device or the name of the user on the remote device

When the access server receives the response, it verifies the secret by performing the same encryption operation as indicated in the response, and by looking up the required host name or username. The secret passwords must be identical on the remote device and the local router.

By transmitting this response, the secret is never transmitted in clear text, preventing other devices from stealing it and gaining illegal access to the system. Without the proper response, the remote device cannot connect to the local router.

The CHAP protocol also allows servers to request that the remote host re-authenticate at any time, which provides another dimension of security. This feature is not typically used with Cisco routers.

The following sections describe how to configure the following:

- PAP authentication
- CHAP authentication
- Both CHAP and PAP authentication

Configuring PAP Authentication

Enable PPP encapsulation and PAP authentication with the following commands:

```
Router(config-if)#encapsulation ppp
Router(config-if)#ppp authentication pap
```

These are the only commands needed to configure the access server to authenticate remote hosts using PAP. However, you must also configure the router with a local username/password database, or point it to a network host that has that information (such as a TACACS+ server). Without access to a username/password database, the router won't know which combinations are authorized and will deny all login attempts. You can configure a local username/password database by using the following command in global configuration mode:

```
Router(config)#username username password password
```

The command in Example 3-6 adds an entry for a user called romeo in the router's local database.

Example 3-6 Configuring a Local Username and Password Database

```
Router(config)#username romeo password juliet
```

In some cases, you must also configure a router's asynchronous interface to place calls to other access servers. If you want to configure an interface to respond to a peer's request to authenticate with PAP, you must use the **ppp pap sent-username** command:

```
Router(config-if)#ppp pap sent-username username password password
```

As an example of when a router needs to authenticate to an access server, look at Figure 3-10. Routers RTA and RTB can dial in to each other through POTS and are configured to use PPP with PAP. In RTA's configuration, the **ppp pap sent-username** command specifies what username/password information to send in the event that it dials RTB and is asked to authenticate. RTB is also configured to send a username and password for PAP, if challenged.

Figure 3-10
RTA and RTB are configured to use PPP with PAP.

```
hostname RTA
username RTB password juliet
interface async 0
    encapsulation ppp
    ppp authentication pap
    ip address 10.0.0.1 255.255.255.0
    dialer-map ip 10.0.0.2 name RTB 5551234
    ppp pap sent-username RTA password romeo
```

```
hostname RTB
username RTA password romeo
interface async 0
    encapsulation ppp
    ppp authentication pap
    ip address 10.0.0.2 255.255.255.0
    dialer-map ip 10.0.0.1 name RTA 5554321
    ppp pap sent-username RTB password juliet
```

WARNING

The name included with the **username** and **dialer map** commands is case sensitive. If the remote host's name is **RTA**, and you create a username entry for **rta** instead, authentication will fail.

To ensure that both systems in the example can communicate properly, their asynchronous interfaces were configured with the **dialer map** command that includes the remote router's name. By configuring each router with a **dialer map** statement, each system knows what to do with authentication issues because the systems have prior knowledge of each other's names. The **dialer map** command also contains the telephone number to dial to reach the specified router.

Figure 3-11 summarizes the PAP authentication process.

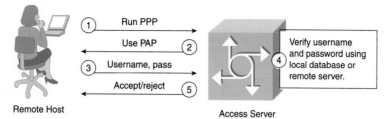

Figure 3-11
The remote user is in control of the frequency and timing of PAP authentication requests.

Configuring CHAP Authentication

When using CHAP authentication, the access server sends a challenge message to the remote node after the PPP link is established (refer to Figure 3-12). The remote node responds with a value calculated by using a one-way hash function, typically Message Digest 5 (MD5). The access server checks the response against its own calculation of the expected hash value. If the values match, the authentication is acknowledged. Otherwise, the connection is immediately terminated. The actual username and password are not actually sent over the media.

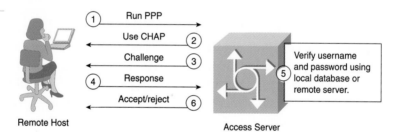

Figure 3-12
The access server is in control of the frequency and timing of CHAP authentication requests, or challenges.

Configure PPP and CHAP authentication using the following commands:

```
Router(config-if)#encapsulation ppp
Router(config-if)#ppp authentication chap
```

Remember that you also have to configure a local username/password database, or point the router to the network TACACS+ or RADIUS server that has that information.

Figure 3-13 presents a CHAP configuration example between RTA and RTB. When using CHAP, an authenticating router uses its host name and enables **secret** (or password if no secret is configured) as the username/password for the one-way hash function.

If you want the router to use a different username and password, you have the option of specifying a different combination with the following commands:

```
Router(config-if)#ppp chap hostname name
Router(config-if)#ppp chap password password
```

Figure 3-13
RTA and RTB are
configured to use
PPP with CHAP.

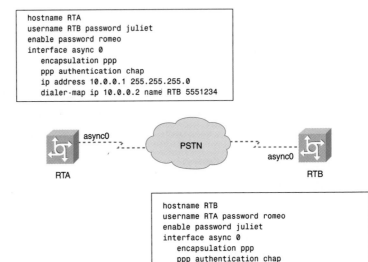

```
hostname RTA
username RTB password juliet
enable password romeo
interface async 0
    encapsulation ppp
    ppp authentication chap
    ip address 10.0.0.1 255.255.255.0
    dialer-map ip 10.0.0.2 name RTB 5551234
```

```
hostname RTB
username RTA password romeo
enable password juliet
interface async 0
    encapsulation ppp
    ppp authentication chap
    ip address 10.0.0.2 255.255.255.0
    dialer-map ip 10.0.0.1 name RTA 5554321
```

Configuring Both CHAP and PAP Authentication

You can enable both PAP and CHAP authentication on an interface. The first method specified is requested during link negotiation. If the peer suggests using the second method, or simply refuses the first method, the second method will be tried. This command can be useful because some remote devices support CHAP only and some PAP only. The commands are as follows:

```
Router(config-if)#ppp authentication pap chap
```

And, alternately

```
Router(config-if)#ppp authentication chap pap
```

PPP Callback

PPP callback is an LCP option used over dial-up links. When configured for PPP callback, a remote client calls the access server, negotiates for PPP callback, and then hangs up. After a configurable period of time, the access server calls the remote client back and the two hosts are free to exchange data.

Why would you use PPP callback?

PPP callback is configured either to control dial-in access or for managing toll charges. As an access control mechanism, the access server can be configured to call back only specific phone numbers and users, thus restricting dial-up sessions. In terms of toll charges, PPP callback places the toll burden on the corporate access server and not the remote host. This might be desirable in order to give mobile users dial-up access at the expense of the corporate office. In other cases, it might actually be cheaper for the access server to make the call than the remote host. From an accounting perspective, PPP callback might simplify billing because the majority of the toll charges are consolidated at one location.

A PPP callback configuration consists of a callback server and at least one callback client. The callback server is an access server (router) located at a central location. The callback client can be a remote router or a PC using a modem.

When PPP callback is configured on two routers, the calling router (the callback client) passes authentication information to the remote router (the callback server), which uses the host name and dial string authentication information to determine whether to place a return call. If the authentication is successful, the callback server disconnects and places a return call. The remote username of the return call associates it with the initial call so that the packets can be transmitted. Remember, the name used with the **dialer map** command is case sensitive. Callback will fail if the **dialer map** name does not match the host name of the callback client.

The following sections describe PPP callback operation, PPP callback server configuration and PPP callback client configuration.

PPP Callback Operation

Figure 3-14 presents a flowchart that describes PPP callback operation using CHAP. An incoming call goes through the CHAP authentication process before callback can occur.

Figure 3-14
PPP callback
operation.

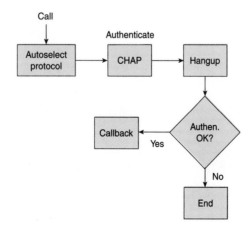

The PPP callback operation consists of the events numbered in Figure 3-15, which are described here:

1. The callback client initiates the call. The client requests callback by using the callback option during the PPP LCP negotiation phase.

2. The callback server acknowledges the callback request and checks its configuration to verify that callback is enabled.

3. The callback client and server authenticate by using either CHAP or PAP authentication. The username identifies the dial string for the return call.

4. After successful initial authentication, the callback server router identifies the callback dial string. The callback server compares the username of the authentication to the host name in a dialer map table. The dial string can be identified by a mapping table or by the Callback Option Message field during the PPP LCP negotiations.

5. If the authenticated username is configured for callback, the initiating call is disconnected by the callback server.

6. The callback server uses the dial string to initiate the callback. If the return call fails, no additional calls are attempted. Callback is not negotiated on the return call.

7. Authentication occurs during the callback.

8. The connection is established and data is exchanged.

NOTE

If a caller requests a callback, but the server is not set to accept a callback, the answering router maintains the initial call.

Figure 3-15
The PPP callback operation includes eight steps.

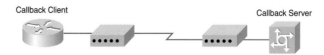

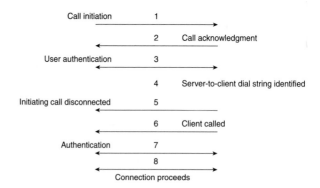

Configuring the Callback Server

Figure 3-16 presents a PPP callback scenario. To configure a router as a callback server, use the commands shown in Table 3-2. Example 3-7 shows that the Server router is configured for TCP/IP over asynchronous PPP.

Figure 3-16
The Server router is configured as a PPP callback server.

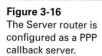 

Example 3-7 Configuring a PPP Callback Server

```
Server(config)#interface async 1
Server(config-if)#ip address 10.1.1.1 255.255.255.0
Server(config-if)#encapsulation ppp
Server(config-if)#ppp authentication chap
Server(config-if)#ppp callback accept
Server(config-if)#dialer in-band
Server(config-if)#dialer-group 1
Server(config-if)#dialer callback-secure
Server(config-if)#dialer map ip 10.1.1.2 name Client class
        DIALBACK modem-script hayes56k broadcast 5556002
Server(config)#username Client password itsasecret
Server(config)#map-class dialer DIALBACK
Server(config-map-class)#dialer callback-server username
Server(config-map-class)#exit
```

Table 3-2   PPP Callback Server Configuration Commands

Command	Purpose
interface *type number*	Specifies the interface and enters interface configuration mode.
dialer in-band [no-parity | odd-parity]	Enables DDR. Specify parity, if needed, on synchronous or asynchronous serial interfaces.
encapsulation ppp	Enables PPP encapsulation.

continues

Table 3-2   PPP Callback Server Configuration Commands (Continued)

Command	Purpose
ppp authentication {chap	pap}	Enables CHAP or PAP authentication.
dialer map *protocol next-hop-address* name *hostname* class *classname dial-string*	Maps the next hop address to the host name and phone number, using the name of the map-class established for PPP callback on this interface.
dialer hold-queue *number* timeout *seconds*	(Optional) Configures a dialer hold queue to store packets to be transferred when the callback connection is established.
dialer enable-timeout *seconds*	(Optional) Configures a timeout period between calls.
ppp callback accept	Configures the interface to accept PPP callback.
dialer callback-secure	(Optional) Enables callback security, if desired.
exit	Returns to global configuration mode.
map-class dialer *classname*	Configures a dialer map class for PPP callback.
dialer callback-server [username]	Configures a dialer map class as a callback server.

To use callback, you must also use CHAP or PAP authentication. The asynchronous interface can then be configured with basic DDR commands: **dialer in-band** and **dialer-group 1**.

Finally, PPP callback is configured with these commands:

```
Server(config)#username Client password itsasecret
Server(config)#map-class dialer DIALBACK
Server(config-map-class)#dialer callback-server username
Server(config-map-class)#exit
```

The **username** command creates an entry for the remote host in the Server's local password database. The **map-class** command creates a dialer configuration called DIALBACK that can be applied to calls on an individual basis with the **dialer map** command. In this case, DIALBACK applies the **dialer callback-server username** command, which enables an interface to make return calls when callback is successfully negotiated. The **map-class** command is discussed further in Chapter 5, "Dialer Profiles." The PPP callback configuration is completed with the following required commands:

```
Server(config)#interface async 1
Server(config-if)#ppp callback accept
Server(config-if)#dialer map ip 10.1.1.2 name Client class DIALBACK modem-script
  hayes56k broadcast 5556002
```

The **ppp callback accept** command enables PPP callback. The **dialer map** statement links the callback client's IP address, username, phone number, and DIALBACK map class (thus applying the **dialer callback-server username** configuration).

In Example 3-7, the Server router's asynchronous interface is configured with this optional command:

```
Server(config-if)#dialer callback-secure
```

This command affects those users that are not authorized to be called back with the **dialer callback-server** command. If the username (*as specified* in the **dialer map** command) is not authorized for callback, the call will be disconnected if the **dialer callback-secure** command is configured. If the **dialer callback-secure** command is not configured, the call will not be disconnected. In either case, callback has not occurred.

Configuring the Callback Client

Configuring a router as a callback client requires the **ppp callback request** command, as shown in Example 3-8. Table 3-3 describes all the commands that configure callback clients.

Example 3-8 Configuring a Callback Client

```
Client(config)#interface async 1

Client(config-if)#encapsulation ppp

Client(config-if)#ppp authentication chap

Client(config-if)#ppp callback request

Client(config-if)#dialer in-band

Client(config-if)#dialer-group 1

Client(config-if)#dialer map ip 10.1.1.1 name Server modem-script hayes56k
  broadcast 5556001
```

Table 3-3   PPP Callback Server Configuration Commands

Command	Purpose
interface *type number*	Specifies the interface.
dialer in-band [no-parity | odd-parity]	Enables DDR. Sets parity on synchronous serial interfaces and asynchronous interfaces.
encapsulation ppp	Enables PPP encapsulation.

continues

> **NOTE**
>
> A dial-up interface cannot be configured to be both a callback server and a call-back client simultaneously.

Table 3-3   PPP Callback Server Configuration Commands (Continued)

Command	Purpose
ppp authentication chap or ppp authentication pap	Enables CHAP or PAP authentication.
dialer map *protocol next-hop-address* **name** *hostname dial-string*	Maps the next hop address to the host name and phone number.
ppp callback request	Enables the interface to request PPP callback for this callback map class.
dialer hold-queue *packets* timeout *seconds*	Configures a dialer hold-queue to store packets for this callback map class (optional).

PPP Compression

PPP can also maximize performance by using data compression, which might provide higher data throughput across low-speed links.

Compression is an option that is negotiated by LCP. If the party you are calling is not configured for compression, no compression will take place. Table 3-4 lists the compression schemes supported by the Cisco IOS.

Table 3-4   IOS Supported Compression Methods

Compression Type	Description
Predictor	Determines whether the data is already compressed. If the data has been compressed by another application, Predictor will not waste time trying to compress it.
Stacker	A Lempel-Ziv (LZ)-based compression algorithm looks at the data and sends each data type only once with information about where the type occurs within the data stream. The receiving side uses this information to reassemble the data stream. (Stacker is the only supported algorithm in the Cisco 700 series.)
MPPC	This protocol (RFC 2118) allows Cisco routers to exchange compressed data with Microsoft clients. MPPC uses an LZ-based compression algorithm.
TCP header compression	This type of compression, also known as Van Jacobson compression, compresses only the TCP headers.

The best compression ratio is usually reached with text files. Some file formats, such as JPEG or MPEG, are already compressed. Also, applications such as Winzip and StuffIt can compress files before they are sent over the network. If a router applies a compression algorithm to a file that is already compressed, the result is a compression ratio of 1:1, or even less.

If you frequently transfer already compressed data, such as graphics and video, you need to consider whether you want to set up compression. Trying to compress already compressed data can take longer than transferring the data without compression. Ideally, you can attain a 2:1 or 3:1 compression ratio for information that was not previously compressed. Expect an average of 1.6:1 compression for mixed compressed and uncompressed source data.

Typically, you should only configure compression on low-speed links because the router compresses data using software, which requires router CPU time and memory. Some algorithms are more memory-intensive; others are more CPU-intensive (see Table 3-5). In either case, the router's ability to route packets is impaired by the drain on its resources. Table 3-5 categorizes the compression algorithms as either processor-intensive or memory-intensive.

Table 3-5   Compression Algorithms and Their Impact on Router Resources

Compression Type	Resource Impact
Stacker MPPC	CPU-intensive
Predictor	Memory-intensive

The IOS commands for configuring PPP to negotiate compression are simple. To configure compression using the Predictor algorithm, use the following command:

```
Router(config-if)#compress predictor
```

To configure Stacker compression, use the following command:

```
Router(config-if)#compress stac
```

MPPC compression is configured with this command:

```
Router(config-if)#compress mppc
```

You need to consider memory and CPU usage when implementing compression on any specific router. Some routers with slow CPUs or inadequate memory can be overloaded when configured to compress traffic.

NOTE

The IOS includes the PPP commands: **ppp compression predictor** and **ppp compression stacker**. Using these commands has exactly the same effect as **compress predictor** and **compress stac**, respectively. For example, if you enter the **ppp compression stacker** command, it will appear as **compress stac** in the configuration file.

These types of compression are performed in software and could significantly affect system performance. Cisco recommends that you disable compression if CPU load exceeds 65 percent. To display the CPU load, use the **show process cpu** command.

Predictor compression is recommended when the bottleneck is caused by high load on the router; Stacker compression is recommended when the bottleneck is caused by a line's bandwidth limitations.

TCP header compression is also an option negotiated by LCP. The *TCP header compression* technique, often referred to by its creator's name—Van Jacobson—is described in RFC 1144. It is supported on serial lines that use HDLC, PPP, or SLIP encapsulation. You must enable TCP header compression on both ends of the connections for it to work. Only TCP headers are compressed—UDP headers are not affected. Header compression is particularly useful on networks with a large percentage of small packets, such as those supporting many Telnet connections. Use the following command:

```
Router(config-if)#ip tcp header-compression
```

The **ip tcp header-compression passive** command specifies that TCP header compression is not required but will be used if the router receives compressed headers from its link partner.

As shown in Example 3-9, you can use the **show compress** command in privileged EXEC mode to view compression statistics.

Example 3-9 Using the show compress Command to Verify Compression

```
SanJose1#show compress
 Serial0/1
        Software compression enabled
        uncompressed bytes xmt/rcv 0/2357
        1  min avg ratio xmt/rcv 0.000/0.000
        5  min avg ratio xmt/rcv 0.000/0.000
        10 min avg ratio xmt/rcv 0.000/2.419
        no bufs xmt 0 no bufs rcv 0
        resyncs 0
      Additional Stacker Stats:
      Transmit bytes:  Uncompressed = 0 Compressed = 0
      Received bytes:  Compressed = 564 Uncompressed = 0
```

MLP

MLP is an LCP option that provides load balancing over dialer interfaces—including ISDN, synchronous, and asynchronous interfaces. MLP can improve throughput and reduce latency between systems by splitting Layer 3 packets and sending the fragments over parallel circuits (refer to Figure 3-17).

Figure 3-17
MLP bundles multiple physical links together to increase bandwidth.

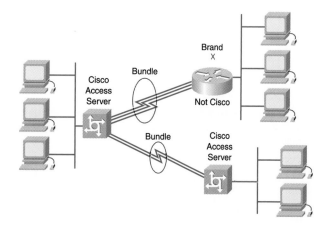

An MLP-capable host indicates to its peer that it can combine multiple physical links into a bundle. Usually, the multiple physical links are the two B channels in an ISDN Basic Rate Interface (BRI).

Before the adoption of MLP (described first in RFC 1717), there was no standardized way to use both of the ISDN B channels of a BRI, and to ensure proper sequencing. MLP is interoperable between Cisco routers running Cisco IOS Software and Cisco 700 series routers, and most routers that comply with the most recent MLP standard, RFC 1990.

Typically, you should use MLP with applications in which bandwidth requirements are dynamic, such as remote LAN access applications for telecommuters, or small office, home office (SOHO) environments. When user traffic exceeds a predefined threshold, an additional physical link (such as a B channel) can be brought up to handle the burst of traffic. If heavy traffic flow is constant, a high-capacity leased line, or some other remote access solution, should be implemented.

During the PPP LCP option negotiation, a system indicates to its peer that it is willing to use MLP as part of the initial LCP option negotiation. The specific option that is

NOTE

MLP works by splitting packets into fragments, not by load-balancing complete packets to a destination.

negotiated is called the Maximum Received Reconstructed Unit (MRRU). MLP systems must be able to do the following:

- Combine multiple physical links into one logical link (bundle)
- Receive and reassemble upper-layer protocol data units (PDUs)
- Receive PDUs of a negotiated size

NOTE

When using the **debug** command to troubleshoot MLP, look for references to the MRRU.

The **ppp multilink** command activates multilink on an interface:

```
Router(config-if)#ppp multilink
```

Example 3-10 presents the output of the **show ppp multilink** command. In the output, you can see the exact number of channels participating in the bundle.

Example 3-10 Verifying MLP by Using the show ppp multilink Command

```
Router#show ppp multilink
Bundle rudder, 3 members, first link is BRI0: B-channel 1
0 lost fragments, 8 reordered, 0 unassigned, sequence 0x1E/0x1E rcvd/sent
```

Transmission channels in the bundle don't have to be the same types. Although rare, asynchronous and synchronous links can simultaneously transmit fragments of one datagram. For example, an ISDN connection can be established when the load on a Frame Relay serial link reaches a certain threshold. The ISDN link and the Frame Relay link can work together as part of the same MLP bundle to share the load.

Configuring MLP is typically done over ISDN and is discussed thoroughly in Chapter 4, "ISDN and DDR."

Verifying PPP Configuration

This section introduces tools for verifying and troubleshooting a PPP session. One way to determine whether PAP or CHAP authentication succeeded is to use the **show dialer** command. This command can be used to view the status of asynchronous dial-up connections.

If the **show dialer** command output displays the name of the remote router, it means that authentication was successful, as shown in Example 3-11. You can check the **show dialer** command on both routers to verify that the name of the other router is displayed. If it is, you know that PAP or CHAP authentication worked. The **show dialer** command output also indicates whether a line is a member of an MLP bundle, as shown in Example 3-11.

Example 3-11 Using show dialer to Verify PPP Operation

```
Capetown#show dialer


BRI0/0 - dialer type = ISDN


Dial String      Successes   Failures    Last DNIS   Last status
5551235                 0          0      never               -
5551234                21          0      00:00:31      successful
0 incoming call(s) have been screened.
0 incoming call(s) rejected for callback.


BRI0/0:1 - dialer type = ISDN
Idle timer (60 secs), Fast idle timer (20 secs)
Wait for carrier (30 secs), Re-enable (15 secs)
Dialer state is multilink member
Dial reason: ip (s=192.168.1.2, d=192.168.0.1)
Connected to 5551234 (SanJose1)


BRI0/0:2 - dialer type = ISDN
Idle timer (60 secs), Fast idle timer (20 secs)
Wait for carrier (30 secs), Re-enable (15 secs)
Dialer state is multilink member
Dial reason: Multilink bundle overloaded
Connected to 5551234 (SanJose1)
```

If you do not see the name of the other host, you know that something was misconfig-
ured because the authentication failed in at least one direction.

The **debug ppp negotiation** command is a great tool for troubleshooting PPP LCP activities, such as authentication, compression, and MLP. When the LCP is in OPEN state,
the NCP negotiation takes place. In the output shown in Example 3-12, you can see
that LCP options are negotiated before any NCP activities take place. The **debug ppp
negotiation** command allows you to observe negotiation of the following activities:

- CHAP authentication
- Compression Control Protocol (CCP)
- NCP protocols IPCP, IPXCP, and so on

Example 3-12 Using debug ppp negotiation to Verify PPP Operation

```
denver#debug ppp negotiation
00:49:11: BR0/0:1 PPP: Treating connection as a callout
00:49:11: BR0/0:1 PPP: Phase is ESTABLISHING, Active Open
00:49:11: BR0/0:1 LCP: O CONFREQ [Closed] id 48 len 15
00:49:11: BR0/0:1 LCP:    AuthProto CHAP (0x0305C22305)
00:49:11: BR0/0:1 LCP:    MagicNumber 0xB091BF2A (0x0506B091BF2A)
00:49:11: BR0/0:1 LCP: I CONFREQ [REQsent] id 47 len 15
00:49:11: BR0/0:1 LCP:    AuthProto CHAP (0x0305C22305)
00:49:11: BR0/0:1 LCP:    MagicNumber 0xB07F4E5E (0x0506B07F4E5E)
00:49:11: BR0/0:1 LCP: O CONFACK [REQsent] id 47 len 15
00:49:11: BR0/0:1 LCP:    AuthProto CHAP (0x0305C22305)
00:49:11: BR0/0:1 LCP:    MagicNumber 0xB07F4E5E (0x0506B07F4E5E)
00:49:11: BR0/0:1 LCP: I CONFACK [ACKsent] id 48 len 15
00:49:11: BR0/0:1 LCP:    AuthProto CHAP (0x0305C22305)
00:49:11: BR0/0:1 LCP:    MagicNumber 0xB091BF2A (0x0506B091BF2A)
00:49:11: BR0/0:1 LCP: State is Open
00:49:11: BR0/0:1 PPP: Phase is AUTHENTICATING, by both
00:49:11: BR0/0:1 CHAP: O CHALLENGE id 31 len 27 from "denver"
00:49:11: BR0/0:1 CHAP: I CHALLENGE id 30 len 28 from "phoenix"
00:49:11: BR0/0:1 CHAP: O RESPONSE id 30 len 27 from "denver"
00:49:11: BR0/0:1 CHAP: I SUCCESS id 30 len 4
00:49:11: BR0/0:1 CHAP: I RESPONSE id 31 len 28 from "phoenix"
00:49:11: BR0/0:1 CHAP: O SUCCESS id 31 len 4
00:49:11: BR0/0:1 PPP: Phase is UP
00:49:11: BR0/0:1 IPCP: O CONFREQ [Closed] id 6 len 10
00:49:11: BR0/0:1 IPCP:    Address 10.1.1.3 (0x03060A010103)
00:49:11: BR0/0:1 CDPCP: O CONFREQ [Closed] id 6 len 4
00:49:11: BR0/0:1 IPCP: I CONFREQ [REQsent] id 5 len 10
00:49:11: BR0/0:1 IPCP:    Address 10.1.1.2 (0x03060A010102)
00:49:11: BR0/0:1 IPCP: O CONFACK [REQsent] id 5 len 10
00:49:11: BR0/0:1 IPCP:    Address 10.1.1.2 (0x03060A010102)
00:49:11: BR0/0:1 CDPCP: I CONFREQ [REQsent] id 5 len 4
00:49:11: BR0/0:1 CDPCP: O CONFACK [REQsent] id 5 len 4
00:49:11: BR0/0:1 IPCP: I CONFACK [ACKsent] id 6 len 10
00:49:11: BR0/0:1 IPCP:    Address 10.1.1.3 (0x03060A010103)
00:49:11: BR0/0:1 IPCP: State is Open
```

Example 3-12 Using debug ppp negotiation to Verify PPP Operation (Continued)

```
00:49:11: BR0/0:1 CDPCP: I CONFACK [ACKsent] id 6 len 4
00:49:11: BR0/0:1 CDPCP: State is Open
00:49:11: BR0/0 IPCP: Install route to 10.1.1.2
```

When specifically debugging CHAP or PAP authentication, the **debug ppp authentication** command can be used in place of **debug ppp negotiation**. The **debug ppp authentication** command gives you the same output as **debug ppp negotiation,** but that output is limited to CHAP and PAP authentication events.

PPP Configuration Example

Now that you have surveyed the various PPP configuration options, let's put what you have learned to work. Figure 3-18 presents a Cisco 2620 router that accepts dial-in calls on its AUX port. This allows a remote Windows PC to dial in to the corporate TCP/IP network or to manage the router remotely.

WARNING
Because debugging output is assigned high priority in the CPU process, it can render the system unusable. For this reason, use **debug** commands only to troubleshoot specific problems or during trouble-shooting sessions with Cisco technical support staff.

Figure 3-18
The central-site router is configured for PPP over an asynchronous line using the AUX port.

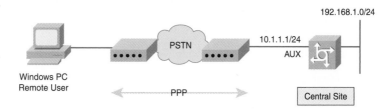

As a first step to configuring the Central router, configure the AUX port for TCP/IP over PPP, as shown in Example 3-13.

Example 3-13 Configuring PPP Authentication on Central

```
Central(config)#interface async 65
Central(config-if)#ip address 10.1.1.1 255.255.255.0
Central(config-if)#encapsulation ppp
Central(config-if)#ppp authentication chap pap
Central(config-if)#exit
Central(config)#username remoteuser password letmein
```

The commands in Example 3-13 set the IP address of the AUX port, which is assigned line 65 on a 2620 router. The **encapsulation ppp** command configures the AUX port to use PPP. The interface is set to request CHAP authentication first but will settle for

PAP if CHAP is not supported by the remote host. The **username** command is used here to build a local database from which to authenticate users.

Next, you can configure PPP options (see Example 3-14).

Example 3-14 Configuring PPP Options on Central

```
Central(config-if)#ppp mode interactive
Central(config-if)#ip peer default ip address 10.1.1.2
Central(config-if)#compress stac
```

The commands in Example 3-14 configure Central's AUX port for PPP interactive mode, which means the remote user can start either an EXEC session or a PPP session (provided you enter the **autoselect ppp** line configuration command later). The **ip peer default ip address** command sets up remote addressing—PPP assigns the remote host the IP address 10.1.1.2. The last command shown in Example 3-14, **compress stac**, configures the AUX port for Stacker compression.

Finally, the physical line, AUX 0, must be configured to use an external modem and allow autoselect PPP, as shown in Example 3-15.

Example 3-15 Configuring the AUX Port for Asynchronous PPP

```
Central(config)#line aux 0
Central(config-line)#login
Central(config-line)#password cisco
Central(config-line)#speed 115200
Central(config-line)#flowcontrol hardware
Central(config-line)#stopbits 1
Central(config-line)#transport input all
Central(config-line)#autoselect ppp
Central(config-line)#modem inout
Central(config-line)#modem autoconfigure type hayes_optima
```

Summary

In this chapter, you learned how to configure PPP between a central site and a remote site, and how to configure PPP LCP options, including CHAP and PAP authentication, compression, MLP, and callback.

The next chapter examines ISDN, which typically uses PPP at the data link layer. Specifically, you learn how to configure MLP on an ISDN BRI.

Review Questions

Use the following review questions to test your understanding of the concepts covered in this chapter. In some cases, there is more than one correct answer, so choose all that apply. Answers are listed in Appendix A, "Answers to Review Questions."

1. Which of the following is not negotiated by LCP?

   A. Authentication

   B. Compression

   C. Encryption ✓

   D. MLP

2. Which of the following protocols are supported by SLIP?

   A. IP ✓

   B. IPX

   C. AppleTalk DDP

   D. DECnet

3. Which of the following is true about PPP?

   A. LCP negotiates Layer 3 options.

   B. NCP negotiates Layer 2 options.

   C. PPP frames are based on HDLC. ✓

   D. PPP does not support IPX.

4. Which of the following commands is used to configure PPP encapsulation?

   A. router(config)#encapsulation ppp

   B. router(config)#ppp encapsulation chap

   C. router(config-if)#ppp encap

   D. router(config-if)#encapsulation ppp ✓

5. Which of the following commands is used to configure CHAP authentication?

   A. router(config-if)#authentication ppp chap

   B. router(config-if)#ppp authentication chap ✓

   C. router(config-if)#ppp encapsulation chap

   D. router(config-if)#chap authentication

6. Which of the following is true about CHAP?

   A. CHAP is a proprietary authentication protocol.

   B. CHAP does not send clear-text passwords across a link. ✓

   C. The remote host is in control of the timing and frequency of login attempts.

   D. The local host is in control of the timing and frequency of login attempts. ✓

7. Which of the following commands can be used to configure Stacker compression?

   A. router(config-if)#**compress stac** ✓

   B. router(config-if)#**ppp stac**

   C. router(config-if)#**compression stacker**

   D. router(config-if)#**ppp compression**

8. Which of the following compression methods is best implemented on networks with a large percentage of small packets, such as those supporting many Telnet connections?

   A. Stacker

   B. Predictor ✓

   C. MPPC

   D. Van Jacobson ✓

9. Which of the following commands configures MLP?

   A. router(config-if)#**ppp mlp**

   B. router(config-if)#**ppp multilink** ✓

   C. router(config-if)#**ip mlp**

   D. router(config-if)#**ip multilink**

10. Which of the following commands can be used to verify and troubleshoot PPP authentication?

   A. **show dialer**

   B. **show ppp** ✓

   C. **debug ppp authentication**

   D. **debug ppp negotiation**

Key Terms

ARAP (AppleTalk Remote Access Protocol) Layer 2 protocol that provides Macintosh users direct access to information and resources at a remote AppleTalk site.

Callback Dial-up feature wherein a remote client calls an access server, hangs up, and then receives a callback from the server. Used to consolidate toll charges and for restricting dial-up access.

CHAP (Challenge Handshake Authentication Protocol) Security feature supported on lines using PPP encapsulation that prevents unauthorized access. CHAP does not prevent unauthorized access; it merely identifies the remote end. The router or access server then determines whether that user is allowed access.

Compression Running of a data set through an algorithm that reduces the space required to store, or the bandwidth required to transmit, the data set.

LCP (Link Control Protocol) PPP protocol that is responsible for negotiating, establishing, and maintaining a data link between end systems.

MLP (Multilink PPP) LCP option that provides load balancing over multiple interfaces. MLP can improve throughput and reduce latency between systems by splitting Layer 3 packets and sending the fragments over parallel circuits.

MPPC (Microsoft Point-to-Point Compression) Scheme that compresses PPP packets between Cisco routers and Microsoft client devices. The MPPC algorithm uses a Lempel-Ziv (LZ)-based algorithm with a continuous history buffer, called a *dictionary*.

NCP (Network Control Protocol) PPP protocol that is responsible for establishing network-layer communication (such as IP) between end systems.

PAP (Password Authentication Protocol) Authentication protocol that allows PPP peers to authenticate one another. The remote router attempting to connect to the local router is required to send an authentication request. Unlike CHAP, PAP passes the password and host name or username in the clear (unencrypted). PAP does not itself prevent unauthorized access but merely identifies the remote end. The router or access server then determines if that user is allowed access. PAP is supported only on PPP lines.

Predictor Compression algorithm that determines whether the data is already compressed. If so, the data is just sent; no time is wasted trying to compress already compressed data.

SLIP (Serial Line Internet Protocol)   Standard protocol for point-to-point serial connections using TCP/IP. Predecessor of PPP.

Stacker   Lempel-Ziv (LZ)-based compression algorithm that looks at the data and sends each data type only once with information about where the type occurs within the data stream. The receiving side uses this information to reassemble the data stream.

TCP header compression   Also known as Van Jacobsen (VJ) compression. This type of compression compresses TCP headers.

Objectives

After completing this chapter, you will be able to perform tasks related to the following:

- ISDN architecture
- ISDN protocol layers
- Configuring ISDN BRI
- Configuring DDR over ISDN
- Verifying ISDN operation
- Configuring PRI

Chapter 4

ISDN and DDR

Introduction

Analog dial-up connections have the advantages of being cheap and readily available in almost every region. Unfortunately, dial-up connectivity over plain old telephone service (POTS) is slow, in terms of both maximum data throughput (56 kbps) and call setup time. Anyone who uses a modem and an ordinary phone line to access the Internet knows that waiting—either for a connection to be made or a Web page to load—comes with the territory.

This chapter introduces and describes a group of technologies called Integrated Services Digital Network (ISDN), which were first proposed over 30 years ago. Recognizing the inherent limitations of POTS, developers envisioned that ISDN would provide a digital pipeline offering integrated access to the broadest range of services. These services were to include voice, packet switching, and even video.

Several ISDN standards were agreed upon over the years. These standards promised to bring high-speed digital service to homes and businesses. But despite ISDN's extensive array of standards, carriers have not uniformly implemented the technology. One reason is that the standardization process often lags behind technological advances. In an effort to offer improved services to customers, some providers have implemented ISDN technologies and features without waiting for industry-wide acceptance or standardization. Another reason for different ISDN implementations is that regional regulations and telecommunications infrastructures dictate the types of services a provider can deliver. Finally, because the standardization process could be politicized by competing vendors, the resultant standards might allow for different technologies. Consequently, ISDN configurations and pricing could vary in significant ways from region to region. Today, customers deploy ISDN primarily as a WAN backup technology, and to provide remote access to telecommuters and small offices. Service providers and large companies use ISDN Primary Rate Interface (PRI) to support large numbers of both POTS (analog modem) and ISDN Basic Rate Interface (BRI) calls. Although ISDN boasts a much faster call setup and higher throughput than POTS, many potential BRI customers are turning to digital subscriber line (DSL) and cable technologies, which offer much higher throughput at a lower cost.

Despite these emerging technologies, ISDN remains a viable remote access solution for several reasons:

- ISDN is more widely available than DSL or cable.
- Many companies and service providers have made a significant investment in ISDN equipment and training, and plan to continue leveraging that investment.
- Remote offices using ISDN can connect to central offices directly, without traversing the public Internet. Most DSL and cable implementations require that the remote host communicate with the central site using a VPN over the Internet.

This chapter covers ISDN technologies and describes how to configure ISDN using the Cisco IOS. This chapter also explores dial-on-demand routing (DDR), which is often used in ISDN configurations.

ISDN Architecture

As its name implies, ISDN uses digital technology. As shown in Figure 4-1, ISDN replaces traditional basic analog telephone service equipment with newer, high-speed digital equipment to provide the customer with a digital local loop. Therefore, ISDN transmissions are digital from end to end. Because POTS uses an analog local loop, the carrier must use Pulse Code Modulation (PCM) to encode the analog signals for digital transmission. This type of analog-to-digital conversion introduces undesired latency and, potentially, noise.

The following sections describe the two different ISDN services available to customers: ISDN BRI and ISDN PRI. This chapter looks specifically at BRI call processing, BRI functional groups, and BRI reference points. Finally, this chapter discusses these same concepts in terms of ISDN PRI.

ISDN Services and Channelized E1 and T1

Customers can connect to the ISDN carrier through two different physical interfaces: BRI and PRI. A single BRI or PRI interface provides a multiplexed *bundle* of B and D channels, as shown in Figure 4-2.

Figure 4-1
Unlike POTS, which
relies on analog local
loops, ISDN provides
digital communica-
tions from end
to end.

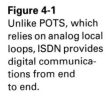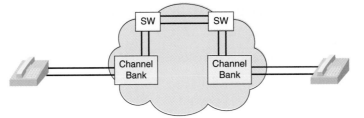

Analog converted to digital and back

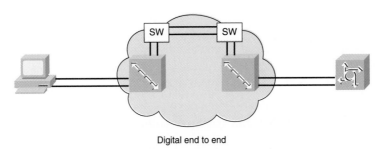

Digital end to end

Figure 4-2
ISDN BRI and PRI are
composed of multi-
ple B channels and
one D channel.

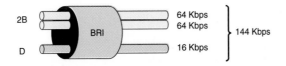

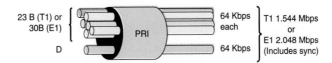

ISDN *B channels* are called bearer channels because they carry voice, data, and fax
transmissions. B channels typically carry this information in frame format by using
either High-Level Data Link Control (HDLC) or Point-to-Point Protocol (PPP) as the
Layer-2 encapsulation protocol for data connections.

The *D channel*, or delta channel, is used for out-of-band signaling. The D channel
carries control messages, such as call setup and teardown. Typically, the D channel
employs what is known as *Link Access Protocol on the D Channel (LAPD)* at Layer 2.

BRI service is provided over a local copper loop that traditionally carries analog phone service. The maximum length of most ISDN local loops in North America is about 18,000 feet (or 5.5 kilometers).

BRI has the following characteristics:

- Two 64-kbps bearer channels
- One 16-kbps delta channel
- 48 kbps of framing and synchronization information
- Total speed of 192 kbps

NOTE

ISDN BRI can be configured for use over leased lines in Japan and Germany. In such cases, the BRI is no longer a dialer interface, and signaling over the D channel no longer applies. The BRI interface is configured as a synchronous serial interface having the default HDLC encapsulation.

When discussing ISDN BRI bandwidth, you need to know which of the BRI characteristics are being referenced. If you are discussing the bandwidth available for user data, ISDN BRI provides 128 kbps (two 64-kbps B channels). If you are discussing the bandwidth of both B channels and the D channel, ISDN BRI provides 144 kbps. Although it is not commonly done, you can reference the total bandwidth of an ISDN BRI, including framing and synchronization, which is 192 kbps.

ISDN PRI service is provided over T1 and E1 leased lines between the customer premise equipment (CPE) and the ISDN switch. PRI over T1 specifies the following:

- Twenty-three 64-kbps bearer channels
- One 64-kbps D channel, carried in timeslot 24
- 8 kbps of framing and synchronization information
- Total speed of 1.544 Mbps

PRI over E1 provides the following:

- Thirty 64-kbps bearer channels
- One 64-kbps D channel, carried in timeslot 16
- 64 kbps of framing and synchronization information
- Total speed of 2.048 Mbps

NOTE

PSTN is a general term referring to the variety of telephone networks and services in place worldwide.

BRI Call Processing

When a BRI call is initiated, the CPE sends the called number to the local ISDN switch using the D channel.

The local switch uses the *Signaling System 7* (*SS7*) protocols to set up a path inside the public switched telephone network (PSTN) and passes the called number to the terminating ISDN switch. This far-end switch brings up the D channel to the destination. Remember that the D channel is used for call setup, signaling, and call termination, which are the call-control functions. ISDN is a local-loop technology; after the ISDN switch processes the call, SS7 is used to traverse the carrier's network.

When the terminating CPE answers, the B channel is connected end to end. The B channel carries the conversation or data. As you will see later in this chapter, both B channels can be used simultaneously to connect to the same destination or to different destinations.

BRI Functional Groups and Reference Points

ISDN is a well-defined set of technologies. The ITU-T (International Telecommunications Union Telecommunication Standardization Sector) groups and organizes the ISDN protocols, or *rules*, according to general topics, as shown in Table 4-1.

Although knowing all the rules is not necessary, it is important that you familiarize yourself with the E, I, and Q designations, and with the general topics that they represent.

Table 4-1   ISDN Protocol Designations

Protocol Series	General Topic	Specific Examples
E	Recommend telephone network standards for ISDN.	E.164. Describes international addressing for ISDN.
I	Define ISDN concepts, terminology, and general methods.	I.430. Describes BRI interface.
Q	Define ISDN switching and signaling. Signaling refers to call setup and teardown.	Q.921. Specifies LAPD. Q.931. Governs the network layer functionality between the terminal endpoint and the local ISDN switch.

In addition to defining protocols, ISDN standards also specify the function of a given device in the network. BRI can involve many functional devices, also known as *functional groups*. The following functional groups are illustrated in Figure 4-3.

- **Terminal equipment 1 (TE1)**—Designates a device that is compatible with the ISDN network. Examples of TE1 include a digital telephone, a router with an ISDN interface, or digital facsimile equipment.

- **Terminal equipment 2 (TE2)**—Designates a device that is not compatible with ISDN and requires a terminal adapter, such as a router without an ISDN interface.

- **Terminal adapter (TA)**—Converts standard electrical signals into the form used by ISDN, so non-ISDN devices can connect to the ISDN network. An example is converting V.35 or EIA/TIA-232 to ISDN.

NOTE

Don't confuse the
ISDN terms TE1
(terminal equip-
ment 1) and *TEI*
(*terminal endpoint
identifier*), which is
a kind of address
assigned to a TE by
an ISDN switch.

- **Network termination type 1 (NT1)**—Connects four-wire ISDN subscriber wiring to the conventional two-wire local-loop facility. The NT1 is part of the CPE in the United States and part of the local exchange in Europe.

- **Network termination type 2 (NT2)**—Directs traffic to and from different subscriber devices and the NT1. The NT2 is an intelligent device that performs switching and concentrating. Often, a private branch exchange (PBX) is the NT2 device.

- **Line termination (LT)**—Located at the exchange side. Its functions are identical to those of an NT1.

- **Exchange termination (ET)**—A subscriber line card in the ISDN exchange. LT and ET are sometimes referred to as the LE (local exchange).

- **Local Exchange (LE)**—The ISDN central office (CO) that houses the ISDN switch. The LE implements the ISDN protocol and is part of the network.

Figure 4-3
ISDN BRI includes
several abstract,
functional groups
and reference points.

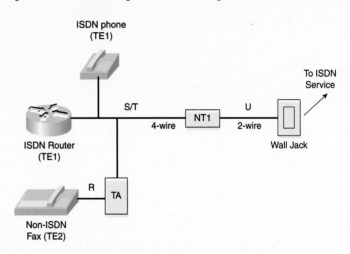

Two types of data terminal equipment (DTEs) can use ISDN services: TE1s and TE2s. A *TE1* is a device such as a phone, router, or PC that has built-in (native) support for ISDN. Conversely, a *TE2* is a device that does not have built-in support for ISDN. A TE2 requires a TA to connect to ISDN.

BRI requires an NT1 to connect to the carrier's ISDN switch. In Europe, the NT1 is maintained by the service provider. In North America, the NT1 belongs to the customer, who is responsible for purchasing and installing it. Some devices, such as routers, can combine both TE1 and NT1 functionality in the same unit.

The ISDN reference points define how the functional groups, such as TE2 and TA, connect to each other. The ISDN reference points are the following:

- **U reference point (user reference point)**—Located between the NT1 and LT (it corresponds with a subscriber line). The U interface has no ITU-T standards. This is the American National Standards Institute (ANSI) standard for the United States.

- **T reference point (terminal reference point)**—Located between the NT1 and NT2 (or between the NT1 and TE1 or TA, if there is no NT2 device). In BRI, the T interface uses the same characteristics as the S interface. Thus, the two reference points are typically combined in a single interface, referenced as an S/T interface.

- **S reference point (system reference point)**—Located between the NT2 and TE1 or TA. It connects the terminals to the ISDN network. This is the most important interface for users. The S interface uses the same characteristics as the T interface.

- **R reference point (rate reference point)**—Located between TA and TE2 (non-ISDN interface). The TE2 connects to the TA through a standard physical-layer interface. These standards include EIA/TIA-232-C (formerly RS-232-C), V.24, X.21, and V.35.

Reference points are architectural definitions that may or may not physically exist as separate elements in a network. For example, some routers have one or more U interfaces, which means they can connect directly to the carrier's ISDN switch. In such a network, the S, T, and R reference points do not exist.

Given all the ISDN abbreviations such as T, S, U, and so on, what do all of these components and reference points look like in the real world?

As shown in Figure 4-3, a connection is made from the wall jack with a standard two-wire cable to the NT1, and then out of the NT1 with a four-wire connection to your ISDN phone, terminal adapter, or Cisco ISDN router or to an ISDN fax. The S/T interface is implemented using an eight-wire connector to allow for powering the NT and TE.

Because all these connectors look similar (such as RJ-11, RJ-45s, and so on), you must be careful about what you plug in and where. The S/T reference point is a four-wire interface (Tx and Rx). It is point-to-point and multipoint (passive bus). It uses the ITU I.430 specification. The S/T interface defines the interface between a TE1 or TA and an NT.

NOTE

Some manufacturers define a V reference point in LEs between LT and ET. This reference point identifies the network node interface and is transparent to users.

The U interface defines the two-wire interface between the NT and the ISDN cloud. The R interface defines the interface between the TA and an attached non-ISDN device (TE2).

An NT1 and NT2 combination device is sometimes referred to as an *NTU*.

A regular ISDN S interface can have several endpoint devices with different capabilities occupying the same bus (the S bus). When the switch can communicate with multiple devices, it is typically referred to as *multipoint*. Unfortunately, this calls for complexity in terms of service profile identifiers (SPIDs) and endpoint identifiers (EIDs), both in ISDN device setup and call processing.

When selecting ISDN equipment, it is important to know the reference point that defines the type of ISDN interface you need. In the United States, you typically need a U interface to connect to your provider. That means if you purchase an ISDN router with an S/T interface, you have to buy additional equipment (an NT1) to connect to your provider's network. Also, if you mistakenly connect a U interface to an NT1, you can cause permanent damage to devices. Knowing the ISDN reference points is key to properly selecting and installing ISDN devices.

NOTE

Internal CSU/DSUs
are common
among modular
routers.

ISDN PRI

Recall that ISDN PRI is delivered through a leased T1 or E1 line. As depicted in Figure 4-4, a channel service unit/data service unit (CSU/DSU) is required to connect a router (the TE) to the carrier network. The PRI reference points are much more straightforward than BRI reference points, which can contain numerous functional groups in a multipoint configuration.

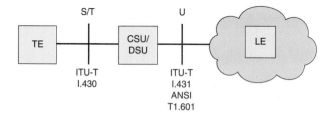

Figure 4-4
In ISDN PRI, a router (TE) is connected to the PSTN through a CSU/DSU and leased line.

If ISDN PRI requires a leased line and offers the same total bandwidth as a leased line, then why not just get a leased line in the first place? In fact, ISDN PRI's primary application is modem aggregation, not high-capacity point-to-point connectivity.

If you need the throughput of a DS1 (1.544 Mbps), then a dedicated line is the appropriate solution. But if you are a service provider, or a large company that supports dozens of dial-up remote access connections, then ISDN PRI offers a powerful solution (see Figure 4-5).

Figure 4-5
ISDN PRI can support both analog and digital dial solutions.

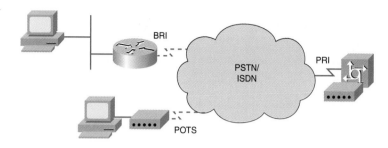

NOTE

The term DS1 stands for digital service 1, which is an interface with a 1.544-Mbps data rate that often carries voice connections on a PBX. Each DS1 has 24 DS0 channels framed together so that each DS0 timeslot can be assigned to a different type of trunk group.

ISDN PRI supports hybrid dial-up access using a single phone number. One PRI over T1 can support up to 23 dial-in calls, which can be either analog POTS calls, or digital ISDN BRI calls. The callers dial the same phone number, although they are each connected to a different channel. Because each channel is a DS0 (64 kbps), PRI makes analog calls at 53.3 kbps (using 56K modems) possible. The D channel's job is to identify if the call is a circuit-switched digital call or an analog modem call. Analog modem calls are decoded and then sent to the onboard modems. Circuit-switched digital calls are directly relayed to the ISDN processor in the router.

In a typical configuration, an access server, such as a Cisco 3660, is outfitted with integrated digital modems and a T1 controller (see Figure 4-5). The T1 controller connects to a leased T1 line, which provides connectivity to the ISDN cloud. This setup allows ISDN routers and analog modems to connect to the access server simultaneously.

ISDN Protocol Layers

Similar to other communication standards, ISDN relies on a combination of protocols. Figure 4-6 illustrates how various ISDN protocols relate to the OSI reference model. The following sections describe the key ISDN protocols at Layers 1, 2, and 3.

NOTE

If you have a single router supporting multiple PRIs, you can use *Non-Facility Associated Signaling (NFAS)*, which is an ISDN service that allows a single D channel to control multiple PRI interfaces. Use of a single D channel to control multiple PRI interfaces can free one B channel on each PRI interface to carry other traffic.

Figure 4-6
ISDN includes protocols that work at the first three layers of the OSI model.

	D Channel	B Channel
Layer 3	DSS1 (Q.931)	IP/IPX
Layer 2	LAPD (Q.921)	HDLC/PPP/FR/ LAPB
Layer 1	1.430/1.431/ANSI T1.601	

ISDN Layer 1

ISDN at Layer 1, the physical layer, is responsible for switching the carrier's circuits to build a connection. ISDN Layer 1 also supports the attachment of various ISDN functional devices. Both the B and the D channels share this physical layer. Layer-1 ISDN standards include the following:

- I.430 for BRI, which defines the communication across the S/T reference point
- I.431 for PRI, which is a full-duplex, point-to-point, serial, synchronous connection
- ANSI T1.601 for BRI, which defines the communication across the U interface for North America

ISDN Layer 2

As shown in Figure 4-6, the D channel and the B channel use different protocols at Layers 2 and 3.

The B channel typically frames data using either PPP or HDLC. Because PPP allows for authentication, ISDN is most commonly configured to use PPP.

As specified by Q.921, the D channel typically frames data using LAPD, which is a version of Link AccessProcedure, Balanced (LAPB) modified especially for the ISDN D channel. At Layer 3, the D channel uses the Q.931 protocol, which is part of the Digital Subscriber Signaling System No. 1 (DSS1) suite of protocols. You can use the 2 in Q.921, and the 3 in Q.931, to remember which layer of the OSI model they are associated with.

With ISDN, all hardware addressing occurs in Layer 2, just as in a traditional local-area network (LAN) environment. It is possible to have up to eight ISDN terminals on an S/T bus. In order for ISDN to differentiate between TEs, each TE must have a unique address. One part of the ISDN Layer-2 address is called a TEI.

The *TEI* is a 7-bit number carried in the address field of the LAPD frame on the D channel. Typically, the TEI is dynamically assigned to a TE, such as an ISDN router, by the ISDN switch. The ISDN switch assigns a TEI upon receiving a request from the TE. Generally, the TE makes this request when it first powers up. Three ranges of TEI addresses exist:

- 0-63 for non-automatic TEI assignment
- 64-126 for automatic TEI assignment
- 127 for group assignment, or broadcast

The TEI works together with the *service access point identifier* (*SAPI*) to complete the Layer-2 address. The *SAPI* is a 6-bit number used to identify and manage different data

NOTE

By default, Cisco routers use a random-length time delay, in the range of 1 to 300 seconds, to prevent mass power failures from overwhelming network ISDN switches with TEI requests when power returns and all the devices start up at the same time. If turned off, this feature can be re-enabled for national ISDN BRI switches by using the **isdn twait-disable** interface configuration command.

types for the same individual device connecting to the ISDN network. Remember, some ISDN messages are for call setup or teardown, while others are actual data. Thus, the TEI represents the specific ISDN device, while the SAPI represents the specific process running on that device. For example, the SAPI value 0 is used to identify call-control procedures, while the SAPI value 63 identifies a Layer-2 management function.

Just as an Ethernet II frame contains the destination MAC address and the protocol type information, the LAPD frame contains a TEI and a SAPI value.

ISDN Layer 3

At Layer 3, the B channel can carry datagrams using a variety of Layer-3 protocols, including IP, IPX, and AppleTalk.

As shown in Figure 4-7, the D channel uses the Q.931 at Layer 3 to communicate between the carrier's ISDN switch and the customer's TE device (for example, a router). In BRI, this protocol is transparent to the NT1 device.

Figure 4-7
Q.931 defines the communication between the ISDN switch (LE) and the TE.

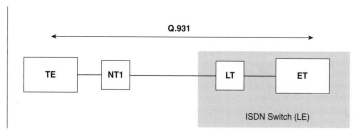

When configuring a router for an ISDN connection, you must specify the type of ISDN switch that it is communicating with. That's because different ISDN switches use different Q.931 messaging procedures. You must match the specific switch-type, or no D-channel communication can occur. When you request ISDN service, your provider furnishes you with the ISDN switch-type information.

An ISDN call can be placed in numerous ways. In an ISDN call, the calling party requests a call setup, as shown in Figure 4-8. Before the actual connect and call proceeding, you might see several different messages, including call proceeding, alerting, and connect messages.

Different ISDN switches use different call setup and teardown procedures. At a minimum, call proceeding, alerting, and connect messages should be exchanged.

NOTE

You can configure a Cisco router to request a TEI when the first ISDN call is placed or received, or when the router is powered on by using the **isdn tei first-call** and **isdn tei powerup** commands, respectively.

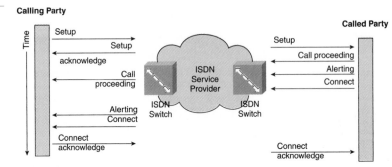

Figure 4-8
The Q.931 protocol runs over the D channel and is responsible for call setup and teardown messages.

Configuring ISDN BRI

To prepare an access server for ISDN BRI, you must specify several global and interface parameters. This section describes the following configuration tasks in detail:

- Configuring the ISDN switch-type
- Configuring the SPIDs
- Configuring the BRI interface encapsulation
- Configuring interface addressing

Configuring the ISDN Switch-Type

Different ISDN providers use different switch-types. In fact, some providers use one type of switch hardware to emulate another type of switch in software. Your ISDN provider provides you the appropriate switch-type information. If your router is not configured with the correct switch-type information, it will not be able to communicate with the ISDN switch using Q.931 at Layer 3. In other words, no ISDN call can be dialed or received.

Cisco IOS release 12.2 supports the switch-types listed in Table 4-2. Types of switches vary depending on the country where the connection is established.

Table 4-2   ISDN Service Provider Switch-Type Keywords by Area

Keyword	Switch-Type
All Countries	
basic-qsig	PINX (PBX) switches with QSIG signaling per Q.931
primary-qsig	Supports QSIG signaling per Q.931
Australia and Europe	
basic-1tr6	German 1TR6 ISDN switches

Table 4-2   **ISDN Service Provider Switch-Type Keywords by Area (Continued)**

Keyword	Switch-Type
basic-net3	NET3 ISDN, Norway NET3, Australian NET3, and New Zealand NET3 switches (covers the Euro-ISDN E-DSS1 signaling system and is ETSI-compliant)
vn3	French VN3 and VN4 ISDN BRI switches
Japan	
ntt	Japanese NTT ISDN switches
North America	
basic-5ess	AT&T basic rate switches
basic-dms100	Northern Telecom DMS-100 basic rate switches
basic-ni	National ISDN switches

You set the switch-type by entering the **isdn switch-type** command. However, you must decide whether to enter this command in either global or interface configuration mode.

The global **isdn switch-type** command sets all ISDN interfaces on the router to be configured for the same switch-type:

```
Router(config)#isdn switch-type type
```

When you issue the **isdn switch-type** command in interface configuration mode, only the interface that you are configuring assumes the switch type:

```
Router(config-if)#isdn switch-type type
```

The interface configuration command overrides the global-level command.

Typically, you specify the switch-type in global configuration mode using the **isdn switch-type** command. However, in some cases—such as when the same router connects to both BRI and PRI—you might need to specify two different ISDN switch-types. For this reason, Cisco extended the use of the command to the interface configuration mode, beginning with IOS release 11.3(T).

The **interface bri** *interface-number* command designates an ISDN interface on a router that natively supports ISDN (TE1). Thus, to configure the first ISDN interface with the AT&T basic rate switch-type, you enter the following commands, shown in Example 4-1.

Example 4-1   **Setting the ISDN switch-type in Interface Configuration Mode**

```
RTA(config)#interface bri 0
RTA(config-if)#isdn switch-type basic-5ess
```

If the router does not have a native BRI (if it is a TE2 device), it must use an external ISDN terminal adapter. On a TE2 router, use the **interface serial** *interface-number* command.

For BRI ISDN service, the switch-type can be one of those listed in Table 4-2. Depending on the version of Cisco IOS Software that you use, you might see different switch-types available for use with this command.

Configuring the SPID

A *service profile identifier* (SPID) is a number provided by the ISDN carrier to identify the line configuration of the BRI service. SPIDs allow multiple ISDN devices, such as phones and routers, to share the local loop. SPIDs are required by DMS-100 and National ISDN-1 switches. Depending on the software version it runs, an AT&T 5ESS switch might also require SPIDs. Your service provider furnishes you with the necessary SPID configuration information.

Each SPID points to line setup and configuration information. When a TE attempts to connect to the ISDN network, it performs a D-channel Layer-2 initialization process that causes a TEI to be assigned to the device. On a Cisco router, this process occurs at either power up, or immediately before the first call is made or received.

The TE then attempts D-channel Layer-3 initialization using Q.931 to communicate with the switch. If SPIDs are required, and are configured incorrectly on the device, the Layer-3 initialization fails, and the ISDN services cannot be used.

The AT&T 5ESS switch supports up to eight SPIDs per BRI. Because multiple SPIDs can be applied to a single B channel, multiple services can be supported simultaneously. For example, the first B channel can be configured for data, and the second B channel can be configured for both voice (using an ISDN telephone) and data.

DMS-100 and National ISDN-1 switches support only two SPIDs per BRI: one SPID for each B channel. If both B channels are being used for data only, configure the router for both SPIDs (one for each B channel). You cannot run data and voice over the same B channel simultaneously. The absence or presence of a channel's SPID in the router's configuration dictates whether that channel can be used for data or voice.

Where do SPID numbers come from? Most telcos use part of the ISDN phone number in the SPID naming system. Therefore, SPIDs are often the ISDN phone number with some optional numbers. For example, the SPID for the phone number (888) 555-1212 could be 888555121200.

A *local directory number* (*LDN*) might also be necessary if the router is to answer calls made to the second directory number. In BRI, the directory number is the local seven-digit ISDN phone number used by the B channel. The commands to set SPIDs and LDNs on both B channels are as follows:

```
Router(config-if)#isdn spid1 spid-number [ldn]
Router(config-if)#isdn spid2 spid-number [ldn]
```

Configuring the Encapsulation Protocol

After DDR (or a user) creates an end-to-end path over the ISDN, some method of datagram encapsulation is needed in order for data to make it from point A to point B. Available encapsulations for ISDN include the following:

- PPP
- HDLC
- Frame Relay
- LAPB
- Combinet Proprietary Protocol (CPP)

As noted earlier in this chapter, you will most likely use PPP as the Layer-2 encapsulation protocol.

The **encapsulation** command is used to configure encapsulation for your ISDN interface:

```
Router(config-if)#encapsulation [ppp | labp | hdlc | x25 | cpp]
```

If you configure PPP encapsulation, you must use Password Authentication Protocol (PAP) or Challenge Handshake Authentication Protocol (CHAP) if you receive calls from more than one dial-up source. Example 4-2 represents a typical BRI encapsulation configuration using PPP with CHAP.

Example 4-2   Configuring a BRI for PPP Encapsulation

```
Router(config)#interface bri 0
Router(config-if)#encapsulation ppp
Router(config-if)#ppp authentication chap
```

Several other important configuration commands can be used with BRI. These commands are examined in the section, "Optional ISDN Configurations," later in this chapter.

Configuring DDR over ISDN

With DDR, connections initiated by remote offices or telecommuters are brought up on an as-needed basis, resulting in substantial cost savings for the company (see Figure 4-9). In DDR scenarios, routers are not connected for long periods of time. Because ISDN provides greater throughput and quicker call setup than POTS, DDR is most often used with ISDN.

Figure 4-9
With DDR, ISDN calls are made only when the router detects interesting traffic.

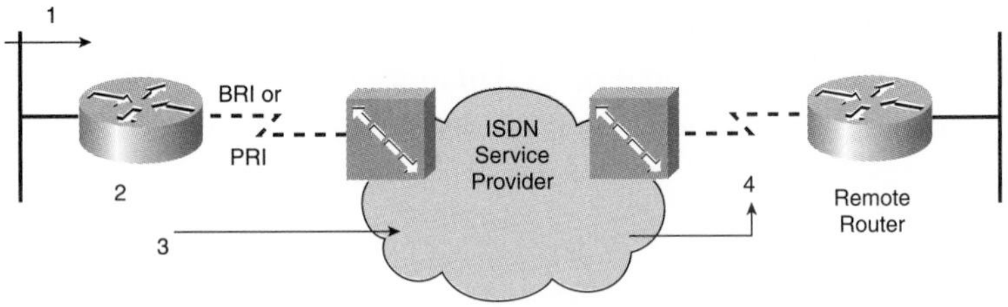

1. Packet arrives
2. Switch packet to DDR interface; determine if interesting
3. If interesting, dial DDR destination via ISDN
4. Connect to remote router

As shown in Figure 4-10, DDR configuration has four basic steps:

1. Define what constitutes interesting traffic by using the **dialer-list** command.

2. Assign this traffic definition to an interface by using the **dialer-group** command.

3. Define the destination address, hostname, and telephone number to dial by using the **dialer map** command.

4. (Optional) Define call parameters by using other **dialer** commands such as **dialer idle-timeout**, **dialer fast-idle**, and **dialer load-threshold**.

These four steps are discussed in the following sections. Although not specific to ISDN configurations, you must also configure routing in order for DDR to work. Different routing methods, including static routing, dynamic routing, route *redistribution*, and *snapshot routing*, are discussed in detail at the end of this section.

Figure 4-10
DDR configuration tasks can be divided into four main steps.

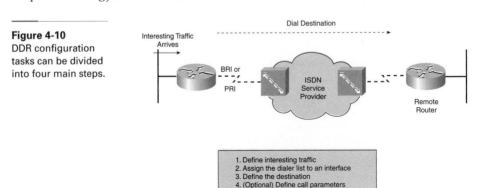

1. Define interesting traffic
2. Assign the dialer list to an interface
3. Define the destination
4. (Optional) Define call parameters

Defining Interesting Traffic

The **dialer-list** command is used to define what type of traffic is *interesting*. A router brings up a DDR interface (if it's not up already) to route interesting traffic. After the call is established, the router does not disconnect the call as long as it continues to receive interesting traffic to route over the DDR link. While the link is up, other *uninteresting* traffic (traffic not defined by the dialer list) can be routed over the link.

If the link is idle for a configurable period of time, the router disconnects the call. The router considers the link idle if it is not being used to route interesting traffic. Every time interesting traffic is routed out a DDR interface, the idle timer is reset. Traffic that is uninteresting does not keep a DDR call established.

The simpler form of the **dialer-list** command specifies whether a whole protocol suite, such as Internet Protocol (IP) or IPX, is permitted to trigger a call. The more complex form of the command references an access list, allowing finer control of the definition of interesting traffic.

Configure a simple dialer list using the following syntax:

```
Router(config)#dialer-list dialer-group-number protocol protocol-name
{permit | deny}
```

The command in Example 4-3 configures a dialer list that triggers a call for any IP traffic.

Example 4-3   Configuring a Simple Dialer List

```
RTA(config)#dialer-list 1 protocol ip permit
```

When the **dialer-list** command is used in conjunction with the access list, the **access-list** command specifies interesting traffic that initiates a DDR call:

```
Router(config)#access-list access-list-number [permit | deny] {protocol | protocol-
keyword}{source source-wildcard | any}{destination destination-wildcard |
  any}[protocol-specific-options] [log]
Router(config)#dialer-list dialer-group list access-list-number
```

By referencing an access list to specify interesting traffic, you have granular control of which protocols, sources, and destinations are worthy of bringing up the link.

An access list and a dialer list can be used together so that only traffic from one host is considered interesting (see Example 4-4).

Example 4-4   Referencing an Access List with the dialer-list Command

```
RTA(config)#access-list 24 permit host 192.168.1.2
RTA(config)#dialer-list 1 list 24
```

Assigning the Dialer List to an Interface

After the dialer list is created, it needs to be assigned to the interface(s) responsible for starting the call. This is accomplished by using the **dialer-group** command. You reference the dialer group in the **dialer-list** command, as shown in Example 4-5.

Example 4-5   Using the dialer-group Command

```
Router(config)#dialer-list 1 protocol ip permit
Router(config)#interface bri 0
Router(config-if)#dialer-group 1
```

NOTE

For a given proto-col and a given dialer group, only one access list can be specified in the **dialer-list** command.

Defining Destination Parameters

After you define what constitutes interesting traffic, you must provide the interface responsibility for starting the call with all the parameters necessary to reach the destination. As you saw in Chapter 2, "Modems and Asynchronous Connections," the **dialer map** command identifies destination information, such as the phone number to dial:

```
Router(config-if)#dialer map protocol next-hop-address [name hostname] [broadcast]
dial-string
```

The **dialer map** command has many other optional parameters available to it. However, using the options shown in Table 4-3 will suffice for most connections.

Table 4-3   Commonly Used Syntax for the dialer map Command

protocol	Protocol keywords; one of the following: appletalk, bridge, clns, decnet, ip, ipx, novell, snapshot, vines, and xns.
next-hop-address	Protocol address used to match against addresses to which packets are destined. This argument is not used with the bridge protocol keyword.
name	(Optional) Indicates the remote system with which the local router or access server communicates. Used for authenticating the remote system on incoming calls.
hostname	(Optional) Case-sensitive name or ID of the remote device (usually the hostname). For routers with ISDN interfaces, if calling line identification—sometimes called (CLID), but also known as caller ID and automatic number identification (ANI) —is provided, the hostname field can contain the number that the calling line ID provides.
broadcast	(Optional) Indicates that broadcasts and multicasts should be forwarded to this protocol address.

Table 4-3   **Commonly Used Syntax for the dialer map Command (Continued)**

dial-string [:*isdn-subaddress*]	(Optional) Telephone number sent to the dialing device when it recognizes packets with the specified next-hop-address that matches the access lists defined, and the optional subaddress number used for ISDN multi-point connections.
	The dial string and ISDN subaddress, if used, must be the last item in the command line.

Cisco IOS commands often contain the word *map*, which is used to map statically Layer-2 addresses to Layer-3 addresses. For example, the command **frame-relay map** is used to define a Layer-3 next-hop-address to its Layer-2 address (DLCI number). With a **dialer map** statement, you associate a Layer-3 address (IP in this chapter) to a dial-up Layer-2 address (which, in this case, is a phone number).

When setting up DDR among more than two sites, it is necessary to use PPP authentication and to use the **name** keyword with the **dialer map** command, as dialer maps for inbound calls are maps between protocol addresses and authenticated user names.

Defining Optional Call Parameters

The following additional call parameters can be added to the interface:

```
Router(config-if)#dialer idle-timeout seconds
Router(config-if)#dialer fast-idle seconds
```

Dial-up connections are subject to an idle timer, which keeps track of how much time has passed since interesting traffic was routed out the interface. By default, the idle-timeout is set to 120 seconds. You can customize this value to make the timer more aggressive, or you can increase the timeout value to keep the connection up longer. To manually set the idle-timeout value, use the **dialer idle-timeout** command.

When the router is waiting to use a line to make another call, it uses a more aggressive idle-timeout called fast-idle. The *fast-idle time* is the number of seconds that a line can remain idle before the current call is disconnected to allow another call that is waiting to use the line. You can configure this value by using the **dialer fast-idle** command. The default value is 20 seconds.

The commands shown in Example 4-6 configure short timeout periods, which might be appropriate for expensive toll lines.

Example 4-6   Configuring dialer idle Timers

```
RTA(config-if)#dialer idle-timeout 60
RTA(config-if)#dialer fast-idle 15
```

Static and Default Routing

DDR does, after all, involve routing. Routers make path determinations based on the information they have in their routing tables. Routing tables are built from administratively defined routes (static routes) and dynamically learned routes.

In a DDR environment, dynamic routing is problematic. Routing protocols such as RIP and OSPF rely on regular communication between link partners. If routers are connected through a dial-up link, active connections could be sporadic, and in some cases, infrequent.

But even though it poses problems over DDR links, dynamic routing could still be necessary in complex networks. Simple distance-vector routing protocols, such as RIP and IGRP, are typically used over DDR connections. However, the WAN core of an enterprise is likely to run a fast-converging routing protocol such as OSPF or EIGRP. OSPF can be used over DDR by configuring OSPF on-demand circuits (see the Tech Note, "Configuring OSPF over On-Demand Circuits").

TECH NOTE: CONFIGURING OSPF OVER ON-DEMAND CIRCUITS

The OSPF on-demand circuit is an enhancement to the OSPF protocol that allows efficient operation over on-demand circuits,such as ISDN, X.25 switched virtual circuits (SVCs), and dial-up lines. This feature supports RFC 1793, *Extending OSPF to Support Demand Circuits*.

Before this feature, OSPF periodic hello and LSA updates were exchanged between routers that connected the on-demand link, even when no changes occurred in the hello or LSA information.

With this feature, periodic hellos are suppressed and the periodic refreshes of LSAs are not flooded over the demand circuit. These packets bring up the link only when they are exchanged for the first time, or when a change occurs in the information they contain. This operation allows the underlying data-link layer to be closed when the network topology is stable.

This feature is useful when you want to connect telecommuters or branch offices to an OSPF backbone at a central site. In this case, OSPF for on-demand circuits allows the benefits of OSPF over the entire domain, without excess connection costs. Periodic refreshes of hello updates, LSA updates, and other protocol overhead are prevented from enabling the on-demand circuit when there is no *real* data to send.

Overhead protocols such as hellos and LSAs are transferred over the on-demand circuit only upon initial setup, and when they reflect a change in the topology. This means that critical changes to the topology that require new OSPF calculations are sent to maintain network topology integrity. Periodic refreshes that do not include changes, however, are not sent across the link.

To configure OSPF for on-demand circuits, use the following command in interface configuration mode, after enabling an OSPF routing process:

```
Router(config-if)#ip ospf demand-circuit
```

If the router is part of a point-to-point topology, then only one end of the demand circuit must be configured with this command. However, all routers must have this feature loaded.

If the router is part of a point-to-multipoint topology, only the multipoint end must be configured with this command.

In cases where the WAN core runs one protocol, and remote sites run another, you might have to use route redistribution to *share* routing information between the different protocols.

Ultimately, you might use static and default routing to address the challenge of routing in a DDR network. You might also use dynamic routing, including route redistribution, to propagate routes. When using a dynamic routing protocol over DDR, you can configure a Cisco router for snapshot routing, which is optimized for use over intermittent, dial-up links. Each of these techniques is discussed in the following sections.

Configuring Static Routes

Static routes are entered manually, eliminating the need for a routing protocol to send routing updates across the DDR connection. Static routes can be effective in small networks that do not change often.

Figure 4-11 shows that, in remote access scenarios, the central site is typically configured with a static route to a remote site's network address, or addresses. Because the remote site is generally a stub, its router is configured with a default route that points back to the central-site router, and the corporate network (represented by the cloud).

Figure 4-11
Typically, you configure a static route to the remote site on the central router, and a default route to the cloud on the remote router.

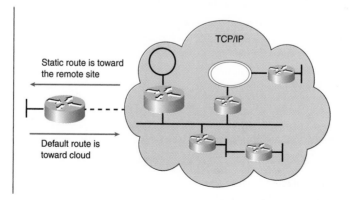

At the central site, you can enter the static route and point it at a remote site's network address, as shown in Figure 4-12 (see Example 4-7).

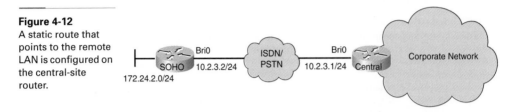

Figure 4-12
A static route that points to the remote LAN is configured on the central-site router.

Example 4-7   Configuring a Static Route by Specifying the next-hop-address

```
Central(config)#ip route 172.24.2.0 255.255.255.0 10.2.3.2
```

If a DDR router configured with the above static route receives an interesting packet destined for the 172.24.2.0 /24 network, the router then looks for a **dialer map** statement that maps a phone number to the next-hop IP address, 10.2.3.2.

Example 4-7 shows how static routes are typically configured for DDR. However, it is possible to use one route to define the next-hop IP address and a second to define the interface on which to find the next-hop (and dialer map). You could configure a static route using the local exit interface (the port from which traffic must exit the local router to reach the destination network), as shown in Example 4-8.

Example 4-8   Configuring a Static Route by Specifying the Exit Interface

```
Central(config)#ip route 172.24.2.0 255.255.255.0 10.2.3.2
Central(config)#ip route 10.2.3.2 255.255.255.255 bri0
Central(config)#interface bri 0
Central(config-if)#dialer map ip 10.2.3.2 name SOHO 5550000
```

A static route pointing to the next-hop IP address is necessary for DDR to work. Take, for example, the configuration shown in Example 4-9.

Example 4-9   Static Route Fails

```
RTA(config)#ip route 192.168.1.0 255.255.255.0 bri 0
RTA(config)#interface bri 0
RTA(config-if)#dialer map ip 10.1.1.1 name RTB 5551111
RTA(config-if)#dialer map ip 10.1.1.2 name RTC 5552222
RTA(config-if)#dialer map ip 10.1.1.3 name RTD 5553333
```

In Example 4-9, RTA's BRI0 has three different dialer maps to three different remote routers. What happens when RTA attempts to route traffic to 192.168.1.0 /24 out BRI0? The router cannot determine the appropriate **dialer map** statement to reach the destination network because no next-hop-address is specified in the static route. Even if RTA had only one **dialer map** statement configured on BRI0, the router would still fail to route the packet.

Under most circumstances, the **ip route** command contains the IP address of the next-hop. However, for routes over unnumbered point-to-point interfaces, you must specify the interface used to reach the destination.

Configuring Default Routes

A default route is likely to be the only route needed on a remote network that has only one outside network connection. Networks that have only one path to the outside world are called *stub networks*. Most remote offices are stub networks, and are therefore often configured with a default route.

To configure a static default route, use the **ip route 0.0.0.0 0.0.0.0** command.

On an IGRP router, you must use the **ip default-network** command if you want that router to include that default route in its updates. IGRP does not understand a route to 0.0.0.0/0. You can also use the **ip default-network** with other routing protocols. For more information on the difference between the **ip route 0.0.0.0 0.0.0.0** command and the **ip default-network** command, see *CCNP Cisco Networking Academy Program: Semester Five Companion Guide, Advanced Routing*.

Example 4-10 shows the commands needed to configure a default route on the router SOHO (see also Figure 4-12).

Example 4-10 Configuring a Default Route

```
SOHO(config)#ip route 0.0.0.0 0.0.0.0 10.2.3.1
SOHO(config)#interface bri 0
SOHO(config-if)#dialer map ip 10.2.3.1 name Central 5551212
```

If configured with this default route and dialer map, the SOHO router routes all non-local traffic over the dial-up link.

Configuring Route Redistribution

When static routes are used on the central-site router, they typically need to be redistributed into a *dynamic routing protocol*. This allows other routers in the enterprise to learn about the remote LAN dynamically. You can configure static route redistribution by using the **redistribute static** command in router configuration mode.

Assume that the corporate network depicted in Figure 4-12 uses EIGRP as its backbone routing protocol. Example 4-11 shows the commands need to redistribute the static route to SOHO's LAN into EIGRP.

Example 4-11   Redistributing Static Routes in to a Dynamic Routing Protocol

```
Central(config)#ip route 172.24.2.0 255.255.255.0 bri 0
Central(config)#router eigrp 100
Central(config-router)#redistribute static
```

Deactivating Routing Updates

Consider the topology shown in Figure 4-13. The Central router is configured with a static route that points to the SOHO's LAN, 172.24.2.0 /24. The Central router is also configured for RIPv2, which is the core routing protocol in the enterprise network (see Example 4-12).

Example 4-12   Configuring RIP

```
Central(config)#ip route 172.24.2.0 255.255.255.0 10.2.3.2
Central(config)#router rip
Central(config-router)#version 2
Central(config-router)#network 10.0.0.0
Central(config-router)#redistribute static
```

Figure 4-13
When configured for RIP, the Central router does not send updates out BRi0 if it is configured as a passive interface.

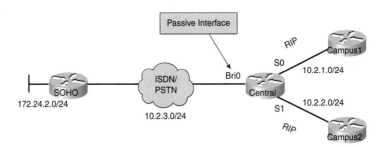

Because RIP accepts only classful addresses, the **network 10.0.0.0** command results in RIPv2 updates being sent on all of Central's interfaces, including its BRI.

By default, RIP sends updates every 30 seconds. If the update qualifies as interesting traffic, Central willplace a call every 30 seconds. If Central is already connected to SOHO, then its idle timer will be reset. With default **dialer idle-timeout** settings, a single update packet sent every 30 seconds would be enough to keep the link up forever, resulting in an unpleasantly large bill.

Typically, if a router is configured for dynamic routing and DDR, you will want to prevent periodic routing updates from establishing a call.

One solution is to configure the dialer list so that RIP is not interesting traffic. This is accomplished by using an access list, as described previously in the section "Defining Interesting Traffic." But because Central and SOHO are using static routes, there's no point in sending useless RIP updates across the dial-up link. In such cases, the routing protocol should be configured to treat the DDR interface as a *passive interface*.

A *passive interface* listens to routing updates but does not send them. You configure a passive interface using the **passive-interface** command in router configuration mode. Example 4-13 shows how Central must be configured so that RIP updates don't bring up the DDR link.

Example 4-13 Configuring a Passive Interface to Prevent Updates from Establishing a Call

```
Central(config)#ip route 172.24.2.0 255.255.255.0 10.2.3.2
Central(config)#router rip
Central(config-router)#version 2
Central(config-router)#network 10.0.0.0
Central(config-router)#redistribute static
Central(config-router)#passive-interface bri 0
```

Snapshot Routing

In most cases, using a combination of static and default routes between dial-up sites is all that's needed to maintain end-to-end connectivity. But situations arise where neither of the link partners connect to a stub network. In such situations, it might be desirable to implement dynamic routing, so complex networks with redundant paths can automatically adapt to topology changes.

Snapshot routing is a method of dynamic routing that is optimized for use of dialer interfaces. When a router is configured for snapshot routing, the interval between updates is controlled so that the routing protocol, such as RIP, doesn't keep a link up constantly.

Snapshot routing works with the following distance-vector protocols:

- RIP for IP
- IGRP for IP
- Novell RIP and SAP for Novell IPX
- Routing Table Maintenance Protocol (RTMP) for AppleTalk
- Routing Table Protocol (RTP) for Banyan VINES

By default, these routing protocols send updates every 10 to 90 seconds. If a router considers these updates as interesting traffic, the DDR link could stay up indefinitely. If the router does not consider these updates as interesting traffic, then updates are not delivered unless the dial-up link is already established. Thus, the routing protocol might be forced to declare routes as down, and remove them from the routing table. Snapshot routing provides a solution to this dilemma.

Unlike distance-vector protocols, link-state routing protocols send periodic hellos to neighbors, in addition to update packets. Typically, hellos are exchanged between neighbors every 5 or 10 seconds. Hellos are required in the operation of link-state protocols because they allow the routers to build relationships for the purpose of exchanging routes. In a DDR environment, link-state protocols trigger a call every few seconds. For this reason, link-state protocols, such as OSPF, are incompatible with snapshot routing. Because EIGRP also relies on the exchange of hellos between neighbors, it can't be used with snapshot routing either.

NOTE

Snapshot routing is available in Cisco IOS Software Release 10.2 or later.

If your network does run OSPF, you should use the OSPF on-demand circuit feature. Alternately, if your network runs OSPF or EIGRP, you can use RIP or IGRP between DDR hosts, and then redistribute these routes into another routing protocol.

Snapshot routing uses the client-server design model (see Figure 4-14). When snapshot routing is configured, one router is designated as the snapshot server and one or more routers are designated as snapshot clients. The server and clients exchange routing information during what is called the *active period* (shown as T1 in Figure 4-14).

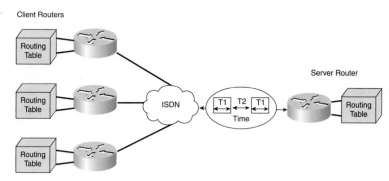

Figure 4-14
When configured for snapshot routing, a snapshot client exchanges routing updates with the snapshot server during the active time (T1).

At the beginning of the active period, the client router dials the server router (or routers) to exchange routing information. At the end of the active period, the router takes a snapshot of the entries in its routing table. These entries remain frozen during what is called the *quiet period* (shown as T2 in Figure 4-14). At the end of the quiet period, another active period begins, and the client router dials the server router to obtain the latest routing information.

The client router determines the frequency at which it calls the server router. The quiet period can be as long as 100,000 minutes (over 69 days).

The following sections describe the snapshot configuration commands and present a configuration example.

Snapshot Configuration Commands

Snapshot routing is enabled through interface configuration commands. The Central router is typically configured as the snapshot server by using the following command:

```
Router(config-if)#snapshot server active-time [dialer]
```

The active-time argument specifies the amount of time, in minutes, that routing updates are regularly exchanged between the client and server routers. This can be an integer in the range 5 to 100. There is no default value. A typical value is 5 minutes.

The **dialer** keyword is used with the **snapshot server** command when you want to allow the client router to dial up the server router in the absence of regular traffic.

To configure a snapshot server client, use the following commands:

```
Router(config-if)#snapshot client active-time quiet-time [suppress-statechange-
  updates]
[dialer]
Router(config-if)#dialer map snapshot sequence-number dial-string
```

The value of the active-time argument must be the same for the client and server routers. The quiet-time parameter specifies the amount of time, in minutes, that routing entries are frozen and remain unchanged between active periods. Routes are not aged during the quiet period, so they remain in the routing table as if they were static entries. This argument can be an integer from 8 to 100,000. There is no default value. The minimum quiet time is generally the active time plus 3.

You must make sure your active time is long enough to allow any routing updates to be sent. For example, IGRP routing updates are sent every 90 seconds by default, so make sure the active time is more than 90 seconds so that the update will be sent in the time allotted.

In addition to the active time, snapshot routing updates might also be triggered whenever the line protocol on an interface changes state (for example, down to up). These conditions can be ignored if the **suppress-statechange-update** configuration option is included. The **suppress-statechange-update** option disables the exchange of routing updates each time the line protocol goes from down to up or from dialer spoofing to fully up. If you use this option, you are effectively telling the router not to send routing updates during a user-initiated exchange of data.

The **dialer map snapshot** command specifies which router to call as the snapshot server. This command includes a sequence number because a given router can be configured with more than one **dialer map snapshot** command. Snapshot servers are dialed in order, starting with the lowest sequence number.

Snapshot Routing Configuration Example

You can configure the West router as the snapshot server by using the syntax shown in Example 4-14 (see Figure 4-15).

Figure 4-15
The West router is acting as the snapshot server, while East is configured as the snapshot client

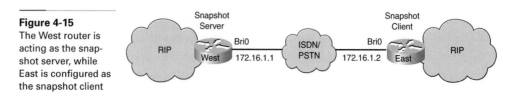

Example 4-14   Configuring a Snapshot Server

```
WEST(config)#interface bri 0
WEST(config-if)#ip address 172.16.1.1 255.255.255.0
WEST(config-if)#encapsulation ppp
WEST(config-if)#ppp authentication chap
WEST(config-if)#dialer map ip 172.16.1.2 255.255.255.0 name EAST broadcast 5559999
WEST(config-if)#snapshot server 5
WEST(config-if)#exit
WEST(config)#router rip
WEST(config-router)#network 172.16.0.0
```

The **snapshot server 5** command (highlighted above) enables snapshot routing and sets the length of the active period to 5 minutes. Example 4-15 shows a possible configuration for the snapshot client. (The key commands are highlighted.)

Example 4-15   Configuring a Snapshot Client

```
EAST(config)#interface bri 0
EAST(config-if)#ip address 172.16.1.2 255.255.255.0
EAST(config-if)#encapsulation ppp
EAST(config-if)#ppp authentication chap
EAST(config-if)#dialer map snapshot 1 name WEST 5558888
EAST(config-if)#dialer map ip 172.16.1.1 255.255.255.0 name WEST broadcast 5558888
```

Example 4-15 Configuring a Snapshot Client (Continued)

```
EAST(config-if)#snapshot client 5 720 suppress-statechange-update dialer
EAST(config)#router rip
EAST(config-router)#network 172.16.0.0
```

The **dialer map snapshot 1** command specifies that the WEST router is the first (and only) snapshot server that should be called.

The **snapshot client** command (highlighted above) defines the quiet time as 720 minutes, or 12 hours. The suppress-statechange-updates keyword prevents the routers from exchanging updates during connections that are established to transfer user data. The **dialer** keyword allows the client router to dial up the server router in the absence of regular traffic, and is required when you use the **suppress-statechange-update** keyword.

Optional ISDN Configurations

This section covers the following optional ISDN configurations and provides an example ISDN BRI configuration:

- B-channel aggregation
- ISDN caller identification
- Called-party number answering
- ISDN rate adaptation

B–Channel Aggregation

The two ISDN B channels in a BRI can be used simultaneously to connect to different destinations. In fact, one channel can be used for voice or fax, while the other is used to transfer data, such as TCP/IP packets. The 64 kbps of bandwidth provided by a single B channel is more than adequate for voice calls. However, in terms of data throughput, the bandwidth needs of today's small offices and power users far outstrip a DS0.

Dialer interfaces, such as BRI and asynchronous interfaces, can be configured for bandwidth on demand (BOD). This means that, after the load on one dial-up link reaches a certain threshold, the dialer can place another call to the same destination, if another available interface belongs to the same rotary group.

This is good news for ISDN users because a BRI's B channels automatically belong to the same rotary group. That means when the first B channel on a BRI is loaded to a threshold that you define (say, 50 percent), the second B channel can be brought up to dial the same destination, potentially doubling your bandwidth. This BOD principal works the same way with PRI, except that all 23 (or 30) channels can belong to the same rotary group. Although it's unlikely, all 23 channels could be used to connect to the same destination!

NOTE

The B channels of a PRI do not belong to the same rotary group by default.

The practice of combining B channels into a single ISDN pipe is called *B-channel aggregation* (see Figure 4-16). Using the Cisco IOS, there are two methods to achieve B-channel aggregation:

- Cisco Proprietary BOD
- Multilink PPP (MLP)

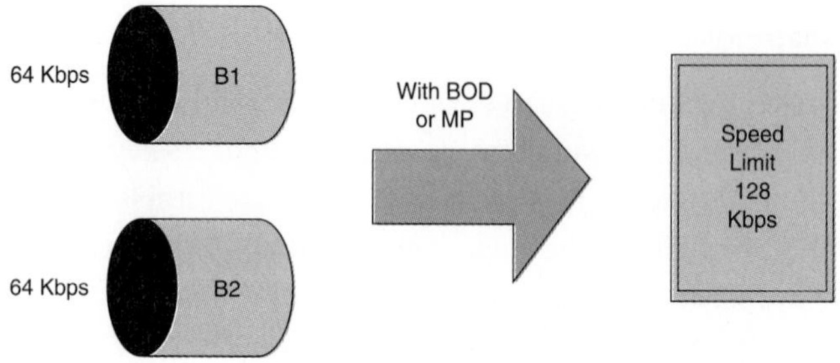

Figure 4-16
B-channel aggregation can be achieved using Cisco Proprietary BOD or MLP.

Both of these methods require the **dialer load-threshold** command. The major difference between the two methods is that Cisco BOD uses a proprietary algorithm to calculate load and bring up additional channels, while MLP uses a standards-based algorithm.

Cisco Proprietary BOD

Cisco Proprietary BOD is triggered by outgoing traffic levels only. When the traffic level reaches a configured level, the access router assigns the other B channel to share the traffic.

Assume you have an access server that is connected to an ISDN BRI with BOD configured, and only one B channel is used for communications. If you transfer a large file, the BOD feature senses the additional outbound traffic and allocates a second B channel. The router load balances the traffic between the two B channels. When you finish transferring the file, the second B channel times out and goes idle, saving you connect time.

To configure Cisco BOD, use the following command:

```
Router(config)#int bri 0
Router(config-if)#dialer load-threshold load
```

The load value is a number from 1 to 255 that is directly related to the bandwidth of the link, which can be specified by the **bandwidth** command. The lowest value, 1, forces the second link up so that both links are always available, regardless of the bandwidth demand. Any value greater than 1 specifies the percentage of bandwidth on the first B channel that must be used before the second B channel is activated for BOD. The bandwidth is defined as a ratio of 255, where 128 is 50 percent and 255 is 100 percent of the available bandwidth.

TECH NOTE: CALCULATING LOAD ON AN INTERFACE

The load value roughly reflects the amount of available bandwidth that is being used on an interface. The Cisco IOS tracks load as two 8-bit numbers, one that describes the amount of bandwidth being used by outbound traffic, and one that describes the amount of bandwidth being used by inbound traffic. As an 8-bit number, the maximum possible value either inbound or outbound is 255. The minimum possible value is 1. The **show interface** command expresses load as a fraction with the denominator of 255:

```
RTA#show interface bri 0/0
BRI0/0 is up, line protocol is up (spoofing)
  Hardware is PQUICC BRI with U interface
  Internet address is 10.1.1.1/24
  MTU 1500 bytes, BW 64 Kbit, DLY 20000 usec,
     reliability 255/255, txload 11/255, rxload 12/255
  Encapsulation PPP, loopback not set
  Last input 00:00:04, output never, output hang never
  Last clearing of "show interface" counters 05:33:55
```

Thus, a load value of 128 indicates that approximately 50 percent of the available bandwidth is used. In the previous example, the receive load value (rxload) is 12 (out of 255), which is about 5 percent.

The IOS bases this calculation on the bandwidth value assigned to an interface. This value can be administratively assigned on some interfaces (including BRI), so it does not necessarily reflect the bandwidth that is actually available. An inaccurate bandwidth value can skew load statistics.

The IOS does not calculate load every second or split second. The overhead associated with such constant calculations would significantly bog down the router. Instead, load data is gathered every 5 seconds. This data is used for a weighted average calculation in which more recent load data has more weight in the computation than older load data. By default, the IOS performs this weighted average calculation using data gathered over the last 300 seconds (5 minutes).

The **load-interval** command allows you to change the default interval of 5 minutes to a shorter or longer period of time. If you change it to a shorter period of time, the input and output statistics that display when you use the **show interface** command are more current and based on more instantaneous data, instead of reflecting a more average load over a longer period of time.

Although the **load-interval** interface configuration command is often used for dial backup purposes to increase or decrease the likelihood of a backup interface being implemented, it can be used on any interface. The default is 300 seconds (5 minutes). The new value must be a multiple of 30, between 30 and 600 seconds.

Using BOD, the load calculation takes into consideration the outbound traffic exclusively. If you want both inbound and outbound traffic to be used in the load calculation, use MLP.

MLP

MLP provides load balancing over multiple WAN links, while providing multivendor interoperability, packet fragmentation, proper sequencing, and load calculation on both inbound and outbound traffic (see Figure 4-17).

Figure 4-17
With MLP, Layer-2 frames are fragmented and sent across parallel paths, which form a bundle.

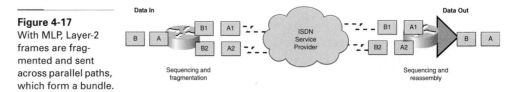

When two or more links are load balancing using MLP, they are referred to as a *bundle*. Layer-2 frames are broken up into fragments that are sequenced and then sent in parallel over the bundled links. These fragments are then reassembled at the destination.

MLP is specified by RFC 1990 (which supercedes the first MLP, RFC 1717). RFC 1990 refers to MLP fragments as *packets*, which can be confusing because the packets are really fragmented Layer-2 frames. Do not confuse MLP packets with the OSI model's Layer-3 packet.

MLP is available in Cisco IOS Release 11.0 and later, and it is available in Cisco 700 series routers with Release 3.2 and later.

Like Cisco proprietary BOD, MLP brings up multiple links when triggered by a load threshold that you define with the **dialer load-threshold** command. Unlike Cisco proprietary BOD, the load can be calculated on inbound traffic, outbound traffic, or in either direction by using the keywords **inbound**, **outbound**, or **either**, as shown here:

```
Router(config-if)#dialer load-threshold [inbound | outbound | either ]
```

In addition to the **dialer load-threshold** command, MLP configuration requires that PPP be configured with authentication and with the **ppp multilink** command, as shown here:

```
Router(config-if)#encapsulation ppp
Router(config-if)#ppp authentication chap
Router(config-if)#ppp multilink
Router(config-if)#dialer load-threshold 128
```

Note that both sides of the connection must be configured for MLP so that the LCP can negotiate this option. If PPP authentication is not configured correctly, MLP does not work properly. The decision to bundle channels is based on the authentication name of the remote router independently on each side of the link. Each router must use a unique hostname for authentication, with a shared password.

MLP is not used exclusively with ISDN B channels. The **ppp multilink** command can be configured on the following interfaces:

- Asynchronous serial interfaces in dialer rotary groups
- Synchronous serial
- BRI
- Multiple BRIs in dialer rotary groups
- Multiple BRIs using dialer profiles
- PRI B channels in dialer rotary groups

When setting up either BOD or MLP, only one end of a link must be configured with the **dialer load-threshold** command. If you need to configure both the caller and answering router, set the threshold at different values. If the calling router is set for an outbound threshold of 50, and the answering router is set for an inbound threshold of 50, they might both attempt to bring up the second link simultaneously. They could get a busy signal from the other end while each is attempting to dial. This is unlikely with ISDN because it sets up calls so quickly, but it can be a problem with slower technologies, such as async dialup.

ISDN Caller Identification

ISDN routers can be configured to screen incoming calls by using *calling line identification (CLID)*. Because the source phone number is included in the callsetup request message, the receiving router can first check the number against a preconfigured list. If the CLID doesn't match an explicitly allowed number, the callsetup request can be rejected. One reason to configure this feature is to prevent charges from calls made by unauthorized numbers.

Caller ID is available only from providers and switches that supply called-number values during the call setup phase. As shown in Figure 4-18, call acceptance does not occur until the router verifies the calling number.

NOTE

In some cases, the provider charges for call setup attempts. Thus, even if the call does not pass caller ID screening, there is a charge for the attempt.

Figure 4-18
When configured for call screening, an ISDN router can accept and reject calls based on the calling-line identification.

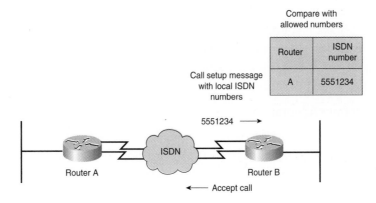

Caller ID screening requires a local switch that is capable of delivering the caller ID to the router or access server. If you enable caller ID screening, but are not connected to such a switch, no calls are allowed in. In addition, caller ID screening records the number exactly as it was sent, with or without an area code prefix.

The **isdn caller** command can be used to configure ISDN caller ID screening:

```
Router(config-if)#isdn caller phone-number
```

The number is a telephone number, up to 25 characters in length. As part of this number, enter an **x** or **X** in any position in the number where you can accept any number as a match (a so-called *wildcard* digit). You can specify up to 64 numbers per interface.

Called-Party Number Answering

Multiple ISDN devices can be physically connected at your site. You can ensure that only a single device answers an incoming call by verifying the number or subaddress in the incoming call against the device configured number, subaddress, or both.

Although the TEI 7-bit code allows up to 127 devices on an S-bus, there are limits to the number of each type that you can attach: up to eight devices with the 5ESS and NI-1 switches, and up to two devices for the DMS-100. Configuring multiple devices on an ISDN line is referred to as *ISDN multipoint*.

You can specify that the router verify a called-party number or subaddress number in the incoming setup message for ISDN BRI calls, if the number is delivered by the ISDN switch. You can do this by configuring the number that is allowed. The following is the interface command that provides a verification of the called-party phone by using the number supplied in the call setup request:

```
Router(config-if)#isdn answer1 [called-party-number][:subaddress]
```

If you want to allow an additional number for the router, you can configure it with the following command:

```
Router(config-if)#isdn answer2 [called-party-number][:subaddress]
```

If you do not specify the **isdn answer1** or **isdn answer2** command, all calls are processed or accepted. If you specify the **isdn answer1** or **isdn answer2** command, the router must verify the incoming called-party number and the subaddress before processing or accepting the call. The called-party number must not be mistaken for the number used by the router to start the call.

ISDN Rate Adaptation

Not all ISDN B channels operate at 64 kbps. Depending on the signaling method, an ISDN B channel might be restricted to 56 kbps. The 56-kbps data rate limitation comes from the restricted digital information (RDI) technique. This method stipulates that

NOTE

B channels that provide a full 64 kbps are called *clear channels*.

octets cannot have all 0s. To meet the RDI requirement of having at least one bit turned on in each octet (called *one-density*) every eighth bit of each octet is set to one. If one bit per octet is borrowed, the data rate drops to 56 kbps for a 64-kbps channel.

Rate adaptation allows a 64-kbps B channel to adjust to 56 kbps, if requested in the call setup message. You must use the rate-adaptation feature for cases in which the destination uses RDI. Figure 4-19 shows a connection with a reduced speed, which is set on the D channel during the call setup process. The manual assignment of calling speed is done on a per-destination basis.

Figure 4-19
By configuring rate adaptation, a router can use the same interface to make 64-kbps and 56-kbps calls on a per-desti-nation basis.

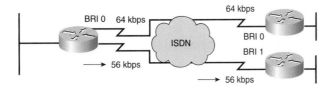

For ISDN interfaces only, you can specify an optional speed parameter for **dialer map** commands, as shown here:

```
Router(config-if)#dialer map protocol next-hop-address [name name] [speed speed]
[broadcast] dial-string
```

This option informs the router whether it must place a call at 56 kbps or 64 kbps. If you omit the ISDN speed parameter, the default is 64 kbps.

Configuring a Router for Initiating an ISDN Call

Let's apply what you have learned about configuring ISDN and DDR to a simple example. In Figure 4-20, the branch-office router, BRANCH1, must be configured to use DDR over ISDN to dial in to the Central office. But the company does not want FTP or Telnet keeping the DDR link active. Also, after the first B channel reaches 50 percent load, the second B channel should be brought up by using MLP.

Figure 4-20
BRANCH1 connects a remote office to the corporate network over ISDN.

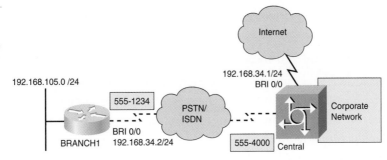

The service provider has assigned the following connection parameters to the branch office site:

- National ISDN-1 Switch
- SPIDs: 51055512340001 and 51055512350001
- LDN 5551234 and 5551235

At this point, you have enough information to configure ISDN DDR on BRANCH1. First, you need to configure the router with the information you received from the provider:

```
BRANCH1(config)#isdn switch-type basic-ni
BRANCH1(config)#interface bri0/0
BRANCH1(config-if)#isdn spid1 51055512340001 5551234
BRANCH1(config-if)#isdn spid2 51055512350001 5551235
BRANCH1(config-if)#no shutdown
```

Next, you can assign the Layer-2 encapsulation and Layer-3 addressing information to the interface:

```
BRANCH1(config-if)#encapsulation ppp
BRANCH1(config-if)#ppp authenticaion chap
BRANCH1(config-if)#ip address 10.0.0.1 255.255.255.0
```

Now you can proceed by configuring DDR over the BRI. The first step is to configure a dialer list, which is tricky in this case because the company requires that FTP and Telnet don't keep a call active. In this situation, you need to define an access list to be referenced by the dialer list.

```
BRANCH1(config-if)#exit
BRANCH1(config)#access-list 155 deny tcp any any eq ftp
BRANCH1(config)#access-list 155 deny tcp any any eq telnet
BRANCH1(config)#access-list 155 permit ip any any
BRANCH1(config)#dialer-list 5 protocol
ip list 155
```

After your dialer list is configured, you can apply it to the BRI with the following command:

```
BRANCH1(config)#interface bri0/0
BRANCH1(config-if)#dialer-group 5
```

The next step is to configure the **dialer map** statement that is used by the router for DDR:

```
BRANCH1(config-if)#dialer map ip 192.168.34.1 name CENTRAL 5554000
```

Because the central-site router is mapped by the hostname in the **dialer map** statement, you must configure a username/password database so that CHAP authentication works. To create a local database, you can enter the following command in global configuration mode:

```
BRANCH1(config-if)#exit
BRANCH1(config)#username CENTRAL password ITSASECRET
```

In interface configuration mode, you can configure optional commands, including MLP:

```
BRANCH1(config)#interface bri0/0
BRANCH1(config-if)#dialer load-threshold 128 either
BRANCH1(config-if)#ppp multilink
BRANCH1(config-if)#dialer idle-timeout 90
```

Because the company requires that the second B channel be triggered when the first channel reaches 50 percent load, the **dialer load-threshold** command is used with a load value of 128, which is approximately one-half of the maximum load, 255.

At this point, the interface configuration is complete. All that remains is to configure routing. Because BRANCH1 connects a stub network, a single default route is appropriate (refer to Figure 4-20):

```
BRANCH1(config-if)#exit
BRANCH1(config)#ip route 0.0.0.0 0.0.0.0 192.168.34.1
```

The BRANCH router's complete configuration looks like this:

```
version 12.0
service timestamps debug uptime
service timestamps log uptime
service password-encryption
!
hostname BRANCH1
!
enable secret 5 $1$obNV$HKkAF5EZlCke7.Rw5NQZc0
enable password 7 00131B1F00520F1F0034484B0A16011206030517
!
username CENTRAL password 7 10673D38363231392930
!
!
!
!
ip subnet-zero
!
ip audit notify log
ip audit po max-events 100
isdn switch-type basic-ni
!
!
!
process-max-time 200
!
interface FastEthernet0/0
 ip address 192.168.105.1 255.255.255.0
 no ip directed-broadcast
!
interface Serial0/0
 no ip address
 no ip directed-broadcast
 no ip mroute-cache
 shutdown
!
interface BRI0/0
 ip address 192.168.34.2 255.255.255.0
 no ip directed-broadcast
```

```
      encapsulation ppp
      dialer idle-timeout 90
      dialer map ip 192.168.34.1 name CENTRA
      dialer load-threshold 128 either
      dialer-group 5
      isdn switch-type basic-ni
      isdn spid1 51055512340001 5551234
      isdn spid2 51055512350001 5551235
      ppp authentication chap
      ppp multilink
     !
     interface FastEthernet0/1
      no ip address
      no ip directed-broadcast
      shutdown
     !
     interface Serial0/1
      no ip address
      no ip directed-broadcast
      shutdown
     !
     ip classless
     ip route 0.0.0.0 0.0.0.0 192.168.34.1
     no ip http server
     !
     access-list 155 deny    tcp any any eq ftp
     access-list 155 deny    tcp any any eq telnet
     access-list 155 permit ip any any
     dialer-list 5 protocol ip list 155
     !
     line con 0
      transport input none
     line aux 0
     line vty 0 4
      password 7 00131B1F00520F1F0034484B0A16011206030517
      login
     !
     !
     no scheduler allocate
     end
```

Verifying ISDN Operation

Several important **show** and **debug** commands can be used to monitor and troubleshoot ISDN operation. The following sections describe how to verify BRI configuration and MLP operation. Finally, these sections survey key **debug** commands used with ISDN.

Verifying BRI Configuration

The **show interface bri** command displays information about the BRI D channel or about one or more B channels, provided that your router is a TE1 (has a native BRI). Sample output for this command is shown in Example 4-16.

Example 4-16   Using the show interface bri Command

```
RTA#show interface bri 0/0
BRI0/0 is up, line protocol is up (spoofing)
  Hardware is PQUICC BRI with U interface
  Internet address is 10.1.1.1/24
  MTU 1500 bytes, BW 64 Kbit, DLY 20000 usec,
     reliability 255/255, txload 1/255, rxload 1/255
  Encapsulation PPP, loopback not set
  Last input 00:00:04, output never, output hang never
  Last clearing of "show interface" counters 05:33:55
  Input queue: 0/75/0 (size/max/drops); Total output drops: 0
  Queueing strategy: weighted fair
  Output queue: 0/1000/64/0 (size/max total/threshold/drops)
     Conversations  0/1/16 (active/max active/max total)
     Reserved Conversations 0/0 (allocated/max allocated)
  5 minute input rate 0 bits/sec, 0 packets/sec
  5 minute output rate 0 bits/sec, 0 packets/sec
     3764 packets input, 15094 bytes, 0 no buffer
     Received 0 broadcasts, 0 runts, 0 giants, 0 throttles
     0 input errors, 0 CRC, 0 frame, 0 overrun, 0 ignored, 0 abort
     3767 packets output, 15160 bytes, 0 underruns
     0 output errors, 0 collisions, 1 interface resets
     0 output buffer failures, 0 output buffers swapped out
     1 carrier transitions
```

Note that the word *spoofing* is highlighted in Example 4-16. Regardless as to whether an ISDN call is established or not, the BRI interface pretends to be up. This pretend state is called spoofing. Spoofing is necessary because the router removes routes pointing to down interfaces from its routing table. Thus, if the BRI was allowed to report its status as down, no routes using the BRI could be included in the routing table. If no routes using the BRI are in the routing table, then DDR cannot route packets to that interface in order to bring the link up.

If the router is a TE2 (has an external terminal adapter), you must use the **show interface serial** command instead of **show interface bri**.

You can also display information on both B channels by using the **show interface bri** [slot/port] **1 2** command (see Example 4-17).

Example 4-17   **Using the show interface bri [slot/port] 1 2 Command**

```
BRI0/0:1 is up, line protocol is up
  Hardware is PQUICC BRI with U interface
  MTU 1500 bytes, BW 64 Kbit, DLY 20000 usec,
     reliability 255/255, txload 1/255, rxload 1/255
  Encapsulation PPP, loopback not set
  Keepalive set (10 sec)
  Time to interface disconnect:  idle 00:00:47
  LCP Open
  Open: IPCP, CDPCP
  Last input 00:00:07, output 00:00:07, output hang never
  Last clearing of "show interface" counters never
  Input queue: 0/75/0 (size/max/drops); Total output drops: 0
  Queueing strategy: weighted fair
  Output queue: 0/1000/64/0 (size/max total/threshold/drops)
     Conversations  0/1/16 (active/max active/max total)
     Reserved Conversations 0/0 (allocated/max allocated)
  5 minute input rate 0 bits/sec, 0 packets/sec
  5 minute output rate 0 bits/sec, 0 packets/sec
     76 packets input, 1224 bytes, 0 no buffer
     Received 0 broadcasts, 0 runts, 0 giants, 0 throttles
     0 input errors, 0 CRC, 0 frame, 0 overrun, 0 ignored, 0 abort
     92 packets output, 2718 bytes, 0 underruns
     0 output errors, 0 collisions, 0 interface resets
     0 output buffer failures, 0 output buffers swapped out
     8 carrier transitions
BRI0/0:2 is down, line protocol is down
  Hardware is PQUICC BRI with U interface
  MTU 1500 bytes, BW 64 Kbit, DLY 20000 usec,
     reliability 255/255, txload 1/255, rxload 1/255
  Encapsulation PPP, loopback not set
  Keepalive set (10 sec)
  LCP Closed
  Closed: IPCP, CDPCP
  Last input never, output never, output hang never
  Last clearing of "show interface" counters never
```

Example 4-17   Using the show interface bri [slot/port] 1 2 Command (Continued)

```
Input queue: 0/75/0 (size/max/drops); Total output drops: 0
Queuing strategy: weighted fair
Output queue: 0/1000/64/0 (size/max total/threshold/drops)
   Conversations  0/0/16 (active/max active/max total)
   Reserved Conversations 0/0 (allocated/max allocated)
5 minute input rate 0 bits/sec, 0 packets/sec
5 minute output rate 0 bits/sec, 0 packets/sec
   0 packets input, 0 bytes, 0 no buffer
   Received 0 broadcasts, 0 runts, 0 giants, 0 throttles
   0 input errors, 0 CRC, 0 frame, 0 overrun, 0 ignored, 0 abort
   0 packets output, 0 bytes, 0 underruns
   0 output errors, 0 collisions, 0 interface resets
   0 output buffer failures, 0 output buffers swapped out
   0 carrier transitions
```

The output shown in Example 4-17 reveals that the B channels do not spoof their status. These lines only show up if a call has been established.

A convenient way to display the operational status of the BRI and both B channels is to use the **show ip interface brief** command, as shown in Example 4-18.

Example 4-18   Using the show ip interface brief Command

```
RTA#show ip interface brief
Interface              IP-Address       OK? Method Status                Protocol
FastEthernet0/0        192.168.0.1      YES NVRAM  up                    up
Serial0/0              unassigned       YES NVRAM  administratively down down
BRI0/0                 10.1.1.1         YES NVRAM  up                    up
BRI0/0:1               unassigned       YES unset  up                    up
BRI0/0:2               unassigned       YES unset  down                  down
```

Note that the output of this command always shows the BRI as up even if both B channels are down. When both B channels are down, the BRI is spoofing.

One of the most important **show** commands used with ISDN is **show isdn status**. This command displays status information for the ISDN on Layer 1, Layer 2, and Layer 3 (as shown by the shaded lines in Example 4-19).

Example 4-19   Using the show isdn status Command

```
RTA#show isdn status
Global ISDN Switchtype = basic-ni
ISDN BRI0/0 interface
        dsl 0, interface ISDN Switchtype = basic-ni
    Layer 1 Status:
        ACTIVE
    Layer 2 Status:
        TEI = 64, Ces = 1, SAPI = 0, State = MULTIPLE_FRAME_ESTABLISHED
        TEI = 65, Ces = 2, SAPI = 0, State = MULTIPLE_FRAME_ESTABLISHED
    Spid Status:
        TEI 64, ces = 1, state = 5(init)
            spid1 configured, spid1 sent, spid1 valid
            Endpoint ID Info: epsf = 0, usid = 70, tid = 1
        TEI 65, ces = 2, state = 5(init)
            spid2 configured, spid2 sent, spid2 valid
            Endpoint ID Info: epsf = 0, usid = 70, tid = 2
    Layer 3 Status:
        2 Active Layer 3 Call(s)
    Activated dsl 0 CCBs = 2
        CCB:callid=8013, sapi=0, ces=1, B-chan=1, calltype=DATA
        CCB:callid=8015, sapi=0, ces=2, B-chan=2, calltype=DATA
    The Free Channel Mask:  0x80000000
    Total Allocated ISDN CCBs = 2
```

The output shown in Example 4-19 was captured on a router while both its B channels were active. The highlighted portions of the output identify the status information associated with Layers 1, 2, and 3. Layer-2 information includes the TEI for each B channel, and is also an indication as to whether the SPIDs have been sent and accepted. At Layer 3, you can see that two calls are active; both of the calltypes are DATA.

The **show isdn status** command is especially useful when you are trying to track down the root of an ISDN connectivity problem. After examining the output in Example 4-20, you can see that TEIs have successfully been assigned to each B channel. However, according to the output, the second B channel has sent its SPID to the ISDN switch and was rejected. The most likely cause of this problem is that the router has been configured with the wrong SPID.

Example 4-20 Using the show isdn status Command to Troubleshoot Connection Problems

```
RTC#show isdn status
Global ISDN Switchtype = basic-ni
ISDN BRI0/0 interface
        dsl 0, interface ISDN Switchtype = basic-ni
    Layer 1 Status:
        ACTIVE
    Layer 2 Status:
        TEI = 64, Ces = 1, SAPI = 0, State = MULTIPLE_FRAME_ESTABLISHED
        TEI = 65, Ces = 2, SAPI = 0, State = MULTIPLE_FRAME_ESTABLISHED
    Spid Status:
        TEI 64, ces = 1, state = 8(established)
            spid1 configured, spid1 sent, spid1 valid
            Endpoint ID Info: epsf = 0, usid = 70, tid = 1
        TEI 65, ces = 2, state = 6(not initialized)
            spid2 configured, spid2 sent, spid2 NOT valid
    Layer 3 Status:
        0 Active Layer 3 Call(s)
    Activated dsl 0 CCBs = 0
    The Free Channel Mask:  0x80000003
    Total Allocated ISDN CCBs = 0
```

You might need to gather information on previous calls, not just those that are currently active. You can view the ISDN call history of a router by issuing the **show isdn history** command (see Example 4-21). This command outputs information on calls that have occurred during the past 15 minutes.

Example 4-21   Using the show isdn history Command

```
RTA#show isdn history
  ------------------------------------------------------------------------
                            ISDN CALL HISTORY
  ------------------------------------------------------------------------
History table has a maximum of 100 entries.
History table data is retained for a maximum of 15 Minutes.
  ------------------------------------------------------------------------
Call    Calling     Called        Remote  Seconds Seconds Seconds Charges
Type    Number      Number        Name    Used    Left    Idle    Units/Currency
  ------------------------------------------------------------------------
Out                 5554000         RTB      39      24      35      0
  ------------------------------------------------------------------------
```

The **show dialer** command is an invaluable monitoring and troubleshooting tool for ISDN interfaces. Example 4-22 displays **show dialer** output during an established call on the first B channel. The second B channel is idle.

Example 4-22   Using the show dialer Command

```
RTA#show dialer

BRI0/0 - dialer type = ISDN

Dial String       Successes   Failures    Last DNIS   Last status
5554000                   2          0    00:00:33       successful
0 incoming call(s) have been screened.
0 incoming call(s) rejected for callback.

BRI0/0:1 - dialer type = ISDN
Idle timer (60 secs), Fast idle timer (20 secs)
Wait for carrier (30 secs), Re-enable (15 secs)
Dialer state is data link layer up
Dial reason: ip (s=10.1.1.1, d=10.1.1.2)
Time until disconnect 30 secs
Connected to 5554000 (RTB)

BRI0/0:2 - dialer type = ISDN
Idle timer (60 secs), Fast idle timer (20 secs)
Wait for carrier (30 secs), Re-enable (15 secs)
Dialer state is idle
```

Verifying MLP

As soon as you configure a BRI interface with the **ppp multilink** command, the router creates a virtual interface called a *virtual access interface*. Example 4-23 illustrates this process.

Example 4-23 Verifying the MLP Virtual Access Interface

```
RTA#show ip interface brief
Interface              IP-Address       OK? Method Status               Protocol
FastEthernet0/0        192.168.0.1      YES NVRAM  up                     up
Serial0/0              unassigned       YES NVRAM  administratively down down
BRI0/0                 10.1.1.1         YES NVRAM  up                     up
BRI0/0:1               unassigned       YES unset  down                   down
BRI0/0:2               unassigned       YES unset  down                   down
RTA#configure terminal
RTA(config)#interface bri0/0
RTA(config-if)#ppp multilink
RTA(config-if)#exit
RTA#show ip interface brief
Interface              IP-Address       OK? Method Status               Protocol
FastEthernet0/0        192.168.0.1      YES NVRAM  up                     up
Serial0/0              unassigned       YES NVRAM  administratively down down
BRI0/0                 10.1.1.1         YES NVRAM  up                     up
BRI0/0:1               unassigned       YES unset  down                   down
BRI0/0:2               unassigned       YES unset  down                   down
Virtual-Access1        unassigned       YES TFTP   down                   down
```

Because both B channels work in parallel to send fragments to the same destination, a virtual access interface is created by the Cisco IOS to represent the multilink bundle. In Example 4-23, that interface is identified as interface Virtual-Access1. This virtual interface goes up after a multilink session is established.

Example 4-24 shows an output of the **show ppp multilink** command, which also references the virtual access interface. The output of this command displays which links are members of the bundle. Note that the bundle is named by using the hostname of the destination, in this case, RTB.

Example 4-24 Using the show ppp multilink Command

```
RTA#show ppp multilink
Virtual-Access1, bundle name is RTB
  Dialer interface is BRI0/0
```

continues

Example 4-24   Using the show ppp multilink Command (Continued)

```
0 lost fragments, 1 reordered, 0 unassigned, sequence 0x2/0x0 rcvd/sent
0 discarded, 0 lost received, 1/255 load
Member links: 2 (max not set, min not set)
  BRI0/0:1
  BRI0/0:2
```

You can also use the following **debug** commands to monitor MLP in an ISDN DDR environment:

- The **debug dialer** command indicates whether the multilink is up after authentication, and also indicates when the overload occurs.
- The **debug ppp multilink** command displays packet sequence numbers. It is useful only as a last resort because it does not help troubleshoot when connections are not being bundled.
- The **debug ppp negotiation** command displays the Maximum-Receive-Reconstructed Unit (MRRU) option negotiation.
- The **debug ppp authentication** command is useful for displaying the steps in the PPP authentication process.
- The **debug isdn events** command displays information that is useful for monitoring and troubleshooting MLP.

ISDN debug Command

You can also use **debug** to troubleshoot negotiations occurring on the D channel with **debug isdn q921** at Layer 2, and **debug isdn q931** at Layer 3.

The **debug isdn q921** command is useful when you want to observe signaling events between the router and the ISDN switch. For instance, consider Example 4-25. The first line of **debug isdn q921** output shows the router sending an Identity Request, indicated by *IDREQ*. Here, the router requests that it be assigned a TEI dynamically. The request includes an action indicator (ai) of 127, which means that the router is requesting a TEI value (127 is the broadcast TEI).

The second line of output is the Identity Assignment (IDASSN) sent by the ISDN switch. The ai in this message contains the assigned TEI number, 64. The third line of output shows the router's response to the assignment. The **SABME** command (set asynchronous balanced mode extended) indicates that the router has accepted the TEI of 64. The fourth line of output shows the ISDN switch's acknowledgement of the **SABME** command. After the router receives this acknowledgment, it brings ISDN Layer 2 up.

Example 4-25

```
RTA#debug isdn q921
00:14:85899345920: ISDN BR0/0: TX ->  IDREQ  ri = 44940  ai = 127
00:14:21: ISDN BR0/0: RX <-  IDASSN  ri = 44940  ai = 64
00:14:90194313216: ISDN BR0/0: TX ->  SABMEp sapi = 0  tei = 64
00:14:21: ISDN BR0/0: RX <-  UAf sapi = 0  tei = 64
00:14:92360871908: %ISDN-6-LAYER2UP: Layer 2 for Interface BR0/0, TEI 64 changed
to up
```

You might likewise use the **debug isdn q931** command to display information about call setup and teardown of ISDN network connections at Layer 3 on the D channel. Sample output from the **debug isdn q931** command shown in Example 4-26 includes a call setup message, indicated by SETUP in the first line. In the second line, the Bearer Capability value of 0x8890 indicates that the coding standard used is ITU-T and the circuit mode is 64 kbps.

Example 4-26   Using the debug isdn q931 Command

```
RTA#debug isdn q931
00:20:77309411328: ISDN BR0/0: TX ->  SETUP pd = 8  callref = 0x50
00:20:79475978700:           Bearer Capability i = 0x8890
00:20:77309411328:           Channel ID i = 0x83
00:20:77309411328:           Keypad Facility i = '5554000'
00:20:18: ISDN BR0/0: RX <-  CALL_PROC pd = 8  callref = 0xD0
00:20:18:          Channel ID i = 0x89
00:20:18: ISDN BR0/0: RX <-  CONNECT pd = 8  callref = 0xD0
00:20:18:          Channel ID i = 0x89
00:20:77309411328: ISDN BR0/0: TX ->  CONNECT_ACK pd = 8  callref = 0x50
00:20:79471047980: %LINK-3-UPDOWN: Interface BRI0/0:1, changed state to up
```

Configuring PRI

Earlier in this chapter, you saw that T1 and E1 leased lines provide two-way service over telephone-switching networks using PRI. A Cisco router that supports PRI interfaces is called a Network Access Server (NAS). This section describes the tasks that are required to configure PRI.

There are four main PRI configuration tasks:

1. Specify the correct PRI switch-type that the router interfaces with at the provider's central office (CO).

2. Specify the T1/E1 controller, framing type, and line coding for the provider's facility.

3. Set a PRI group timeslot for the T1/E1 facility and indicate the speed used.

4. Identify the interface that you will configure to act with DDR.

Because routers connect to PRI using T1/E1, there is no *interface pri*. Instead, the physical interface on the router that connects to the leased line is called a *T1 controller* (or E1 controller, if you are using E1). This controller must be configured properly to interface with the carrier network. The ISDN PRI D and B channels are configured separately from the controllerby using the **interface serial** command.

Configuring PRI Switch-Type

Use the **isdn switch-type** command to specify the provider's ISDN switch to which the NAS's PRI connects. As with BRI, this command can be issued globally or in interface configuration mode. You might need to use the **isdn switch-type** command in interface configuration mode when a single NAS supports multiple PRIs and you need to configure each controller with a different switch-type.

Table 4-4 lists the options for the PRI **isdn switch-type** command. An incompatible switch-selection configuration can result in failure to make ISDN calls. Reloading the router after changing the switch-type is typically required to make the new configuration effective.

Table 4-4   ISDN PRI Switch-Types by Area

Switch-Type Keyword	Description
Australia and Europe	
primary-net5	European, Australian, New Zealand, and Asian ISDN PRI switches (covers the Euro-ISDN E-DSS1 signaling system and is ETSI-compliant).
Japan	
primary-ntt	Japanese ISDN PRI switches.
North America	
primary-4ess	AT&T 4ESS switch-type for North America.
primary-5ess	AT&T 5ESS switch-type for North America.

Table 4-4   ISDN PRI Switch-Types by Area (Continued)

Switch-Type Keyword	Description
primary-dms100	NT DMS-100 switch type for North America.
primary-ni	National ISDN switch-type.
primary-qsig-slave	Specifies the Cisco MC3810 router or the interface to act as the primary QSIG slave when the PINX is the primary QSIG master.
primary-qsig-master	Specifies the Cisco MC3810 router or the interface to act as the primary QSIG master.

Configuring the T1/E1 Controller for PRI

You can begin configuring a T1 or E1 controller using the following command in global configuration mode:

```
Router(config)#controller {t1 | e1} {slot/port | unit number}
```

The command shown in Example 4-27 is used to enter interface configuration mode for a T1 controller on a 2620 router:

Example 4-27   Specifying a T1 Controller

```
Router(config)#controller t1
Router(config-controller)#
```

After you enter interface configuration mode, you can configure the framing, linecoding, and clocking, as dictated by your service provider.

The **framing** command is used to select the frame type used by the PRI service provider (see Table 4-5). For T1, use the following command syntax:

```
Router(config-controller)#framing {sf | esf}
```

And for E1 lines, use the **framing** command with the following options:

```
Router(config-controller)#framing {crc4 | no-crc4} [australia]
```

Table 4-5   Keywords Used with the framing interface configuration Command

Keyword	Description
sf	Specifies Super Frame as the T1 frame type.
esf	Specifies Extended Super Frame as the T1 frame type.

continues

Table 4-5   Keywords Used with the framing interface configuration Command (Continued)

Keyword	Description
crc4	Specifies CRC4 frame as the E1 frame type.
no-crc4	Specifies no CRC4 frame as the E1 frame type.
australia	(Optional) Specifies the E1 frame type used in Australia.

Use the **linecode** command to identify the physical-layer signaling method to satisfy the 1s density requirement on the provider's digital facility:

```
Router(config-controller)#linecode {ami | b8zs | hdb3}
```

Table 4-6 describes the keywords used with this command. Without a sufficient number of 1s in the digital bitstream, the switches and multiplexers in a WAN can lose their synchronization for transmitting and receiving signals. In North America, the B8ZS signaling method accommodates the 1s density requirements for T1 carrier facilities by using special bipolar signals encoded over the digital transmission link. It allows a full 64 kbps for each ISDN channel.

Table 4-6   Keywords Used with the linecode Command

Keyword	Description
ami	Specifies alternate mark inversion for T1 configurations.
b8zs	Specifies binary 8-zero substitution for T1 PRI configurations.
hdb3	Specifies High-Density Bipolar 3 for E1 PRI configurations.

Example 4-28 shows the typical configuration used with a T1 controller in North America.

Example 4-28   Typical T1 Configuration

```
RTA(config)#controller t1
RTA(config-controller)#framing esf
RTA(config-controller)#linecode b8zs
```

The typical configuration for E1 is shown in Example 4-29.

Example 4-29 Typical E1 Configuration

```
RTB(config)#controller e1
RTB(config-controller)#framing crc4
RTB(config-controller)#linecode hdb3
```

Use the **line** and **internal** options of the **clock source** command to configure the T1 clock source for the Cisco 7000 family, and the Cisco 3600 and 4000 series modules. The AS5000 access server series uses the **line primary** and **secondary** version of the command to select either the primary or secondary time-division multiplexing (TDM) as the clock source. With two controllers in an AS5000 series, one is primary and one is secondary. With four controllers, one is still primary with multiple secondaries:

```
Router(config-controller)#clock source {line [primary | secondary] | internal}
```

The **clock source line** command is the most common configuration. One instance in which you would use **clock source internal** is when two routers are connected back to back in a test environment.

Additional ISDN PRI Configuration Parameters

Additional ISDN PRI configuration parameters include the following:

- **pri-group** command
- D-channel selection
- Accepting analog calls

The **pri-group** command configures the specified interface for PRI operation and the number of fixed timeslots that are allocated on the provider's digital facility:

```
Router(config-controller)#pri-group [timeslots range]
```

The **interface serial** command specifies an interface for PRI D-channel operation. The interface is a serial interface to a T1/E1 on the router or access server:

```
Router(config)#interface serial { slot/port: | unit:}{23 | 15}
```

Within an E1 or T1 facility, the channels start numbering at 1 (1 to 31 for E1 and 1 to 24 for T1). Serial interfaces in the Cisco router start numbering at 0. Therefore, channel 16, the E1 signaling channel, is serial port subinterface 15. Channel 24, the T1 signaling channel, becomes serial subinterface 23. Thus, **interface serial 1/0:23** refers to the D channel of a T1 PRI (see Table 4-7).

Table 4-7   An Example of Channel-to-Interface Mapping for a T1 Using all 24 Channels on Serial 0/0

Channel	Example Interface Designation
1 (B channel)	S0/0:0
2 (B channel)	S0/0:1
3 (B channel)	S0/0:2
4 (B channel)	S0/0:3
5 (B channel)	S0/0:4
6 (B channel)	S0/0:5
7 (B channel)	S0/0:6
8 (B channel)	S0/0:7
9 (B channel)	S0/0:8
10 (B channel)	S0/0:9
11 (B channel)	S0/0:10
12 (B channel)	S0/0:11
13 (B channel)	S0/0:12
14 (B channel)	S0/0:13
15 (B channel)	S0/0:14
16 (B channel)	S0/0:15
17 (B channel)	S0/0:16
18 (B channel)	S0/0:17
19 (B channel)	S0/0:18
20 (B channel)	S0/0:19
21 (B channel)	S0/0:20
22 (B channel)	S0/0:21
23 (B channel)	S0/0:22
24 (D channel)	S0/0:23

The **isdn incoming-voice modem** command allows incoming analog calls to be switched to internal modems that are installed on a digital network module. Software examines the bearer capability fields of the D-channel data and determines whether a call is a normal ISDN call or an analog call being carried on an ISDN B channel. If it is an analog call, it is switched to internal modems. This command is available only for those access servers with the capability for internal modems:

```
Router(config-if)#isdn incoming-voice modem
```

PRI Configuration Example

Figure 4-21 presents an example PRI implementation on a 3600 series router, NAS-1. You can configure NAS-1 for the appropriate ISDN switch by using the following command:

```
NAS-1(config)#isdn switch-type primary-5ess
```

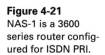

Figure 4-21
NAS-1 is a 3600
series router config-
ured for ISDN PRI.

Next, you can configure NAS-1's T1 controller using parameters provided by the ISDN carrier:

```
NAS-1(config)#controller t1
NAS-1(config-controller)#framing esf
NAS-1(config-controller)#linecode b8zs
NAS-1(config-controller)#clock source line primary
NAS-1(config-controller)#pri-group timeslots 1-24
```

The **clock source line primary** command specifies that NAS-1 receives its clock source from the T1 line. The **pri-group timeslots 1-24** command configures all 24 possible timeslots for use by the PRI. If you assume the controller is Serial interface S1/0, this command creates channel serial interfaces Serial 1/0:0 through Serial 1/0:23. The timeslots (DS0s) 1-23 are used for the B channels. The last timeslot (DS0), which is 24 (or Serial 1/0:23), is used as the D channel.

With the T1 controller configured, you can now turn your attention to the interface configuration:

```
NAS-1(config)#interface serial0/0:23
NAS-1(config-if)#ip unnumbered fastethernet0/0
NAS-1(config-if)#encapsulation ppp
NAS-1(config-if)#ppp authentication chap pap
NAS-1(config-if)#no cdp enable
NAS-1(config-if)#dialer-group 1
```

The **interface serial0/0:23** command specifies channel 24 of the T1, which is the D channel. When you configure the D channel, its configuration is applied to all the individual B channels. Specifically, when calls are made or received on the B channels, the configuration is copied, or cloned, from dialer interface, serial0/0:23.

In this case, you are using IP unnumbered, so the PRI borrows **fastethernet0/0**'s IP address.

For an E1 example, the timeslot argument for the **pri-group** command is 1-31 rather than 1-24, as shown for a T1 example; and the **interface** command is 0/0:15 instead of 0/0:23

Summary

In this chapter, you learned the difference between ISDN BRI and PRI, and how to select either one of these services, depending on the applications. You examined the signaling and call sequences of the Q.921 and Q.931 protocols, and learned how to configure and troubleshoot ISDN for DDR and for accepting calls. In Chapter 5, you learn how to optimize the configuration of DDR.

Review Questions

Use the following review questions to test your understanding of the concepts covered in this chapter. In some cases, there is more than one correct answer, so choose all that apply. Answers are listed in Appendix A, "Answers to Review Questions."

1. Which of the following is true about BRI?

   A. BRI has two 64-kbps B channels.

   B. BRI has one 64-kbps D channel.

   C. BRI has a total speed of 128 kbps.

   D. BRI has a total speed of 192 kbps.

2. Which of the following is true about the ISDN D channel?

   A. It typically uses PPP at Layer 2.

   B. It typically uses LAPD at Layer 2.

   C. It typically uses Q.921 at Layer 3.

   D. It does not function at Layer 3.

3. Which ISDN reference point connects the NT1 to the LE?

   A. V

   B. S/T

   C. U

   D. R

4. How many B channels are supported in ISDN PRI over T1?

   A. 23

   B. 24

   C. 30

   D. 31

5. Which of the following routing protocols are compatible with snapshot routing?

   A. RIPv1

   B. RIPv2

   C. IGRP

   D. RTMP

6. Which of the following is NOT true about SPIDs?

    A. SPIDs are ISDN phone numbers.

    B. SPIDs are assigned by the provider.

    C. SPIDs are always needed in order to properly establish Layer-2 communication with an ISDN BRI switch.

    D. The AT&T 5ESS supports up to 8 SPIDs per BRI channel.

7. Which of the following syntax correctly defines the entire TCP/IP protocol suite as interesting traffic?

    A. (config-if)#**dialer-list 1 permit ip any any**

    B. (config-if)#**dialer-list 5 ip permit**

    C. (config-if)#**dialer-list 7 protocol permit ip**

    D. (config-if)#**dialer-list 2 protocol ip permit**

8. Which of the following syntax correctly defines the number of seconds that a line can remain idle before the current call is disconnected to allow another call that is waiting to use the line?

    A. (config-if)#**dialer wait-for-timeout 10**

    B. (config-if)#**dialer fast-idle 10**

    C. (config-if)#**dialer idle-timeout 10**

    D. (config-if)#**dialer idle-wait 10**

9. Which IOS command correctly configures bandwidth on demand to trigger a second dial-up link when the first reaches 50percent load?

    A. (config-if)#**dialer load-threshold 50**

    B. (config-if)#**dialer load-threshold 5**

    C. (config-if)#**dialer load-threshold 50**

    D. (config-if)#**dialer load-threshold 128**

10. Which of the following commands could be used to enter configuration mode for the D channel of a PRI over T1?

    A. (config-if)#**controller t1**

    B. (config-if)#**interface serial 0/0:23**

    C. (config-if)#**interface pri**

    D. (config-if)#**interface t1**

Key Terms

Active period In snapshot routing, the period of time during which a client and server exchange routing updates.

B channel An ISDN communication channel that bears or carries voice or dat The bearer channel is the fundamental component of ISDN interfaces. It carries 64,000 bits per seconds (64 kbps) in either direction.

Bundle Group of links being used together for MLP.

CLID (calling line identification) The ISDN number of the calling source. This is provided by the Telco in the call setup messages. You can screen calls based on CLI for added security.

D channel An ISDN communication channel used for sending information between the ISDN equipment and the ISDN central-office switch. The delta channel carries the signaling and call progress messages.

LAPD (Link Access Protocol-D) The data link Layer-2 protocol that manages the exchange of information to the ISDN network. LAPD is defined in Q.921.

LE (Local Exchange) The ISDN central office (CO) that houses the ISDN switch. The LE implements the ISDN protocol and is part of the network.

LDN (local directory number) Used for call routing, the LDN is associated with a SPID (and therefore with North American BRI interfaces) and is necessary for receiving incoming calls on the second B channel.

Passive interface An interface that listens for routing updates, but does not send them.

Q.921 (also referred to as LAPD) Specifies the data link protocol used over ISDN's D channel.

Q.931 ITU-T specification for signaling to establish, maintain, and clear ISDN network connections.

Quiet period In snapshot routing, the period of time during which no routing updates are exchanged, and routing table entries are frozen.

Redistribution The process of importing static, connected, or dynamically learned routes into a routing protocol.

SS7 (Signaling System 7) On the PSTN, SS7 is a system that puts the information required to set up and manage telephone calls in a separate network rather than within the same network that the telephone call is made on.

SAPI (service access point identifier)   An address used at Layer 2 to manage different data types for the same individual device connecting to the ISDN network. The SAPI and TEI together form the Layer-2 address.

Snapshot routing   Method of gathering routing information during an *active time*, taking a snapshot of the information, and using that routing information for a configured length of time (referred to as the *quiet time*).

Stub network   Network that has only one entry/exit point.

TEI (terminal endpoint identifier)   An address used at Layer 2 to manage individual devices connecting to the ISDN network. The TEI is typically dynamically negotiated with the ISDN switch.

Objectives

After completing this chapter, you will be able to perform tasks related to the following:

- Legacy DDR
- Rotary groups
- Dialer profiles
- Dialer map-classes

Chapter 5

Dialer Profiles

Introduction

The dial-on-demand routing (DDR) configurations introduced in previous chapters are examples of what Cisco terms *legacy DDR*. A *legacy* is something that's received from the past. In this case, legacy DDR refers to the old way of configuring DDR, which is characterized by the application of **dialer** commands directly on the physical interface (such as BRI0, Async0, etc.), or by the use of rotary groups.

This chapter examines the weaknesses of legacy DDR (including rotary groups) and details a newer, alternate method of DDR configuration using dialer profiles. DDR with dialer profiles allows for the most flexible and efficient dial configurations.

Legacy DDR

Legacy DDR is powerful and comprehensive; it supports Frame Relay, the International Organization for Standardization Connectionless Network Service (ISO CLNS), the Link Access Procedure Balanced (LAPB) protocol, snapshot routing, and all routed protocols that are supported on Cisco routers. However, legacy DDR's limitations can adversely affect growth.

Legacy DDR is based on a static binding between the per-destination call specification and the physical interface configuration (see Figure 5-1).

Figure 5-1
Using legacy DDR,
each physical
interface is locked
in to a single logical
configuration.

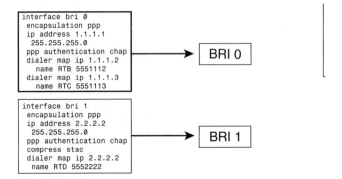

```
interface bri 0
  encapsulation ppp
  ip address 1.1.1.1
    255.255.255.0
  ppp authentication chap
  dialer map ip 1.1.1.2
    name RTB 5551112
  dialer map ip 1.1.1.3
    name RTC 5551113
```
→ BRI 0

```
interface bri 1
  encapsulation ppp
  ip address 2.2.2.2
    255.255.255.0
  ppp authentication chap
  compress stac
  dialer map ip 2.2.2.2
    name RTD 5552222
```
→ BRI 1

The problem with this method is that legacy DDR locks a physical interface into one configuration. For example, BRI0 can have only one Internet Protocol (IP) address, one encapsulation type, and one set of dialer timers. Consider the configuration in Example 5-1.

Example 5-1 Using a Single Dialer Map with Legacy DDR

```
RTA#show running-config interface bri 0
Building configuration...

Current configuration:
!
interface BRI0
 description connected to ntt 81012345678902
 ip address 7.1.1.7 255.255.255.0
 encapsulation ppp
 dialer idle-timeout 30
 dialer load-threshold 40 either
 dialer map ip 7.1.1.8 name atlanta 81012345678901
 dialer-group 1
 ppp authentication pap
 ppp multilink
end
```

Legacy DDR configurations use **dialer map** statements, which are convenient when one physical interface is responsible for calling one destination. As configured, the

BRI0 can only dial a host named Atlanta, and can only use Point-to-Point Protocol (PPP) with a **dialer idle-timeout** of 30 seconds when connected (refer to Example 5-1).

The **dialer map** command can also be used if your router calls multiple destinations that all use the same communication parameters. Example 5-2 shows that three separate **dialer map** statements can be configured on the same interface. But this means that each call must also use the other configured parameters, such as the dialer idle timer values and PPP authentication method.

Example 5-2 Using Multiple Dialer Maps with Legacy DDR

```
RTA#show running-config interface bri 0
Building configuration...

Current configuration:
!
interface BRI0
 description connected to ntt 81012345678902
 ip address 7.1.1.7 255.255.255.0
 encapsulation ppp
 dialer idle-timeout 30
 dialer load-threshold 40 either
 dialer map ip 7.1.1.8 name RTB 81012345678901
 dialer map ip 7.1.1.9 name RTC 81012345671234
 dialer map ip 7.1.1.4 name RTD 81012345671122
 dialer-group 1
 ppp authentication pap
 ppp multilink
end
```

What if your router is responsible for reaching three separate locations that use different communication parameters? Suppose that one location requires Password Authentication Protocol (PAP) authentication when another is doing Challenge Handshake Authentication Protocol (CHAP) authentication. One location might require an Integrated Services Digital Network (ISDN) speed of 56 Kbps, whereas the other destinations communicate at 64 Kbps. If this is the case, specific call parameters must be defined under three separate physical interfaces, each of them connected to a separate line (see Figure 5-2).

Figure 5-2
Using legacy DDR,
three separate physi-
cal interfaces are
required to connect
to remote sites using
different call parame-
ters and timer values.

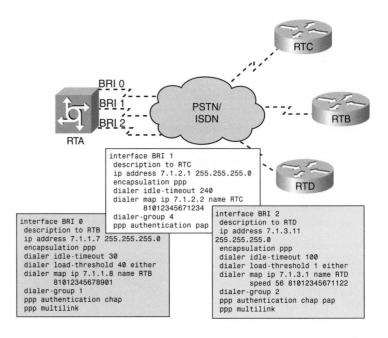

```
interface BRI 1
  description to RTC
  ip address 7.1.2.1 255.255.255.0
  encapsulation ppp
  dialer idle-timeout 240
  dialer map ip 7.1.2.2 name RTC
         81012345671234
  dialer-group 4
  ppp authentication pap
```

```
interface BRI 0
  description to RTB
  ip address 7.1.1.7 255.255.255.0
  encapsulation ppp
  dialer idle-timeout 30
  dialer load-threshold 40 either
  dialer map ip 7.1.1.8 name RTB
         81012345678901
  dialer-group 1
  ppp authentication chap
  ppp multilink
```

```
interface BRI 2
  description to RTD
  ip address 7.1.3.11
255.255.255.0
  encapsulation ppp
  dialer idle-timeout 100
  dialer load-threshold 1 either
  dialer map ip 7.1.3.1 name RTD
         speed 56 81012345671122
  dialer-group 2
  ppp authentication chap pap
  ppp multilink
```

The previous scenario might result in wasted resources and money. You would have to procure a router with three dial-up WAN interfaces, and you would have to pay for three lines that might be used for only a few minutes daily.

A more efficient solution might be a mechanism in which physical interfaces are not locked in to permanent configurations. Instead, this mechanism assumes call parameters on an as-needed basis (see Figure 5-3). When the call is finished, the same interface is freed of the previous configuration and is ready to service another calling destination. This method, called *DDR with dialer profiles*, is discussed in the section, "Dialer Profiles," later in this chapter.

Consider another scenario. What if you have multiple physical interfaces that all need to be configured with the exact same communication parameters? For example, you might have eight asynchronous interfaces that each answer calls using the same IP address, same encapsulation, and same **dialer** configuration commands. The solution is to use dialer rotary groups (see Figure 5-4).

Figure 5-3
Using DDR with dialer profiles, you can propagate logical configurations from multiple dialer interfaces to a physical interface.

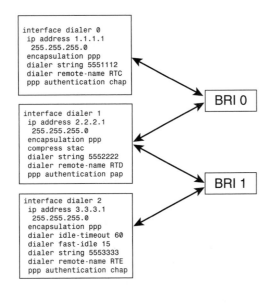

Figure 5-4
Using legacy DDR with rotary groups, you can propagate a single logical configuration from the dialer interface to multiple physical interfaces.

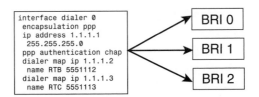

The following sections describe how to use dialer rotary groups, including how to configure dialer rotary groups for ISDN. Asynchronous interface groups are also discussed. Finally, this section looks at the limitations of legacy DDR.

Rotary Groups

Dialer rotary groups allow you to apply a single interface configuration to a set of physical interfaces. Dialer rotary groups are useful in environments that have multiple callers and calling destinations.

You define a dialer rotary group by specifying a dialer interface. The dialer interface is not a physical interface; it is an entity that allows you to propagate an interface configuration to multiple interfaces. After you define the dialer interface by a number, such as interface dialer 1, you can then configure parameters for that interface. Finally, physical interfaces are assigned to the dialer rotary group. Physical interfaces inherit the dialer interface configuration parameters (see Figure 5-5).

Figure 5-5
You can propagate a single logical configuration from the dialer interface to multiple physical interfaces using rotary groups.

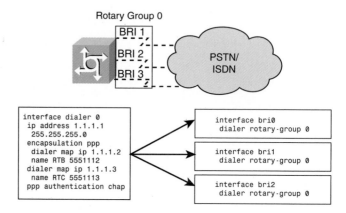

NOTE

You can define up to 256 dialer interfaces.

The telephone company also has rotary groups, called *hunt groups*, which allow you to dial one phone number and get connected to one of several different phone numbers. In other words, a hunt group is a series of telephone lines that are programmed so that as incoming calls arrive, if the first line is busy the second line is tried, and then the third line is tried, and so on, until a free line is found. This way, an incoming call should not end up with a busy signal, as shown in Figure 5-6. If your telephone company has provided you with a hunt group, it is a good idea to configure dialer rotary groups on the router. Most ISPs use a hunt group for their customer access numbers. This is why several customers of an ISP can dial the same number and connect at the same time.

Figure 5-6
If you use a hunt group, configure dialer rotary groups so that incoming calls are routed to the first available free line.

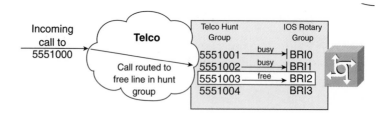

Rotary groups can also be used for outgoing calls. After a dialer interface configuration is propagated to a set of physical interfaces, you can use those interfaces to place calls using standard DDR criteria. When many destinations are configured, any of the physical interfaces in a rotary group can be used for outgoing calls. When traffic arrives, an interface from the rotary group is dialed. When traffic for a different host arrives, another interface is dialed. Using the dialer interface allows you to specify one set of dialer maps that can apply to multiple physical lines.

The **interface dialer** command in global configuration mode creates a dialer rotary group:

```
Router(config)#interface dialer group-number
```

You can assign an interface to a dialer rotary group using the following command:

```
Router(config-if)#dialer rotary-group group-number
```

When many destinations are configured, any of the physical interfaces in a rotary group can be used for outgoing calls.

If you want to use the same logical configuration on three of the asynchronous lines of a Cisco 2511 access server, you can use the configuration shown in Example 5-3 and Figure 5-7.

Figure 5-7
As members of rotary group 1, the three asynchronous interfaces use the logical configuration defined by interface Dialer1.

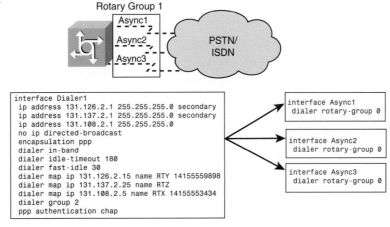

```
interface Dialer1
 ip address 131.126.2.1 255.255.255.0 secondary
 ip address 131.137.2.1 255.255.255.0 secondary
 ip address 131.108.2.1 255.255.255.0
 no ip directed-broadcast
 encapsulation ppp
 dialer in-band
 dialer idle-timeout 180
 dialer fast-idle 30
 dialer map ip 131.126.2.15 name RTY 14155559898
 dialer map ip 131.137.2.25 name RTZ
 dialer map ip 131.108.2.5 name RTX 14155553434
 dialer group 2
 ppp authentication chap
```

```
interface Async1
 dialer rotary-group 0
```

```
interface Async2
 dialer rotary-group 0
```

```
interface Async3
 dialer rotary-group 0
```

WARNING

The console line (line 0) cannot be in a rotary group.

NOTE

It is not necessary to configure rotary groups for the B channels of a single BRI or Primary Rate Interface (PRI). ISDN B channels are automatically placed into a rotary group. However, multiple BRI or PRI interfaces can be grouped using the **dialer rotary-group** command.

NOTE

An ISDN BRI is a rotary group of B channels. An ISDN interface can be part of a rotary group comprising other interfaces (synchronous, asynchronous, ISDN BRI, or ISDN PRI). However, Cisco supports, at most, one level of recursion; that is, a rotary of rotaries is acceptable, but a rotary of rotaries of rotaries is not supported.

Example 5-3 Using Dialer Rotary Groups

```
RTA(config)#interface dialer 1
RTA(config-if)#encapsulation ppp
RTA(config-if)#ppp authentication chap
RTA(config-if)#dialer in-band
RTA(config-if)#dialer-group 2
RTA(config-if)#dialer idle-timeout 180
RTA(config-if)#dialer fast-idle 30
RTA(config-if)#ip address 131.108.2.1 255.255.255.0
RTA(config-if)#ip address 131.126.2.1 255.255.255.0 secondary
RTA(config-if)#ip address 131.137.2.1 255.255.255.0 secondary
RTA(config-if)#dialer map ip 131.108.2.5 name RTX 14155553434
RTA(config-if)#dialer map ip 131.126.2.15 name RTY 14155559898
RTA(config-if)#dialer map ip 131.137.2.25 name RTZ

RTA(config-if)#interface async 1
RTA(config-if)#dialer rotary-group 1
RTA(config-if)#interface async 2
RTA(config-if)#dialer rotary-group 1
RTA(config-if)#interface async 3
RTA(config-if)#dialer rotary-group 1
```

The **interface dialer 1** command creates the logical interface configuration that is shared among the members of the rotary group. Because this interface is numbered 1, a physical line must belong to dialer rotary group 1 to use this configuration.

The **secondary** parameter is used with the **ip address** command to assign additional logical addresses. In Example 5-3, interface Dialer1 is configured so that members of rotary group 1 can assume one of three IP addresses depending on which **dialer map** statement is used.

The **dialer map** statement referencing RTZ does not include a phone number, which allows the remote router RTZ to call the access server, but RTA cannot call RTZ.

Finally, interfaces async 1, async 2, and async 3 are each placed in rotary group 1 using the **dialer rotary-group** command. No other logical configuration for these interfaces is necessary because they inherit the parameters configured for interface Dialer1.

Configuring ISDN for Dialer Rotary Groups

A physical interface can belong to only one dialer rotary group. But the **dialer rotary-group** command can be used with any dial-up interface, async, BRI, PRI, and serial. In Example 5-4, the shaded commands assign all the BRIs to dialer rotary-group 2 so that the BRIs answer calls made to the same phone number as part of the hunt group (see Figure 5-8).

Figure 5-8
Multiple BRI interfaces can belong to the same rotary group.

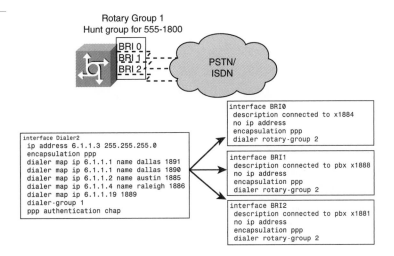

```
interface Dialer2
 ip address 6.1.1.3 255.255.255.0
 encapsulation ppp
 dialer map ip 6.1.1.1 name dallas 1891
 dialer map ip 6.1.1.1 name dallas 1890
 dialer map ip 6.1.1.2 name austin 1885
 dialer map ip 6.1.1.4 name raleigh 1886
 dialer map ip 6.1.1.19 1889
 dialer-group 1
 ppp authentication chap
```

```
interface BRI0
 description connected to x1884
 no ip address
 encapsulation ppp
 dialer rotary-group 2
```

```
interface BRI1
 description connected to pbx x1888
 no ip address
 encapsulation ppp
 dialer rotary-group 2
```

```
interface BRI2
 description connected to pbx x1881
 no ip address
 encapsulation ppp
 dialer rotary-group 2
```

Example 5-4 Configuring Multiple BRIs as Part of a Dialer Rotary-Group

```
interface BRI0

description connected to x1884

no ip address

encapsulation ppp

dialer rotary-group 2

!

interface BRI1

description connected to pbx line 1888

no ip address

encapsulation ppp

dialer rotary-group 2
```

continues

Example 5-4 Configuring Multiple BRIs as Part of a Dialer Rotary-Group (Continued)

```
!
interface BRI2
no ip address
encapsulation ppp
dialer rotary-group 2
!
interface Dialer2
ip address 6.1.1.3 255.255.255.0
encapsulation ppp
dialer map ip 6.1.1.1 name dallas 1891
dialer map ip 6.1.1.1 name dallas 1890
dialer map ip 6.1.1.2 name austin 1885
dialer map ip 6.1.1.4 name raleigh 1886
dialer map ip 6.1.1.19 1889
dialer-group 1
ppp authentication chap
dialer-list 1 protocol ip permit
```

You might still have to perform some of the configuration on the physical interface rather than at the dialer rotary interface. For example, if you connect to a switch that requires service profile identifiers (SPIDs) (remember that not all ISDN switches require them), you have to enter each of the SPIDs separately at each of the physical BRI interfaces. The rest of the interface configuration is done on the dialer interface.

If you install multiple BRIs or PRIs to service remote users, you need to ask your provider for one phone number to be used as a hunt group. You can configure the appropriate interfaces as members of the same rotary group so that remote users need to dial only one number. Using one number requires only one set of **dialer map** statements on the remote routers instead of multiple statements, a scenario that also makes configuration and debugging much less complicated.

Asynchronous Interface Groups

A dialer rotary group propagates a single configuration to multiple interfaces. Similarly, the **interface group-async** command configures a group interface. You can configure the group interface to include multiple asynchronous interfaces as members; members share the group configuration. Example 5-5 shows how to use the **interface group-async** command.

Example 5-5 Configuring Asynchronous Interface Groups

```
RTB(config)#interface group-async 1
RTB(config-if)#group-range 1 16
```

You assign interfaces to a group using the **group-range** command. In Example 5-5, asynchronous interfaces 1 through 16 are assigned to the group with the command **group-range 1 16**. After assigning asynchronous interfaces to a group, you cannot configure these interfaces separately. This method of configuring an asynchronous group is limited to asynchronous terminal lines and, unlike dialer rotary groups, cannot be used with other kinds of interfaces.

Legacy DDR Limitations

Whether you use a dialer rotary group or an asynchronous group interface, your physical interfaces (BRIs, asyncs, and so on) can use only a single configuration. Consider the following example depicted in Figure 5-9.

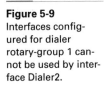

Figure 5-9
Interfaces configured for dialer rotary-group 1 cannot be used by interface Dialer2.

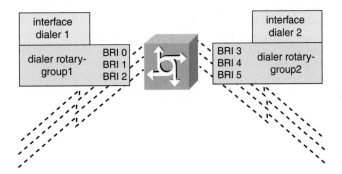

Dialer rotary group 1 includes BRI0, BRI1, and BRI2. What happens if all three of these interfaces are in use and another call arrives for interface Dialer1? Even if BRI3, BRI4, and BRI5 are not in use, they cannot be used by interface Dialer1 because they have been assigned to dialer rotary group 2. This example shows that it is possible for an access server to have available interfaces, yet not be able to use them to answer or make a call. This is the major drawback of legacy DDR. A physical dial interface can have only one logical configuration.

Dialer Profiles

The newer way of configuring DDR is called DDR with dialer profiles. Dialer profiles separate the logical configuration from the interface that receives or makes calls. Profiles can define encapsulation, access control lists (ACLs), and minimum or maximum calls, and can turn features on or off.

With dialer profiles, the logical and physical configurations are dynamically bound to each other on a per-call basis, allowing physical interfaces to dynamically take on different characteristics based on incoming or outgoing calls, as shown in Figure 5-10.

Figure 5-10
Interface BRI0 can be bound to either dialer interface on an as-needed basis.

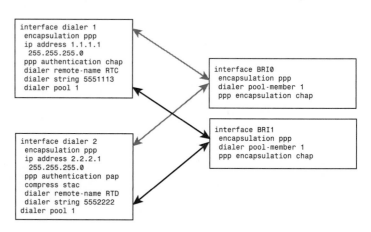

```
interface dialer 1
  encapsulation ppp
  ip address 1.1.1.1
   255.255.255.0
  ppp authentication chap
  dialer remote-name RTC
  dialer string 5551113
  dialer pool 1
```

```
interface BRI0
  encapsulation ppp
  dialer pool-member 1
  ppp encapsulation chap
```

```
interface dialer 2
  encapsulation ppp
  ip address 2.2.2.1
   255.255.255.0
  ppp authentication pap
  compress stac
  dialer remote-name RTD
  dialer string 5552222
  dialer pool 1
```

```
interface BRI1
  encapsulation ppp
  dialer pool-member 1
  ppp encapsulation chap
```

Similar to dialer rotary groups, dialer profiles use the dialer interface to separate the logical configuration—such as an IP address, Layer 2 encapsulation, and dialer parameters—from the physical interface that places or receives calls. But unlike a dialer rotary group, a physical interface can be used by multiple dialer interfaces.

Essentially, each dialer interface is a dialer profile that can be bound to any member of the *dialer pool*. You can configure a dialer profile for each remote user or router that you plan on establishing a call with (see Figure 5-11). When the access server needs to place a call, it looks for the appropriate dialer profile. After it identifies the correct profile, the access server attempts to find an available physical interface that belongs to the appropriate dialer pool. If a physical interface is available, the access server temporarily binds the dialer profile to that interface and makes the call.

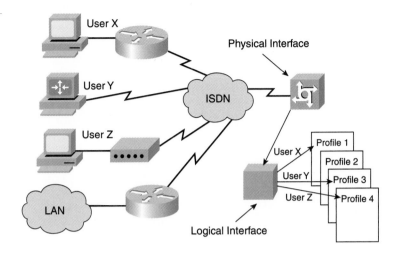

Figure 5-11
Dialer profiles can
be created for each
remote host that
dials in or receives
calls.

Example 5-6 presents a dialer profile configuration on an access server, called Central.

Example 5-6 An Example Dialer Profile Configuration

```
interface Dialer0
 ip address 172.16.1.1 255.255.255.0
 encapsulation ppp
 dialer remote-name RTX
 dialer idle-timeout 240
 dialer fast-idle 45
 dialer string 5551111
 dialer pool 1
 dialer-group 1
 ppp authentication chap pap
!
interface Dialer1
 ip address 172.16.2.1 255.255.255.0
 encapsulation ppp
 dialer remote-name user1
 dialer idle-timeout 100
```

continues

Example 5-6 An Example Dialer Profile Configuration (Continued)

```
 dialer pool 1
 dialer-group 4
 ppp authentication chap
!
interface Dialer2
 ip address 172.16.3.1 255.255.255.0
 encapsulation ppp
 dialer remote-name RTY
 dialer string 5552222
 dialer string 5552223
 dialer pool 1
 dialer-group 1
 ppp authentication chap pap
!
access-list 101 permit tcp any any eq smtp
access-list 101 permit tcp any any eq ftp
access-list 101 permit tcp any any eq www
dialer-list 1 protocol ip permit
dialer-list 4 protocol ip list 101
```

Example 5-6 shows three dialer profiles. None of these profiles includes a **dialer map** statement. When you are using dialer profiles, the IOS does not allow you to configure the dialer interface with a **dialer map** command.

Recall that **dialer map** statements are used with legacy DDR so that a single interface can call, or receive calls from, multiple hosts. The purpose of the **dialer map** command is to map the phone number to an IP, and to identify the remote host's name for the purposes of CHAP or PAP authentication.

With dialer profiles, you typically configure a profile for each remote host the router connects with, so connecting to multiple destinations is not an issue. Instead of specifying the phone number using a **dialer map** command, you use the **dialer string** command with dialer profiles. The **dialer string** command specifies the phone number to dial when placing a call from an interface to a specific destination. The syntax is as follows:

```
Router(config-if)#dialer string dial-string
```

In some cases, you might want an interface to only receive calls, making the **dialer string** command unnecessary.

You also need some way to specify the hostname of the remote system in order for PPP authentication to work with a dialer profile. Use the **dialer remote-name** command to specify the authentication name of the host:

```
Router(config-if)#dialer remote-name username
```

Returning to Example 5-6, interface Dialer1 is a profile for calling, or receiving calls from a router called RTX.

The second profile, interface Dialer0, has no dialer string configured. This profile is used to receive incoming calls only. Assume that user1 is a telecommuter calling from a home office. In such cases, the central-site router does not need to dial out. The **dialer remote-name user1** command is included so that user1 can authenticate using CHAP.

Finally, the third profile, interface Dialer2, is configured so that the router can either make or receive a call to RTY. Two **dialer string** commands specify two different phone numbers that can be used to connect with this host.

All three of these dialer profiles are configured to use any interfaces in dialer pool 1, as shown in Figure 5-12. A dialer pool is a collection of dial interfaces that can be used by a dialer profile. In this case, BRI0, BRI1, and BRI2 belong to dialer pool 1, as shown in Example 5-7.

Figure 5-12
The Central router is configured with one dialer pool, which can be used by multiple dialer interfaces.

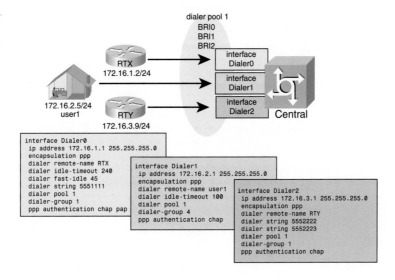

Any of the three dialer profiles defined in Example 5-6 can use any of the interfaces that belong to dialer pool 1. You configure an interface to belong to a dialer pool using the following command:

```
Router(config-if)# dialer pool-member number [priority priority]
[min-link minimum] [max-link maximum]
```

The **priority** keyword can be used with the **dialer pool-member** command to prioritize which interfaces must be used first if more than one interface in the pool is available. The priority value can be set from 0 (lowest) to 255 (highest). Interfaces with the highest priority are selected first for dialing out. The default value is 0.

The **min-link** and **max-link** keywords are only used with ISDN interfaces. The **min-link** keyword configures the minimum number of B channels on the interface that are reserved for the dialing pool, in the range 0 to 255. The default value is 0. A reserved channel is inactive until the specified dialer interface uses it to place calls. The **max-link** keyword defines the maximum number of B channels on the interface that can be used by the dialing pool, in the range 0 to 255. The default max-link value is 255.

To configure central's BRI0, BRI1, and BRI2 to belong to the same dialer pool, use the commands shown in Example 5-7.

Example 5-7 Assigning Interfaces to a Dialer Pool

```
Central(config)#interface bri0
Central(config-if)#dialer pool-member 1
Central(config-if)#interface bri1
Central(config-if)#dialer pool-member 1
Central(config-if)#interface bri2
Central(config-if)#dialer pool-member 1
```

If needed, you can also configure an interface to belong to multiple dialer pools (see Example 5-8).

Example 5-8 Assigning an Interface to Multiple Dialer Pools

```
RTA(config)#interface bri2
RTA(config-if)#dialer pool-member 2
RTA(config-if)#dialer pool-member 3
```

Likewise, a dialer profile can be configured to use interfaces from multiple dialer pools, as shown in Example 5-9.

Example 5-9 Configuring a Dialer Interface to Use Multiple Dialer Pools

```
RTA(config)#interface dialer 4
RTA(config-if)#dialer pool 2
RTA(config-if)#dialer pool 3
```

Each dialer profile on a router can specify a different dialer-group. Dialer profiles allow you to control what constitutes interesting traffic on a per-caller basis. For example, if user1 is connected to BRI1, interface dialer 1 is used. As shown in Example 5-6, this dialer profile (interface dialer 1) is configured with the **dialer-group 4** command. Dialer-list 4 determines what is interesting traffic during user1's call.

On the other hand, if RTX connects to central's BRI1, interface dialer 0 is used. Because interface dialer 0 is configured with the **dialer-group 1** command, dialer-list 1 defines interesting traffic.

If user1 sends only continuous pings to central's BRI1, central brings down the link after the idle timer expires. Dialer-list 4 does not specify ICMP as interesting traffic. But if RTX sends continuous pings to the same interface, central resets the idle timer and keeps the line up because dialer-list 1 defines all IP protocols as interesting.

The following sections discuss how dialer profiles are bound to calls when they are made and received by the router. In addition, the following topics are covered:

- Using dialer profiles with ISDN B channels
- Dialer rotary groups versus dialer profiles
- Dialer map classes

Placing Calls with Dialer Profiles

With no dialer map, how does the router know which dialer profile to use when placing a call?

Look at the configuration and routing table shown in Example 5-10. If Central2 receives interesting traffic destined for the 10.0.0.0 network, it checks its routing table. The routing table indicates that the next-hop IP address for the 10.0.0.0 network is 1.1.1.2. Of the three configured dialer profiles, only interface Dialer1 is configured with an IP address (1.1.1.1) that is in the same subnet as 1.1.1.2. Therefore, interface Dialer1 is bound to the first available interface in dialer pool 1 and the call is made to 5551111.

Example 5-10 Dialer Profiles and Routing Table Example

```
Central2#show run
<output omitted>
interface Dialer1
 ip address 1.1.1.1 255.255.255.0
 encapsulation ppp
 dialer remote-name RTA
 dialer string 5551111
 dialer pool 1
 dialer-group 1
 ppp authentication chap pap
!
interface Dialer2
 ip address 2.2.2.2 255.255.255.0
 encapsulation ppp
 dialer remote-name RTB
 dialer string 5552222
 dialer pool 1
 dialer-group 1
 ppp authentication chap
!
interface Dialer3
 ip address 3.3.3.3 255.255.255.0
 encapsulation ppp
 dialer remote-name RTC
 dialer string 5553333
 dialer pool 1
 dialer-group 1
 ppp authentication chap pap
!
dialer-list 1 protocol ip permit
<output omitted>


Central2#show ip route
<output omitted>


Gateway of last resort is 1.1.1.3 to network 0.0.0.0
```

Example 5-10 Dialer Profiles and Routing Table Example (Continued)

```
     1.0.0.0/24 is subnetted, 1 subnets
C       1.1.1.0 is directly connected, Dialer1
     2.0.0.0/24 is subnetted, 1 subnets
C       2.2.2.0 is directly connected, Dialer2
     3.0.0.0/24 is subnetted, 1 subnets
C       3.3.3.0 is directly connected, Dialer3
S    20.0.0.0/8 [1/0] via 2.2.2.1
S    10.0.0.0/8 [1/0] via 1.1.1.2
S    30.0.0.0/8 [1/0] via 3.3.3.1
S*   0.0.0.0/0 [1/0] via 1.1.1.2
```

The same process is repeated when Central2 receives interesting traffic destined for 30.1.15.4. After checking its routing table, Central2 finds that the next-hop to the 30.0.0.0/8 network is 3.3.3.1. Central2 then scans its configured dialer profiles and finds that interface Dialer3 is configured with an IP address on the same subnet as the next-hop. In this case, interface Dialer3 is bound to an interface in dialer pool 1 so that the call can be made to 5553333.

If Central2 receives traffic destined for the 172.16.0.0/16 network, it does not find a specific route to that network in its table. Thus, Central2 uses the default route (0.0.0.0/0) with a next-hop of 1.1.1.2. Again, interface Dialer1 is used to make the call.

Receiving Calls with Dialer Profiles

How does the router know which dialer profile to use when receiving a call? If an interface in Central2's dialer pool 1 receives a call, it can bind to any of the three dialer profiles shown in Example 5-10. Assume that the dialer pool 1 members are BRI0 and BRI1, as shown in Example 5-11.

Example 5-11 Dialer Pools and ISDN BRI

```
Central2#show run
<output omitted>
interface BRI0
 encapsulation ppp
 dialer pool-member 1
 ppp authentication chap
!
interface BRI1
 encapsulation ppp
 dialer pool-member 1
 ppp authentication chap
<output omitted>
```

Although all three dialer profiles are configured for PPP and CHAP, the BRIs that make up the dialer pool are also configured for PPP and CHAP. This might seem redundant, but it is required for this configuration to work. When RTB places a call to Central2, it dials a phone number that establishes a call with Central2's BRI0. At this point, Central2 does not know which dialer profile to bind to BRI0. Because RTB is using PPP with CHAP, Central2's BRI0 needs to support this in order for the call to proceed. That's why dialer pool members (physical interfaces) must have encapsulation, PPP authentication, and multilink PPP (MLP) already configured. As part of the PPP Link Control Protocol (LCP) link establishment process, RTB then sends its username to Central2. Central2 learns that a host called RTB is calling in, and looks for a dialer profile that includes the **dialer remote-name RTB** command. In this case, Central2 finds that interface dialer 2 is configured with RTB's hostname. Thus, Central2 binds interface dialer 2 to BRI0 and the call continues (see Figure 5-13).

Although it is common to configure dialer profiles with PPP and CHAP, it is not required. The dialer profile software binds an incoming call on a physical interface according to the following events, and in the order listed:

1. There is only one dialer profile configured to use the pool of which the physical interface is a member; this condition is the default bind. The physical interface must be a member of only this one pool. A default bind is possible only to a dialer profile when no **dialer caller** or **dialer called** commands are configured on that profile.

2. The calling line ID (CLID) matches what is configured in a **dialer caller** command on a dialer profile using a pool of which the physical interface is a member.

3. The Digital Number Identification Service (DNIS) that is presented matches what is configured in a **dialer called** command on a dialer profile using a pool of which the physical interface is a member.

4. If a bind has not yet occurred, but the physical interface is configured for PPP encapsulation and CHAP or PAP authentication, and the CHAP or PAP name presented matches a **dialer remote-name** command configuration on a dialer profile using a pool of which the physical interface is a member, the dialer profile software binds to that dialer profile. This is the method shown in Figure 5-13.

Figure 5-13
When Central2 receives a call from RTB on BRI0 or BRI1, it looks for the appropriate dialer profile to bind to the physical interface.

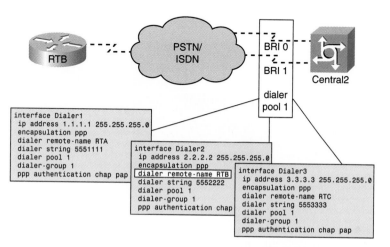

```
interface Dialer1
  ip address 1.1.1.1 255.255.255.0
  encapsulation ppp
  dialer remote-name RTA
  dialer string 5551111
  dialer pool 1
  dialer-group 1
  ppp authentication chap pap
```

```
interface Dialer2
  ip address 2.2.2.2 255.255.255.0
  encapsulation ppp
  dialer remote-name RTB
  dialer string 5552222
  dialer pool 1
  dialer-group 1
  ppp authentication chap
```

```
interface Dialer3
  ip address 3.3.3.3 255.255.255.0
  encapsulation ppp
  dialer remote-name RTC
  dialer string 5553333
  dialer pool 1
  dialer-group 1
  ppp authentication chap pap
```

If none of the previous events is successful, the call is not answered. The call is also disconnected during any of the first three events when, after the bind occurs and the physical interface is configured for PPP encapsulation and CHAP or PAP authentication, the CHAP or PAP presented does *not* match what is configured in a **dialer remote-name** command on the dialer profile that was bound to the call.

Using Dialer Profiles with ISDN B Channels

Before the Cisco IOS supported dialer profiles, all ISDN B channels inherited the physical interface configuration. Dialer profiles let you create different configurations for B channels on an ISDN PRI or BRI. Using dialer profiles, you can do the following:

- You can configure B channels of an ISDN interface with different IP subnets or IPX networks.

- You can use different encapsulations on B channels of an ISDN interface.

- You can set different DDR parameters for B channels of an ISDN interface.

- You can optimize the use of available ISDN B channels by letting ISDN BRIs belong to multiple dialer pools.

You do not have to enter any special configuration commands to have one B channel use one profile, while the other channel uses a different one. Figure 5-14 shows the first B channel of a BRI bound to interface dialer 0. When user2 dials the second B channel, interface dialer 1 is bound to that channel.

Figure 5-14
BRI 0:1 uses one logical configuration while BRI 0:2 uses another.

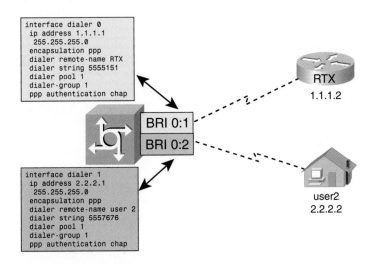

```
interface dialer 0
  ip address 1.1.1.1
   255.255.255.0
  encapsulation ppp
  dialer remote-name RTX
  dialer string 5555151
  dialer pool 1
  dialer-group 1
  ppp authentication chap
```

```
interface dialer 1
  ip address 2.2.2.1
   255.255.255.0
  encapsulation ppp
  dialer remote-name user 2
  dialer string 5557676
  dialer pool 1
  dialer-group 1
  ppp authentication chap
```

When a BRI or PRI is used to back up an interface, all the B channels are down and the entire interface is idle. By using dialer profiles, B channels can be freed up for DDR.

Dialer Rotary Groups Versus Dialer Profiles

The main difference between a dialer rotary group and a dialer profile is that a physical interface participates in only one rotary group. With a dialer profile, a physical interface can belong to many different pools.

You configure both dialer rotary groups and dialer profiles by creating a dialer interface (interface dialer 0, interface dialer 1, etc.). When configuring a dialer interface, if you use the **dialer pool** command, you have created a dialer profile. Remember, when you use the **dialer pool** command, you cannot also use **dialer map** commands. You must use **dialer string** and **dialer remote-name** instead.

Dialer Map Class

The *dialer map class* is an optional element that defines specific characteristics for a call to a specified dial string.

For example, the map class for one destination might specify an ISDN speed of 56 Kbps, whereas a map class for a different destination might specify an ISDN speed of 64 Kbps. The dialer map class can also contain optional dialer-timing parameters.

A map class is an optional element of a dialer profile. When you create a map class, it is separate from the dialer interface. Because it is separate, it can be used by more than one dialer interface. To create a dialer map class, use the following command syntax:

```
Router(config)#map-class dialer classname
```

After you enter this command, you enter map-class configuration mode, where you can enter the commands shown in Example 5-12.

Example 5-12 Available dialer Commands in Map-Class Configuration Mode

```
Router(config)#map-class dialer MAPME
Router(config-map-class)#dialer ?
  callback-server       Enable callback return call
  enable-timeout        Set length of time an interface stays down before it
                        is available for dialing
  fast-idle             Set idle time before disconnecting line with an
                        unusually high level of contention
  idle-timeout          Set idle time before disconnecting line
  isdn                  ISDN Settings
  outgoing              Dial using the selected ISDN dialing plan
  voice-call            Dial the configured number as a voice call
  wait-for-carrier-time How long the router will wait for carrier
```

Example 5-13 creates a map class called MYMAPCLASS, which defines two dialer timers.

Example 5-13 Configuring a Dialer Map Class

```
RTA(config)#map-class dialer MYMAPCLASS
RTA(config-map-class)#dialer fast-idle 15
RTA(config-map-class)#dialer idle-timeout 60
```

MYMAPCLASS can now be applied on a per-destination basis. You specify a dialer map class when using the **dialer string** command, which has the following syntax:

```
Router(config-if)#dialer string dial-string class classname
```

Any **dialer string** command in any dialer profile can use MYMAPCLASS (see Example 5-14).

Example 5-14 Apply a Dialer Map-Class

```
RTA#show run
<output omitted>
interface Dialer1
 ip address 1.1.1.1 255.255.255.0
 encapsulation ppp
 dialer remote-name RTA
 dialer string 5551111 class MYMAPCLASS
 dialer pool 1
 dialer-group 1
 ppp authentication chap pap
!
interface Dialer2
 ip address 2.2.2.2 255.255.255.0
 encapsulation ppp
 dialer remote-name RTB
 dialer string 5552222 class MYMAPCLASS
 dialer pool 1
 dialer-group 1
 ppp authentication chap
!
interface Dialer3
 ip address 3.3.3.3 255.255.255.0
 encapsulation ppp
 dialer remote-name RTC
 dialer string 5553333 class MYMAPCLASS
 dialer pool 1
 dialer-group 1
 ppp authentication chap pap
```

Example 5-14 shows how you can use a single dialer map class with multiple dialer profiles. The primary use of the dialer map class is to enable a single dialer profile to use a variety of dialer settings, as shown in Example 5-15.

Example 5-15 Partial Configuration Using Two Map Classes on the Same Dialer Interface

```
interface Dialer1
 dialer string 5552222 class 64k
 dialer string 5551111 class 56k
!
map-class dialer 56K
 dialer isdn speed 56
!
map-class dialer 64K
 dialer idle-timeout 100
```

In this case, interface Dialer1 uses the map class 56k when dialing 5551111, and the map class 64k when dialing 5552222. Without a dialer map class configuration, the same **dialer** parameters must be used for all calls made by the dialer interface.

Dialer commands can be configured under the dialer interface directly. The same command might appear more than once, possibly with different parameters, as shown in Example 5-16.

Example 5-16 Configuring Dialer Parameters with a Dialer Map

```
interface Dialer1
 dialer idle-timeout 240
 dialer string 5552222 class 64k
 dialer string 5551111 class 56k
 dialer string 5553333 class 64k
!
map-class dialer 56K
 dialer isdn speed 56
!
map-class dialer 64K
 dialer idle-timeout 100
```

In a case where the dialer interface and a dialer map class specify different values for the same parameter, the value assigned by the dialer map class is used.

Summary

Legacy DDR forces a physical interface into a single logical configuration. A dialer interface can be used to configure dialer rotary groups so that multiple physical interfaces can use the same logical configuration. In a complex DDR environment, legacy DDR can lead to scaling problems and complex **dialer map** statements. The preferred way to configure DDR is to use dialer profiles, which results in simpler and more flexible configurations. Dialer map classes are an optional component of a dialer profile. By using a dialer map class you can configure some dialer settings based on which number the interface dials.

Review Questions

1. Which of the following is true about physical dial interfaces configured for legacy DDR?

   A. A physical dial interface can have only one logical configuration.

   B. A physical dial interface can have up to three logical configurations.

   C. A physical dial interface can have up to 255 logical configurations.

   D. A physical dial interface must be assigned to a dialer pool.

2. Which of the following is true about the **dialer map** command?

   A. A physical interface can be configured with more than one **dialer map** command.

   B. The **dialer map** command cannot be used with legacy DDR.

   C. The **dialer map** command cannot be used with dialer rotary groups.

   D. The **dialer map** command cannot be used with dialer profiles.

3. Which of the following is true about ISDN and dialer rotary groups?

   A. You must manually configure both B channels of a BRI as a dialer rotary group.

   B. Multiple BRIs on a router are automatically part of the same dialer rotary group.

   C. Multiple PRIs on a router are automatically part of the same dialer rotary group.

   D. Both B channels of a BRI are automatically part of the same dialer rotary group.

4. You can configure an interface to belong to rotary group 2 using which command?

   A. (config-if)#**dialer-group 2**

   B. (config-if)#**dialer pool-member 2**

   C. (config-if)#**dialer rotary-group 2**

   D. (config-if)#**dialer rotary 2**

5. When can you use asynchronous group interfaces?

   A. When you need a single asynchronous line to have multiple logical connections.

   B. When you need to assign the same logical configuration to a group of asynchronous interfaces.

   C. When you need to assign the same logical configuration to more than one dialer interface.

   D. When you need to create a rotary group.

6. Which of the following commands would you use to assign asynchronous interfaces to a group interface?

   A. (config-if)#dialer-group 65 70

   B. (config-if)#rotary-group 65 70

   C. (config-if)#group-range 65 70

   D. (config-if)#dialer group-interface 65 70

7. Which of the following commands would you use to assign a physical interface to belong to dialer pool 2 so that it can be used in a dialer profile configuration?

   A. (config-if)#dialer pool 2

   B. (config-if)#dialer pool-member 2

   C. (config-if)#dialer rotary-group 2

   D. (config-if)#dialer rotary 2

8. Which of the following commands creates a dialer map class called DIALMAP?

   A. (config-if)#dialer map-class DIALMAP

   B. (config-if)#map-class dialer DIALMAP

   C. (config-map-class)#dialer map DIALMAP

   D. (config)#map-class dialer DIALMAP

9. Which of the following commands configures the interface to use the dialer map class DIALMAP when dialing 5551212?

   A. (config-if)#dialer string 5551212 class DIALMAP

   B. (config-if)#dialer map-class DIALMAP 5551212

   C. (config-if)#dialer map ip 1.1.1.1 name DIALMAP 5551212

   D. (config-if)#dial 5551212 DIALMAP

10. Which of the following commands specify that the remote dial-in host is RTB?

  A. (config-if)#**dialer remote-host RTB**

  B. (config-if)#**dialer remote-name RTB**

  C. (config-if)#**username RTB password cisco**

  D. (config-if)#**dialer map ip 1.1.1.1 name RTB 5551111**

Key Terms

Dialer pool A collection of physical interfaces that are grouped together to be used by a dialer profile.

Dialer map class Optional configuration that allows different characteristics for different types of calls to be assigned on a per-call-destination basis.

Hunt group A series of telephone lines that are programmed so that as incoming calls arrive, if the first line is busy the second line is tried, and then the third line is tried, and so on, until a free line is found

Legacy DDR Method of configuring DDR that restricts a physical dial interface to a single logical configuration.

Objectives

After completing this chapter, you will be able to perform tasks related to the following:

- Packet switching
- X.25 operation
- X.121 addressing
- X.25 configuration

Chapter 6

X.25

Introduction

Dial-up technologies, such as plain old telephone service (POTS) and Integrated Services Digital Network Basic Rate Interface (ISDN BRI), limit users to intermittent, low-bandwidth connections. Such on-demand WAN circuits do not provide the bandwidth and constant connectivity required by many of today's applications. Small offices and even home users are moving toward always on, high-speed Internet connections using digital subscriber line (DSL) or cable. But for many branch offices and remote sites, *packet-switched network* (*PSN*) services present the most flexible, secure, and affordable WAN solution.

PSNs offer permanent, always on connections, and temporary switched circuits. These circuits can provide guaranteed bandwidth at a fraction of the cost of leased lines.

This chapter introduces PSNs and focuses on one of the earliest and most widespread packet-switching specifications, X.25. We will explore fundamental X.25 concepts, X.25 operation, X.121 addressing, and X.25 configuration. In the next chapter, we will examine a more modern and efficient packet-switching technology, Frame Relay.

Packet Switching

PSNs use shared transmission facilities to provide customers with cost-effective WAN services. Before PSNs were widely available, customers could choose either a dial-up connection or a dedicated one. Both types of connections can be inefficient for applications that involve bursty, intermittent transfers of data.

Applications such as e-mail, Telnet, and HTTP typically result in bursts of traffic rather than steady streams of data. In other words, data is sent only after a user clicks the mouse or types a character. The bottom line: The link might be idle for much of the time when using these applications.

Dial-up WAN connections offer flexibility in such cases because circuits are built on demand. When a burst of traffic needs to be sent, the WAN connection is established. When there is no more traffic to send, the connection is torn down.

NOTE

The acronym PSN refers to a packet-switched network. Alternately, a PSN is called a packet-switched data network, or PSDN. The acronym *PDN* is also used to describe X.25 networks. PDN can mean public, private, or packet data network. This acronym can refer to any packet-based network. When discussing X.25 and Frame Relay, PDN often refers to public carrier networks that charge a fee for the use of their packet-switching facilities.

But dial-up over POTS is slow (53 Kbps or less). When X.25 packet switching was first developed more than 25 years ago, data transmission over POTS links was extremely slow (speeds of 300 bps were common) and prone to a high rate of errors. Unlike today's modems, modems at that time were quite expensive despite their low transfer rates.

Lack of bandwidth isn't the only problem with dial-up connections. Dial-up WAN services typically result in a charge based on the duration of a call. If a remote site posts transactions every few minutes, the dial-up link might be needed all day. Consider a ticket reservation system for a major airline. A given office might need to send bursts of ticketing data to a central database every few minutes. If an office requires that the call be up for most of the day, dial-up might no longer be a cost-effective solution.

Dedicated lines provide guaranteed bandwidth and constant connectivity. If a customer purchases dedicated services, such as a full T1 between remote sites, the carrier must reserve a path in its network for the customer's traffic. Typically, the reserved physical path is created by switching several of the provider's links, or channels on those links, to form an end-to-end path from one site to the other.

However, a dedicated link is often not the most efficient solution for a customer. Consider the ticket reservation system for the airline again. Although a busy office might use the WAN connection every minute or so, the traffic is still bursty in nature. The customer might be paying for a full T1 that is idle the majority of the time. Such underutilization is not efficient or cost-effective.

PSNs provide remote offices with either permanent or switched connections that feature high levels of throughput (typically up to DS1, although DS3 implementations are becoming increasingly popular). An important advantage of PSNs is that they offer customers a way to share facilities with other customers, thereby reducing the cost of WAN service. The customer typically leases a connection to the provider's PSN, and then shares the facilities in that network with other customers. One customer might be sending a large amount of data across the network, while another customer is idle, or vice versa.

Paths through the PSN are called *virtual circuits* (*VCs*). A VC is a logical path, not a physical one. VCs make it possible for a remote site to maintain connections to multiple sites over the same physical interface. A site can send data directly to several other remote sites via different VCs in the carrier network. This requires that the customer mark, or tag, each unit of data in some way so that the provider's WAN switch can determine which destination to route the traffic through the cloud (see Figure 6-1). In Frame Relay networks, the VC information is called a Data Link Control Identifier (DLCI) and is included in the frame header. In X.25 networks, the VC information is called the *Logical Channel Identifier* (*LCI*) and is included in the packet header.

Figure 6-1
Using a VC identi-
fier, RTA can send
a packet to RTB or
RTC using the same
physical interface
connected to a PSN.

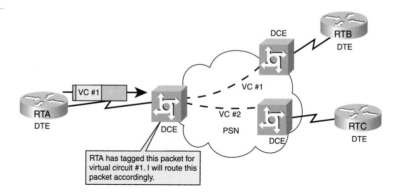

PSNs allow providers to charge their customers on the basis of the number of packets transmitted. Because customers can pay as they go, PSNs can provide optimal cost-effectiveness.

X.25 was one of the earliest packet-switched technologies and the first to be deployed worldwide. In fact, X.25 continues to be world's most common packet-switched technology, and can be found in virtually every region that supports data communications.

X.25 Concepts

X.25 is a standard that defines the connection between a terminal and a PSN. In other words, X.25 is an interface specification. It does not specify the characteristics of the PSN itself. The networking industry commonly uses the term X.25 to refer to the entire suite of X.25 protocols.

Developed in the early 1970s, X.25 was designed to transmit and receive data between alphanumeric dumb terminals through analog telephone lines. X.25 enabled dumb terminals to remotely access applications on mainframes or minicomputers. Later, X.25 was enhanced to support a variety of networking protocols, including IP, Novell IPX, and AppleTalk (see Figure 6-2).

The following sections describe the X.25 protocol stack, X.25 devices, VCs, X.25 encapsulation, and X.25 addressing (X.121).

X.25 Protocol Stack

The X.25 suite of protocols includes *Packet-Layer Protocol* (*PLP*), *Link Access Procedure, Balanced* (*LAPB*), and various Layer-1 standards (such as X.21bis, EIA/TIA-232, EIA/TIA-449, EIA-530, and G.703). Figure 6-3 maps the key X.25 protocols to the layers of the OSI reference model.

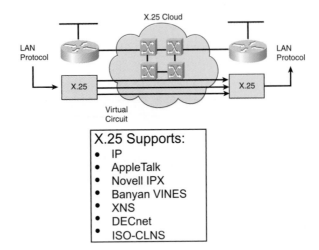

Figure 6-2
X.25 can transport
local-area network
(LAN) packets end to
end through a PSN.

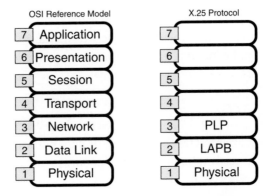

Figure 6-3
The X.25 protocol
stack maps to the
first three layers of
the OSI model.

PLP operates at the network layer (Layer 3) while LAPB operates at the data link layer (Layer 2). Both PLP and LAPB include mechanisms for error checking, flow control, and reliability. By including these mechanisms at both layer 2 and layer 3, X.25 provides a high level of reliability. Such reliability was critical in early implementations of X.25. These implementations typically used analog copper circuits that were prone to a higher rate of errors than modern fiber circuits. If a network is built on unreliable circuits, error checking at the data-link layer can handle transmission errors more efficiently than processes in software (the network layer and above).

X.25's high level of reliability comes at the price of relatively high overhead, and thus, low performance. Today's digital transmission facilities and fiber-optic links have much lower error rates than their predecessors. Thus, X.25 proves over-engineered when implemented over modern WAN links. Newer technologies, such as Frame Relay, have taken advantage of lower error rates by providing a stripped-down, unreliable data link. Such technologies rely on error detection and correction in the upper layers (typically the transport layer).

Today's applications place increasing demands on the WAN for more bandwidth and speed. Because of X.25's inherent overhead, it is typically implemented when supporting a legacy application, or when more modern technologies are not available.

X.25 Network Devices

X.25 network devices fall into three general categories:

- Data terminal equipment (DTE)
- Data communications equipment (DCE)
- *Packet switching exchange* (PSE)

In terms of X.25, DTE devices are end systems that communicate across the X.25 network. They are usually terminals, routers, or network hosts, and are located on the premises of individual subscribers.

In terms of X.25, DCE devices are communications devices, such as packet switches. They provide the interface between DTE devices and a PSE. X.25 DCEs are typically located in the carrier's facilities. The X.25 protocol implements virtual circuits between the X.25 DTE and the X.25 DCE.

PSEs are switches that compose the bulk of the carrier's network. They transfer data from one DTE device to another through the X.25 PSN. Figure 6-4 illustrates the relationships between the three types of X.25 network devices.

Both the X.25 DTE and the X.25 DCE are made up of two physical devices: a DTE (router or switch) and a DCE (modem or CSU/DSU). Equipment is categorized as an X.25 DTE or X.25 DCE based on the role it plays in the X.25 network. This role is not necessarily dependent on the type of physical interface used, or whether the device is acting as a clock source.

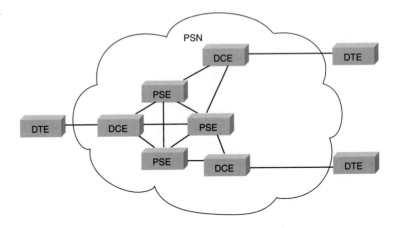

Figure 6-4
An X.25 network
typically includes
several DTEs, DCEs,
and PSEs.

The way X.25 traffic is carried within the carrier cloud depends on the implementation. The carrier might deploy any number of technologies within the cloud, including ATM, or even X.25.

X.25 PAD

The *packet assembler/disassembler* (PAD) is a device commonly found in X.25 networks. PADs are used when a DTE device, such as a character-mode terminal, is too simple to implement the full X.25 functionality. The PAD is located between a DTE device and a DCE device, and it performs three primary functions:

- Buffering
- Packet assembly
- Packet disassembly

The PAD buffers data sent to or from the DTE device. It also assembles outgoing data into packets and forwards them to the DCE device. This operation includes adding an X.25 header. Finally, the PAD disassembles incoming packets before forwarding the data to the DTE. This includes removing the X.25 header. Figure 6-5 illustrates the basic operation of the PAD when receiving packets from the X.25 WAN.

The operation of the terminal-PAD interface, the services offered by a PAD, and the X.25 host control interaction are defined by the International Telecommunication Union Telecommunication Standardization Sector (ITU-T) recommendations.

Figure 6-5
The X.25 PAD buffers, assembles, and disassembles data packets.

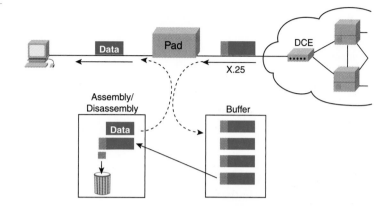

Some ITU-T recommendations defining the PAD are as follows:

- **X.3**—Specifies the parameters for terminal-handling functions (such as baud rate, flow control, character echoing, and other functions) for a connection to an X.25 host. The X.3 parameters are similar in function to Telnet options.

- **X.28**—Specifies the user interface for locally controlling a PAD. X.28 identifies the keystrokes that you must enter at a terminal to set up the PAD, similar to the AT command set for modems.

- **X.29**—Specifies a protocol for setting the X.3 parameters through a network connection. When a connection is established, the destination host can request that the PAD or terminal change its parameters by using the X.29 protocol. A PAD cannot tell the destination host to change its X.3 parameters, but it can communicate that its own parameters were changed.

- **X.75**—Specifies the gateway between the X.25 clouds. It defines the signaling system between two PDNs. X.75 is essentially a Network-to-Network Interface (NNI).

Virtual Circuits

When discussing X.25, the term *virtual circuit (VC)* is used interchangeably with the terms *Logical Channel Identifier (LCI)*, *virtual circuit number (VCN)*, *logical channel number (LCN)*, and *virtual channel identifier (VCI)*. An X.25 connection can be a *Permanent Virtual Circuit* (PVC) or, more commonly, a *Switched Virtual Circuit* (SVC). Figure 6-6 depicts these two types of VCs.

Figure 6-6
An X.25 VC can
either be switched
(SVC) or permanent
(PVC).

Switched Virtual Circuits   **Permanent Virtual Circuits**
(SVCs)   **(PVCs)**

A PVC is similar to a leased line. Both the network provider and the attached X.25 subscriber must provision the VC. PVCs use no call setup or call clear phases that are apparent to the subscriber. Any provisioned PVCs are always present, even when no data traffic is being transferred. Unlike Frame Relay, which typically uses PVCs, it is more common to implement X.25 using SVCs.

An SVC exists only for the duration of the session. Three phases are associated with X.25 SVCs:

- Call setup
- Information transfer
- Call clear

The X.25 protocol offers simultaneous service to many hosts. An X.25 network can support configurations of multiple SVCs and PVCs over the same physical circuit attached to the X.25 interface. Cisco routers provide numbering for up to 4095 VCs per X.25 interface. VCs are identified using the LCI.

X.25 Encapsulation

NOTE

The encapsulation of IP and other network-layer protocols over X.25 networks is discussed in RFC 1356.

Delivery of network-layer data through the internetwork usually involves encapsulation of Layer-3 packets inside Layer-2 frames. The type and format of the Layer-2 frame depends on the type of media used. In an X.25 environment, a LAPB frame is used. When a frame arrives at a router, the Layer-2 header is stripped off. Then, the router analyzes the Layer-3 packet and places it inside a new frame as it is forwarded.

In an X.25 WAN, the Layer-3 packet must include X.25 PLP. The Layer-3 PLP header provides reliability through sequencing, and manages packet exchanges between DTE devices across VCs. If X.25 includes a header at Layer 3, where do Layer-3 protocols such as Internet Protocol (IP) and IPX fit in?

Figure 6-7 shows that Layer 3 occurs twice in an X.25 TCP/IP packet: once for the IP datagram and once for X.25 PLP.

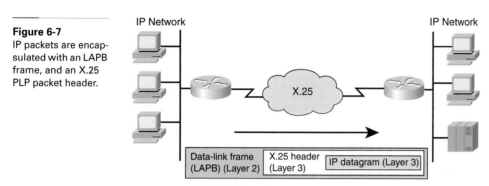

Figure 6-7
IP packets are encapsulated with an LAPB frame, and an X.25 PLP packet header.

When configuring X.25 on a Cisco router's interface, you can choose between Cisco's encapsulation type, or the Internet Engineering Task Force (IETF) type. The Cisco encapsulation method is the default.

The Layer-3 X.25 header is made up of the following components:

- **A general format identifier (GFI)**—The GFI is a 4-bit field that indicates the general format of the packet header.
- **An LCI**—The LCI is a 12-bit field that identifies the VC. The LCI is locally significant at the DTE/data communications equipment DCE interface.
- **A packet type identifier (PTI)**—The PTI field identifies one of X.25's 17 packet types.

Thus, in an X.25 environment, the VC information (the LCI) is carried in the Layer-3 header. An end-to-end VC is established in the PSN via two logical channels, each with an independent LCI, on two DTE/DCE interfaces, one at each end of the VC.

X.121—The X.25 Addressing Standard

Addressing fields in PLP call setup packets provide source and destination DTE addresses. These are used to establish the VCs that constitute X.25 communication.

ITU-T Recommendation X.121 specifies the source and destination address formats. X.121 addresses (also referred to as *international data numbers* [IDNs]) vary in length and can be up to 14 decimal digits long.

The first four digits of an IDN are called the *data network identification code* (*DNIC*). The DNIC is divided into two parts, the first three digits specifying the country and the last digit specifying the PSN itself. The remaining digits are called the *national terminal number* (*NTN*) and are used to identify the specific DTE on the PSN. The X.121 address format is shown in Figure 6-8.

Figure 6-8
The X.121 address is divided into two parts, the DNIC and the NTN.

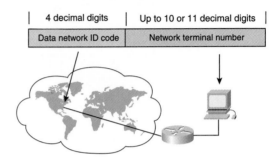

X.25(X.121 Addressing Format)

For your specific DNIC code, consult your service provider. For a listing of ITU-T country code assignments, refer to the ITU-T Recommendation X.121. A sample of the DNIC country codes is listed in Table 6-1.

Table 6-1   X.121 DNIC Country Codes

Country	Country Code Range
Belgium	206
France	208-209
Austria	232
United Kingdom	234-237
Germany	262-265
Canada	302-303
United States	310-316
Jamaica	338
Japan	440-443
Australia	505
New Zealand	530
Morocco	604

Table 6-1   X.121 DNIC Country Codes (Continued)

Country	Country Code Range
South Africa	655
Argentina	722
Brazil	724

For different network protocols to connect across X.25, mapping statements are entered on the router. These statements map the next-hop network-layer address to an X.121 address. For example, an IP network-layer address is mapped to an X.121 address to identify the next-hop host on the other side of the X.25 network.

Configuring X.25

When you select X.25 as a WAN protocol, you must set appropriate interface parameters. The interface configuration tasks include the following:

- Defining the X.25 encapsulation (DTE is the default).
- Assigning the X.121 address (usually supplied by the PDN service provider).
- Defining map statements to associate X.121 addresses with higher-level protocol addresses.

Other configuration tasks can be performed to control data throughput and to ensure compatibility with the X.25 network service provider. Commonly used parameters include the number of VCs allowed, and packet size negotiation.

X.25 is a flow-controlled protocol. The default flow-control parameters must match on both sides of a link. Mismatches because of inconsistent configurations can cause severe internetworking problems.

The following sections describe X.25 SVC configuration, X.25 PVC configuration, and optional configurations, including:

- VC ranges
- Packet sizes
- Window parameters

Configuring X.25 SVCs

To activate X.25 on an interface, you must enter the **encapsulation x25** command to specify the encapsulation type to be used:

```
Router(config-if)#encapsulation x25 [dte | dce] [ddn | bfe] | [ietf]
```

The router can be an X.25 DTE device, which is typically used when the X.25 PSN is used to transport various protocols. The router can also be configured as an X.25 DCE device, which is typically used when the router acts as an X.25 switch. You can choose between two encapsulation methods, Cisco and IETF. The default is Cisco and is not specified by a keyword. Table 6-2 describes the command syntax used with the **encapsulation x25** command.

Table 6-2   Syntax Descriptions for the Encapsulation x25 Command

dte	(Optional) Specifies operation as a DTE. This is the default X.25 mode.
dce	(Optional) Specifies operation as a DCE.
ddn	(Optional) Specifies Defense Data Network (DDN) encapsulation on an interface using DDN X.25 Standard Service.
bfe	(Optional) Specifies Blacker Front End (BFE) encapsulation on an interface attached to a BFE device.
ietf	(Optional) Specifies that the interface's datagram encapsulation defaults to the IETF standard method, as defined by RFC 1356.

NOTE

The **x25 map** command, which has a similar function to the **frame-relay map** command, maps the remote x121 address to the remote IP address. This contrasts with the **frame-relay map** command, which maps the local DLCI address to the remote IP address.

The **x25 address** command defines the local router X.121 address (one address per interface). The value specified must match the address designated by the X.25 PDN:

```
Router(config-if)#x25 address x.121-address
```

The **x25 map** command provides a static map of higher-level addresses to X.25 addresses. The command maps the network-layer addresses of the remote host to the X.121 address of the remote host:

```
Router(config-if)#x25 map protocol address x.121-address [options]
```

Table 6-3 describes the **x25 map** command syntax. A common option used with this command is the **broadcast** keyword. This command causes the Cisco IOS to direct any broadcasts sent through this interface to the specified X.121 address.

Table 6-3   Syntax Description of the x25 Map Command

protocol	Protocol type, entered by keyword. As many as nine protocol and address pairs can be specified in one command line.
address	Protocol address.
x121-address	X.121 address of the remote host.
options	(Optional) Additional functionality that can be specified for originated calls.

Let's put these commands together in an example X.25 SVC configuration. Figure 6-9 presents an example topology.

Figure 6-9
The central site connects to the branch office using an X.25 SVC.

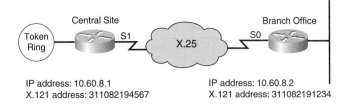

IP address: 10.60.8.1
X.121 address: 311082194567

IP address: 10.60.8.2
X.121 address: 311082191234

The central-site router has an IP route to the branch office's LAN through 10.60.8.2. To reach 10.60.8.2, the central-site router must use its serial 1 interface, which is configured as shown in Example 6-1.

Example 6-1 Central Site SVC Configuration

```
Central(config)#interface serial 1
Central(config-if)#ip address 10.60.8.1 255.255.248.0
Central(config-if)#encapsulation x25
Central(config-if)#x25 address 311082194567
Central(config-if)#x25 map ip 10.60.8.2 311082191234 broadcast
```

The **x25 map** statement maps 10.60.8.2 to an X.25 address. In this typical configuration, the central router tries to establish an SVC to the branch router using its X.121 source address (311082194567) and a destination X.121 address of 311082191234.

The branch router is configured according to Example 6-2.

Example 6-2 Branch Office SVC Configuration

```
Branch(config)#interface serial 0
Branch(config-if)#encapsulation x25
Branch(config-if)#x25 address 311082191234
Branch(config-if)#ip address 10.60.8.2 255.255.248.0
Branch(config-if)#x25 map ip 10.60.8.1 311082194567 broadcast
```

Upon receipt of the setup request, the branch router identifies the remote IP address from the source X.121 address and accepts the connection. After the SVC is connected, each router uses it as a point-to-point data link for the identified destination. Examples 6-1 and 6-2 demonstrate that the two X.25 hosts need complementary map configurations to establish the VC that will encapsulate IP datagrams.

Figure 6-10 presents a scenario in which multiple X.25 circuits are established from the central router.

Figure 6-10
The central router
uses multiple X.25
circuits to connect to
remote sites.

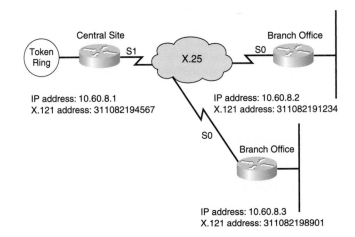

Example 6-3 shows that separate **x25 map** statements are configured to create separate links to each branch office. In this case, the same network layer protocol, IP, is used.

Example 6-3 Configuring Multiple SVCs on the Same Interface

```
Central(config)#interface serial 1
Central(config-if)#encapsulation x25
Central(config-if)#x25 address 311082194567
Central(config-if)#ip address 10.60.8.1 255.255.248.0
Central(config-if)#x25 map ip 10.60.8.2 311082191234 broadcast
Central(config-if)#x25 map ip 10.60.8.3 311082198901 broadcast
```

Configuring X.25 PVCs

When configuring a PVC, you must configure the interface using the **encapsulation x25** command. You must also assign an X.121 address using the **x25 address** command. These tasks are the same, whether you are configuring an SVC or a PVC.

However, instead of using the **x25 map** command to establish a PVC, you use the **x25 pvc** command. PVCs are the X.25 equivalent of leased lines; they are never disconnected. You do not need to configure an address map before defining a PVC because the **x25** command does the mapping for you, as shown in the following code:

```
Router(config-if)#x25 pvc circuit protocol address [protocol2 address2
  [...[protocol9 address9]]] x121-address [option]
```

Table 6-4 describes the **x25 pvc** command syntax.

Table 6-4   **Syntax Descriptions for the x25 pvc Command**

circuit	VC channel number, which must be less than the number of VCs assigned to the SVCs. X.25 VC numbering is explained later, in the section "Configuring X.25 VC Ranges."
protocol	Protocol type, entered by keyword. As many as nine protocol and address pairs can be specified in one command line.
address	Protocol address of the host at the other end of the PVC.
x121-address	X.121 address.
option	(Optional) Provides additional functionality, or allows X.25 parameters to be specified for the PVC.

Multiple protocols can be routed on the same PVC. Multiple circuits can also be established on an interface by specifying another PVC with the **x25 pvc** command.

In addition to configuring X.25 parameters, you must enter interface configuration mode and assign a higher-layer address, such as an IP address, to the interface.

Figure 6-11 shows that the carrier has established a PVC through its network, connecting PVC 3 to PVC 4. On the central router, the **x25 pvc** command associates the PVC number with both the X.121 address and the IP address of the branch router (see Example 6-4).

Figure 6-11
The site uses an X.25
PVC to connect to
the branch office.

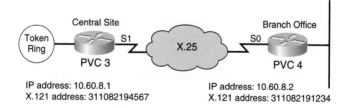

Example 6-4 Configuring a PVC on the Central Router

```
Central(config)#interface serial 1
Central(config-if)#encapsulation x25
Central(config-if)#x25 address 311082194567
Central(config-if)#ip address 10.60.8.1 255.255.248.0
Central(config-if)#x25 pvc 4 ip 10.60.8.2 311082191234 broadcast
```

NOTE

In a typical X.25 implementation, a single router is rarely configured for more than 50 VCs. The number of VCs configured on a router varies depending on the size of an organization. Larger organizations will have more remote sites, and therefore might require more VCs.

On the branch router, the **x25 pvc** command links PVC 3 with the X.121 and IP addresses of the central office (see Example 6-5).

Example 6-5 Configuring a PVC on the Branch Router

```
Branch(config)#interface serial 0
Branch(config-if)#encapsulation x25
Branch(config-if)#x25 address 311082191234
Branch(config-if)#ip address 10.60.8.2 255.255.248.0
Branch(config-if)#x25 pvc 3 ip 10.60.8.1 311082194567 broadcast
```

Configuring X.25 VC Ranges

X.25 can maintain up to 4095 VCs. Recall that a VC is identified by its LCI.

An important part of X.25 operation is the range of VC numbers. These numbers are broken into the following four ranges:

1. PVCs

2. Incoming-only circuits

3. Two-way circuits

4. Outgoing-only circuits

The incoming-only, two-way, and outgoing-only ranges define the VC numbers over which an SVC can be established by the placement of an X.25 call, much as a telephone network establishes a switched voice circuit when a call is placed.

The rules about DCE and DTE devices initiating calls are as follows:

- Only the DCE can initiate a call in the incoming-only range.
- Only the DTE can initiate a call in the outgoing-only range.
- Both the DCE and DTE can initiate a call in the two-way range.

There is no difference in how the SVCs operate in the different ranges, except for the aforementioned restrictions on which device can initiate a call. These ranges can be used to prevent one side from monopolizing the VCs, which is important for X.25 interfaces with a small number of SVCs available. Six X.25 parameters define the upper and lower limit of each of the three SVC ranges. These ranges cannot overlap. A PVC must be assigned a number lower than those assigned to the SVC ranges.

To configure X.25 VC ranges, use the interface configuration commands listed in Table 6-5.

Table 6-5   X.25 VC Ranges Configuration Commands

Command	Purpose
Router(config-if)#**x25 lic** *circuit-number*	Sets the lowest incoming-only circuit number. The default is 0.
Router(config-if)#**x25 hic** *circuit-number*	Sets the highest incoming-only circuit number. The default is 0.
Router(config-if)#**x25 ltc** *circuit-number*	Sets the lowest two-way circuit number. The default is 1.
Router(config-if)#**x25 htc** *circuit-number*	Sets the highest two-way circuit number. The default is 1024 for X.25; 4095 for Connection-Mode Network Service (CMNS).
Router(config-if)#**x25 loc** *circuit-number*	Sets the lowest outgoing-only circuit number. The default is 0.
Router(config-if)#**x25 hoc** *circuit-number*	Sets the highest outgoing-only circuit number. The default is 0.

Each parameter can range from 1 to 4095. The values for these parameters must be the same on both ends of the X.25 link. For connection to a PDN, these values must be set to the values assigned by the network. An SVC range is unused if its lower and upper limits are set to 0. Other than this use for marking unused ranges, VC 0 is not available.

Example 6-6 sets the VC ranges of 5 to 20 for incoming calls only (from the DCE to the DTE) and 25 to 1024 for either incoming or outgoing calls. It also specifies that no VCs are reserved solely for outgoing calls (from the DTE to the DCE). Up to four permanent VCs can be defined on VCs 1 through 4. In this configuration, VCs 21 to 24 are unused, but can later be reconfigured for incoming calls, or two-way calls, as needed.

Example 6-6 Configuring a PVC on the Branch Router

```
RTX(config)#interface serial 0
RTX(config-if)#encapsulation x25
RTX(config-if)#x25 lic 5
RTX(config-if)#x25 hic 20
RTX(config-if)#x25 ltc 25
```

Configuring X.25 Packet Sizes

The **x25 ips** and **x25 ops** commands set the default maximum input/output packet size. Configuring the input/output packet size is an optional configuration task, and might not be necessary for basic X.25 operation. You might need to configure these parameters to optimize performance, or to match the packet-size values set on the remote router at the other end of the VC.

To set the incoming packet size, use the **x25 ips** command:

```
Router(config-if)#x25 ips bytes
```

To set the outgoing packet size, use the **x25 ops** command:

```
Router(config-if)#x25 ops bytes
```

The default bytes value is 128. Supported values are 16, 32, 64, 128, 256, 512, 1024, 2048, and 4096. The input and output values should match unless the network supports asymmetric transmissions. If the stations of an X.25 attachment conflict on the maximum packet size of the VC, the VC is unlikely to work.

Fragmentation is a feature of X.25. The PAD reassembles the IP packet at the destination.

The typical default packet size provided worldwide by PDNs is 128 bytes. In the United States and Europe, default packet sizes of 1024 are common. Other countries can also provide higher packet sizes.

Before configuring the maximum packet size on your X.25 WAN connection, ask your service provider the maximum packet size it supports.

Example 6-7 shows the commands needed to configure both the incoming and outgoing packet size to 1024.

Example 6-7 Configuring X.25 Maximum Packet Sizes

```
RTX(config-if)#encapsulation x25
RTX(config-if)#x25 ips 1024
RTX(config-if)#x25 ops 1024
```

Configuring Window Parameters

X.25 uses a sliding window for flow control. Larger windows allow more packets to be in transit. A larger VC window size allows more packets in the network between the two VC endpoints. Configuring window parameters is an optional configuration task, and might not be necessary for basic X.25 operation. You might need to configure window parameters to optimize performance, or to match the window parameters set on the remote router at the other end of the VC.

Use the **x25 win** and **x25 wout** commands to set the default window size. The window size specifies the number of packets that can be received or sent without receiving or sending an acknowledgment. Both ends of an X.25 link must use the same default window size.

Therefore, to specify default unacknowledged packet limits, use the following commands:

```
Router(config-if)#x25 win packets
Router(config-if)#x25 wout packets
```

The packet value used in the **x25 win** and **x25 wout** commands is the number of unacknowledged packets. The default value is 2 packets. This value is used only on VCs that do not negotiate a window size. The minimum window size is 1 packet. The maximum number of unacknowledged packets is one less than a value called the *modulus*.

The **x25 modulo** command specifies the packet-numbering modulus, which determines the maximum size of the window. There are two possible modulus values: 8 and 128. Modulo 8 is widely used and allows VC window sizes up to 7 packets. Modulo 128 is rare, but it allows VC window sizes up to 127 packets. Why are these the only two modulus values? The reason for the two modulo values is that modulo 8 sequence numbers are encoded in 3 bits of information, while modulo 128 sequence numbers are encoded in 7 bits of information.

The command to define packet-level window counter limits is the following:

```
Router(config-if)#x25 modulo modulus
```

Window sizes and modulo values should match at both ends of the X.25 link. A larger window size allows more frames to be in transit between the immediate DTE/DCE connection.

Assuming that the **modulo** is 8 (the default setting), Example 6-8 shows the commands needed to increase both window sizes to the maximum 7 packets.

Example 6-8 Configuring X.25 Window Sizes

```
RTX(config-if)#encapsulation x25
RTX(config-if)#x25 win 7
RTX(config-if)#x25 wout 7
```

Example 6-9 increases the window size to 127, which first requires that the **modulo** be set to 128.

Example 6-9 Configuring the X.25 Modulus to Increase Maximum Window Size

```
RTX(config-if)#encapsulation x25
RTX(config-if)#x25 modulo 128
RTX(config-if)#x25 win 127
RTX(config-if)#x25 wout 127
```

X.25 Configuration Example

Example 6-10 shows an example X.25 interface configuration that uses the commands discussed in the previous sections.

Example 6-10 X.25 Interface Configuration

```
Central(config)#interface serial 0/0
Central(config-if)#encapsulation x25
Central(config-if)#x25 address 311082194567
Central(config-if)#ip address 10.60.8.1 255.255.248.0
Central(config-if)#x25 pvc 1 ip 10.60.8.2 311082191234 broadcast
Central(config-if)#x25 pvc 2 ip 10.60.8.3 311082198901 broadcast
Central(config-if)#x25 map ip 10.60.8.4 311082194321 broadcast
Central(config-if)#x25 map ip 10.60.8.5 311082195151 broadcast
Central(config-if)#x25 lic 5
Central(config-if)#x25 hic 20
Central(config-if)#x25 ltc 25
Central(config-if)#x25 ips 1024
Central(config-if)#x25 ops 1024
Central(config-if)#x25 win 7
Central(config-if)#x25 wout 7
```

Using this configuration, VCs 1-4 are available for PVCs because the **x25 lic 5** command specifies that the lowest SVC can be VC 5. The two **x25 pvc** commands configure PVCs 1 and 2. The **ips** and **ops** commands set the incoming and outgoing packet sizes to 1024. The **win** and **wout** commands set the sliding acknowledgment window to 7 packets.

Verifying X.25 Configuration

Use the **show interfaces** command to display status and counter information about the X.25 interface that was configured in the previous section.

```
Central#show interfaces serial 0/0
serial 0/0 is up, line protocol is up
  Hardware is HD64570 with 5-in-1 module
  Internet address is 10.60.8.1/21
  MTU 1500 bytes, BW 1544 Kbit, DLY 20000 usec,
    reliability 255/255, txload 1/255, rxload 1/255
  Encapsulation X25, loopback not set
  X.25 DTE, address 311082194567, state R1, modulo 8, timer 0
    Defaults: idle VC timeout 0
      cisco encapsulation
      input/output window sizes 7/7, packet sizes 1024/1024
    Timers: T20 180, T21 200, T22 180, T23 180
    Channels: Incoming-only 5-20, Two-way 25-1024, Outgoing-only none
    RESTARTs 0/0 CALLs 0+0/0+0/0+0 DIAGs 0/0
  LAPB DTE, state CONNECT, modulo 8, k 7, N1 12056, N2 20
    T1 3000, T2 0, interface outage (partial T3) 0, T4 0
    VS 3, VR 1, tx NR 1, Remote VR 3, Retransmissions 0
    Queues: U/S frames 0, I frames 0, unack. 0, reTx 0
    IFRAMEs 27/17 RNRs 0/0 REJs 0/0 SABM/Es 0/1 FRMRs 0/0 DISCs 0/0
  Last input 00:01:05, output 00:00:49, output hang never
  Last clearing of "show interface" counters 00:01:41
  Queueing strategy: fifo
  Output queue 0/40, 0 drops; input queue 0/75, 0 drops
  5 minute input rate 0 bits/sec, 0 packets/sec
  5 minute output rate 0 bits/sec, 0 packets/sec
    45 packets input, 645 bytes, 0 no buffer
    Received 0 broadcasts, 0 runts, 0 giants, 0 throttles
    0 input errors, 0 CRC, 0 frame, 0 overrun, 0 ignored, 0 abort
    36 packets output, 3087 bytes, 0 underruns
    0 output errors, 0 collisions, 0 interface resets
    0 output buffer failures, 0 output buffers swapped out
    0 carrier transitions
    DCD=up  DSR=up  DTR=up  RTS=up  CTS=up
Central#
```

The first shaded line in the previous example indicates that this interface is configured to use X.25 encapsulation. The second shaded line reports that this interface is an X.25 DTE and has the X.121 address of 311082194567. The third shaded line shows the X.25 encapsulation type is set to Cisco, as opposed to IETF. The fourth shaded line displays the window size and maximum packet size, as configured by the **x25 win/x25 wout** and **x25 ips/x25 ops** commands, respectively. The last shaded line lists the configured VC ranges, set by the commands: **x25 lic 5, x25 hic 20**, and **x25 ltc 25**.

Summary

In this chapter, you learned how to configure an X.25 WAN connection and assign X.121 addresses to the router interfaces. You also learned how to map higher-level addresses to X.25 addresses and how to verify the X.25 configuration of your router. In Chapter 7, you learn about the successor of X.25, Frame Relay.

Review Questions

Use the following review questions to test your understanding of the concepts covered in this chapter. In some cases, there is more than one correct answer, so choose all that apply. Answers are listed in Appendix A, "Answers to Review Questions."

1. Which of the following is not a packet-switching technology?

   A. POTS

   B. X.25

   C. Frame Relay

   D. ISDN BRI

2. X.25 VCs are identified using which of the following?

   A. LCI

   B. DLCI

   C. X.121

   D. X.75

3. At which of the following layers of the OSI model does the X.25 protocol suite operate?

   A. Layer 1

   B. Layer 2

   C. Layer 3

   D. Layer 4

4. Which of the following statements best describes the function of an X.25 DCE?

   A. Customer device that provides access to the customer network

   B. Device that assembles and disassembles X.25 packets

   C. Provider device that provides access to the X.25 cloud

   D. An asynchronous dumb terminal

5. Which of the following statements best describes the function of an X.25 PAD?

   A. Customer device that provides access to the customer network

   B. Device that assembles and disassembles X.25 packets

   C. Provider device that provides access to the X.25 cloud

   D. An asynchronous dumb terminal

6. An X.121 address consists of which of the following components?

   A. Country Code

   B. PSN ID

   C. NTN

   D. LCI

7. Which of the following commands configures an interface to use the Cisco X.25 encapsulation type?

   A. Router(config)#encapsulation x25 dte

   B. Router(config)#encapsulation x25 cisco

   C. Router(config-if)#encapsulation x25

   D. Router(config-if)#encapsulation x25 cisco

8. Which of the following commands correctly configures an X.25 SVC?

   A. x25 svc 4 ip 1.6.8.1 311082191234 broadcast

   B. x25 map ip 1.6.8.1 311082191234

   C. x25 map svc 5 ip 1.6.8.1 311082191234 broadcast

   D. x25 svc map ip 1.6.8.1 311082191234

9. Which of the following commands correctly configures an X.25 PVC?

   A. x25 pvc 4 ip 1.6.8.1 311082191234 broadcast

   B. x25 map ip 1.6.8.1 311082191234

   C. x25 map pvc 5 ip 1.6.8.1 311082191234 broadcast

   D. x25 svc map ip 1.6.8.1 311082191234

10. If the X.25 modulo is set to 8, what is the maximum packet size for the sliding window?

    A. 7

    B. 8

    C. 127

    D. 128

Key Terms

DNIC (Data Network Identification Code)   Part of an X.121 address. DNICs are divided into two parts: the first specifying the country in which the addressed PSN is located, and the second specifying the PSN itself.

LAPB (Link Access Procedure, Balanced)   Data-link layer protocol in the X.25 protocol stack. LAPB is derived from High-Level Data Link Control (HDLC).

LCI (Logical Channel Identifier)   Number used to identify X.25 VCs. Also called Virtual Circuit Number (VCN).

NTN (National Terminal Number)   Part of an X.121 address. Used to identify the specific DTE on the PSN.

PAD (packet assembler/disassembler)   Device used to connect simple devices (such as character-mode terminals) that do not support the full functionality of a particular protocol to a network. PADs buffer data and assemble and disassemble packets sent to such end devices.

PDN (Public Data Network)   Network operated either by a government (as in Europe) or by a private concern to provide computer communications to the public, usually for a fee.

PLP (Packet-Layer Protocol)   Network layer protocol in the X.25 protocol stack.

PSE (Packet switching exchange)   Typically, a switch in an X.25 PSN.

PSN (Packet-switched network)   Network that uses packet-switching technology for data transfer. Sometimes called a packet-switched data network (PSDN).

PVC (permanent virtual circuit)   See VC.

SVC (switched virtual circuit)   See VC.

VC (virtual circuit)   Logical circuit created to ensure reliable communication between two network devices. A VC is defined by some kind of identifier, such as a DLCI or VPI/VCI pair. A VC can be either permanent (PVC) or switched (SVC).

Objectives

After completing this chapter, you will be able to perform tasks related to the following:

- Frame Relay Virtual Circuits
- Frame Relay DLCIs
- Frame Relay LMI
- Configuring Frame Relay
- Verifying Frame Relay configurations
- Frame Relay topologies
- Frame Relay subinterfaces

Chapter 7

Frame Relay

Introduction

In Chapter 6, "X.25," you were introduced to packet-switched networks (PSNs) and the X.25 protocol. X.25 achieves an exceptionally high level of reliability at the cost of increased overhead.

Frame Relay has replaced X.25 as the packet-switching technology of choice in developed nations, particularly the United States. First standardized in 1990, Frame Relay streamlines Layer-2 functions and provides only basic error checking. This low-overhead approach to switching packets increases performance and efficiency. Today's fiber optic links and digital transmission facilities offer much lower error rates than their copper predecessors. For that reason, X.25's reliability mechanisms at Layers 2 and 3 are no longer seen as worth the added overhead.

This chapter presents Frame Relay technology, including its benefits and requirements. This chapter explores how Frame Relay can be used to connect a central site with its branch offices. You are introduced to the routing issues caused by split horizon, and you learn how to configure subinterfaces to solve this problem.

Frame Relay Concepts

Frame Relay is an International Telecommunication Union Telecommunication Standardization Sector (ITU-T) and American National Standards Institute (ANSI) standard that defines the process for sending data over a PSN. It is a connection-oriented, data-link layer technology that is optimized to provide high performance and efficiency.

Today's telecommunications networks are characterized by relatively error-free digital transmission and highly reliable fiber infrastructures. Frame Relay takes advantage of these technologies by relying almost entirely on upper-layer protocols to detect and recover from errors. Frame Relay does not have the sequencing, windowing, and retransmission mechanisms used by X.25. Without the overhead associated with such comprehensive error detection, Frame Relay's streamlined frame outperforms X.25. As a result,

Frame Relay is appropriate for uses that require high throughput, such as local-area network (LAN) interconnection. It uses the services of many different physical-layer facilities at speeds that typically range from 56 Kbps up to 2 Mbps, although higher speeds are possible. The network providing the Frame Relay service can be either a carrier-provided public network or a network of privately owned equipment serving a single enterprise.

Similar to X.25, Frame Relay defines the interconnection process, or interface, between the customer's data terminal equipment (DTE) and the service provider's data communications equipment (DCE). Frame Relay DTEs and DCEs are defined by their role in the Frame Relay network. A typical Frame Relay DTE consists of the customer's router and attached CSU/DSU. Frame Relay DCEs are usually a provider's switch and attached CSU/DSU.

Frame Relay does not define the way the data is transmitted within the service provider's network after the traffic reaches the provider's switch (see Figure 7-1). Thus, a Frame Relay provider could use a variety of technologies, such as Asynchronous Transfer Mode (ATM) and Point-to-Point Protocol (PPP), to move data from one end of its network to the other.

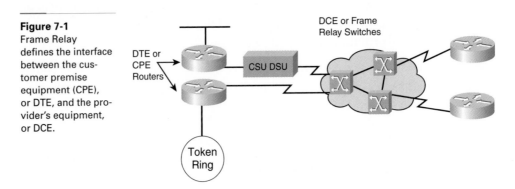

Figure 7-1
Frame Relay defines the interface between the customer premise equipment (CPE), or DTE, and the provider's equipment, or DCE.

The following sections describe the types of Frame Relay devices, Frame Relay operation, Frame Relay Data Link Connection Identifiers (DLCIs), and Frame Relay frame format. Also, Frame Relay status messaging and dynamic address mapping are discussed.

Frame Relay Devices

Devices attached to a Frame Relay WAN fall into two general categories: DTE and DCE. DTEs generally are considered to be terminating equipment for a specific customer network and typically are located on the customer's premises. In fact, they usually are owned by the customer. Examples of DTE devices are routers and *Frame Relay Access Devices* (*FRADs*). A FRAD is a specialized device designed to provide a connection between a LAN and a Frame Relay WAN.

DCEs are carrier-owned internetworking devices. The purpose of DCE equipment is to provide clocking and switching services in a network. Frame Relay DCEs are packet switches, which are the devices that actually transmit data through the WAN. Figure 7-1 shows the relationship between the two categories of devices.

Frame Relay Operation

Generally, the greater the distance covered by a leased line, the more expensive the service. Maintaining a full mesh of leased lines to remote sites proves too expensive for many organizations. On the other hand, PSNs provide a means for multiplexing several logical data conversations over a single physical transmission link. Figure 7-2 shows how packet-switched networks use virtual circuits (VCs) to deliver packets from end-to-end over a shared infrastructure.

Figure 7-2
PSNs use VCs to enable multipoint connections over shared facilities.

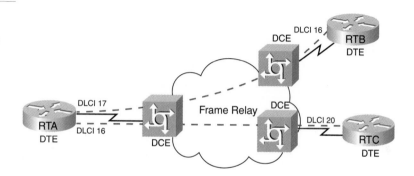

A packet-switched service such as Frame Relay requires that a customer maintain only one circuit (typically a T1) to the provider's central office (CO). This circuit is sometimes referred to as an access circuit. Frame Relay provides tremendous cost-effectiveness because one site can connect to many geographically distant sites using a single T1— and a single channel service unit/data service unit (CSU/DSU) to the local CO.

Frame Relay networks, such as X.25 networks, support both Permanent Virtual Circuits (PVCs) and Switched Virtual Circuits (SVCs). The PVC is the most common type of Frame Relay VC. PVCs are permanently established connections that are used when there is frequent and consistent data transfer between DTE devices across a Frame Relay network.

SVCs are temporary connections, used when there is only sporadic data transfer between DTE devices across the Frame Relay network. Because they are temporary, SVC connections require call setup and termination for each connection. Cisco IOS

Release 11.2 or later supports Frame Relay SVCs. You need to determine whether your carrier supports SVCs before implementing them because many Frame Relay providers only support PVCs.

SVCs offer several advantages for a Frame Relay provider, including easier management of the Frame Relay cloud and the use of its bandwidth. However, because the pricing of SVCs is higher than PVCs and the standards are still fairly new, the vast majority of Frame Relay network providers use PVCs.

Frame Relay DLCIs

In a packet-switched network such as Frame Relay, each end of the VC is assigned a connection identifier. The service provider's switching equipment maintains a table that maps these connection identifiers to outbound ports. When a frame is received, the Frame Relay switch analyzes the connection identifier and delivers the frame to the appropriate outbound port.

Just because a company has access circuits doesn't mean that they are able to communicate directly with other companies connected to the same Frame Relay provider. Each VC needs to be created in advance by the provider, and the customer typically pays for each and every VC.

In X.25 environments, the VC identifier is called a logical channel identifier (LCI). In Frame Relay networks, a *Data Link Connection Identifier* (*DLCI*) (pronounced *del*-see) identifies the logical VC between the CPE (typically a router) and the Frame Relay switch. The Frame Relay switch maps the DLCIs between each pair of routers to create a PVC.

DLCIs have local significance. The DLCI references the point between the local router and the Frame Relay switch to which the router is connected. A locally significant DLCI does not reference the other end of the PVC. In other words, two DTE devices connected by a VC might use a different DLCI value to refer to the same connection.

As an example, consider Figure 7-2. The PVC linking RTA and RTB is identified by DLCI 17. But this association between the RTA-RTB PVC and DLCI 17 is significant only to RTA and its directly connected switch. The same PVC is identified by DLCI 16 on RTB's side of the connection. Meanwhile, RTA uses DLCI 16 to reference the PVC that connects RTA with RTC.

Because multiple Frame Relay VCs can terminate at a single physical interface, several addressing and routing issues must be addressed. Consider RTA in Figure 7-3.

Figure 7-3
RTA must determine
which of the three
available PVCs
connects to RTB.

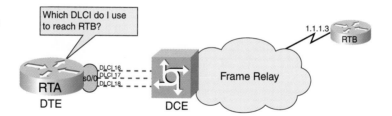

RTA can use only one of three configured PVCs to reach RTB. How does RTA know which PVC to use? In order for the customer's router to know which PVC to use, Layer-3 addresses must be mapped to DLCI numbers.

Figure 7-4 shows that RTA must map Layer-3 addresses to the available DLCIs. RTA maps RTB's IP address, 1.1.1.3, to DLCI 17. When RTA needs to route traffic to RTB, RTA consults its Frame Relay map to find the appropriate DLCI number. After RTA knows which DLCI to use, RTA can encapsulate the IP packet with a Frame Relay frame. The frame contains, among other things, the destination DLCI value.

Figure 7-4
RTA maps IP
addresses to
DLCI numbers.

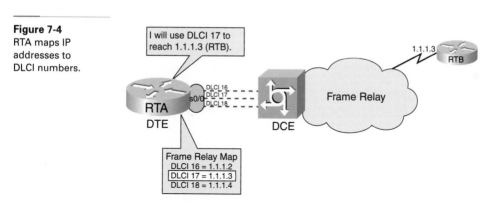

By including a destination DLCI in the Frame Relay header, RTA can talk to RTB and other nodes over the same physical circuit. This technique of allowing multiple logical channels to transmit across a single physical circuit is called *statistical multiplexing*. Statistical multiplexing dynamically allocates bandwidth to active channels. If RTA has no packets to send to RTB, RTA can use all the available bandwidth to communicate with RTC. The DLCI value carried in the Layer-2 frame determines the destination of the packet (and the path through the PSN).

This method of multiplexing contrasts with *time-division multiplexing* (*TDM*). TDM is typically used over dedicated circuits (leased lines). Using TDM, information from multiple channels can be allocated bandwidth on a single wire based on pre-assigned time slots. Unfortunately, TDM allocates bandwidth to each channel regardless of whether the station has data to transmit.

X.25 performs statistical multiplexing using LCIs, which are part of the X.25 Layer-3 header. Unlike X.25, Frame Relay does not operate at Layer 3. Multiplexing is achieved at Layer 2 by using the DLCI fields.

DLCIs are typically assigned by the service provider. Currently, 10 bits are used in the frame to represent the DLCI number, yielding 1024 possibilities (0–1023). Not all 1024 of these DLCI numbers are available to identify customer PVCs. In fact, providers typically assign DLCIs from 16 to 1007.

DLCIs 0–15 and 1008–1023 are reserved for special purposes. Depending on your provider's configuration, DLCI 0 or DLCI 1023 is used to send status messages. DLCIs 19 and 20 are reserved for multicast traffic.

In order to build a map of DLCIs to Layer-3 addresses, the router must first know what VCs are available. Typically, the process of learning about available VCs and their DLCI values is handled by a signaling standard and keepalive mechanism called *Local Management Interface* (*LMI*). LMI is discussed in the next section.

After the DLCIs for available VCs are known, the router must learn which Layer-3 addresses map to which DLCIs. The address mapping can be configured either manually or dynamically (see the section, "Inverse ARP," later in this chapter).

Frame Relay Frame Format

Cisco routers support two types of Frame Relay headers: a 4-byte header and a 2-byte header that conforms to the Internet Engineering Task Force (IETF) standards. Figure 7-5 depicts the components of the IETF Frame Relay frame in detail. The 4-byte header is proprietary to Cisco and cannot be used if the router is connected to another vendor's equipment across a Frame Relay network.

After examining Figure 7-5, you might conclude that, because there are two DLCI fields, the frame carries both a source and a destination DLCI. In fact, the first DLCI field (6 bits) and the second DLCI field (4 bits) are concatenated (used together) to represent the 10-bit destination DLCI number. Because DLCI numbers typically have only local significance, including a source DLCI in the frame would be meaningless. Table 7-1 briefly defines the function of each field in the frame.

Figure 7-5
The IETF Frame
Relay frame is
2 bytes long.

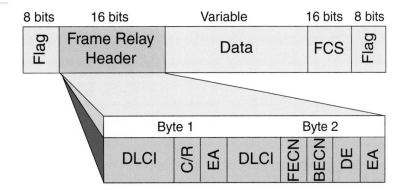

Table 7-1   Frame Relay IETF Frame Field Definitions

Field	Definition
Flags	Delimit the beginning and end of the frame. The value of this field is always the same and is represented either as the hexadecimal number 7E or the binary number 01111110.
DLCI	The 10-bit DLCI value represents the virtual connection between the DTE device and the switch.
Extended Address (EA)	The EA is used to indicate whether the byte in which the EA value is 1 is the last addressing field. If the value is 1, the current byte is determined to be the last octet. Although current Frame Relay implementations all use a two-octet header, this capability does allow for longer headers, and thus, longer DLCIs, to be used in the future.
C/R	The C/R is the bit that follows the most significant DLCI byte in the Address field. The C/R bit is not currently used.
FECN	Forward-explicit congestion notification (FECN) is a single-bit field that can be set to a value of 1 by a switch to indicate to an end DTE device, such as a router, that congestion was experienced in the direction of the frame transmission from source to destination.

continues

Table 7-1   Frame Relay IETF Frame Field Definitions (Continued)

Field	Definition
BECN	Backward-explicit congestion notification (BECN) is a single-bit field that, when set to a value of 1 by a switch, indicates that congestion was experienced in the network in the direction opposite of the frame transmission from source to destination. See Chapter 8, "Shaping Frame Relay Traffic," for more information on FECN and BECN.
DE	Discard eligibility (DE) is set by a DTE device, such as a router, to indicate that the marked frame is of lesser importance relative to other frames being transmitted. Frames that are marked as "discard eligible" should be discarded before other frames in a congested network. This allows for a fairly basic prioritization mechanism in Frame Relay networks. See Chapter 8 for more information on the DE bit.
Data	Contains encapsulated upper-layer data. Each frame in this variable-length field includes a user data or payload field that varies in length up to 16,000 octets. This field serves to transport the higher-layer protocol data unit (PDU) through a Frame Relay network.
FCS	Frame Check Sequence (FCS) ensures the integrity of transmitted data. This value is computed by the source device and verified by the receiver to ensure integrity of transmission.

Frame Relay LMI

LMI is a signaling standard between the CPE device (typically a router) and the Frame Relay switch. LMI is responsible for managing the connection and maintaining status between the devices (see Figure 7-6). It includes support for the following:

- **A keepalive mechanism**—This verifies that data is flowing.
- **A status mechanism**—These messages provide communication and synchronization between the network and the user device. They periodically report the existence of new PVCs and the deletion of already existing PVCs, and generally provide information about PVC integrity. VC status messages prevent the sending of data into black holes—that is, over PVCs that no longer exist.

- **A multicast mechanism**—Multicasting allows a sender to transmit a single frame, but have it delivered by the network to multiple recipients. Multicasting supports the efficient conveyance of routing protocol messages and address-resolution procedures that typically must be sent to many destinations simultaneously.

- **Global addressing**—This gives connection identifiers global rather than local significance, which allows them to be used to identify a specific interface to the Frame Relay network. Global addressing makes the Frame Relay network resemble a LAN in terms of addressing. Therefore, address resolution protocols perform over Frame Relay exactly as they do over a LAN.

NOTE

Although global addressing is possible, it is rarely implemented by providers. The majority of Frame Relay implementations use locally significant addressing.

Figure 7-6
The Frame Relay switch uses LMI to send status messages to the CPE.

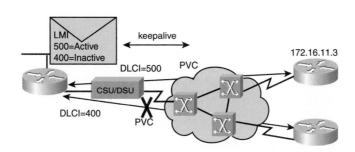

In order to deliver LMI and its services to customers as soon as possible, vendors and standards bodies worked separately to deploy LMI in early Frame Relay implementations. This resulted in three types of LMI, none of which is compatible with the other. Cisco, StrataCom, Northern Telecom, and Digital Equipment Corporation, collectively known as the Gang of Four, released one type of LMI, while the ANSI and the ITU-T each released their own versions (see Table 7-2).

NOTE

Because the Gang of Four standardized their own version of LMI, Cisco Systems acquired StrataCom; Northern Telecom is now Nortel Networks; and Digital Equipment Corporation was purchased by Compaq Computer Corporation.

Table 7-2   The Three Frame Relay LMI Types

Cisco IOS Keyword	Description
ansi	Annex D defined by ANSI standard T1.617
cisco	LMI type defined jointly by Cisco and three other companies
q933a	ITU-T Q.933 Annex A

The LMI type used by the provider's Frame Relay switch and the CPE must match. In Cisco IOS releases before 11.2, you must manually configure a Frame Relay interface to use the correct LMI type using the keywords shown in Table 7-2. Your provider will furnish you with this information.

If you are using Cisco IOS Release 11.2 or later, the router attempts to automatically detect the type of LMI being used by the provider's switch. This automatic detection process is called LMI autosensing. When using LMI autosensing, the router sends one or more requests to the Frame Relay switch. The Frame Relay switch responds with one or more LMI types. The router configures itself to use the last LMI type received.

The Frame Relay switch uses LMI to report the status of each configured PVC. The three possible PVC states are

- **Active state**—Indicates that the connection is active and that routers can exchange data.
- **Inactive state**—Indicates that the local connection to the Frame Relay switch is working, but the remote router connection to the Frame Relay switch is not working.
- **Deleted state**—Indicates that no LMI is being received from the Frame Relay switch, or that there is no service between the CPE router and the Frame Relay switch.

If the router reports that a DLCI is deleted, this means that the service provider's switch is not programmed to handle this DLCI. The local router is most likely configured with the wrong static DLCI or **frame-relay map** statement.

Inverse ARP

You can map DLCIs to Layer-3 addresses manually on a router using the appropriate configuration commands. But building static maps can require a great deal of administrative overhead in complex networks, and static maps cannot adapt to changes in the Frame Relay topology. Through the exchange of LMI, a Frame Relay switch can announce a new VC with its corresponding DLCI. Unfortunately, Layer-3 protocol addressing is not included in the announcement. The station receiving such an indication learns of the new connection, but is unable to address the other side. Without a new configuration or a mechanism for discovering the protocol address of the other side, this new VC is unusable.

Inverse ARP was developed to provide a mechanism for dynamic DLCI-to-Layer-3 address maps. Inverse ARP works much the same way Address Resolution Protocol (ARP) works on a LAN. After the router learns from the switch about available PVCs and their corresponding DLCIs, the router can send an Inverse ARP request to the other end of the PVC. The router sends an Inverse ARP request to each DLCI for each protocol configured on the interface. The Inverse ARP request asks the remote station for its Layer-3 address, while at the same time providing the remote system with the local system's Layer-3 address. Figure 7-7 illustrates the Inverse ARP process. The return information from the Inverse ARP is then used to build the Frame Relay map.

Figure 7-7
Using Inverse
ARP, a router can
dynamically map IP
addresses to DLCIs.

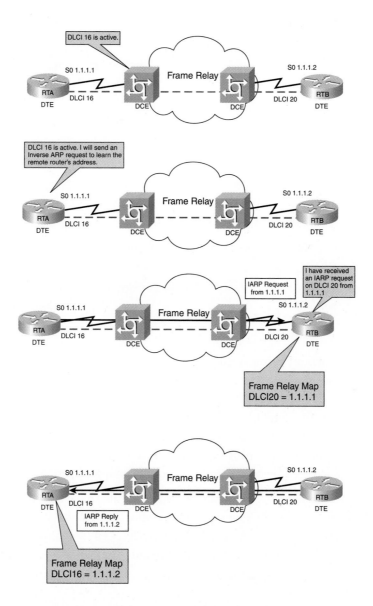

On a Cisco router, Inverse ARP is on by default when you configure an interface to use
Frame Relay encapsulation. If you configure static mapping for a specific DLCI,
Inverse ARP is disabled for that DLCI. You must use static mapping if the router at the
other end either does not support Inverse ARP at all, or does not support Inverse ARP
for a specific protocol that you want to use over Frame Relay.

Configuring Frame Relay

To configure an interface for Frame Relay, you must select the encapsulation type used to encapsulate data traffic at each end. There are two possible Frame Relay encapsulations: the Cisco encapsulation and the IETF encapsulation. By default, an interface uses the Cisco Frame Relay encapsulation method. This method is proprietary to Cisco and should not be used if the router is connected to another vendor's equipment across a Frame Relay network. Use the following command to configure a serial interface to use Frame Relay encapsulation:

```
Router(config-if)#encapsulation frame-relay [ietf]
```

If you are using Cisco IOS Release 11.1 or earlier, you must manually define the LMI type used by the Frame Relay switch using the following command:

```
Router(config-if)#frame-relay lmi-type {ansi | cisco | q933i}
```

With Cisco IOS Release 11.2 or later, the LMI type is autosensed, so no configuration is needed. If you specify an LMI type, autosensing is disabled.

The following sections describe how to configure Frame Relay maps and how to use the map configurations to apply Frame Relay encapsulation types on a per-PVC basis.

Configuring Frame Relay Maps

If you use dynamic address mapping, Inverse ARP requests a next-hop protocol address for each active PVC. After the requesting router receives an Inverse ARP response, it updates its DLCI to Layer-3 address mapping table. Dynamic address mapping is enabled by default for all protocols enabled on a physical interface. If your Frame Relay environment supports LMI and Inverse ARP, dynamic address mapping will take place. Therefore, no static address mapping is required.

Depending on your configuration, you might also have to manually configure a Frame Relay map. Use the **frame-relay map** command to configure static address mapping. After you configure a static map for a given DLCI, you have disabled Inverse ARP on that DLCI. The **frame-relay map** command uses the following syntax:

```
Router(config-ig)#frame-relay map protocol protocol-address dlci [broadcast]
  [ietf | cisco]
```

In Figure 7-8, the headquarters router is configured with a static map to the branch router. The commands needed to configure Frame Relay on RTX are shown in Example 7-1.

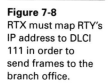

Figure 7-8
RTX must map RTY's IP address to DLCI 111 in order to send frames to the branch office.

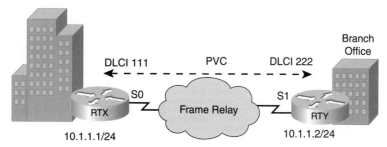

Example 7-1 Configuring a Static Frame Relay Map on RTX

```
RTX(config)#interface s0
RTX(config-if)#ip address 10.1.1.1 255.255.255.0
RTX(config-if)#encapsulation frame-relay ietf
RTX(config-if)#frame-relay map ip 10.1.1.2 111 broadcast
```

On the other side of the connection, RTY is configured, as shown in Example 7-2.

Example 7-2 Configuring a Static Frame Relay Map on RTY

```
RTY(config)#interface s1
RTY(config-if)#ip address 10.1.1.2 255.255.255.0
RTY(config-if)#encapsulation frame-relay ietf
RTY(config-if)#frame-relay map ip 10.1.1.1 222 broadcast
```

The **broadcast** keyword is commonly used with the **frame-relay map** command. The **broadcast** keyword provides two functions: It forwards broadcasts when multicasting is not enabled, and it simplifies the configuration of OSPF for nonbroadcast networks that use Frame Relay.

The **broadcast** keyword might also be required for some routing protocols—for example, AppleTalk—that depend on regular routing table updates, especially when the router at the remote end is waiting for a routing update packet to arrive before adding the route.

By requiring selection of a designated router, OSPF treats a nonbroadcast, multiaccess network such as Frame Relay in much the same way as it treats a broadcast network. In previous releases of the IOS, selection of a designated router required manual assignment in the OSPF configuration using the **neighbor interface** router command. When the **frame-relay map** command (with the **broadcast** keyword) and the **ip ospf network** command (with the **broadcast** keyword) are configured, there is no need to configure any neighbors manually. OSPF now automatically runs over the Frame Relay network as a broadcast network.

Configuring Encapsulation Per PVC

If the Cisco encapsulation is configured on a serial interface, that encapsulation applies to all VCs on that serial interface, by default. If some of the equipment at the destination is non-Cisco equipment and some is Cisco equipment, you can configure the Cisco encapsulation on the interface and selectively configure IETF encapsulation per DLCI (or vice versa). Because the default encapsulation is Cisco, you do not have to reference it explicitly in the **encapsulation frame-relay** command, as shown in Example 7-3.

Example 7-3 Using the frame-relay map Command to Specify an Encapsulation Type

```
RTB(config)#interface serial 0
RTB(config-if)#encapsulation frame-relay
RTB(config-if)#frame-relay map ip 131.108.123.2 48 broadcast
RTB(config-if)#frame-relay map ip 131.108.123.3 49 broadcast ietf
RTB(config-if)#frame-relay map ip 131.108.123.4 50 broadcast
```

Figure 7-9 depicts the router in this configuration scenario.

Figure 7-9
RTB is configured for
Cisco Frame Relay
encapsulation on all
PVCs, except for the
PVC specified by
DLCI 49.

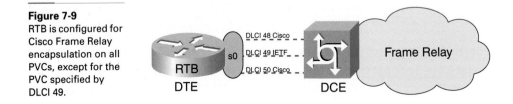

The **encapsulation frame-relay** command configures the Cisco Frame Relay encapsulation for all PVCs on the serial interface. But the **frame-relay map ip 131.108.123.3 49 broadcast ietf** command sets the encapsulation type to IETF for the PVC identified by DLCI 49.

Verifying Frame Relay Operation

After you configure Frame Relay, you can verify that the connections are active by using different show commands. The following examples of various **show** commands apply to the router, RTA, as depicted in Figure 7-10.

Figure 7-10
RTA connects to
RTB and RTC over
Frame Relay.

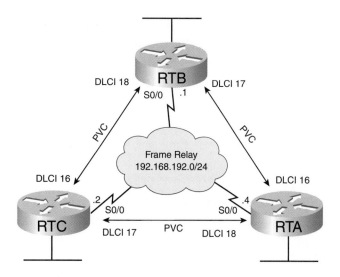

The **show interface serial** command displays information regarding the encapsulation, Layer-1, and Layer-2 status (see Example 7-4). It also displays the LMI type and the DLCI used for the LMI signaling, shown by the shaded line in Example 7-4.

Example 7-4 Using the show interface serial Command

```
RTA#show interface serial 0/0
Serial0/0 is up, line protocol is up
  Hardware is PowerQUICC Serial
  Internet address is 192.168.192.4/24
  MTU 1500 bytes, BW 1544 Kbit, DLY 20000 usec,
      reliability 255/255, txload 1/255, rxload 1/255
  Encapsulation FRAME-RELAY, loopback not set
  Keepalive set (10 sec)
  LMI enq sent  109, LMI stat recvd 109, LMI upd recvd 0, DTE
LMI up
  LMI enq recvd 0, LMI stat sent  0, LMI upd sent  0
  LMI DLCI 1023  LMI type is CISCO  frame relay DTE
  Broadcast queue 0/64, broadcasts sent/dropped 36/0, interface
broadcasts 17
  Last input 00:00:05, output 00:00:05, output hang never
  Last clearing of "show interface" counters 00:18:15
!
<output omitted>
```

A typical Frame Relay WAN is composed of numerous sites that are connected to central offices through a local loop. The telco identifies these individual local loops with a circuit number, such as: 05QHDQ101545-080TCOM-002. Telco technicians typically label the terminated circuit with the circuit number. When you call the telco for help with troubleshooting your Frame Relay WAN, you might be required to provide the circuit number.

To simplify the management of your WAN, use the **description** command at the interface level to record the circuit number, as shown by Example 7-5.

Example 7-5 Using the description Command

```
RTC(config)#interface serial 0
RTC(config-if)#description Circuit-05QHDQ101545-080TCOM-002
RTC(config-if)#^z
RTC#show interface serial 0
Serial 0 is up, line protocol is up
Hardware is MCI Serial
Description: Circuit-05QHDQ101545-080TCOM-002
Internet address is 192.168.0.192, subnet mask 255.255.255.0
<output omitted>
```

The **show frame-relay pvc** command displays the status of each configured connection, and traffic statistics (see Example 7-6). This command is also useful for viewing the number of BECN and FECN packets received by the router.

Example 7-6 Using the show frame-relay pvc Command

```
RTA#show frame-relay pvc

PVC Statistics for interface Serial0/0 (Frame Relay DTE)

              Active      Inactive      Deleted        Static
 Local          2            0             0             0
 Switched       0            0             0             0
 Unused         0            0             0             0
DLCI = 16, DLCI USAGE = LOCAL, PVC STATUS = ACTIVE, INTERFACE = Serial0/0
  input pkts 676           output pkts 470          in bytes 92211
  out bytes 86466          dropped pkts 0           in FECN pkts 0
```

Example 7-6 Using the show frame-relay pvc Command (Continued)

```
 in BECN pkts 0          out FECN pkts 0          out BECN pkts 0
 in DE pkts 0            out DE pkts 0
 out bcast pkts 372        out bcast bytes 76274
 pvc create time 03:32:04, last time pvc status changed 03:32:04


DLCI = 18, DLCI USAGE = LOCAL, PVC STATUS = ACTIVE, INTERFACE = Serial0/0
 input pkts 433          output pkts 436          in bytes 81309
 out bytes 82942         dropped pkts 0           in FECN pkts 0
 in BECN pkts 0          out FECN pkts 0          out BECN pkts 0
 in DE pkts 0            out DE pkts 0
 out bcast pkts 371        out bcast bytes 76182
             pvc create time 03:32:05, last time pvc status changed 03:32:05
```

The **show frame-relay map** command displays the current map entries and information about the connections, as shown in Example 7-7.

Example 7-7 Using the show frame-relay map Command

```
RTA#show frame-relay map
Serial0/0 (up): ip 192.168.192.1 dlci 16(0x10,0x400), dynamic,
              broadcast,, status defined, active
Serial0/0 (up): ip 192.168.192.2 dlci 18(0x11,0x410), dynamic,
                  broadcast,, status defined, active
```

The **show frame-relay lmi** command displays LMI traffic statistics, as shown in Example 7-8. This command shows the number of status messages exchanged between the local router and the Frame Relay switch. The shaded output shows the LMI type for the interface.

Example 7-8 Using the show frame-relay lmi Command

```
RTA#show frame-relay lmi
LMI Statistics for interface Serial0/0 (Frame Relay DTE) LMI TYPE = ANSI
  Invalid Unnumbered info 0           Invalid Prot Disc 0
  Invalid dummy Call Ref 0            Invalid Msg Type 0
  Invalid Status Message 0            Invalid Lock Shift 0
  Invalid Information ID 0            Invalid Report IE Len 0
```

continues

Example 7-8 Using the show frame-relay lmi Command (Continued)

```
Invalid Report Request 0        Invalid Keep IE Len 0

Num Status Enq. Sent 2523       Num Status msgs Rcvd 2522

Num Update Status Rcvd 0        Num Status Timeouts 7
```

Frame Relay Topologies

Frame Relay allows you to interconnect your remote sites in a variety of ways. Example topologies, as shown in Figure 7-11, include the following:

- A *star topology*, also known as a *hub-and-spoke* configuration, is the most popular Frame Relay network topology because it is the most cost-effective. In this topology, remote sites are connected to a central site that generally provides a service or application. This is the least expensive topology because it requires the fewest PVCs. In this scenario, the central router provides a multi-point connection because it is typically using a single interface to interconnect multiple PVCs.

- In a *full-mesh topology*, all routers have VCs to all other destinations. This method, although more costly than other Frame Relay topologies, provides direct connections from each site to all other sites, and allows for redundancy. When one link goes down, a router at site A can reroute traffic through site C, for example. As the number of nodes in the full-mesh topology increases, the topology becomes increasingly more expensive. The formula to calculate the total number of VCs with a fully meshed WAN is $[n(n-1)]/2$, where n is the number of sites.

- In a *partial-mesh topology*, not all sites have direct access to each other.

Depending on the traffic patterns in your network, you might want to have additional PVCs connect to remote sites that send or receive a heavy amount of traffic.

If you choose a star or partial-mesh topology for your Frame Relay WAN, you must account for potential problems created by Frame Relay's *Non-Broadcast Multiaccess (NBMA)* nature, in particular routing issues with split horizon. These issues are discussed in the next section.

Figure 7-11
Frame Relay networks can have full-mesh or partial-mesh (including hub-and-spoke) topologies.

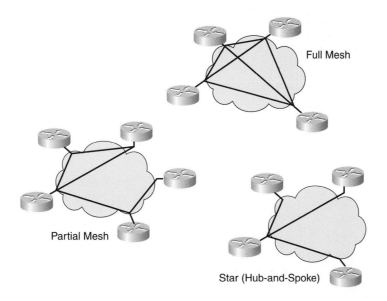

Reachability Issues with Routing Updates

A Frame Relay network provides NBMA connectivity between remote sites. An NBMA network is a *multiaccess network*, which means more than two nodes can connect to the network. Ethernet is another example of multiaccess architecture. In an Ethernet LAN, all nodes see all broadcast frames. However, in a non-broadcast network, such as Frame Relay, nodes cannot see each other's broadcasts unless they are directly connected through a VC. This means that Branch A cannot see Branch B's broadcasts directly because they are connected using a hub-and-spoke topology (see Figure 7-12). The central router must receive Branch A's broadcast and then send the broadcast to Branch B. This scenario is problematic when dealing with routing protocols because of the *split horizon* rule.

The split horizon rule reduces the chance of a routing loop by preventing a routing update received on one interface to be forwarded through the same interface. If the central router learns about Network X from Branch A, that update is learned through S0. According to the split horizon rule, central could not update Branch B or Branch C about Network X because that update would be sent using the same interface that received the update, S0.

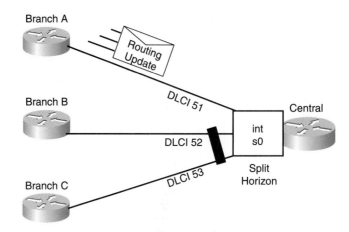

Figure 7-12
Split horizon pre-
vents the central
router from updat-
ing Branch B and
Branch C with routes
learned from
Branch A.

To remedy this situation, you can turn off split horizon for IP. When you configure an interface for Frame Relay encapsulation, split horizon for IP is automatically turned off for the main interface. Of course, if you disable split horizon, you lose the protection it affords against routing loops. And, in some cases, you might not be able to disable split horizon. The only way that you can disable split horizon when routing IPX and AppleTalk is if you are using Enhanced Interior Gateway Routing Protocol (EIGRP). When split horizon can't be turned off, or when you need split horizon to protect against routing loops, you can configure Frame Relay using subinterfaces. This configuration approach is covered in the next section.

There are other routing issues with multipoint connections on a single interface. When multiple DLCIs terminate in a single interface, the router must replicate routing updates and service advertisements for each PVC. The updates can consume access-link bandwidth and cause significant latency variations in user traffic. The updates can also consume interface buffers and lead to higher packet-rate loss for both user data and routing updates.

The amount of broadcast traffic and the number of VCs terminating at each router should be evaluated during the design phase of a Frame Relay network. Overhead traffic, such as routing updates, can affect the delivery of critical user data, especially when the delivery path contains low-bandwidth (56-Kbps) links.

Frame Relay Subinterfaces

Subinterfaces are logical subdivisions of a physical interface. In split-horizon routing environments, routing information received on one subinterface can be sent out on another subinterface. In subinterface configuration, each VC can be configured as a point-to-point connection, allowing each subinterface to act similar to a leased line.

A key reason for using subinterfaces is to allow distance-vector routing protocols to perform properly in an environment in which split horizon is activated. The router receiving a broadcast on subinterface s0.1, for example, is capable of sending the received routing information out of interfaces s0.2 and s0.3.

Reconsider the situation in which Branch A sends a routing update to Central (see Figure 7-13). With subinterfaces, Central receives the update on its interface s0.1 and is able to pass the routing information to Branch B and Branch C, sending it out through interfaces s0.2 and s0.3.

Figure 7-13
Because the Central router is configured with three subinterfaces, Central can update the other branch routers with routes received from Branch A.

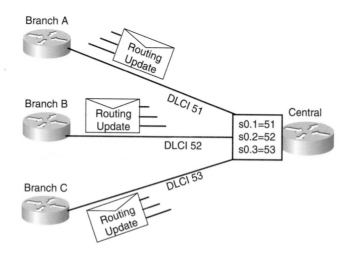

There are two types of Frame Relay subinterfaces, as shown in Figure 7-14:

- **Point to point**—A single subinterface is used to establish one PVC connection to another physical interface or subinterface on a remote router. In this case, the interfaces are in the same subnet, and each interface has a single DLCI. In this environment, broadcasts are not a problem because the routers are point-to-point and act similar to a leased line.

- **Multipoint**—A single subinterface is used to establish multiple PVC connections to multiple physical interfaces or subinterfaces on remote routers. In this case, all the participating interfaces are in the same subnet, and each interface has its own local DLCI. Because the subinterface is acting as a regular NBMA Frame Relay network, broadcast traffic is subject to the split-horizon rule.

Figure 7-14
RTA connects to RTB and RTC using a multipoint subinterface, while using a point-to-point subinterface to connect to RTD.

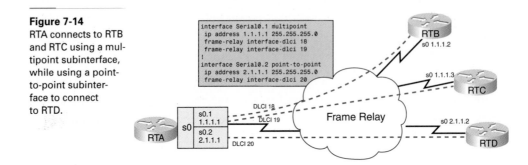

Figure 7-14 illustrates a Frame Relay point-to-point and multipoint subinterface configuration example.

To configure subinterfaces on a physical interface, you must configure the interface for Frame Relay encapsulation (either Cisco or IETF). Also, you must remove any configured IP address on the physical interface because each subinterface will have its own IP address. If the physical interface has an address, frames will not be received by the local subinterfaces. Example 7-10 shows how these commands are applied to RTA in Figure 7-14.

Example 7-9 Configuring a Physical Interface to Use Frame Relay Subinterfaces

```
RTA(config)#interface s0
RTA(config-if)#encapsulation frame-relay ietf
RTA(config-if)#no ip address
```

Next, you can specify the subinterface or subinterfaces you want to create using the following command:

```
Router(config-if)#interface serial number.subinterface-number {multipoint |
  point-to-point}
```

The following command creates a point-to-point subinterface 2 on Serial 0, as shown in Figure 7-14:

```
RTA(config-if)#interface serial s0.2 point-to-point
RTA(config-subif)#
```

The prompt changes after you enter this command. The "subif" in the prompt indicates that you are in subinterface configuration mode.

As another subinterface configuration example, this command creates subinterface 5 on Serial 2:

```
RTX(config)#interface serial s2.5 multipoint
RTX(config-subif)#
```

You can specify subinterface numbers in interface configuration mode, or global configuration mode. The Cisco IOS accepts any number from 1 to 4294967295 as a subinterface number. The number 0 refers to the physical interface and not a subinterface.

The wide range of possible subinterface numbers gives you some measure of flexibility. When configuring a point-to-point subinterface, it is common practice to number the subinterface according to the PVC's DLCI value. For example, if you are going to create a subinterface on Serial 0 that connects to the PVC using DLCI 16, you could use the following command:

```
RTX(config-if)#interface serial s0.16 point-to-point
RTX(config-subif)#
```

After you create the subinterface, you can then specify logical configuration parameters, such as an IP address. For RTA in Figure 7-14, you can use the following command:

```
RTA(config-subif)#ip address 2.1.1.1 255.255.255.0
```

If you are assigning an IP address to a point-to-point subinterface, you also have the option of specifying IP unnumbered, as shown here:

```
Router(config-if)#ip unnumbered interface
```

At this point in the subinterface configuration, you can either configure a static Frame Relay map or use the **frame-relay interface-dlci** command. The **frame-relay interface-dlci** command associates the selected subinterface with a DLCI. This command is required for all point-to-point subinterfaces. It is also required for multipoint subinterfaces for which Inverse ARP is enabled. It is not required for multipoint subinterfaces that are configured with static maps.

To understand what the **frame-relay interface-dlci** command does, and why it is needed, consider Figure 7-14 again. The Frame Switch uses LMI to inform RTA that three active PVCs are available, and that the DLCIs associated with these PVCs are 18, 19, and 20. When RTA learns about DLCIs 18, 19, and 20 on interface S0, how will RTA know which DLCI to use with which subinterface? LMI provides no way of telling RTA that DLCI 20 should be used by interface s0.2 and not s0.1. Therefore, you must manually associate each subinterface with the appropriate DLCI numbers.

> **NOTE**
>
> The **frame-relay interface-dlci** command is typically used only on subinterfaces. In fact, you might be told never to use this command on the main interface. However, the **frame-relay interface-dlci** command can also be applied to main interfaces. The **frame-relay interface-dlci** command is used to support routing protocols on main interfaces that are configured to use Inverse ARP. This command is also helpful for assigning a specific map class to a single PVC on a multipoint subinterface.

RTA in Figure 7-14 is configured according to Example 7-10.

Example 7-10　Using the frame-relay interface-dlci Command

```
RTA(config)#interface serial s0.1 multipoint
RTA(config-subif)#ip address 1.1.1.1 255.255.255.0
RTA(config-subif)#frame-relay interface-dlci 18
RTA(config-fr-dlci)#exit
RTA(config-subif)#frame-relay interface-dlci 19
RTA(config-fr-dlci)#exit
RTA(config-subif)#exit
RTA(config)#interface serial s0.2 point-to-point
RTA(config-subif)#ip address 2.1.1.1 255.255.255.0
RTA(config-subif)#frame-relay interface-dlci 20
RTA(config-fr-dlci)#^Z
```

If you define a subinterface for point-to-point communication, you cannot reassign the same subinterface number to be used for multipoint communication without first rebooting the router.

Summary

This chapter discussed the differences between Frame Relay and its predecessor, X.25. You learned that VCs are identified by DLCIs, and that the LMI is used to communicate status information between the Frame Relay switch and the CPE. Also, you saw how Inverse ARP and static configurations are used to map Layer-3 addresses to DLCIs. This chapter presented the types of Frame Relay topologies, including partial-mesh topologies. Because of the split horizon rule, partial-mesh topologies might result in routing problems. Subinterfaces are often used to circumvent routing issues caused by partial-mesh topologies.

Chapter 8 describes how Frame Relay traffic is controlled and metered by service providers and customers. This type of control is sometimes called traffic shaping.

Review Questions

Use the following review questions to test your understanding of the concepts covered in this chapter. In some cases, there is more than one correct answer, so choose all that apply. Answers are listed in Appendix A, "Answers to Review Questions."

1. Which of the following is not true about Frame Relay?

   A. Frame Relay specifies Layer-3 reliability mechanisms.

   B. Frame Relay is a packet-switched technology.

   C. Frame Relay offers fewer error-correction mechanisms than X.25.

   D. Frame Relay describes the connection between the provider's equipment and the CPE.

2. What is the range of DLCIs available to Frame relay customers?

   A. 0–1024

   B. 0–1023

   C. 16–1007

   D. 16–1023

3. Which of the following is not a valid Frame Relay LMI Type?

   A. ANSI

   B. TU-T Q.933a

   C. Cisco

   D. IETF

4. What version of the Cisco IOS was the first to support LMI autosensing?

   A. 11.0

   B. 11.1

   C. 11.2

   D. 11.3

5. Which of the following commands correctly configures Cisco Frame Relay encapsulation?

   A. Router(config-subif)#**encapsulation frame-relay**

   B. Router(config-if)#**encapsulation frame-relay**

   C. Router(config-subif)#**encapsulation frame-relay cisco**

   D. Router(config-if)#**encapsulation frame-relay cisco**

6. Which of the following commands correctly maps the IP address 1.1.1.1 to DLCI 24?

    A. frame-relay map 1.1.1.1 24 broadcast ietf

    B. frame-relay map ip 1.1.1.1 broadcast 24

    C. frame-relay map ip 1.1.1.1 24

    D. frame-relay ip map 1.1.1.1 24 broadcast ietf

7. Which of the following commands correctly configures a Frame Relay subinterface?

    A. Router(config)#**interface s3.3 multipoint**

    B. Router(config-if)#**interface s0/0.1 point-to-multipoint**

    C. Router(config)#**interface s0/0:1**

    D. Router(config-if)#**interface s0/1**

8. Which of the following statements is true about split horizon?

    A. Split horizon cannot be disabled on IP interfaces.

    B. Split horizon is disabled by default on all interfaces.

    C. Split horizon is disabled by default on Frame Relay serial interfaces.

    D. Split horizon interfaces cannot be configured for Frame Relay.

9. When are you most likely to use the **frame-relay interface-dlci** command?

    A. When configuring a point-to-point subinterface.

    B. When configuring a main interface for multipoint Frame Relay.

    C. When static DLCI-to-Layer-3-address mappings are present.

    D. Whenever you disable LMI.

10. What command allows you to configure Frame Relay encapsulation types on a per-PVC basis?

    A. frame-relay pvc

    B. frame-relay interface-dlci

    C. frame-relay map

    D. frame-relay encapsulation

Key Terms

DLCI (Data-Link Connection Identifier)   Value that specifies a PVC or an SVC in a Frame Relay network.

FRAD (Frame Relay Access Device)   Any network device that provides a connection between a LAN and a Frame Relay WAN.

Inverse ARP (Inverse Address Resolution Protocol)   Method of building dynamic routes in a network. Allows an access server to discover the network address of a device associated with a VC.

LMI (Local Management Interface)   Set of enhancements to the basic Frame Relay specification. LMI includes support for a keepalive mechanism, which verifies that data is flowing; a multicast mechanism, which provides the network server with its local DLCI and the multicast DLCI; global addressing, which gives DLCIs global rather than local significance in Frame Relay networks; and a status mechanism, which provides an on-going status report on the DLCIs known to the switch.

NBMA (Non-Broadcast Multiaccess)   Describes a multiaccess network that does not support broadcasting (such as X.25), or one in which broadcasting is not feasible.

Split horizon   A routing technique in which information about routes is prevented from exiting the router interface through which that information was received.

Statistical multiplexing   Technique whereby information from multiple logical channels can be transmitted across a single physical channel. Statistical multiplexing dynamically allocates bandwidth only to active input channels, making better use of available bandwidth and allowing more devices to be connected than with other multiplexing techniques. Packet switching networks typically employ statistical multiplexing.

Subinterfaces   One of several virtual interfaces on a single physical interface.

TDM (time-division multiplexing)   Technique in which information from multiple channels can be allocated bandwidth on a single wire based on preassigned time slots. Bandwidth is allocated to each channel regardless of whether the station has data to transmit.

Objectives

After completing this chapter, you will be able to perform tasks related to the following:

- Frame Relay traffic shaping
- Traffic shaping using rate enforcement
- Traffic shaping using rate adaption
- Traffic shaping using queuing
- On-demand routing

Shaping Frame Relay Traffic

Chapters 6, "X.25," and 7, "Frame Relay," describe two common packet-switching technologies. In a packet-switched network, connections between remote sites are established using virtual circuits (VCs). Service providers deploy switching equipment to build and manage these VCs. In Figure 8-1, the Frame Relay provider's network of switches is depicted as a cloud.

Figure 8-1
A customer can configure Frame Relay traffic management to alleviate congestion and prevent packet loss.

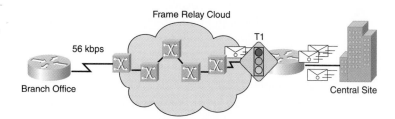

The architecture of packet-switched networks gives providers and their customers a great deal of control over how traffic is managed. Providers can raise or lower the rate at which customer data flows by reconfiguring their switching equipment. Frame Relay switches are typically configured to drop traffic under certain circumstances, or prioritize traffic in other cases. None of this control is implemented on a dedicated circuit, such as a dedicated point-to-point T1.

Unlike a leased line, which provides a fixed amount of bandwidth at all times, a packet-switched network can provide multiple levels of bandwidth and service.

In a Frame Relay network, customers can control, or shape, traffic so that certain protocols and VCs conform to specified transmission rates.

Customers might turn to *traffic shaping* because of a policy or an application. An application might dictate that the rate of a given interface not exceed a certain rate—even though the physical line is capable of higher transmission speeds.

Customers also shape traffic to avoid having a high-capacity link overwhelm a branch-office router that has a low speed connection.

Frame Relay traffic shaping relies on parameters that are useful for managing network traffic congestion. These include committed information rate (*CIR*), forward and backward explicit congestion notification (*FECN/BECN*), and the discard eligibility (*DE*) bit.

This chapter explores Frame Relay traffic shaping from the customer's perspective, including rate enforcement, rate adaption, and queuing.

Finally, this chapter explores on-demand routing, an alternative to configuring and managing the routing process over Frame Relay hub-and-spoke networks.

Overview of Frame Relay Traffic Shaping

Several factors determine the rate at which a customer can send data on a Frame Relay network. Foremost in limiting the maximum transmission rate is the capacity of the local loop to the provider. If the local loop is a T1, you can't send more than 1.544 Mbps. The provider typically provides a clocking signal, which determines the speed of the local loop. In Frame Relay terminology, the speed of the local loop is called the *local access rate*.

Providers use the CIR parameter to provision network resources and regulate usage. For example, a company with a T1 connection to the packet-switched network (PSN) might agree to a CIR of 768 Kbps. This means that the provider guarantees 768 Kbps of bandwidth to the customer's link at all times.

Typically, the higher the CIR, the higher the cost of service. Customers can choose the CIR that's most appropriate to their bandwidth needs, as long as the CIR is less than or equal to the local access rate.

If a customer's CIR is less than the local access rate, the customer and provider agree on whether bursting above the CIR is allowed. Consider Figure 8-2. If the local access rate is T1 (1.544 Mbps), and the CIR is 768 Kbps, half of the potential bandwidth (as determined by the local access rate) remains available.

NOTE

Many providers allow their customers to purchase a CIR of 0. This means that the provider does not guarantee any throughput. In practice, customers usually find that their provider allows them to burst over the 0 CIR virtually all the time. If you purchase a CIR of 0, you must monitor performance carefully to determine whether it is acceptable.

Figure 8-2
When the CIR is less than the local access rate (in this case, 1.544 Mbps), bursting is possible.

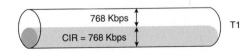

Frame Relay allows a customer and provider to agree that under certain circumstances, the customer can burst over the CIR. Because burst traffic is in excess of the CIR, the provider does not guarantee that it will deliver the frames.

Either a router or a Frame Relay switch tags each frame that is transmitted beyond the CIR as eligible to be discarded. A single bit in the Frame Relay frame is set to 1. This bit is known as the *discard eligible* (*DE*) bit. The provider's switches or the customer's routers can selectively set the DE bit in frames and then drop these frames when congestion occurs.

The Frame Relay specification also includes a protocol for congestion notification. This mechanism relies on the FECN/BECN bits in the header of the frame.

You need to be familiar with some terminology related to Frame Relay traffic management, including the following:

- **Local access rate**—The clock speed (port speed) of the connection (local loop) to the Frame Relay cloud. It is the rate at which data travels into or out of the network, regardless of other settings.

- **CIR**—The rate, in bits per second, at which the Frame Relay switch agrees to transfer data. The rate is usually averaged over a period of time, referred to as the committed rate measurement interval (Tc). In general, the duration of Tc is proportional to the burstiness of the traffic.

- *Oversubscription*—Oversubscription is when the sum of the CIRs on all the VCs exceeds the access line speed. Oversubscription can also occur when the access line can support the sum of CIRs purchased, but not of the CIRs plus the bursting capacities of the VCs. Oversubscription increases the likelihood of packets being dropped.

- *Committed Burst* (Bc)—The maximum number of bits that the switch agrees to transfer during any Tc. The higher the Bc-to-CIR ratio, the longer the switch can handle a sustained burst. For example, if the Tc is 2 seconds and the CIR is 32 Kbps, the Bc is 64 Kbps. The Tc calculation is $Tc = Bc/CIR$.

- *Excess Burst* (**Be**)—The maximum number of uncommitted bits that the Frame Relay switch attempts to transfer beyond the CIR. Be is dependent on the service offerings available from your vendor, but it is typically limited to the port speed of the local access loop.

- **Excess Information Rate (EIR)**—Defines the maximum bandwidth available to the customer, that is, the CIR plus the Be. Typically, the EIR is set to the local access rate. In the event the provider sets the EIR to be lower than the local access rate, all frames beyond that maximum can be discarded automatically, even if there is no congestion.

- **FECN**—When a Frame Relay switch recognizes congestion in the network, it sends an FECN packet to the destination device, indicating that congestion has occurred.

NOTE

It's typically not in a customer's best interest to mark his own traffic as eligible for discard. For this reason, when the DE bit is set, it is most commonly done by the provider's equipment.

NOTE

Tc is not a recurrent time interval. It is used strictly to measure inbound data, during which time it acts as a sliding window. Inbound data triggers the Tc interval.

- **BECN**—When a Frame Relay switch recognizes congestion in the network, it sends a BECN packet to the source router, instructing the router to reduce the rate at which it is sending packets. With Cisco IOS Release 11.2 or later, Cisco routers can respond to BECN notifications. This topic is discussed later in this chapter.

- **DE bit**—When the router detects network congestion, it marks the packet Discard Eligible. The DE bit is set on the traffic that was received after the CIR was met. These packets are normally delivered, but in periods of congestion, the Frame Relay switch drops packets with the DE bit set first.

Types of Frame Relay Traffic Management

The traffic shaping over Frame Relay feature provides the following capabilities:

- **Rate enforcement on a per-virtual-circuit basis**—You can configure a peak rate to limit outbound traffic to either the CIR or some other defined value, such as the excess information rate (EIR).

- **Generalized BECN support on a per-VC basis**—The router can monitor BECNs and throttle traffic based on BECN-marked packet feedback from the Frame Relay network.

- **Priority/Custom/Weighted Fair Queuing (PQ/CQ/WFQ) support at the VC level**—This allows for finer granularity in the prioritization and queuing of traffic, thus giving you more control over the traffic flow on an individual VC.

Configuring Traffic Shaping over Frame Relay

The traffic shaping over Frame Relay feature can be used in the following situations:

- When you have a Frame Relay network topology that consists of a high-speed (T1 line speed or greater) connection at the central site and low-speed (56 Kbps or less) connections at the branch sites

- When you have a Frame Relay network that is constructed with many VCs to different locations on a single physical line into the network

- If you notice that your Frame Relay connections occasionally get congested

- When you have several different types of traffic (such as Internet Protocol [IP], Systems Network Architecture [SNA], or IPX) to transmit on the same Frame Relay VC, and want to ensure that the different traffic types receive a certain amount of bandwidth

When you have a Frame Relay network topology that consists of a high-speed (T1 or greater) connection at the central site and a low-speed (56 Kbps or less) connection at the branch sites, you can use the traffic shaping over Frame Relay feature, as shown in Figure 8-3).

Figure 8-3
Because the central and branch sites have different connection speeds to the PSN, traffic shaping might be necessary to improve performance.

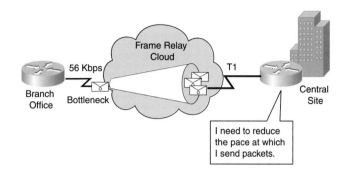

Because of the speed mismatch, a bottleneck often exists for traffic on a VC when the central site tries to communicate with the branch site. This bottleneck results in poor response times for traffic, such as SNA or interactive Telnet when it is stuck behind a large File Transfer Protocol (FTP) packet flow on a low-speed line. Packets get dropped at the bottleneck, resulting in lost SNA sessions and possibly causing the central site to retransmit unacknowledged packets—making the congestion problem worse. The rate enforcement capability of the traffic-shaping feature can be used to limit the rate at which data is sent on the VC at the central site. Rate enforcement can also be used in conjunction with the existing Data Link Control Identifier (DLCI) prioritization feature to further improve performance in this situation.

When you have a Frame Relay network that is constructed with many VCs to different locations on a single physical line into the network, these VCs send traffic as fast as the physical line speed allows. The rate enforcement capability enables you to control the transmission speed used by the router by other criteria, such as the CIR or EIR. The rate enforcement feature can preallocate the bandwidth that each VC receives on the physical line into the Frame Relay network, effectively creating a virtual time-division multiplexing (TDM) network.

If you notice that your Frame Relay connections occasionally get congested, you might want the router to throttle traffic instead of sending it in to the network. Throttling the traffic might help prevent packet loss in the network. The BECN-based throttling capability that is provided with the traffic-shaping feature allows you to have the router dynamically throttle traffic, based on receiving BECN-tagged packets from the network. This throttling holds packets in the router buffers to reduce the data flow from the router into the Frame Relay network. The throttling is done on a per-VC basis, and the rate of transmission is dynamically increased as fewer BECNs are received.

You might have several different types of traffic, such as IP, SNA, or IPX, to transmit on the same Frame Relay VC, and want to ensure that the different traffic types receive a certain amount of bandwidth. Using CQ, with the per-VC queuing and rate enforcement capabilities, enables you to configure VCs to perform this task. Prior to Cisco IOS Release 11.2, CQ was defined only at the interface level. Now it can be defined at the VC level.

Traffic Shaping Configuration Steps

To enable Frame Relay traffic shaping, perform the following steps:

1. *Specify a map class.* Specify a map class to be defined with the **map-class frame-relay** command:

   ```
   Router(config)#map-class frame-relay map-class-name
   ```

2. *Configure the map class.* When you define a map class for Frame Relay, you can do the following:

   - Define the average and peak rates (in bits per second) that are allowed on VCs associated with the map class.

   - Specify that the router dynamically fluctuates the rate at which it sends packets, depending on the BECNs it receives.

   - Specify either a custom queue list or a priority queue group to use on VCs associated with the map class.

   When in map class configuration mode, you can define the average and peak rates, specify that the router dynamically fluctuate the rate at which it sends packets—depending on the BECNs it receives—or specify either a CQ list or a PQ group to use on VCs associated with the map class.

3. *Enable Frame Relay on an interface.* After you define a map class with queuing and traffic-shaping parameters, enter interface configuration mode and enable Frame Relay encapsulation on an interface with the **encapsulation frame-relay** command:

   ```
   Router(config-if)#encapsulation frame-relay
   ```

4. *Enable Frame Relay traffic shaping on an interface.* Enabling Frame Relay traffic shaping on an interface, using the **frame-relay traffic-shaping** command, enables both traffic shaping and per-VC queuing on all the Permanent Virtual Circuits (PVCs) and Switched Virtual Circuits (SVCs) on the interface. Traffic shaping enables the router to control the circuit output rate and react to congestion notification information.

5. *Add the map class to VCs on the interface.* Add a map class to all VCs on the interface with the **frame-relay class** *map-class-name* command. The *map-class-name* argument must match the map-class-name of the map class you configured:

   ```
   Router(config-if)#frame-relay class map-class-name
   ```

> **NOTE**
>
> The map class can be mapped to the interface or to a specific sub-interface on the interface.

Traffic Shaping Through Rate Enforcement

Figure 8-4 presents a scenario that warrants Frame Relay traffic shaping. The central site has a T1 connection to the Frame Relay cloud. But the branch offices only have a 9600 bps connection. The CIR for each PVC going from the central site to each branch office is set at 9.6 Kbps.

Figure 8-4
Without traffic shaping, the central site's T1 connection to the Frame Relay cloud might overwhelm the branch offices.

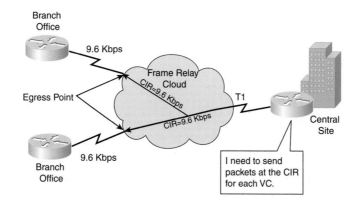

In this environment, the following occurs:

- The central site might send data across the T1 line. Even though the CIR is 9.6 Kbps, the router continues to send data based on the T1 rate.

- The data goes through the cloud.

- When the data reaches the local loop that is connected to the branch office, a bottleneck occurs because the data is being sent faster than the speed of the branch-office local loop. At this point, packets are buffered at the egress point of the network, increasing line response time and (possibly) causing problems, particularly for latency-sensitive protocols such as SNA.

The solution is to slow the speed at which the central-site router is sending data. With the traffic shaping over Frame Relay feature, you can define and enforce a rate on the VC at which the router sends data. The pace you set can be the CIR, EIR, or some other value.

Perform the following steps to configure Frame Relay rate enforcement:

1. Define a map class and enter map class configuration mode:
   ```
   Router(config)#map-class frame-relay map-class-name
   ```

2. Define the rate enforcement parameters to use:
   ```
   Router(config-map-class)#frame-relay traffic-rate average [peak]
   ```

   The *average* value is the average rate (equivalent to CIR).

The *peak* value is the peak rate, equivalent to CIR + Be/t = CIR(1 + Be/Bc). The default peak value is the line rate (derived from the **bandwidth** command). For SVCs, the configured peak and average rates are converted to the equivalent CIR, Be, and Bc values for use by SVC signaling. Only one command format (*traffic rate* or CIR, Be, and Bc) can be accepted in one map class. The user is warned when entering a second command type that the previous one is being overwritten.

3. Enable both traffic shaping and per-VC queuing for all VCs (PVCs and SVCs) on a Frame Relay interface:
   ```
   Router(config-if)#frame-relay traffic-shaping
   ```

   For VCs where no specific traffic shaping or queuing parameters are specified, a set of default values is used.

4. Associate a map class with an interface or subinterface:
   ```
   Router(config-if)#frame-relay class name
   ```

   Each VC created on the interface/subinterface inherits all the relevant parameters defined in the **frame-relay class** *name*. For each VC, the precedence rules are as follows:

   Use a map class associated with VC if it exists.

   - If not, use a map class associated with subinterface, if it exists.

   - If not, use a map class associated with interface, if it exists.

   - If not, use the default parameters.

Example 8-1 shows the commands needed to configure the central-site router shown in Figure 8-4.

Example 8-1 Configuring Frame Relay Rate Enforcement

```
Central(config)#interface serial 2
Central(config-if)#encapsulation frame-relay
Central(config-if)#frame-relay traffic-shaping
Central(config-if)#frame-relay class branch
Central(config)#map-class frame-relay branch
Central(config-map-class)#frame-relay traffic-rate 9600 19200
```

Traffic Shaping Through Rate Dynamic Enforcement

Figure 8-5 illustrates a Frame Relay environment in which different sites have different speeds for local-loop connections to the Frame Relay cloud.

Figure 8-5
The central-site router might send bursts of traffic above the rate the branch-office router can handle, resulting in occasional packet loss.

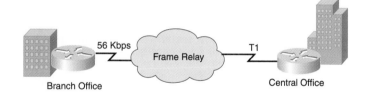

56 Kbps

Frame Relay

T1

Branch Office

Central Office

In this environment, the following process occurs:

1. The central site sends data to the branch-site router. During peak usage times, the central site sends data at a rate faster than the branch office's 56 Kbps connection can handle.

2. One of the switches within the cloud determines that it is getting congested with traffic. In this case, the congested switch sends a BECN packet to the central router.

   Prior to configuring the traffic shaping-over-Frame Relay feature, the central router notes that the BECN is received but does not slow its transmission rate.

3. At this point, packets begin dropping within the switch that is encountering the congestion. As previously discussed, this environment can cause problems, particularly for latency-sensitive protocols such as SNA.

In this scenario, the solution is to enable the central router to dynamically fluctuate the rate at which it sends packets, depending on the BECNs that it receives. For example, if the central router begins receiving many BECNs, it will reduce the packet transmit rate. As the BECNs become intermittent, the router will increase the packet transmit rate.

Perform the following steps to configure traffic shaping-over-Frame Relay BECN support:

1. Define a map class and enter map class configuration mode, as previously discussed.

2. Use the following command to enable BECN support:
   ```
   Router(config-map-class)#frame-relay adaptive-shaping becn
   ```

When enabled, BECNs received from the network on this VC are used to further regulate the output rate on the VC. As the frequency of BECNs increases, the output rate is steadily reduced from *peak to average* (equivalent of CIR). As congestion eases in the network and the frequency of BECNs decreases, the output rate is allowed to increase gradually to its configured *peak*.

3. Enable both traffic shaping and per-VC queuing for all VCs (PVCs and SVCs) on a Frame Relay interface:

Router(config-if)#**frame-relay traffic-shaping**

For VCs, where no specific traffic shaping or queuing parameters are specified, a set of default values is used.

4. Associate a map class with an interface or subinterface, as previously discussed:

Router(config-if)#**frame-relay class** *name*

Example 8-2 presents the commands needed to configure RTA for adaptive traffic shaping (see Figure 8-5).

Example 8-2 Configuring Frame Relay Rate Enforcement

```
Central(config)#interface serial 0
Central(config-if)#encapsulation frame-relay
Central(config-if)#frame-relay traffic-shaping
Central(config-if)#frame-relay class BECCNNOTIFY
Central(config-if)#exit
Central(config)#map-class frame-relay BECNNOTIFY
Central(config-map-class)#frame-relay adaptive-shaping becn
```

Traffic Shaping with Queuing

A third method of Frame Relay traffic shaping involves the use of queuing—specifically, PQ, and CQ. Queuing methods are described in Chapter 10, "Queuing and Compression."

Queue lists prioritize traffic based on protocol type. By referencing access lists, queue lists can even prioritize traffic based on the source or destination address of a packet.

You can use queue lists when configuring the router to shape Frame Relay traffic. Example 8-3 illustrates how queue lists can be used in a traffic-shaping configuration.

In Example 8-3, a Frame Relay map class is used to set the peak and average rates for individual VCs. By defining a peak rate at which the router can dispatch packets, you force the router to temporarily hold packets in a memory buffer during periods of high use. The memory buffer is a kind of waiting room for outbound packets.

As the router shapes traffic so that it does not exceed the defined rate, it schedules buffered packets for transmission. This scheduling process is called *queuing*. PQ and CQ lists configure the router to prioritize certain traffic over other traffic, regardless of which packets arrive in the buffer first. In effect, queuing allows packets to cut in line.

Why would you configure queuing, rather than let the first packet to be buffered be the first packet dispatched? Typically, you configure queuing so that delay-sensitive application traffic, such as voice or Telnet, is as unaffected as possible by the shaping process. For example, you can configure a queue so that voice traffic is given priority over FTP traffic. Adding a few seconds to the time it takes to download a file is preferable to adding even a half second of delay in a stream of voice traffic.

By applying a Frame Relay map class to a VC, you can specify different peak and average rates on a per-VC basis. Example 8-3 shows how this can be done in conjunction with queuing.

Example 8-3 Frame Relay Traffic Shaping with Queuing

```
interface Serial0
 no ip address
 encapsulation frame-relay
 frame-relay lmi-type ansi
 frame-relay traffic-shaping
 frame-relay class slow_vcs
!
interface Serial0.1 point-to-point
 ip address 10.128.30.1 255.255.255.248
 ip ospf cost 200
 bandwidth 10
 frame-relay interface-dlci 101
!
interface Serial0.2 point-to-point
 ip address 10.128.30.9 255.255.255.248
 ip ospf cost 400
 bandwidth 10
 frame-relay interface-dlci 102
   class fast_vcs
!
interface Serial0.3 point-to-point
 ip address 10.128.30.17 255.255.255.248
 ip ospf cost 200
 bandwidth 10
 frame-relay interface-dlci 103
```

continues

Example 8-3 Frame Relay Traffic Shaping with Queuing (Continued)

```
!
map-class frame-relay slow_vcs
 frame-relay traffic-rate 4800 9600
 frame-relay custom-queue-list 1
!
map-class frame-relay fast_vcs
 frame-relay traffic-rate 16000 64000
 frame-relay priority-group 2
!
access-list 100 permit tcp any any eq 2065
access-list 115 permit tcp any any eq 256
!
priority-list 2 protocol decnet high
priority-list 2 protocol ip normal
priority-list 2 default medium
!
queue-list 1 protocol ip 1 list 100
queue-list 1 protocol ip 2 list 115
queue-list 1 default 3
queue-list 1 queue 1 byte-count 1600 limit 200
queue-list 1 queue 2 byte-count 600 limit 200
queue-list 1 queue 3 byte-count 500 limit 200
```

In Example 8-3, the VCs on subinterfaces Serial0.1 and Serial0.3 inherit class parameters from the main interface, namely those defined in *slow_vcs*, but the VC defined on subinterface Serial0.2 (DLCI 102) is specifically configured to use map class *fast_vcs*.

Map class *slow_vcs* uses a peak rate of 9600 and an average rate of 4800 bps. Because BECN feedback is enabled by default, the output rate is cut back as low as 4800 bps in response to received BECNs. This map class is configured to use CQ using queue-list 1. In this example, queue-list 1 has three queues, with the first two being controlled by access lists 100 and 115.

Map class *fast_vcs* uses a peak rate of 64,000 and an average rate of 16,000 bps. Because BECN feedback is enabled by default, the output rate is cut back to as low as 16,000 bps in response to received BECNs. This map class is configured for PQ using priority-group 2.

Verifying Frame Relay Traffic Shaping

This section explains the following specific **show** commands available for Frame Relay traffic shaping:

- **show frame-relay pvc** *dlci*
- **show traffic-shape**
- **show traffic-shape statistics**

The show frame-relay pvc Command

The **show frame-relay pvc** command output provides the information shown in Table 8-1.

Table 8-1   The show frame-relay pvc Command Output

Field	Description
CIR	Current committed information rate (CIR), in bits per second (bps).
Bc	Current committed burst size, in bits.
Be	Current excess burst size, in bits.
Limit	Maximum number of bytes transmitted per internal interval (excess plus sustained).
Interval	Interval being used internally (might be smaller than the interval derived from Bc/CIR; this happens when the router determines that traffic flow is more stable with a smaller configured interval).
Mincir	Minimum CIR for the PVC.
Increment	Number of bytes that are sustained per internal interval.
BECN response	Frame Relay has BECN adaption configured.
List Queue Args	Identifier and parameter values for a custom queue list defined for the PVC. These identifiers and values correspond to the command queue-list 1 queue 4 byte-count 100.
Output queues	Output queues used for the PVC, with the current size, the maximum size, and the number of dropped frames shown for each queue.

Example 8-4 provides sample output for the **show frame-relay pvc** command.

Example 8-4 Using the show frame-relay pvc Command

```
RTA#show frame-relay pvc 130
PVC Statistics for interface Serial1 (Frame Relay DTE)
DLCI = 130, DLCI USAGE = LOCAL, PVC STATUS = ACTIVE, INTERFACE = Serial1.1
```

continues

Example 8-4 Using the show frame-relay pvc Command (Continued)

```
input pkts 4                output pkts 6                in bytes 180

out bytes 824               dropped pkts 0              in FECN pkts 0

in BECN pkts 0              out FECN pkts 0            out BECN pkts 0

 in DE pkts 0                         out DE pkts 0

 out bcast pkts 6                     out bcast bytes 824

 pvc create time 00:02:27, last time pvc status changed 00:02:27

 cir 64000      bc 64000       be 64000      byte limit 9000     interval 125

 mincir 32000   byte increment  1000         Adaptive Shaping none

 pkts 7         bytes 854      pkts delayed 0        bytes delayed 0

 shaping inactive

 traffic shaping drops 0

 Queueing strategy: fifo

 Output queue 0/40, 0 drop, 0 dequeued
```

The show traffic-shape Command

Use the **show traffic-shape** command to display the current traffic-shaping configuration. The command output contains the following fields described in Table 8-2.

Table 8-2　　The show traffic-shape Command Output

Field	Description
Target Rate	Rate that traffic is shaped to in bps.
Byte Limit	Maximum number of bytes transmitted per internal interval.
Sustain bits/int	Configured sustained bits per interval.
Excess bits/int	Configured excess bits in the first interval.
Interval (ms)	Interval being used internally. This interval might be smaller than the Bc divided by the CIR if the router determines that traffic flow is more stable with a smaller configured interval.
Increment (bytes)	Number of bytes that are sustained per internal interval.
Adapt Active	Contains BECN if Frame Relay has BECN adaption configured.

Figure 8-6 provides sample output for the **show traffic-shape** command.

Figure 8-6
The show traffic-shape command includes the CIR and Bc values.

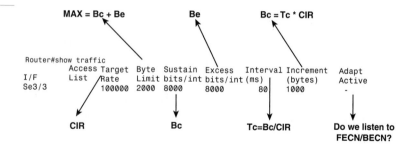

The show traffic-shape statistics Command

Use the **show traffic-shape statistics** command to display the current traffic-shaping statistics. The command output contains the fields listed in Table 8-3.

Table 8-3 The show traffic-shape statistics Command Output

Field	Description
Queue Depth	Number of messages in the queue.
Packets	Number of packets sent through the interface.
Bytes	Number of bytes sent through the interface.
Packets Delayed	Number of packets sent through the interface that were delayed in the traffic-shaping queue.
Bytes Delayed	Number of bytes sent through the interface that were delayed in the traffic-shaping queue.
Shaping Active	Contains yes when timers indicate that traffic shaping is occurring and no if traffic shaping does not occur.

Figure 8-7 maps the described fields to some sample output shown by the **show traffic-shape statistics** command.

Figure 8-7
The show traffic-shape statistics command includes the queue depth and the number of packets delayed.

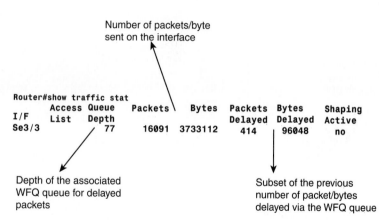

On-Demand Routing

The configuration of static routes is a fairly simple process in a hub-and-spoke Frame Relay topology, such as the network shown in Figure 8-8. However, many network administrators still view static routes as administratively undesirable. The difficulty is not so much adding routes as new stub networks are brought online, as it is remembering to remove routes when stub networks or stub routers are taken offline. Beginning with the release of IOS 11.2, Cisco offers a proprietary alternative for hub routers called on-demand routing (ODR).

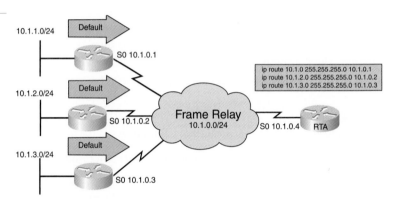

Figure 8-8
Although static routes can be used on both the spoke and hub routers, ODR presents a more scalable solution.

With ODR, a hub router can automatically discover stub networks while the stub routers still use a default route to the hub (see Figure 8-9). ODR conveys address prefixes—that is, only the network portion of the IP address as opposed to the entire address. The network portion does not have to be strictly *classful*; that is, Variable-Length Subnet Masking (VLSM) is supported. Further, because only minimal route information is traversing the link between the stub and hub routers, bandwidth is conserved.

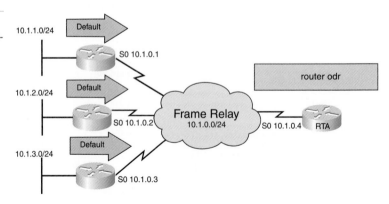

Figure 8-9
In an ODR configuration, spoke routers keep their default route, but the hub router learns about spoke networks dynamically through ODR.

ODR is not a true routing protocol. It discovers information about stub networks, but does not provide any routing information to the stub routers. The link information is conveyed by a data link protocol and, therefore, does not go further than from the stub router to the hub router. However, ODR-discovered routes can be redistributed into dynamic routing protocols.

Example 8-5 shows a routing table containing ODR entries. The table shows that the administrative distance is 160 and the metric of the routes is 1. Because ODR routes are always from a hub router to a stub router, the metric (hop count) is never more than 1.

Example 8-5 Sample Routing Table with ODR Entries

```
RTA#show ip route
Codes: C - connected, S - static, I - IGRP, R - RIP, M - mobile, B - BGP
       D - EIGRP, EX - EIGRP external, O - OSPF, IA - OSPF inter area
       N1 - OSPF NSSA external type 1, N2 - OSPF NSSA external type 2
       E1 - OSPF external type 1, E2 - OSPF external type 2, E - EGP
       i - IS-IS, L1 - IS-IS level-1, L2 - IS-IS level-2, ia – IS-IS inter area
       * - candidate default, U - per-user static route, o - ODR
       P - periodic downloaded static route


Gateway of last resort is not set
10.0.0.0/8 is subnetted, 4 subnets, 1 mask
C    10.1.0.0/24 is directly connected, Serial0
o    10.1.1.0/24 [160/1] via 10.1.0.1, 00:00:32, Serial0

o    10.1.2.0/24 [160/1] via 10.1.0.2, 00:00:32, Serial0
o    10.1.3.0/24 [160/1] via 10.1.0.3, 00:00:32, Serial0
RTA#
```

The transport mechanism for ODR routes is the Cisco Discovery Protocol (CDP), a proprietary data-link protocol that gathers information about neighboring network devices. CDP runs on any media that supports the subnetwork access protocol (SNAP), which means that ODR also depends on SNAP support. Although CDP is enabled by default on all interfaces of all Cisco devices running IOS 10.3 and later, ODR support does not begin until Release 11.2. ODR is configured on the hub router only. However, the stub routers must run IOS 11.2 or later for the hub router to discover their attached networks.

ODR is enabled with a single command, **router odr**. No networks or other parameters must be specified. CDP is enabled by default; it needs to be enabled only if it has been turned off for some reason. The command to enable the CDP process on a router is **cdp run**. To enable CDP on a specific interface, the command is **cdp enable**.

Figure 8-10 shows a typical hub-and-spoke topology. To configure ODR, use the **router odr** command on the hub router. As long as all routers are running IOS 11.2 or later and the connecting medium supports SNAP (such as the Frame Relay shown), ODR is operational and the hub will learn the stub networks. The only configuration necessary at the stub routers is a static default route to the hub router.

Figure 8-10
Baghdad is the hub router and can be configured for ODR.

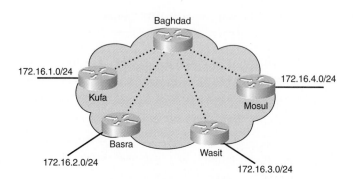

ODR routes can also be redistributed into routing protocols. If the Baghdad router in the graphic needed to advertise the ODR-discovered routes into OSPF, Baghdad's configuration could therefore include the commands shown in Example 8-6.

Example 8-6 Configuring ODR with Redistribution

```
Router odr
!
router ospf 1
redistribute odr metric 100 subnets
network 172.16.0.0 0.0.255.255 area 1
```

Summary

This chapter introduced the concept of traffic shaping, and provided examples and descriptions of commands that can be used for traffic shaping in a Frame Relay network. The three methods of Frame Relay traffic shaping presented are traffic shaping with rate enforcement, traffic shaping with rate adaption, and traffic shaping with queuing.

This chapter also introduced ODR, which can be used as an alternative to a routing protocol in Frame Relay hub-and-spoke networks. ODR allows administrators to easily manage the addition and removal of stub networks.

Review Questions

Use the following review questions to test your understanding of the concepts covered in this chapter. In some cases, there is more than one correct answer, so choose all that apply. Answers are listed in Appendix A, "Answers to Review Questions."

1. Which of the following terms is used to refer to the port speed of the router's interface connected to a local loop?

   A. CIR

   B. FECN

   C. Local access rate

   D. Committed access rate

2. Which of the following terms is used to refer to the guaranteed level of bandwidth agreed upon by the Frame Relay provider and customer?

   A. CIR

   B. FECN

   C. Local access rate

   D. Oversubscription

3. Which of the following is a Frame Relay congestion notification?

   A. CIR

   B. FECN

   C. BECN

   D. DE

4. Which of the following commands configures Frame Relay rate enforcement?

   A. (config-map-class)#frame-relay traffic-rate 9600 19200

   B. (config-subif)#frame-relay traffic-rate 9600 19200

   C. (config-map-class)#frame-relay adaptive-shaping becn

   D. (config-subif)#frame-relay adaptive-shaping becn

5. Which of the following commands configures Frame Relay rate adaption?

   A. (config-map-class)#frame-relay traffic-rate 9600 19200

   B. (config-subif)#frame-relay traffic-rate 9600 19200

   C. (config-map-class)#frame-relay adaptive-shaping becn

   D. (config-subif)#frame-relay adaptive-shaping becn

6. Which of the following commands enables Frame Relay traffic shaping?

   A. (config-map-class)#**frame-relay traffic-shaping**

   B. (config)#**traffic-shape**

   C. (config-if)# **frame-relay traffic-shaping**

   D. (config-if)#**traffic-shape**

7. What kinds of queuing are configured in conjunction with Frame Relay traffic shaping?

   A. FIFO

   B. WFQ

   C. Priority Queuing

   D. Custom Queuing

8. What is true about ODR?

   A. ODR is a routing protocol.

   B. ODR routes have an administrative distance of 60.

   C. ODR is primarily used in full-mesh Frame Relay networks.

   D. ODR requires CDP.

9. Which of the following commands enables ODR?

   A. (config)#**router odr**

   B. (config)#**router odr 10**

   C. (config)#**odr routing**

   D. (config)#**odr enable**

10. Which of the following commands is required in order for ODR routes to be propagated by EIGRP?

   A. (config-router)#**odr enable**

   B. (config-router)#**redistribute odr**

   C. (config-router)#**traffic-share odr**

   D. (config-router)#**odr traffic-share**

Key Terms

BECN (Backward Explicit Congestion Notification)   Bit set by a Frame Relay network in frames traveling in the opposite direction of frames encountering a congested path. Data terminal equipment (DTE) receiving frames with the BECN bit set can request that higher-level protocols take flow control action as appropriate.

Bc (Committed Burst)   Negotiated tariff metric in Frame Relay network. The maximum amount of data (in bits) that a Frame Relay network is committed to accept and transmit at the CIR.

DE (Discard Eligible)   If the network is congested, DE traffic can be dropped to ensure the delivery of higher priority traffic.

Be (Excess Burst)   Negotiated tariff metric in Frame Relay internetworks. The number of bits that a Frame Relay internetwork attempts to transmit after Bc is accommodated. Be data, in general, is delivered with a lower probability than Bc data because Be data can be marked as DE by the network.

FECN (Forward Explicit Congestion Notification)   Bit set by a Frame Relay network to inform the DTE receiving the frame that congestion was experienced in the path from source to destination. DTE receiving frames with the FECN bit set can request that higher-level protocols take flow-control action as appropriate.

Local access rate   The clock speed (port speed) of the connection (local loop) to the Frame Relay cloud. It is the rate at which data travels into or out of the network, regardless of other settings.

Oversubscription   Oversubscription is when the sum of the CIRs on all the VCs coming in to a device exceeds the access line speed. Oversubscription can also occur when the access line can support the sum of CIRs purchased, but not of the CIRs plus the bursting capacities of the VCs.

Traffic shaping   Configuration that limits surges that can congest a network. Data is buffered and then sent into the network in regulated amounts to ensure that the traffic fits within the promised parameters. Also called *smoothing*.

Objectives

After completing this chapter, you will be able to perform tasks related to the following:

- Configuring dial-backup
- Configuring load-backup
- Routing with load-backup
- Configuring DDR backup with the Dialer Watch feature
- Verifying dial-backup configurations

Chapter 9

WAN Backup Connections

Introduction

In today's enterprise, Frame Relay Permanent Virtual Circuits (PVCs) and leased lines typically connect remote sites that require continuous access to the central site. How can you maintain connectivity between two sites if the permanent connection goes down? One way is to configure a backup solution using a dial-up technology, such as plain ordinary telephone service (POTS) or Integrated Services Digital Network (ISDN). This technique is called *dial-backup*.

A dial-backup link can be established after the primary link fails, or after the primary link reaches a pre-defined utilization level. In both cases, the backup link provides temporary bandwidth.

This chapter describes how to configure dial-backup and load-backup, including how to do so using dialer profiles. In addition, this chapter discusses routing issues when using a secondary link, specifically with OSPF, Interior Gateway Routing Protocol (IGRP), and Enhanced Interior Gateway Routing Protocol (EIGRP). Finally, this chapter looks at how to configure dial-backup using DDR and the Dial Watch feature.

Configuring Dial-Backup

As a networking professional, you might determine that certain mission-critical applications require additional WAN links to prevent downtime. You can provision multiple T1s for a particular application and even back that up with a Frame Relay PVC. Although you might lease additional lines for backup purposes, you will still use these lines for load balancing or to route certain traffic. Strictly speaking, such links are redundant links, not backup links.

From the point of view of the Cisco IOS, backup links are dial-up technologies. A *backup interface* is an interface that stays shut down until one of two things happens to the primary link:

- The primary link goes down.
- The primary link reaches or exceeds an administratively defined load.

The *primary link* is typically a Frame Relay PVC, or a leased line.

NOTE

If you administratively shut down the primary interface, the backup interface will not activate.

A backup interface can be a physical interface, or a logical interface such as a dialer profile. Typical backup interfaces include ISDN Basic Rate Interface (BRI) and asynchronous interfaces. Serial interfaces connected to either an asynchronous modem or ISDN BRI can also be backup interfaces. The backup interface and its associated WAN connection are also called the *secondary link*. Figure 9-1 illustrates an ISDN secondary link, which backs up a Frame Relay primary link.

Figure 9-1
RTA uses ISDN BRI as a secondary link to RTB.

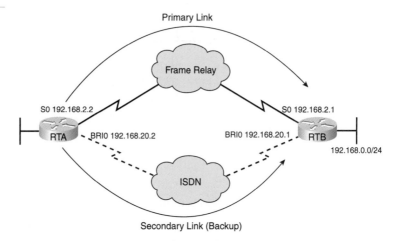

Configuring a backup link requires only two commands:

```
Router(config-if)#backup interface interface-type number
Router(config-if)#backup delay {enable-delay | never} {disable-delay | never}
```

After configuring the primary interface with a Layer-3 address and Layer-2 encapsulation, you can use the **backup interface** command to specify which interface is used as the backup. You can then use the **backup delay** command to configure how long the router must wait to bring up the secondary link after the primary interface fails. The **backup delay** command is also used to configure how long to wait before disabling the secondary link after the primary interface comes back up.

Table 9-1 describes the parameters that you can use with the **backup delay** command.

Table 9-1   Syntax Description for the backup delay Command

enable-delay	Number of seconds that elapse after the primary line goes down.
disable-delay	Number of seconds that elapse after the primary line comes up before the secondary line is deactivated.
never	Prevents the secondary line from being activated or deactivated.

After you use the **backup interface** command to specify a backup interface, the router places that interface in *standby mode*. In standby mode, an interface cannot be used to accept calls. Moreover, an interface in standby mode cannot be used to make a call using DDR. The only call a backup interface can make is for the purposes of establishing the backup link. For more details, see the section, "Standby Mode" later in this chapter.

In Figure 9-1, interface serial 0 (S0) is the primary interface. Example 9-1 shows the commands needed to configure serial 0 to use BRI0 as the backup interface.

Example 9-1 Configuring a Backup Interface

```
RTA(config)#interface serial 0
RTA(config-if)#backup interface bri0
RTA(config-if)#backup delay 20 15
```

The **backup delay 20 15** command configures the backup link to activate after the primary has been down for 20 seconds. The backup link stays active until the primary link has come back up, and has stayed up for 15 seconds.

By configuring the router to wait several seconds before bringing up the backup interface, you prevent a flapping interface from initiating a dial connection (which is typically a toll call). Also, by configuring the router to wait before disabling the backup interface, you decrease the likelihood of a flapping interface prematurely terminating the dial-up session.

The **backup interface** command must be configured only on one side of the secondary link.

In cases when you are not using a dynamic routing protocol, you must configure a *floating static route* for the backup interface configuration to work. A *floating static route* is a static route that has an administrative distance greater than the administrative distance of corresponding dynamic routes. When using dial-backup and static routing, you need to configure a floating static route that uses the dialer interface (BRI, Async, Dialer, and so on).

NOTE

A *flapping* interface is an interface that is rapidly vacillating from an up state to a down state. Typically, faulty media or malfunctioning interfaces are the cause of flapping links.

Figure 9-2 presents a floating static route scenario. In this scenario, a floating static route is configured without using the **backup interface** command. This approach is favored by administrators who do not want to place a dialer interface in standby mode. RTA has the following dynamic route, learned through RIP:

```
R      192.168.0.0/24 [120/1] via 192.168.2.1, 00:00:25, Serial0
```

RIP's administrative distance is 120. You can configure a floating static route to the same network, but with a higher administrative distance, as shown here:

```
ip route 192.168.0.0 255.255.255.0 192.168.20.1 130
```

This route, with an administrative distance of 130, will not make it in the routing table until the dynamic route is lost due to a link failure, or some other cause. Thus, the BRI is not used to teach 192.168.0.0/24 when the dynamic route is available.

Figure 9-2
RTA is configured with a floating static route so that it uses BRI0 to reach 192.168.0.0/24 in the event that its serial interface goes down.

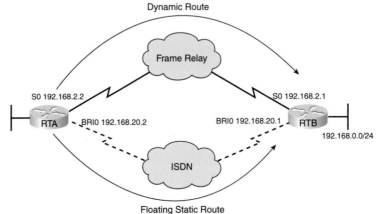

Using Dial-Backup to Support the Primary Link

Using Dial-Backup to Support the Primary Link

You can configure dial-backup to activate the secondary link after the primary reaches a certain level of utilization. During periods of high utilization, you can use the secondary link and the primary link at the same time, which reduces the load on the primary link. The Cisco IOS monitors the traffic load and computes a five-minute moving average every 5 seconds (see Chapter 4's sidebar, "Tech Note: Calculating Load on an Interface"). If this average exceeds the value you set for the line (as shown in Figure 9-3), the secondary line is activated. Depending on the configuration, some or all of the traffic flows onto the secondary dial-up line.

Figure 9-3
RTX activates the
secondary link after
the primary reaches
75 percent use.

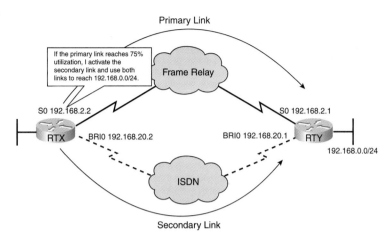

To configure a backup line to activate when the primary exceeds a certain threshold,
use the following commands:

```
Router(config-if)#backup interface interface-type number
Router(config-if)#backup load {enable-threshold | never} {disable-load | never}
```

The secondary line is disabled when one of the following conditions occurs:

- The transmitted load on the primary line plus the transmitted load on the
  secondary line is less than the value entered for the disable-load argument.
  This value is a percentage of the primary link's bandwidth.
- The received load on the primary line plus the received load on the secondary
  line is less than the value entered for the disable-load argument.

Table 9-2 describes the parameters that you can use with the **backup load** command.

Table 9-2   Syntax Description for the backup load Command

enable-threshold	Percentage of available bandwidth of the primary line that the traffic load must *exceed* to enable dial backup (five minute moving average).
disable-load	Percentage of available bandwidth of the primary line that the traffic load must be *less than* to disable dial backup.
never	Prevents the secondary line from being activated or deactivated.

NOTE

The **backup load**
command cannot
be configured on
Frame Relay sub-
interfaces.

To configure RTX in Figure 9-3, use the following commands, shown in Example 9-2.

Example 9-2 Using the backup load command

```
RTX(config)#interface serial 0
RTX(config-if)#backup interface bri0
RTX(config-if)#backup load 75 10
```

In Figure 9-3, interface serial 0 is RTX's primary interface. The **backup interface bri0** command specifies that BRI0 is the backup interface. The **backup load 75 10** command instructs the router to bring the secondary interface up after the primary reaches 75 percent load. The secondary link deactivates after the primary link traffic load drops to 10 percent use.

Use both the **backup delay** and **backup load** commands to configure a backup interface to activate either when the primary link fails or when the primary link reaches a certain load threshold.

Standby Mode

When a backup interface is specified on a primary line, the backup interface is placed in *standby mode* (as shown by the shaded portion of Example 9-3). When in standby mode, the backup interface is effectively shut down until enabled. The backup route between the two company sites is not usable and it does not appear in the routing table.

Example 9-3 Verify the Backup Interface's Status

```
RTA#show interface bri0
BRI0 is standby mode, line protocol is down
  Hardware is PQUICC BRI with U interface
  Internet address is 192.168.20.2/24
  MTU 1500 bytes, BW 64 Kbit, DLY 20000 usec,
      reliability 252/255, txload 1/255, rxload 1/255
  Encapsulation PPP, loopback not set
  Last input 00:00:21, output never, output hang never
  Last clearing of "show interface" counters 01:52:18
  Input queue: 0/75/87 (size/max/drops); Total output drops: 0
  Qeueuing strategy: weighted fair
  Output queue: 0/1000/64/0 (size/max total/threshold/drops)
      Conversations  0/1/16 (active/max active/max total)
      Reserved Conversations 0/0 (allocated/max allocated)
```

Example 9-3 Verify the Backup Interface's Status (Continued)

```
5 minute input rate 0 bits/sec, 0 packets/sec
5 minute output rate 0 bits/sec, 0 packets/sec
   155 packets input, 738 bytes, 0 no buffer
   Received 0 broadcasts, 0 runts, 0 giants, 0 throttles
   87 input errors, 87 CRC, 0 frame, 0 overrun, 0 ignored, 56 abort
   188 packets output, 1029 bytes, 0 underruns
   0 output errors, 0 collisions, 13 interface resets
   0 output buffer failures, 0 output buffers swapped out
   41 carrier transitions
```

The primary link shown in Figure 9-4 is the only route appearing in the routing table.
The branch-office router (RTA) continues to monitor the following two events:

- Carrier detect
- Keepalives

If RTA does not receive either a keepalive or a carrier-detect response, it assumes that
the primary line is down and activates the backup link. If a primary line fails, the primary interface goes down and the backup is enabled. The routing table now reflects
the backup route as the only usable route between the two company sites.

Figure 9-4
On RTA, BRI0 is in
standby mode until
the primary inter-
face fails, or until
load on the primary
interface reaches a
certain percentage.

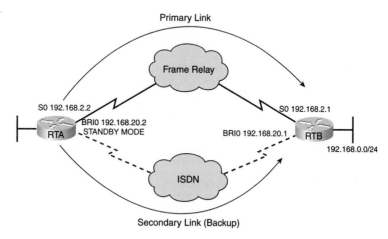

If a physical link is used as a backup to a primary connection, it is in standby mode
and cannot be used as a link to another site.

In Figure 9-5, RTA wants to back up its Frame Relay connection with ISDN BRI. RTA also wants to use the same BRI interface as a dial-on-demand routing (DDR) link to RTC. If Branch Office A places the physical BRI link in standby mode, it is deactivated and does not activate until the primary line fails or reaches a specified threshold. Thus, the BRI link cannot be used to connect to RTC.

Figure 9-5
With its BRI0 in standby mode, RTA cannot use it to place DDR calls, even when the secondary link is inactive.

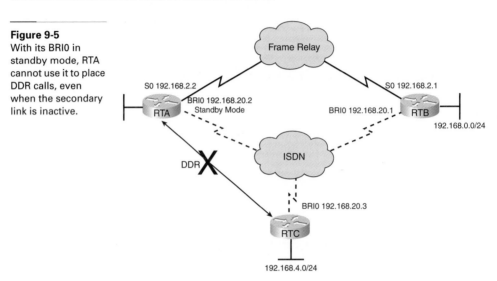

Using Dialer Profiles as Backup Interfaces

With dialer profiles, the BRI connection in Figure 9-5 can be used to back up the primary Frame Relay link between RTA and RTB. At the same time, it can be configured for DDR between RTA and RTC. With dialer profiles, the same physical interface can assume multiple logical configurations (see Figure 9-6).

Figure 9-6
Dialer profiles can be used to apply either a DDR or dial-backup configuration to the same interface.

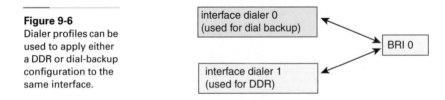

To prevent a physical interface from being locked into standby mode, configure a dialer profile to act as the backup line. This profile is in standby mode until engaged. You can then configure another dialer profile for DDR. To complete your configuration, make the physical interface a member of the appropriate dialer pool, or pools, so that both profiles can use the interface.

For example, consider RTA in Figure 9-5. Rather than locking BRI0 in as the secondary interface, you can configure the primary interface (serial 0) to use interface dialer 0. Example 9-4 shows the commands that are used to make the dialer profile a backup interface.

Example 9-4 Configuring a Dialer Profile as a Backup Interface

```
RTA(config)#interface serial 0
RTA(config-if)#backup interface dialer 0
RTA(config-if)#backup delay 25 20
```

Meanwhile, you can configure two or more dialer profiles. Example 9-5 presents two sample configurations.

Example 9-5 Sample Dialer Profiles for dial-backup and DDR

```
interface Dialer0
 ip address 192.168.20.2 255.255.255.0
 encapsulation ppp
 dialer remote-name RTB
 dialer string 5551111
 dialer pool 1
 ppp authentication chap pap
!
interface Dialer1
ip address 192.168.10.2 255.255.255.0
 encapsulation ppp
 dialer remote-name RTC
 dialer string 5552222
 dialer pool 1
 dialer-group 4
 ppp authentication chap
```

Finally, Example 9-6 shows how you can assign a physical interface to be a member of the dialer pool (or dialer pools) associated with both the dial-backup and DDR profiles.

Example 9-6 Assigning a Physical Interface to Dialer Pools

```
RTA(config)#interface bri0
RTA(config-if)#dialer pool-member 1
```

Using dialer profiles for dial-backup has tremendous advantages, especially with ISDN BRI. Because ISDN BRI is typically more costly than POTS, it is important to maximize your ISDN resources. When you use a BRI for dial-backup without dialer profiles, neither of the B channels can be used while the interface is in standby mode. After the backup is initiated over one B channel, the second B channel remains unavailable for use by DDR. If you configure dial-backup with dialer profiles, it is possible to use one B channel for DDR and the other for dial-backup simultaneously.

Routing with the Load-Backup Feature

When using the load-backup feature, load sharing and load balancing work differently depending on the routing protocol used. After the secondary link is made active, the router must decide how to use the secondary path. Virtually all interior gateway routing protocols keep and use multiple routes to the same destination. However, some routing protocols, such as OSPF, will not install additional routes to a network unless they have a metric equal to the best route. IGRP and EIGRP will not use routes of unequal metrics unless an administrator configures them to do so.

The following sections describe load-backup issues and configuration strategies with OSPF and IGRP/EIGRP.

Load Backup with OSPF

If you are using OSPF, the load-backup feature load shares between the primary and backup links after the backup link is activated, but only if certain conditions are met.

> **NOTE**
>
> Configuring OSPF over dial-up links is typically done using the on-demand circuit feature. See Chapter 4's Tech Note, "Configuring OSPF over On-Demand Circuits," for more information.

OSPF uses cost as the sole routing metric. Cost is based on bandwidth. For example, a 64-kbps link gets a metric of 1562, while a T1 link gets a metric of 604. Unless both the primary link and the secondary link have the same cost (which is unlikely unless your primary link is 128 Kbps or less), OSPF will not install both routes in the routing table. If one link has a lower cost than the other, all routing occurs over the link with the lower cost, even if both lines are up (see Figure 9-7).

When the OSPF interface costs for the primary and secondary links are unequal, you can configure the costs to be the same by using the following command:

```
Router(config-if)#ip ospf cost interface-cost
```

OSPF's cost can be a value in the range from 1 to 65,535.

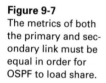

Figure 9-7
The metrics of both the primary and secondary link must be equal in order for OSPF to load share.

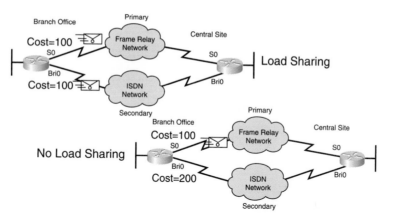

Load Backup with IGRP and EIGRP

By default, IGRP and EIGRP do not use more than one route to a destination unless the routes have equal metrics. You can tweak the IGRP/EIGRP metric values of the primary and secondary links so that both routes have equal metrics. However, this method is not recommended because, unlike OSPF, EIGRP and IGRP can be configured to use unequal-cost routes to the same destination.

Use the **variance** *multiplier* command to configure unequal-cost load balancing by defining the difference between the best metric and the worst acceptable metric. Setting this value lets the router determine the feasibility of a potential route. A route is feasible if the next router in the path is closer to the destination than the current local router, and if the metric for the entire path is within the variance. Only paths that are feasible can be used for load balancing and can be included in the routing table.

In Figure 9-8, RTA's EIGRP routing process has two 192.168.0.0/24 routes to choose from after the secondary link becomes active. In this case, EIGRP chooses only the route using the primary link because its metric of 5,639,936 is better than the metric of the secondary route, which is 40,640,000.

For the secondary link to be of any use, you must configure the variance multiplier (see Example 9-7).

Example 9-7 Using the Variance Command

```
RTA(config)#router eigrp 1
RTA(config-router)#variance 10
```

Figure 9-8
EIGRP chooses the route(s) with the best metric, unless the variance value is configured to allow for unequal-cost load sharing.

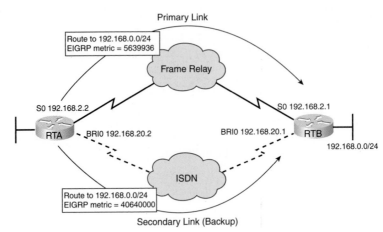

IGRP also uses the variance command, with the same effect.

This increases the poorest allowable metric to 56,399,360 (10 * 5,639,936 = 56,399,360). EIGRP includes all the routes that have a metric under 56,399,360, which includes the route using the secondary link (40,640,000). Example 9-8 shows what RTA's routing table looks like after setting the variance to 10. Both routes to 192.168.0.0/24 are installed in the routing table.

Example 9-8 RTA's Routing Table

```
RTA>show ip route
Codes: C - connected, S - static, I - IGRP, R - RIP, M - mobile, B - BGP
       D - EIGRP, EX - EIGRP external, O - OSPF, IA - OSPF inter area
       N1 - OSPF NSSA external type 1, N2 - OSPF NSSA external type 2
       E1 - OSPF external type 1, E2 - OSPF external type 2, E - EGP
       i - IS-IS, L1 - IS-IS level-1, L2 - IS-IS level-2, * - candidate default
       U - per-user static route, o - ODR


Gateway of last resort is not set

C       192.168.6.0/24 is directly connected, Ethernet0
        192.168.20.0/24 is variably subnetted, 2 subnets, 2 masks
C       192.168.20.0/24 is directly connected, BRI0
C       192.168.20.2/32 is directly connected, BRI0
D    192.168.0.0/8 [90/5639936] via 192.168.2.1, 00:00:24, Serial0
                   [90/40640000] via 192.168.20.1, 00:00:24, BRI0
C    192.168.2.0/24 is directly connected, Serial0
```

Verifying Dial-Backup Configurations

To verify a backup line link for a primary line connection, enter the **show interface** *type number* command. The primary interface output shown in Example 9-9 illustrates that Dialer1 is specified as a backup, if the serial interface fails. The first shaded line in the output shows that the backup is enabled 20 seconds after the primary interface fails and is deactivated 40 seconds after the serial interface reactivates. The second shaded line shows that the backup interface is activated if load on the primary reaches or exceeds 60 percent (kickin load). The backup is deactivated after load on the primary interface reaches 10 percent (kickout load).

Example 9-9 Verifying dial-backup Using the show interface Command

```
Capetown#show interface s0/0
Serial0/0 is up, line protocol is up
  Hardware is PowerQUICC Serial
  Internet address is 192.168.192.4/24
  Backup interface BRI0/0, failure delay 20 sec, secondary disable delay 40 sec,
  kickin load 60%, kickout load 10%
  MTU 1500 bytes, BW 384 Kbit, DLY 20000 usec,
     reliability 255/255, txload 1/255, rxload 1/255
  Encapsulation FRAME-RELAY, loopback not set
<output omitted>
```

You can use the **show backup** command to output status information on all configured backup interfaces. Example 9-10 shows the output of this command before the backup interface is activated, Example 9-11 shows the output of this command when the backup interface is active due to primary link failure, and Example 9-12 shows the output of this command when the backup interface is active for load backup.

Example 9-10 Using the show backup Command (Secondary Interface in Standby)

```
RTA#show backup
Primary Interface    Secondary Interface   Status
-----------------    -------------------   ------
Serial0/0            BRI0/0                normal operation
```

Example 9-11 Using the show backup Command (Primary Interface Down)

```
RTA#show backup
Primary Interface    Secondary Interface   Status
```

continues

Example 9-11 *Using the show backup Command (Primary Interface Down) (Continued)*

```
. . . . . . . . . . . . . . . . .      . . . . . . . . . . . . . . . . . .       . . . . . .
Serial0/0               BRI0/0                      backup mode
```

Example 9-12 *Using the show backup Command (Primary Interface over Load Threshold)*

```
RTA#show backup
Primary Interface    Secondary Interface    Status
. . . . . . . . . . . . . . . . .      . . . . . . . . . . . . . . . . . .       . . . . . .
Serial0/0               BRI0/0                      overload mode
```

Configuring Dial-Backup Using Dialer Watch

Using the backup interface feature might not provide optimum performance on some networks, such as those using Frame Relay multipoint subinterfaces or Frame Relay connections that do not support end-to-end PVC status updates. The Dialer Watch needs to be used in such cases.

Dialer Watch is a backup feature that integrates dial-backup with routing capabilities. Dialer Watch provides reliable connectivity without relying solely on defining interesting traffic to trigger outgoing calls at the central router. Hence, Dialer Watch can also be considered regular DDR with no requirement for interesting traffic other than lost routes. By configuring a set of watched routes that define the primary interface, you are able to monitor and track the status of the primary interface as watched routes are added and deleted.

Monitoring the watched routes is done in the following sequence:

1. Whenever a watched route is deleted, Dialer Watch checks to see if there is at least one valid route for any of the defined watched IP addresses.

2. If no valid route exists, the primary line is considered down and unusable.

3. If a valid route exists for at least one of the defined IP addresses, and if the route is pointing to an interface other than the backup interface configured for Dialer Watch, the primary link is considered up.

4. In the primary link goes down, Dialer Watch is immediately notified by the routing protocol and the secondary link is brought up.

5. After the secondary link is up, at the expiration of each idle timeout, the primary link is rechecked.

6. If the primary link remains down, the idle timer is indefinitely reset.

7. If the primary link is up, the secondary backup link is disconnected. Additionally, you can set a disable timer to create a delay for the secondary link to disconnect, after the primary link is reestablished.

Dialer Watch provides the following advantages:

- **Routing**—Backup initialization is linked to the dynamic routing protocol, rather than a specific interface or static route entry. Therefore, both primary and backup interfaces can be any interface type, and can be used across multiple interfaces and multiple routers. Dialer Watch also relies on convergence, which is sometimes preferred over traditional DDR links.

- **Routing protocol independent**—Static routes or dynamic routing protocols, such as IGRP, EIGRP, or OSPF can be used.

- **Nonpacket semantics**—Dialer Watch does not exclusively rely on interesting packets to trigger dialing. The link is automatically brought up when the primary line goes down without postponing dialing.

- **Dial backup reliability**—DDR redial functionality is extended to dial indefinitely in the event that secondary backup lines are not initiated. Typically, DDR redial attempts are affected by enable-timeouts and wait-for-carrier time values. Intermittent media difficulties or flapping interfaces can cause problems for traditional DDR links. However, Dialer Watch automatically reestablishes the secondary backup line on ISDN, synchronous, and asynchronous serial links.

To support Dialer Watch, the router must be configured for DDR. Currently, the Dialer Watch feature only supports IP.

Configuring Dialer Watch

Perform the following tasks to configure Dialer Watch. All tasks are required, except the last task, to set a disable timer:

- Determine the Primary and Secondary Interfaces
- Determine the Interface Addresses and Networks to Watch
- Configure the Interface to Perform DDR Backup
- Create a Dialer List
- Set the Disable Timer on the Backup Interface (optional)

Decide which interfaces on which routers are to act as primary and secondary interfaces. Unlike traditional backup methods, you can define multiple interfaces on multiple routers instead of a singly defined interface on one router.

Determine which addresses and networks are to be monitored or watched. Typically, this is an interface on a remote router or a network advertised by a central or remote router.

To initiate Dialer Watch, you must configure the interface to perform DDR and backup. Use traditional DDR configuration commands, such as dialer maps, for DDR capabilities. To enable Dialer Watch on the backup interface, perform the following task in interface configuration mode:

```
dialer watch-group group-number
```

To define the IP addresses you want watched, use the following command in global configuration mode:

```
dialer watch-list group-number ip ip-address address-mask
```

The **dialer watch-list** command is the means to detect if the primary interface is up or down. The primary interface is determined to be up when there is an available route with a valid metric to any of the addresses defined in this list, and it points to an interface other than the interface on which the **dialer watch-group** is defined. The primary interface is determined to be down when there is no available route to any of the addresses defined in the **dialer watch-list** command.

Under some conditions, you might want to implement a delay before the backup interface is dropped after the primary interface recovers. This delay can ensure stability, especially for flapping interfaces or interfaces experiencing frequent route changes. To apply a disable time, use the following command in interface configuration mode:

```
dialer-watch-disable seconds
```

Dialer Watch Configuration Example

In Figure 9-9, RTA and RTB are connected through Frame Relay. RTC is configured to perform Dialer Watch and it watches networks 3.0.0.0, 4.0.0.0, and 5.0.0.0. If routing updates are deleted for these three networks, RTC implements Dialer Watch by initiating the call to RTA.

Examples 9-13, 9-14, and 9-15 present the relevant configurations for RTA, RTB, and RTC, respectively. Only RTC is configured with the Dialer Watch feature.

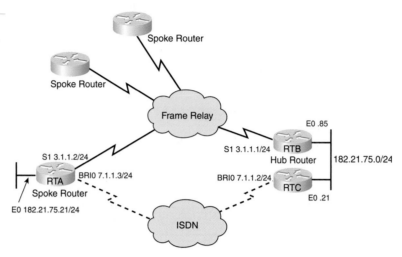

Figure 9-9
Dialer Watch is configured on RTC to back up the Frame Relay link between RTA and RTB.

Example 9-13 Dialer Watch Scenario Configuration for RTA

```
! Remote site username and password.
username RTC password cisco
interface ethernet0
 ip address 182.21.75.21 255.255.255.0
interface serial1
 ! This is Primary interface on the remote end
 ip address 3.1.1.2 255.255.255.0
 encapsulation frame-relay
 frame-relay map ip 3.1.1.1 100
!
interface bri0
 ! This is where the secondary dials in. This router does not require a dialer map
 ! statement because it is receiving the call.
 ip address 7.1.1.3 255.255.255.0
 encapsulation ppp
 ! The dialer idle-timeout command prevents premature hangup
 dialer idle-timeout 10000
 dialer-group 1
 ppp authentication chap
```

continues

Example 9-13 Dialer Watch Scenario Configuration for RTA (Continued)

```
!
access-list 100 permit ip any any
dialer-list 1 protocol ip list 100
!
! The interfaces are configured to use EIGRP routing
router eigrp 190
network 3.0.0.0
network 7.0.0.0
network 182.21.0.0
!
end
```

Example 9-14 Dialer Watch Scenario Configuration for RTB

```
interface Ethernet0
 ! RTB and RTC are on same LAN
 ip address 172.21.24.85 255.255.255.0

interface serial1
 ! This is the Primary multipoint interface
 ip address 3.1.1.1 255.255.255.0
 encapsulation frame-relay
 frame-relay map ip 3.1.1.2 200
 frame-relay map ip 3.1.1.3 300
 frame-relay map ip 3.1.1.4 400

! The interfaces are configured to use EIGRP routing
router eigrp 190
network 3.0.0.0
network 172.21.0.0
!
end
```

Example 9-15 Dialer Watch Scenario Configuration for RTC

```
! Remote site username and password.
username RTA password cisco
interface Ethernet0
 ! This is in the same LAN as RTB Ethernet 0
 ip address 172.21.24.86 255.255.255.0
!
interface bri0
 ! This is the secondary backup line
 ip address 7.1.1.2 255.255.255.0
 encapsulation ppp
 dialer idle-timeout 5
 ! Use a dialer map for the IP address/network which is the same network as
 ! being watched
 dialer map ip 3.1.1.0 name RTA 5551111 broadcast
 ! Add a dialer map for remote end's IP address to make routing work over this
interface
 dialer map ip 7.1.1.3 name RTA 5551111 broadcast
 dialer-group 1
 ! Enable Dialer Watch on this interface
 dialer watch-group 1
 ppp authentication chap
!
! The interfaces are configured to use EIGRP routing
router eigrp 190
network 7.0.0.0
network 172.21.0.0
!
access-list 100 deny    eigrp any any
access-list 100 permit ip any any
! Watch IP network 3.1.1.0
dialer watch-list 1 ip 3.1.1.0 255.255.255.0
dialer-list 1 protocol ip list 100
!
end
```

This multiple router backup example scenario highlights the strengths of the Dialer Watch feature. RTC's BRI backs up RTB's serial interface. Also, this configuration shows how Dialer Watch can be used with a multipoint Frame Relay connection. In contrast, the backup interface feature is not designed to support multiple router backup, or per-PVC backup.

Although Dialer Watch can support a more complex variety of configurations, it is more difficult to configure than a backup interface. Table 9-3 summarizes the characteristics of the three dial backup methods.

Table 9-3   Summary of Dial Backup Methods

Backup Interface	Floating Static Route	Dialer Watch
Easiest to configure.	Moderately difficult to configure.	More difficult to configure.
Dependent on line protocol status of primary interface and requires that the primary interface go down.	Employs static routes with higher administrative distance to trigger DDR call.	Watches specific routes in the routing table and initiates backup link if the route is missing.
Encapsulation is a factor. For example, Frame Relay backup might not work correctly with backup interface.	Encapsulation independent.	Encapsulation independent.
Does not consider end-to-end connectivity. Problems with end-to-end connectivity, such as routing errors, do not trigger backup links.	Evaluates status of primary link based on the existence of routes to the peer. Hence it considers primary link status based on the ability to pass traffic to the peer.	Evaluates status of primary link based on the existence of routes to the peer. Hence it considers primary link status based on the ability to pass traffic to the peer.
Needs interesting traffic to trigger dialing the backup link.	Needs interesting traffic to trigger dialing the backup link even after the route to the peer is lost.	Does not rely exclusively on interesting packets to trigger dialing. Dialing the backup link is done immediately when the primary route is lost.

Table 9-3   Summary of Dial Backup Methods (Continued)

Backup Interface	Floating Static Route	Dialer Watch
Routing protocol independent.	Dependent on the routing protocol convergence time.	Dependent on the routing protocol convergence time.
Routing protocol independent.	All routing protocols supported.	EIGRP/IGRP/OSPF supported.
Limited to one router, one interface.	Typically limited to single router, but with multiple interface/networks.	Supports multiple router backup scenario. For example, one router monitors the link between two other routers and initiates the backup if that link fails.
Can be used to provide bandwidth on demand. The backup interface can be set up to activate when the primary link reaches a specified threshold.	Bandwidth on demand is not possible because the route to the peer exists regardless of the load on the primary link.	Bandwidth on demand is not possible because the route to the peer exists regardless of the load on the primary link.

Summary

In this chapter, you learned how to configure a backup connection that activates upon primary line failures, or when the primary line reaches a specified threshold. You learned how to configure a dialer interface to act as a backup to physical interfaces. You also learned how to configure the Dialer Watch feature.

Review Questions

Use the following review questions to test your understanding of the concepts covered in this chapter. In some cases, there is more than one correct answer, so choose all that apply. Answers are listed in Appendix A, "Answers to Review Questions."

1. Which circumstances can activate a backup interface?

    A. Primary interface is administratively shut down.

    B. Primary interface reaches or exceeds a load threshold.

    C. Primary interface goes down due to link failure.

    D. Secondary interface receives DDR traffic.

2. Which of the following commands configures BRI0 to activate 30 seconds after Serial0 fails?

    A. (config-if)#**backup interface bri0**
       (config-if)#**backup delay 20 30**

    B. (config-if)#**backup interface bri0**
       (config-if)#**backup delay 30 20**

    C. (config-if)#**backup interface serial0**
       (config-if)#**backup delay 20 30**

    D. (config-if)#**backup interface serial0**
       (config-if)#**backup delay 30 20**

3. Which of the following configures BRI0 to back up Serial0?

    A. (config)#**interface serial0**
       (config-if)#**backup interface bri0**

    B. (config)#**interface bri0**
       (config-if)#**backup interface serial0**

    C. (config)#**interface bri0**
       (config-if)#**interface backup serial0**

    D. (config)#**interface serial0**
       (config-if)#**interface backup serial0**

4. Which of the following commands activates the backup interface after load on the primary interface reaches or exceeds a 70 percent load?

   A. (config-if)#**backup load 30 70**

   B. (config-if)#**backup load 70 30**

   C. (config-if)#**load backup 30 70**

   D. (config-if)#**load backup 70 30**

5. While the primary interface is up and under load, what mode is a backup interface in?

   A. Backup

   B. Administrative shutdown

   C. Spoofing

   D. Standby

6. Which of the following commands assigns a dialer profile as the backup interface?

   A. (config-if)#**interface dialer0**

   B. (config-if)#**backup interface dialer-pool 1**

   C. (config-if)#**backup interface dialer0**

   D. (config-if)#**interface backup dialer0**

7. Which of the following commands can be used to modify the cost of an OSPF interface?

   A. (config)#**ip ospf cost 10**

   B. (config-if)#**ip ospf cost 10**

   C. (config-if)#**ospf cost 10**

   D. (config)#**ospf cost 10**

8. Which of the following commands is used to configure IGRP and EIGRP to use unequal-cost load balancing?

   A. (config-route-map)#**variance** *multiplier*

   B. (config)#**variance** *multiplier*

   C. (config-if)#**variance** *multiplier*

   D. (config-router)#**variance** *multiplier*

9. Which of the following commands can be used to determine the state of a backup interface?

   A. show interface

   B. show backup interface

   C. show backup

   D. show interface backup

10. What does "kickout load 20%" mean?

   A. The secondary interface deactivates after its load drops to 20 percent.

   B. The secondary interface deactivates after its combined load on the primary and secondary interfaces drops to 20 percent or less.

   C. The secondary interface deactivates after the load on the primary link drops to 20 percent or less.

   D. The secondary interface deactivates after its transmit load (txload) drops to 20 percent or less.

Key Terms

Backup interface   An interface that remains in standby mode until the primary link goes down, or until the load on the primary link reaches (or exceeds) a predefined threshold.

Floating static route   An administratively defined route that is assigned an administrative distance, which is higher than an existing route. A floating static route is not installed in the routing table until the route with the lower administrative distance is flushed from the table.

Primary link   A WAN link, such as a leased line or PVC, that is assigned a backup interface.

Secondary link   A backup WAN link that is activated after the primary link fails, or after the primary link reaches (or exceeds) a predefined load threshold.

Standby mode   On a backup interface, an interface state wherein the interface is shut down and awaiting primary link failure, or primary link overload.

Objectives

After completing this chapter, you will be able to perform tasks related to the following:

- FIFO queuing
- Weighted fair queuing
- Priority queuing
- Custom queuing
- Compression

Chapter 10

Queuing and Compression

Introduction

With today's applications placing an increasing emphasis on bandwidth, a remote site's need for bandwidth increases even if business doesn't. It is common for a remote site to outgrow its WAN connection. For example, consider a small branch office that was originally allocated an Integrated Services Digital Network Basic Rate Interface (ISDN BRI). What if this office experiences a rapid increase in productivity or sales? More employees and more transactions result in greater bandwidth demands as data flows to and from the central site.

When a remote site's bandwidth demands outstrip its link's capacity, the best solution is to provision more bandwidth. However, in some cases, leasing an additional line or adding additional circuits might not be practical, especially if the bandwidth demands are sudden and unexpected.

This chapter discusses queuing and compression. These two techniques are used to handle congestion on WAN links, particularly links that offer less than T1/E1 bandwidth (1.544/2.048) Mbps.

Queuing Overview

Routers have a protocol-dependent switching process that handles traffic as it arrives on an interface. The switching process includes the delivery of traffic to an outgoing interface *buffer*. A *buffer* is an area of memory that is used to store data that is awaiting action. If the outgoing interface is congested, the interface buffer fills with traffic waiting to be sent (see Figure 10-1). When the router is able to send traffic out the interface, it must choose which of the packets waiting in the buffers to send first.

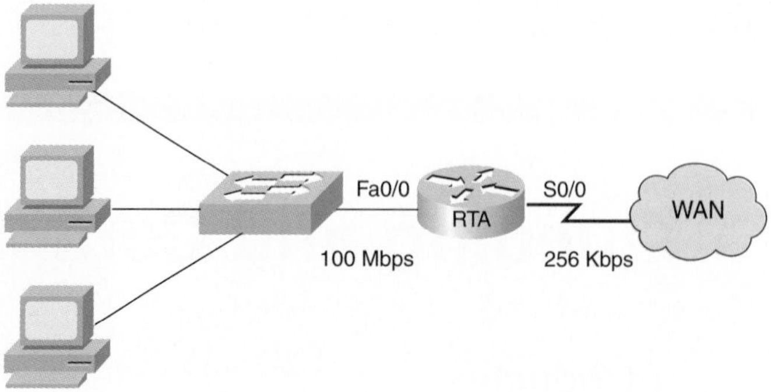

Figure 10-1
Speed mismatch is
the most frequent
cause of congestion.

Fa0/0   RTA   S0/0   WAN

100 Mbps   256 Kbps

It seems obvious to conclude that a router should send the packet that has been waiting in the buffer the longest before it sends any other packet. However, there are many cases where sending the first packet to arrive is not desirable. In some cases, there is more important data that should be given priority and sent first, even if it wasn't received first.

Queuing refers to the process the router uses to schedule packets for transmission during periods of congestion. You can configure a congested router to reorder packets so that mission-critical and delay-sensitive traffic gets sent out first—even if other low-priority packets arrive before them.

The Cisco IOS supports four methods of queuing, as described in the following sections: *first-in, first out* (FIFO) *queuing*; *priority queuing* (PQ); *custom queuing* (CQ); and *weighted fair queuing* (WFQ). Only one of these queuing methods can be applied per interface, because each method handles traffic in a unique way:

- **FIFO**—FIFO entails no concept of priority or classes of traffic. With FIFO, transmission of packets out the interface occurs in the order the packets arrive.
- **WFQ**—WFQ offers dynamic, fair queuing that divides bandwidth across queues of traffic based on weights. (WFQ ensures that all traffic is treated fairly, given its weight. To help understand how WFQ works, consider the queue for a series of File Transfer Protocol (FTP) packets as a queue for the collective, and the queue for discrete interactive traffic packets as a queue for the individual. Given the weight of the queues, WFQ ensures that for all FTP packets sent as a collective an equal number of individual interactive traffic packets are sent.)

  Given this handling, WFQ ensures satisfactory response time to critical applications, such as interactive, transaction-based applications, that are intolerant of performance degradation. For serial interfaces at E1 (2.048 Mbps) and below, flow-based WFQ is used by default. When no other queuing strategies are configured, all other interfaces use FIFO by default.

- CQ—With CQ, bandwidth is allocated proportionally for each different class of traffic. CQ allows you to specify the number of bytes or packets to be drawn from the queue, which is especially useful on slow interfaces.
- PQ—With PQ, packets belonging to one priority class of traffic are sent before all lower priority traffic to ensure timely delivery of those packets.

FIFO queuing is the simplest algorithm for packet transmission. With FIFO, transmission occurs in the same order as messages are received. Until recently, FIFO queuing was the default for all router interfaces.

The biggest problem with FIFO queuing is that it sends out packets in the order they are received. Therefore, a small Telnet or voice packet could get stuck behind two or more large file transfer packets simply because of the order in which they arrive at the router. The end result is a delay in service or eventual timeout of a session associated with the smaller packets.

If traffic needs to be reordered, you must configure WFQ, CQ, or PQ.

The need to prioritize packets arises from the diverse mixture of protocols and applications found in today's networks.

Depending on the application and overall bandwidth, users may or may not perceive any real performance degradation when congestion is present. For example, end users are accustomed to waiting for a file to download when using a file transfer protocol such as FTP. If the download takes an extra 5 or even 10 seconds to complete, the typical end user is not likely to notice or care. On the other hand, some applications cannot tolerate even less than 1 second of delay. Voice traffic and other interactive applications are extremely delay-sensitive. Human beings typically can't tolerate much more than 200 milliseconds of delay when listening to voice traffic.

What if a large file transfer and *Voice over IP* (*VoIP*) traffic both started to fill the buffer of a congested interface? Which traffic would you want sent first?

Prioritization is most effective on WAN links in which the combination of bursty traffic and relatively lower data rates can cause temporary congestion. Depending on the average packet size, prioritization is most effective when applied to links at T1/E1 bandwidth speeds or lower. If there is never congestion on the WAN link, there is no reason to implement traffic prioritization.

Prioritization is effective on WAN links that experience temporary congestion. If a WAN link is constantly congested, traffic prioritization might not resolve the problem. Adding bandwidth might be the appropriate solution.

Establishing a Queuing Policy

A queuing policy helps the network manager meet two major challenges: provide an appropriate level of service for all users and control expensive WAN costs.

Typically, the corporate goal is to deploy and maintain a single enterprise network, even though the network supports disparate applications, organizations, technologies, and user expectations. Consequently, network managers are concerned about providing all users with an appropriate level of service, while continuing to support mission-critical applications and having the ability to integrate new technologies at the same time.

Because a major cost of running a network is also related to WAN circuit charges, network managers must strike the appropriate balance between the capacity and cost of these WAN circuits, and the level of service provided to the users.

To help meet these challenges, queuing allows network managers to prioritize, reserve, and manage network resources—and to ensure the seamless integration and migration of disparate technologies without unnecessary costs.

Determining the best Cisco IOS queuing option for your traffic needs involves the following general guidelines (as represented in Figure 10-2):

1. Determine whether the WAN is congested. If no traffic congestion exists, there is no need to sort the traffic—it is serviced as it arrives. However, if the traffic load exceeds the transmission capacity for periods of time, one of Cisco's IOS-queuing options might be the solution.

2. Decide whether strict control over traffic prioritization is necessary and whether automatic configuration is acceptable. Proper queuing configuration is not necessarily a simple task. To effectively perform this task, the network manager must study the types of traffic using the interface, determine how to distinguish them, and decide their relative priority. This done, the manager must install the filters and test their effect on the traffic. Traffic patterns change over time, so the analysis must be repeated periodically.

3. Establish a queuing policy. A queuing policy results from the analysis of traffic patterns and the determination of the relative traffic priorities discussed in Step 2.

4. Determine whether any of the traffic types you identified in your traffic pattern analysis can tolerate a delay.

Figure 10-2
Queuing should
be enabled only
on congested
interfaces.

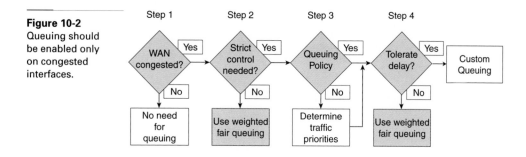

FIFO

As its name implies, FIFO queuing does not prioritize packets according to type of traffic or protocol. FIFO merely queues packets for transmission according to the order in which they arrive. Because of its simplicity, FIFO is the fastest of the four queuing methods, and should be used on all non-congested interfaces. It is the Cisco default queuing mode for all interfaces faster than E1 (2.048 Mbps).

FIFO has several shortcomings. Because FIFO queuing makes no decision about packet priority, order of arrival always determines quality of service. This means that high-volume conversations, such as FTP, can cause long delays in delivering time-sensitive application traffic and essential signaling messages. Large file transfers and other high-volume network applications often generate series of packets of associated data. These related packets are known as *packet trains*.

As shown in Figure 10-3, packet trains are groups of packets that tend to move together through the network. These packet trains can consume all available bandwidth and starve out other traffic.

WFQ

CQ and PQ require that an administrator predefine priorities and configure access lists. In other words, you have to know what the priorities are in advance, and you have to do some complex configuration on the router to implement congestion management. If network conditions change, routers using these static queuing methods can't adapt to the changes.

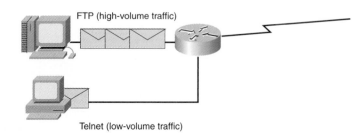

Figure 10-3
High-volume traffic sources, such as FTP, create packet trains, which can consume buffer space and delay low-volume traffic.

FTP (high-volume traffic)

Telnet (low-volume traffic)

For administrators looking for a dynamic, fair method to prioritize traffic on a congested interface, WFQ is the answer. WFQ automatically allocates bandwidth to all types of network traffic, but prioritizes delay-sensitive packets so that high-volume conversations don't consume all the available bandwidth.

By using a complex algorithm, WFQ sorts the packets that make up the different conversations on an interface, and then assigns a precedence, or weight, to traffic so that each conversation gets its fair share of bandwidth. WFQ breaks up large trains of packets so that low-volume conversations don't get overrun by large file transfers or any other heavy traffic. Thus, the router can prioritize traffic based on the actual network conditions at the time, without complex administration.

As the only dynamic queuing strategy of the four queuing methods, WFQ is used by default on serial interfaces at E1 speeds (2.048 Mbps) and below. WFQ is disabled on serial interfaces that use X.25, Synchronous Data Link Control (SDLC), or compressed Point-to-Point Protocol (PPP). Local-area network (LAN) interfaces and serial lines, operating at E3 or T3 speeds, are not available for WFQ.

The WFQ algorithm arranges traffic into conversations. The discrimination of traffic into conversations is based on packet-header addressing.

Common conversation discriminators include the following:

- Source/destination network address
- Source/destination MAC address
- Source/destination port or socket numbers
- Frame Relay Data Link Connection Identifier (DLCI) value
- Quality of service/type of service (QoS/ToS) value

The WFQ algorithm places packets of the various conversations in the fair queue before transmission (see Figure 10-4). The order of removal from the fair queue is determined by the virtual delivery time of the last bit of each arriving packet. Small, low-volume packets are given priority over large, high-volume conversation packets.

Figure 10-4
The WFQ algorithm classifies incoming packets and schedules them to be dispatched.

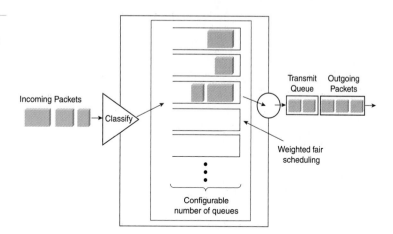

As a result of the queuing order, short messages, (ones that do not require much bandwidth) are given priority. After low-volume conversations are serviced, high-volume conversations share the remaining link capacity fairly, and interleave (alternate) transmission timeslots. The queuing algorithm ensures the proper amount of bandwidth for each message. With WFQ, two equal-size file transfers get equal bandwidth, rather than the first file transfer using most of the link's capacity.

Configuring WFQ

The **fair-queue** command enables fair queuing on an interface:

```
Router(config-if)#fair-queue {congestive-discard-threshold}
```

The *congestive-discard-threshold* is the number of messages to queue for high-volume traffic—in other words, the maximum packets in a conversation held in a queue before they are discarded. Valid values range from 1 to 512. The default is 64 messages. The command shown in Example 10-1 sets the congestive discard threshold number to 128.

Example 10-1 Configuring WFQ

```
RTA(config-if)#fair-queue 128
```

The congestive-discard-threshold policy applies only to high-volume conversations that have more than one message in the queue. The discard policy tries to control conversations that could monopolize the link.

If an individual conversation queue contains more messages than the congestive-discard threshold, that conversation will not have any new messages queued until the content of that queue drops below one-fourth of the congestive-discard value. For example, if the congestive-discard value is set to 128, the queue must contain fewer than 32 entries (1/4 of 128) before new messages can enter the queue.

Figure 10-5 illustrates a WFQ configuration scenario.

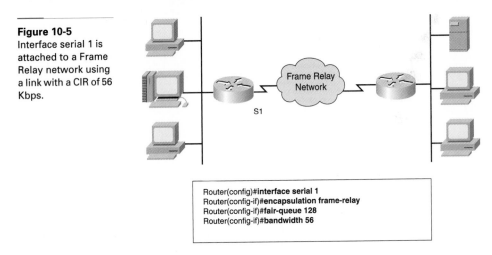

Figure 10-5
Interface serial 1 is attached to a Frame Relay network using a link with a CIR of 56 Kbps.

Router(config)#**interface serial 1**
Router(config-if)#**encapsulation frame-relay**
Router(config-if)#**fair-queue 128**
Router(config-if)#**bandwidth 56**

Use the **no fair-queue** command to disable WFQ and enable FIFO queuing on an interface.

PQ

You can use PQ to prioritize one type of traffic over others, so that the highest-priority traffic always gets dispatched before any other packets. To implement PQ, you classify traffic according to various criteria, including protocol type, and then assign that traffic to one of four output queues: high, medium, normal, or low priority (see Figure 10-6). When the router is ready to send a packet, it checks the high queue first. After the high queue is empty, the router checks the medium queue, and so on. This process (starting with the high-priority queue) is repeated every time the router is ready to send a packet (see Figure 10-7).

With PQ, the high-priority queue is always emptied before the medium-priority queue, and so on. Among the available congestion management protocols, PQ provides the network administrator the most control over deciding which traffic gets forwarded.

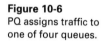

Figure 10-6
PQ assigns traffic to
one of four queues.

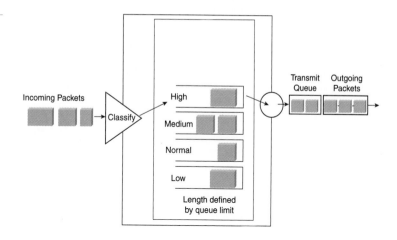

Figure 10-7
In PQ, all other
queues must be
empty before traffic
in the low priority
queue can be
serviced.

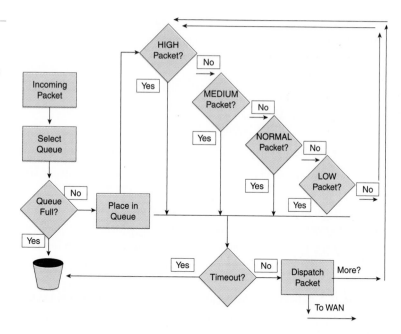

One drawback to PQ is that if a link is exceptionally busy with higher-priority traffic,
the lower-priority queue might not be serviced within an acceptable time frame, or

even at all. Because of its limitations, PQ should only be used on low-speed WAN links; it is rarely implemented on interfaces at 1.544 Mbps or greater.

PQ is useful in environments in which traffic has a hierarchy of importance, and more important traffic should not be delayed by less important traffic. For example, one organization might determine that voice traffic should always be prioritized over FTP traffic.

An incoming packet is compared with the priority list to select a queue. If there is room, the packet is buffered in memory and waits to be dispatched after the queue is selected. If the queue is full, the packet is dropped. For this reason, controlling queue size is an important configuration task.

Be careful when you define the packets that belong in the high queue because these packets are always processed first. If the high queue is always filled, packets in other queues do not have a chance to be transmitted.

WFQ automatically prioritizes traffic to ensure that all traffic is given fair access to bandwidth. Use PQ when you must guarantee that certain types of traffic receive as much of the available bandwidth as needed.

Configuring PQ

A *priority list* is a set of rules that describe the way packets should be assigned to PQs. You can establish queuing priorities based on the protocol type, an access list, or on packets entering from a specific interface.

Create an output PQ list with the **priority-list protocol** command, as shown here:

```
Router(config)#priority-list list-number protocol protocol-name
  {high | medium | normal | low} queue-keyword keyword-value
```

The *list-number* is used to identify the list, and can be any number from 1 to 16. Use the **protocol** keyword to specify the name of the protocol to prioritize. All protocols supported by the Cisco IOS are allowed. You can use the help feature by typing a "?" to determine what protocols are available on your platform, as shown in Example 10-2.

Example 10-2 Determining the Protocols Available with the priority-list Command

```
RTA(config)#priority-list 1 protocol ?
  arp          IP ARP
  bridge       Bridging
  bstun        Block Serial Tunnel
  cdp          Cisco Discovery Protocol
  compressedtcp Compressed TCP
```

Example 10-2 Determining the Protocols Available with the priority-list Command (Continued)

```
dlsw           Data Link Switching
ip             IP
llc2           llc2
pad            PAD links
qllc           qllc protocol
rsrb           Remote Source-Route Bridging
snapshot       Snapshot routing support
stun           Serial Tunnel
```

The *queue-keyword* argument provides additional options including byte count, TCP service and port number assignments, and AppleTalk, IP, IPX, VINES, or XNS access list assignments. Example 10-3 shows a sample command using the **tcp** keyword to specify that Telnet traffic should be placed in the high priority queue.

Example 10-3 Configuring Telnet as High Priority

```
RTA(config)#priority-list 1 protocol ip high tcp 23
```

In addition to specifying TCP and UDP port numbers, you can also use an access list to identify Internet Protocol (IP) traffic for queuing, as shown in Example 10-4.

Example 10-4 Using an Access List to Specify Packets for Prioritization

```
RTA(config)#access-list 10 permit 239.1.1.0 0.0.0.255
RTA(config)#priority-list 1 protocol ip high list 10
```

In this case, traffic matching access-list 10 is placed in the high queue.

You can also create an output PQ list with the **priority-list interface** command:

```
Router(config)#priority-list list-number interface interface-type
 interface-number {high | medium | normal | low}
```

Use this command to set queuing priorities for all traffic arriving on an incoming interface.

Example 10-5 shows the command necessary to specify that traffic arriving on Ethernet 0 be placed in the medium priority queue.

NOTE

Remember that, when using multiple rules for a single protocol, the system reads the priority settings in the order of appearance.

Example 10-5 Using the priority-list interface Command

```
RTA(config)#priority-list 2 interface ethernet 0 medium
```

You can explicitly assign a queue for packets that were not specified in the priority list. The packets are assigned to the normal queue by default. Use the **priority-list default** command to assign packets to a queue if no other priority list conditions are met:

```
Router(config)#priority-list list-number default {high | medium | normal | low}
```

The following sections describe how to configure priority queue sizes, and how to apply priority lists to an interface.

Specifying the Maximum Size of the Priority Queues

You can specify the maximum number of allowable packets in each queue. In general, it is recommended that the default queue sizes not be changed.

Use the optional **priority-list queue-limit** command to change the default maximum number of packets in each queue.

```
Router(config)#priority-list list-number queue-limit
high-limit medium-limit normal-limit low-limit
```

The default queue limit arguments are listed in Table 10-1.

Table 10-1   Default Priority Queue Limits

Queue Argument	Packet Limits
high-limit	20
medium-limit	40
normal-limit	60
low-limit	80

The command shown in Example 10-6 changes the maximum number of packets in the high priority queue to 10. The medium-, normal-, and low-limit queue sizes remain at their default 40-, 60-, and 80-packet limits.

Example 10-6 Configuring Priority Queue Limits

```
RTA(config)#priority-list 4 queue-limit 10 40 60 80
```

Assigning the Priority List to an Interface

Only one priority list can be assigned per interface. When assigned, the priority list rules are applied to all traffic that passes through the interface.

After you define the priority list, enter interface configuration mode and enter the
priority-group command to link a priority list to an interface:

```
Router(config-if)#priority-group list
```

The configuration shown in Example 10-7 shows a priority list that places Telnet traffic in the high queue, FTP traffic in the low queue, and applies the list to interface s0.

Example 10-7 Applying a Priority List to an Interface

```
RTA(config)#priority-list 1 protocol ip high tcp 23
RTA(config)#priority-list 1 protocol ip low tcp 21
RTA(config)#interface s0
RTA(config-if)#priority-group 1
```

CQ

Whereas PQ might result in an unacceptable delay of low-priority traffic, CQ allows
an administrator to reserve a minimum amount of bandwidth for every kind of traffic
(see Figure 10-8). Each traffic type gets a share of the available bandwidth, although
these amounts don't have to be equal. Thus, delay-sensitive and mission-critical traffic
can be assigned a large percentage of available bandwidth, while low-priority traffic
receives a smaller portion.

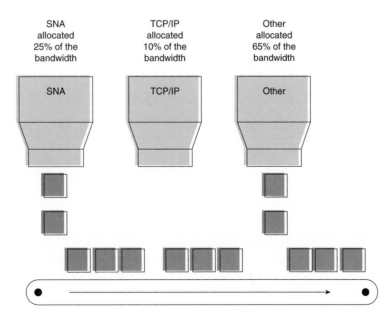

Figure 10-8
Custom queuing
allows you to guarantee bandwidth for
traffic by assigning
queue space to each
protocol.

SNA allocated 25% of the bandwidth

TCP/IP allocated 10% of the bandwidth

Other allocated 65% of the bandwidth

CQ prioritizes multiprotocol traffic. An administrator can configure up to 16 queues, which makes it ideal for networks that must provide a minimum level of responsiveness for several different protocols. Each queue is serviced sequentially until the number of bytes sent exceeds the configurable byte count, or until the queue is empty.

CQ is particularly important for time-sensitive protocols, such as voice, video, and IBM's Systems Network Architecture (SNA), which require predictable response time. Queue 0 is a system queue that handles system packets such as keepalives. Queue 0 is emptied before the other custom queues.

Configuring CQ

You can configure CQ to filter for an interface or a protocol. For example, you can do the following:

- Send all traffic from Ethernet interface 0 to custom queue 1.
- Send all IP traffic to custom queue 2.
- Send all IPX traffic to custom queue 3.
- Send all AppleTalk traffic to custom queue 4.

As with PQ, you can create a CQ list by using the protocol or the interface as discriminating criteria.

Use the **queue-list protocol** command to specify inclusion of a protocol in a particular queue:

```
Router(config)#queue-list list-number protocol protocol-name queue-number
    queue-keyword keyword-value
```

NOTE

In Cisco IOS Release 11.0, the maximum number of queues that can be used for CQ increased from 10 to 16. Sixteen queues are assigned by default.

You can also create an output CQ list with the **queue-list interface** command. Use the **queue-list interface** command to establish queuing priorities on incoming interfaces:

```
Router(config)#queue-list list-number interface interface-type interface-number
    queue-number
```

Similar to PQ, CQ has a default queue used for those packets that do not match a CQ list. If no default queue is specified, default traffic is assigned to queue 1. You can assign default traffic to another queue using the following syntax:

```
Router(config)#queue-list list-number default queue-number
```

Example 10-8 assigns traffic that matches IP access list 10 to queue number 1, Telnet packets to queue number 2,and UDP Domain Name System (DNS) packets to queue number 3. The **queue-list 4 interface serial 0 10** command assigns packets entering on serial interface 0 to queue 10. Finally, the default queue for list 4 is set to queue number 4.

Example 10-8 Configuring CQ

```
RTA(config)#queue-list 4 protocol ip 1 list 10
RTA(config)#queue-list 4 protocol ip 2 tcp 23
RTA(config)#queue-list 4 protocol ip 3 udp 53
RTA(config)#queue-list 4 interface serial 0 10
RTA(config)#queue-list 4 default 4
```

The following sections describe how to configure CQ sizes, and how to apply CQ lists to an interface.

Specifying the Maximum Size of the CQs

You can designate the maximum number of packets that a queue can contain. If a queue is full, incoming packets for that queue are dropped. To specify the length of a particular queue, use the optional **queue-list** *queue limit* command, as shown here:

```
Router(config)#queue-list list-number queue queue-number limit limit-number
```

To allocate more bandwidth to the traffic of a protocol or traffic from an interface, you increase the size of a queue.

Use the **queue-list** *queue byte-count* command to set the minimum byte count transferred from a given queue at a time. This value is specified on a per-queue basis, as shown here:

```
Router(config)#queue-list list-number queue queue-number byte-count
  byte-count-number
```

If a queue threshold (the maximum byte count) is reached during the transmission of a packet, the whole packet is still allowed to go through because the router will not split a packet for the purpose of queuing.

For example, the default threshold of 1500 bytes is used on a given queue. The first packet assigned to that queue is 1100 bytes, and the second packet is 300 bytes. The threshold has not been reached yet because the byte count is currently at 1400 bytes. The next packet assigned to the same queue is therefore processed, regardless of its size. If the third packet is 1000 bytes, the whole packet is processed, for a total byte count of 2400 bytes. The fourth packet is put on hold while the router services the subsequent queues.

For example, the **queue-list 1 queue 1 byte-count 4500** command allocates 4500 bytes to queue 1. This command increases the transfer capacity of queue 1 from the default of 1500 bytes to 4500 bytes.

NOTE

You can define multiple rules; the system reads the priority settings in order of appearance. The Cisco IOS searches the list in the order it is specified, and the first matching rule terminates the search. When a match is found, the packet is assigned to the appropriate queue.

NOTE

The **queue-limit** keyword specifies the size of a queue. The **byte-count** keyword specifies how many bytes of a queue are transmitted before proceeding to the next queue.

Assigning the CQ List to an Interface

You must assign the CQ list to an interface to enable queuing. The filters of the queue list are applied to all traffic that passes through the interface.

Use the **custom-queue-list** command to link a queue list to an interface, as shown here:

```
Router(config-if)#custom-queue-list list
```

Verifying Queuing Operation

Use the **show queueing** command to display detailed queuing information about all interfaces where queuing is enabled.

You can also use the **show interfaces** command to display queuing information for the router interfaces (see the shaded portion of the output in Example 10-9).

Example 10-9 Using the show interface Command to Display Queuing Statistics

```
RTA#show interface s1/0
Serial1/0 is up, line protocol is up
  Hardware is QUICC Serial
  Internet address is 192.168.0.1/30
  MTU 1500 bytes, BW 1544 Kbit, DLY 20000 usec,
      reliability 255/255, txload 1/255, rxload 6/255
  Encapsulation PPP, loopback not set
  Keepalive set (10 sec)
  LCP Open
  Listen: CDPCP
  Open: IPCP
  Last input 00:00:00, output 00:00:00, output hang never
  Last clearing of "show interface" counters 1d12h
  Input queue: 0/75/59/0 (size/max/drops/flushes); Total output drops: 0
  Queueing strategy: weighted fair
  Output queue: 0/1000/64/0 (size/max total/threshold/drops)
     Conversations  0/27/256 (active/max active/max total)
     Reserved Conversations 0/0 (allocated/max allocated)
     Available Bandwidth 1158 kilobits/sec
  3 minute input rate 37000 bits/sec, 10 packets/sec
  3 minute output rate 4000 bits/sec, 8 packets/sec
```

Example 10-9 Using the show interface Command to Display Queuing Statistics (Continued)

```
    3531088 packets input, 595969122 bytes, 0 no buffer
    Received 0 broadcasts, 0 runts, 0 giants, 0 throttles
    0 input errors, 0 CRC, 0 frame, 0 overrun, 0 ignored, 0 abort
    4100136 packets output, 3204946448 bytes, 0 underruns
    0 output errors, 0 collisions, 0 interface resets
    0 output buffer failures, 0 output buffers swapped out
    0 carrier transitions
    DCD=up  DSR=up  DTR=up  RTS=up  CTS=up
```

Use the **show queueing custom** command to display CQ information, as shown in
Example 10-10.

Example 10-10 Using the show queueing custom Command

```
RTB#show queueing custom
Current custom queue configuration:

List    Queue   Args
1       3       default
1       1       protocol ip     tcp port ftp
1       2       protocol ip     tcp port www
1       4       protocol ip     list 111
1       4       byte-count 3000
```

You can use the **show queueing priority** command and **show queueing fair** command
to display PQ and WFQ information, respectively (see Examples 10-11 and 10-12).

Example 10-11 Using the show queueing priority Command

```
RTC#show queueing priority
Current priority queue configuration:

List    Queue   Args
3       high    protocol ip     list 121
3       medium  protocol ip     list 122
3       low     protocol ip     list 123
```

Example 10-12 Using the show queueing fair Command

```
RTD#show queueing fair
Current fair queue configuration:

   Interface          Discard   Dynamic  Reserved  Link    Priority
                      threshold queues   queues    queues  queues

   Serial1/0          64        256      0         8       1
   Serial1/1          64        256      0         8       1
```

NOTE

The configuring
compression
using PPP is also
discussed in
Chapter 3, "PPP."

Optimizing Traffic Flow with Data Compression

Many strategies and techniques exist for optimizing traffic over WAN links, including queuing and access lists. One of the more effective methods is compression. This section discusses how to optimize the WAN traffic over the WAN link by compressing data on the WAN link.

Data compression works by identifying patterns in a stream of data, and choosing a more efficient method of representing the same information. Essentially, an algorithm is applied to the data to remove as much redundancy as possible. The efficiency and effectiveness of a compression scheme is measured by its *compression ratio*, the ratio of the size of uncompressed data to compressed data. A compression ratio of 2:1 (relatively common) means that the compressed data is half the size of the original data.

Many different algorithms are available to compress data. Some are designed to take advantage of a specific medium and the redundancies found in them, but do a poor job when applied to other sources of data. For example, the MPEG standard was designed to take advantage of the relatively small difference from one frame to another in video data and so does an excellent job of compressing motion pictures, but would do a terrible job of compressing text.

One of the most important points in compression theory is that there exists a theoretical limit, known as *Shannon's Limit*, to how much a given source of data can be compressed. Beyond that point, it is impossible to reliably recover compressed data. Modern compression algorithms coupled with today's fast processors are allowing us to approach Shannon's Limit, but we will never be able to cross it.

Data-compression technology maximizes bandwidth and increases WAN link throughput by reducing frame size and thereby allowing more data to be transmitted over a link.

Figure 10-9 graphically illustrates the following types of data compression that Cisco equipment supports:

■ Link compression (also known as per-interface compression)

- Payload compression (also known as per-virtual-circuit compression)
- TCP header compression

Figure 10-9
Link compression compresses the entire frame, while other forms of compression compress only parts of the frame.

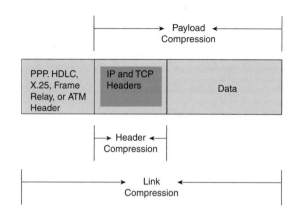

By default, data is transmitted across a serial link uncompressed. This allows headers to be used in the normal switching operation but can consume more bandwidth than desired.

Link Compression Over a Point-to-Point Connection

Link compression (also known as *per-interface compression*) involves compressing both the header and payload sections of a data stream. Unlike header compression, link compression is protocol independent.

Link compression uses either the Predictor or STAC algorithm to compress the traffic in another link layer, such as PPP or Link Access Procedure, Balanced (LAPB). To ensure error correction and packet sequencing (Cisco High-Level Data Link Control [HDLC] uses STAC compression only):

- **Predictor**—Predicts the next sequence of characters in the data stream by using an index to look up a sequence in a compression dictionary. It then examines the next sequence in the data stream to see if it matches. If it does, that sequence replaces the looked-up sequence in a maintained dictionary. If it does not, the algorithm locates the next character sequence in the index, and the process begins again. The index updates itself by hashing a few of the most recent character sequences from the input stream.

- **STAC**—Developed by STAC Electronics, STAC is a Lempel-Ziv (LZ)-based compression algorithm. It searches the input data stream for redundant strings and replaces them with what is called a *token*, which turns out to be shorter than the original redundant data string.

Microsoft Point to Point Compression (MPPC) is a scheme used to compress PPP packets between Cisco and Microsoft client devices. The MPPC algorithm is designed to optimize bandwidth use in order to support multiple simultaneous connections. The MPPC algorithm uses an LZ-based algorithm with a continuous history buffer called a *dictionary*.

Exactly one MPPC datagram is encapsulated in the PPP information field. The PPP protocol field indicates the hexadecimal type of 00FD for all compressed datagrams. The maximum length of the MPPC datagram sent over PPP is the same as the Maximum Transmission Unit (MTU) of the PPP interface; however, this length cannot be greater than 8192 bytes because the history buffer is limited to 8192 bytes. If compressing the data results in data expansion, the original data is sent as an uncompressed MPPC packet.

If the data flow traverses a point-to-point connection, use link compression. In a link-compression environment, the complete frame is compressed and the switching information in the frame or packet headers is not available for WAN-switching networks. Thus, the best applications for link compression are point-to-point environments with a limited hop path. Typical examples are leased lines or ISDN.

Use the **compress [predictor | stac | mppc]** command to configure point-to-point software compression for a LAPB, PPP, or HDLC link. Data-compression schemes used in internetworking devices are referred to as *lossless compression algorithms*. These schemes reproduce the original bit streams exactly, with no degradation or loss, a feature that is required by routers and other devices to transport data across the network:

```
Router(config-if)#compress [predictor | stac | mppc]
```

Payload Compression

Payload compression (also known as *per-virtual-circuit compression*) compresses only the data portion (including the Layer-3 and Layer-4 headers) of the data stream. The frame header is left untouched.

When designing an internetwork, the customer cannot assume that an application will go over point-to-point lines. If link compression is used, the header might not be readable at a particular hop. For example, if a Frame Relay switch receives a compressed Layer-2 header, it would not be able to read the DLCI and make the appropriate routing decision. To avoid compressing the Layer-2 headers, the customer can use payload compression instead (see Figure 10-10).

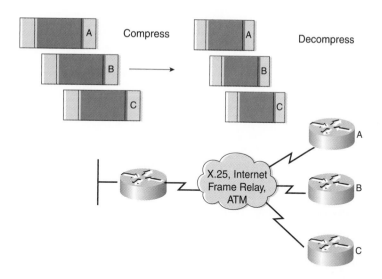

Figure 10-10
Payload compression leaves Layer-2 headers untouched so that header information can be used to route data in a packet-switched network.

Payload compression is appropriate for virtual network services such as Switched Multi-megabit Data Service (SMDS), Frame Relay, and Asynchronous Transfer Mode (ATM).

Use the **frame-relay payload-compress** command to enable STAC compression on a specified Frame Relay point-to-point interface or subinterface:

```
Router(config-if)#frame-relay payload-compress
```

TCP/IP Header Compression

The TCP header compression subscribes to the Van Jacobson Algorithm, which is defined in RFC 1144. TCP/IP header compression lowers the overhead generated by the disproportionately large TCP/IP headers as they are transmitted across the WAN (see Figure 10-11).

TCP header compression is protocol specific and compresses only the TCP/IP header, which leaves the Layer-2 header intact to allow a packet with a compressed TCP/IP header to travel across a WAN link.

Use the **ip tcp header-compression** command to enable TCP header compression. The **passive** keyword compresses outgoing TCP packets, only if incoming TCP packets on the same interface are compressed. If passive is not specified, the router compresses all traffic:

```
Router(config-if)#ip tcp header-compression [passive]
```

NOTE

You must *not* implement both Layer 2 payload compression and TCP/IP header compression concurrently because it is redundant and wasteful. It is also possible that the link will not come up or pass IP traffic if you enable both forms of compression.

Figure 10-11
Van Jacobson compression affects the TCP header only.

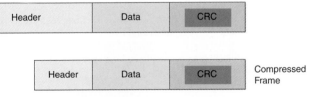

TCP header compression is beneficial on small packets with few bytes of data, such as Telnet. Cisco header compression supports X.25, Frame Relay, and dial-on-demand WAN link protocols.

Because of processing overhead, header compression is generally used at lower speeds, such as 64-Kbps links.

Compression Considerations

Other considerations for selecting a compression algorithm to optimize your WAN use are the following:

- **Modem compression**—In dial environments, compression can occur in the modem. Two common modem-compression standards are Microcom Networking Protocol 5 (MNP5) and the International Telecommunication Union (ITU) V.42bis. MNP5 and V.42bis offer up to two times and four times compression, respectively. The two specifications are not compatible. The modems at both ends of the connection negotiate the standard to use. If compression is being done at the modem, do not configure the router to run compression because some modems, such as a V.42bis and MNP5 modem, cannot compress a file that is already compressed by software. In the case of MNP5, it will even try to compress a precompressed file and actually expand it, thus slowing the file transfer.

- **Encrypted data**—Compression is a Layer 2 function. When a data stream is encrypted by the client application, it is then passed onto the router for routing or compression services. When the compression engine receives the encrypted data stream, which by definition has no repetitive patterns, the data expands and does not compress. The compression algorithm then compares the before and after images to determine which is the smallest, and then sends the uncompressed data as it was originally received if expansion occurred. So, if data is encrypted, do not compress the encrypted data using a Layer-2 compression algorithm.

The solution to this problem is to compress at Layer 3 and then encrypt at the same layer. Cisco actively provides a solution to this problem with its work on the IP Security (IPSec) and IP Compression (IPComp) Protocols. IPSec is a standards-based method of providing privacy, integrity, and authenticity to information transferred across IP networks. IPSec provides IP network-layer encryption. IPComp is a mechanism to reduce the size of IP datagrams and is especially useful when encryption is applied to IP datagrams, in which Layer-2 (PPP) compression is not effective.

<table>
<tr><td></td><td>

WARNING

Never recompress data. Compressed data does not compress; it actually expands.
</td></tr>
</table>

- **CPU cycles versus memory**—The amount of memory that a router must have varies according to the protocol being compressed, the compression algorithm, and the number of concurrent circuits on the router. Memory requirements are higher for Predictor than for STAC, and payload uses more memory than link compression. Likewise, link compression uses more CPU cycles.

Summary

In this chapter, you learned when to enable queuing. You learned how to configure WFQ, PQ, and CQ on router interfaces; and how to verify proper queuing configuration. This chapter also reviewed link compression algorithms and configuration commands, in addition to introducing payload compression.

Review Questions

Use the following review questions to test your understanding of the concepts covered in this chapter. In some cases, there is more than one correct answer, so choose all that apply. Answers are listed in Appendix A, "Answers to Review Questions."

1. Which method of queuing allows an administrator to configure up to 16 different queues?

   A. FIFO

   B. WFQ

   C. PQ

   D. CQ

2. Which method of queuing allows an administrator to configure four total queues: high, medium, normal, and low?

   A. FIFO

   B. WFQ

   C. PQ

   D. CQ

3. Which method of queuing schedules packets based on the order in which they arrive?

   A. FIFO

   B. WFQ

   C. PQ

   D. CQ

4. Which method of queuing is the default method on E1, T1, and slower interfaces?

   A. FIFO

   B. WFQ

   C. PQ

   D. CQ

5. Which method of queuing is the default method on interfaces with higher bandwidth than E1?

   A. FIFO

   B. WFQ

   C. PQ

   D. CQ

6. Which of the following commands correctly assigns a CQ to an interface?

   A. (config)#custom-queue-list 1

   B. (config-if)#custom-queue-list 1

   C. (config)#queue-list 1

   D. (config-if)#queue-list 1

7. Which of the following commands correctly assigns a PQ to an interface?

   A. (config)#priority-queue-list 1

   B. (config-if)#priority-queue-list 1

   C. (config)#priority-list 1

   D. (config-if)#priority-group 1

8. Which of the following commands correctly assigns Telnet to the high priority queue?

   A. (config)#priority-list 1 protocol ip high tcp 23

   B. (config)#priority-list 2 protocol tcp high 23

   C. (config)#queue-list 3 protocol tcp high 23

   D. (config)#queue-list 4 protocol ip high tcp 23

9. In the priority-list 1 protocol ip high list 10 command, to what does the 10 refer?

   A. Sequence number

   B. Queue number

   C. Protocol number

   D. An access list

10. In terms of router resources, which of the following is true about Stacker and Predictor?

A. Stacker is memory intensive and Predictor is CPU intensive.

B. Predictor is memory intensive and Stacker is CPU intensive.

C. Both Predictor and Stacker are CPU intensive.

D. Both Predictor and Stacker are memory intensive.

Key Terms

Buffer　An area of memory shared by hardware devices or program processes that operate at different speeds or with different sets of priorities.

CQ (custom queuing)　Queuing method in which bandwidth is allocated proportionally for each different class of traffic. CQ allows the configuration of the number of bytes or packets to be drawn from the queue, which is especially useful on slow interfaces.

FIFO queuing (first-in, first-out queuing)　Queuing method that involves buffering and forwarding of packets in the order of arrival. FIFO embodies no concept of priority or classes of traffic. There is only one queue, and all packets are treated equally. Packets are sent out an interface in the order in which they arrive.

Link compression　Method of compression that involves compressing both the header and payload sections of a data stream. Unlike header compression, link compression is protocol independent. Also known as *per-interface compression*.

Payload compression　Method of compression that involves compressing only the data portion (including the Layer-3 and Layer-4 headers) of the data stream. The frame header is left untouched. Also known as *per-virtual-circuit compression*.

PQ (priority queuing)　Queuing method in which packets belonging to one priority class of traffic are sent before all lower priority traffic to ensure timely delivery of those packets.

VoIP (Voice over Internet Protocol)　The capability to carry normal telephony-style voice over an IP-based Internet with POTS-like functionality, reliability, and voice quality.

WFQ (weighted fair queuing)　Congestion management algorithm that identifies conversations (in the form of traffic streams), separates packets that belong to each conversation, and ensures that capacity is shared fairly between these individual conversations. WFQ is an automatic way of stabilizing network behavior during congestion and results in increased performance and reduced retransmission.

Objectives

After completing this chapter, you will be able to perform tasks related to the following:

- NAT terminology
- Dynamic NAT
- Static NAT
- NAT overload
- TCP load distribution

Chapter 11

NAT

Introduction

There is a limited supply of Internet Protocol (IP) version 4 addresses. In the early 1990s, many experts believed that we would run out of IP addresses (if the Internet didn't collapse under the weight of too many IP networks first). Today, IPv4 is no longer in immediate danger of failing, thanks to new technologies and enhancements. One of the technologies that helped IPv4 stave off address depletion is *Network Address Translation(NAT)*.

NAT, as defined in RFC 1631, is the process of swapping one address for another in the IP packet header. In practice, NAT is used to allow hosts that are privately addressed to access the Internet.

NAT is particularly effective when connecting a small office or home office (SOHO) to the corporate network. By using NAT, a company does not have to allocate a real IP address for each of its remote users.

This chapter provides an overview of NAT, and describes how to configure NAT functions, including static NAT, dynamic NAT, NAT overload, and TCP distribution. Finally, this chapter discusses the drawbacks of NAT and how its operation can be monitored using the Cisco IOS.

NAT Overview

Strictly speaking, NAT is the process of altering the IP header of a packet so that the destination address, the source address, or both addresses are replaced in the header by different addresses. This swapping process is performed by a router with specialized NAT software or hardware. Such a NAT-enabled device is often called a NAT *box* because it can be a Cisco router, a UNIX system, a Windows host, or any number of other systems.

A NAT-enabled device typically operates at the border of a *stub domain.* A stub domain is a network that has a single connection to the outside world. Figure 11-1 presents a simple example of a stub domain. When a host inside the stub domain, such as 10.1.1.6, wants to transmit to a host on the outside, it forwards the packet to its default gateway. In this case, the host's default gateway is also the NAT box.

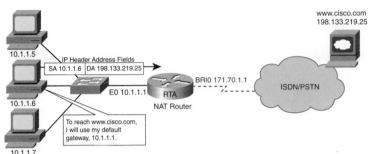

Figure 11-1
A host inside the stub domain sends packets to the Internet via a NAT router.

The NAT process then looks inside the IP header and, if appropriate, replaces the local IP address with a globally unique IP address. Figure 11-2 illustrates this address translation. RTA, the NAT router, determines that the source IP address of the packet (10.1.1.6) should be swapped. In this case, RTA replaces the private address with a global (real) address, 171.70.2.1. RTA also keeps a record of this translation in a NAT translation table.

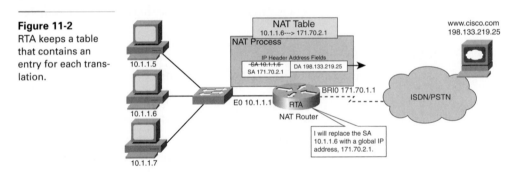

Figure 11-2
RTA keeps a table that contains an entry for each translation.

When an outside host sends a response (see Figure 11-3), the NAT router receives it, checks the current table of network address translations, and replaces the destination address with the original inside source address (see Figure 11-4).

NAT translations can occur dynamically or statically and can be used for a variety of purposes. The following sections describe these key NAT concepts and configurations:

- Private addressing
- NAT terminology
- Dynamic NAT
- Static NAT
- NAT overload
- TCP load distribution

Figure 11-3
An outside host replies to translated address 171.70.2.1.

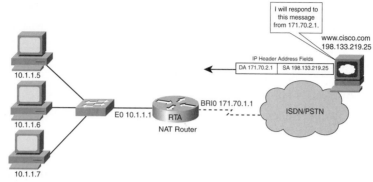

Figure 11-4
RTA checks incoming packets on BRI0 against its translation table and swaps the destination address, if necessary.

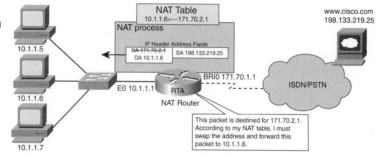

Private IP Addresses

RFC 1918 sets aside three blocks of IP addresses—a Class A, a Class B, and a Class C range—for private, internal use (see Table 11-1). These three ranges provide more than 17 million addresses for internal use.

Table 11-1   RFC 1918 Addresses

Class	RFC 1918 Internal Address Range	CIDR Prefix
A	10.0.0.0–10.255.255.255	10.0.0.0/8
B	172.16.0.0–172.31.255.255	172.16.0.0/12
C	192.168.0.0–192.168.255.255	192.168.0.0/16

Public addresses must be registered by an organization or leased from a provider (almost always for a fee). On the other hand, private IP addresses are set aside to be used by anyone. That means two networks, or two million networks, can each use the same private address. The restriction is that private addresses cannot be used on the public Internet. A private address cannot be used on the Internet because ISPs typically configure their routers to prevent privately addressed customer traffic from being forwarded.

NAT provides tremendous benefits to individual companies and the Internet, as well. Before NAT, a host with a private address could not access the Internet. With NAT, individual companies can address some, or all, of their hosts with private addresses and then use NAT to access the public Internet. At the same time, these hosts connect to the Internet without necessarily depleting its address space.

NAT Terminology

When configuring NAT using the Cisco IOS, it's critical that you understand NAT terminology. In particular, you must have a strong grasp of the following terms:

- **Inside addresses**—The set of networks that are subject to translation. Inside addresses are typically RFC 1918 addresses, but they can be any valid IP address.
- **Outside addresses**—All other addresses. Usually, these are valid addresses located on the Internet.

Inside addresses are associated with hosts inside the NAT boundary, regardless of whether they are private (RFC 1918) or public addresses. Inside addresses are part of your network. Outside addresses are typically associated with all Internet addresses. However, in some cases, outside addresses can be associated with hosts on your own network, beyond the NAT boundary. Two different kinds of inside addresses and two different types of outside addresses exist:

- *Inside local address*—Configured IP address assigned to a host on the inside network. Address might be globally unique, allocated out of the private address space defined in RFC 1918, or officially allocated to another organization (see Figure 11-5).
- *Inside global address*—The IP address of an inside host as it appears to the outside network (see Figure 11-5). The inside global address is the translated address. These addresses are typically allocated from a globally unique address space, typically provided by the Internet Service Provider (ISP) (if the enterprise is connected to the global Internet).
- *Outside local address*—The IP address of an outside host as it appears to the inside network. These addresses can be allocated from the RFC 1918 space if desired (see Figure 11-6).
- *Outside global address*—The configured IP address assigned to a host in the outside network (see Figure 11-6).

Figure 11-5
Typically, inside local addresses are private addresses that are translated into real inside global addresses.

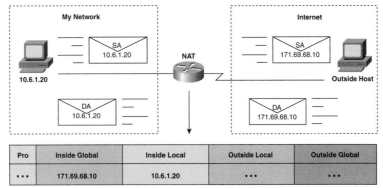

10.6.1.20 is Inside Local Address
171.69.68.10 is Inside Global Address

Figure 11-6
NAT translates outside local addresses, which are addresses that your inside hosts use to reach outside hosts.

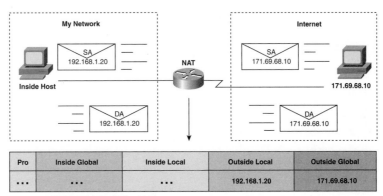

192.168.1.20 is Outside Local Address
171.69.10 is Outside Global Address

Dynamic NAT

With *dynamic NAT*, translations don't exist in the NAT translation table until the router receives traffic that requires translation (such traffic is defined by an administrator). Dynamic translations are temporary and eventually time out.

For example, host 10.4.1.1 transmits a packet to an Internet host, as shown in Figure 11-7. Because a private address can't be routed on the Internet, this host uses the services of a router configured for NAT.

Figure 11-7
NAT routers keep a table that maps global IP addresses to private, internal addresses.

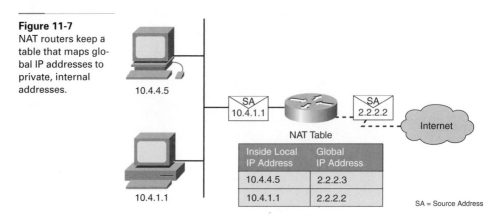

The NAT router alters the IP packet by removing the original source address, 10.4.1.1, and replacing it with a globally unique address from a pool defined by an administrator.

As shown in Figure 11-7, the inside host is dynamically assigned 2.2.2.2 from the address pool. The NAT box keeps a record of this address translation in its NAT table. When an Internet host's reply packet is sent to 2.2.2.2, it arrives at the NAT router, which checks its NAT table for the mapping to the local inside address. The NAT router then replaces the destination address with the original local address, 10.4.1.1. The translation mapping is not permanent; it ages out after a configurable period of time.

When configuring dynamic NAT, you typically create a pool of global addresses to be allocated as needed. Use the **ip nat pool** command to configure the address pool, as shown here:

```
Router(config)#ip nat pool name start-ip end-ip {netmask netmask | prefix-length
  prefix-length}
```

You must also specify which packets should be translated. Typically, you specify packets matching a certain range of source addresses to be translated. Use the **access-list** global configuration command to create an access list to match addresses that the router should translate:

```
Router(config)#access-list access-list-number permit source [source-wildcard]
```

To establish a dynamic translation based on source address, use the **ip nat inside source list** command:

```
Router(config)#ip nat inside source list access-list-number pool name
```

This command must specify the number of the access list.

Finally, you must configure at least one interface on the router as the inside interface by using the following interface configuration command:

```
Router(config-if)#ip nat inside
```

The router only creates dynamic entries in the translation table for packets arriving on interfaces configured with the **ip nat inside** command.

Use the **ip nat outside** command to mark an interface as an outside interface:

```
Router(config-if)#ip nat outside
```

Following these steps, you can configure RTA; the NAT router is shown in Figure 11-8.

Figure 11-8
RTA is configured for dynamic NAT.

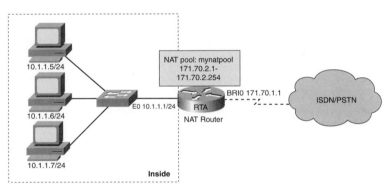

First, define the NAT pool, as shown in Example 11-1.

Example 11-1 Defining a NAT Pool

```
RTA(config)#ip nat pool mynatpool 171.70.2.1 171.70.2.254 netmask 255.255.255.0
```

This command creates a pool of global addresses called **mynatpool** that can be used by inside local hosts. But which local hosts are allowed to use this pool? Example 11-2 uses an access list to match the source addresses to be translated.

NOTE

When using the **ip nat pool** command, you have the option of specifying the subnet mask or the prefix length. The **netmask** keyword uses a dotted-decimal argument, such as 255.255.255.0. A 24-bit mask can also be specified using the **prefix-length 24** command.

Example 11-2 Using Access Lists with NAT Pools

```
RTA(config)#access-list 24 permit 10.1.1.0 0.0.0.255
RTA(config)#ip nat inside source list 24 pool mynatpool
```

The last command configures the router to use **access-list 24** to decide whether to translate the IP source address using **mynatpool**.

As the final configuration steps on the NAT router, Example 11-3 configures the appropriate interfaces to take on the role of **outside** and **inside**.

Example 11-3 Configuring NAT Interfaces

```
RTA(config)#interface bri0
RTA(config-if)#ip nat outside
RTA(config-if)#interface e0
RTA(config-if)#ip nat inside
```

If the host at 10.1.1.6 sends an IP packet to an outside host, such as 4.4.4.1, RTA translates the source address and creates a NAT table entry. Use the **show ip nat translations** command, as shown in Example 11-4, to view the translation table.

Example 11-4 Using the show ip nat translations Command

```
RTA#show ip nat translations
Pro Inside global     Inside local     Outside local     Outside global
--- 171.70.2.1        10.1.1.6         ---               ---
```

Example 11-4 shows that the inside local address 10.1.1.6 has been translated to the inside global address 171.70.2.1. Although this table entry exists, outside hosts can use the global IP address 171.70.2.1 to reach the host at 10.1.1.6.

On a Cisco router, dynamic NAT table entries remain in the table for 24 hours by default. After the entry ages out, outside hosts can no longer reach 10.1.1.6 until a new table entry is created. The table entry can be created only from the inside.

A 24-hour timeout is relatively long. You can adjust the translation timeout using the following command:

```
Router(config)#ip nat translation timeout seconds
```

One of the primary advantages to dynamic NAT is the ability to serve a large number of hosts with a smaller number of globally routable IP addresses. It is important for translation table entries to timeout so that addresses in the pool become available again for other hosts.

For example, you could configure a pool of 30 inside global addresses for 250 inside local hosts. Only 30 of the inside hosts can use a global address at any one time. This configuration might work well in an environment where outside (Internet) connectivity is infrequent and short-lived. If the inside hosts are using outside connections for occasional Web surfing or e-mail, this configuration might be appropriate. However, if translation table entries don't age out fast enough, the entire pool of addresses could be in use, and additional hosts would be unable to access the Internet. To serve a large number of hosts with just a handful of addresses, you might have to use address overloading (see the section, "NAT Overload").

Although NAT is not a security firewall, it can prevent outsiders from initiating connections with inside hosts, unless a permanent global address mapping exists in the NAT table (static NAT). Because outside hosts never see the "pretranslated" inside addresses, NAT has the effect of hiding the inside structure of a network.

Static NAT

Static translation occurs when you specifically configure addresses in a lookup table. A specific inside local address maps to a prespecified outside global address. The inside and outside addresses are statically mapped one for one. This means that for every inside local address, static NAT requires an inside global address. If you used static NAT exclusively, you would not conserve real IP addresses.

For this reason, static NAT is typically used in conjunction with dynamic NAT, in cases where you have overlapping networks (see the section, "Overlapping Networks" later in this chapter), or in cases when you have changed from one numbering scheme to another (if you change providers, etc.).

Consider how static NAT can be used in conjunction with dynamic NAT. Company XYZ uses dynamic NAT to allow inside hosts to access the Internet. But what if the company wants outside users to access an internally addressed Web server? Without a permanent global address, outside hosts are unable to consistently access the server.

Company XYZ can statically map a global address (170.70.2.10) to an inside address (10.1.1.7). Static mappings exist in the NAT table until an administrator removes them. Internet hosts, and Domain Name System (DNS), can use the global address (170.70.2.10) to access the privately addressed Web server.

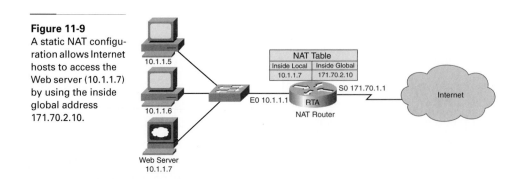

Figure 11-9
A static NAT configuration allows Internet hosts to access the Web server (10.1.1.7) by using the inside global address 171.70.2.10.

Use the following command to configure a static translation between an inside local address and an inside global address:

```
Router(config)#ip nat inside source static local-ip global-ip
```

After you configure the static mapping(s), you must specify an inside and outside interface, as shown in Example 11-5.

Example 11-5 Configuring Static NAT

```
RTA(config)#ip nat inside source static 10.1.1.7 172.70.2.10
RTA(config)#interface bri0
RTA(config-if)#ip nat outside
RTA(config-if)#interface e0
RTA(config-if)#ip nat inside
```

The ability to create static mappings makes NAT a useful tool if Company XYZ were ever to change providers. If the company moves from one ISP to another, it might have to completely readdress its systems. Instead of readdressing, NAT can be deployed to temporarily translate the old addresses to new ones, with static mappings in place to keep Web and other public services available to the outside.

NAT Overload

One of the most powerful features of NAT routers is their capability to use *Port Address Translation (PAT)*, which allows multiple inside addresses to map to the same global address. This is sometimes called a many-to-one NAT, or *address overloading*. With address overloading, literally hundreds of privately addressed nodes can access the Internet using a single global address. The NAT router keeps track of the different conversations by mapping TCP and UDP port numbers in the translation table. A translation entry that maps one IP address and port pair to another is called an *extended table entry*.

For example, Figure 11-10 shows three inside nodes using the same translated global address of 170.70.2.2. Each of these hosts can communicate with different Internet hosts, or even with the same outside host.

According to the NAT table shown in Figure 11-10, RTA translates the packet from the inside local address, 10.1.1.5, TCP port 1232. The translated inside global address is 171.70.2.2, also on port 1232.

NOTE

TCP and UDP use a 16-bit field to represent port numbers. Port numbers range from 1 to 65,535. Port numbers are used by applications to send data and listen for connections. Client applications, such as Web browsers, typically use port numbers in the range 1024 to 65,535.

Figure 11-10
With NAT overload, TCP and UDP port numbers can be used to keep track of address translations in the NAT table.

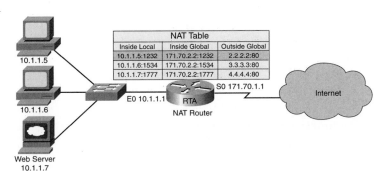

With the outside host at 2.2.2.2, TCP port 80 replies to the address 171.70.2.2, on port 1232. When RTA (the NAT router) receives this reply, it uses the destination port number to determine whether the destination IP address should be translated to 10.1.1.5, 10.1.1.6, or 10.1.1.7.

As long as the inside global port numbers are unique for each inside local host, NAT overload works. For example, if the host at 10.1.1.5 and 10.1.1.6 both use TCP port 1234, the NAT router can create the extended table entries mapping 10.1.1.5:1234 to 171.70.2.2:1234 and 10.1.1.6:1234 to 171.70.2.2:1235. NAT implementations don't necessarily try to preserve the original port number.

NAT FOR THE HOME USER

The advent of broadband Internet connections in the home has had an interesting side effect: Home users are networking their own computers with the goal of sharing a single high-speed Internet connection. Recognizing this new market, vendors quickly packaged affordable NAT solutions for the home. Some products are stand-alone solutions, or appliances, that provide many-to-one NAT along with Dynamic Host Configuration Protocol (DHCP) services—all with little or no configuration. Other products are software solutions that run on a computer with multiple logical addresses. Notable among these software solutions is Internet Connection Sharing, which ships with Microsoft's latest versions of Windows. With NAT now built into the world's most ubiquitous operating system, you can bet its popularity will only increase.

NAT overload can go a long way to alleviate address depletion, but its capabilities are limited. Over 65,000 inside addresses can theoretically map to a single outside address. However, the actual number of translations supported by a Cisco router varies.

NAT overload can be used in conjunction with dynamic mappings to a NAT pool. A NAT device, such as a Cisco PIX Firewall, can use a one-to-one dynamic mapping until the available addresses are almost depleted, at which time NAT can overload the remaining address or addresses. However, on a Cisco IOS router, NAT overloads the first address in the pool until it's maxed out and then moves on to the second address, and so on.

Configure NAT overload by using the keyword **overload**:

Router(config)#**ip nat inside source list** *access-list-number* **pool** *name* **overload**

RTA (Figure 11-10) is configured as shown in Example 11-6.

Example 11-6 Configuring NAT Overload

```
RTA(config)#ip nat pool mypatpool 171.70.2.1 171.70.2.30 netmask 255.255.255.0
RTA(config)#access-list 24 permit 10.1.1.0 0.0.0.255
RTA(config)#ip nat inside source list 24 pool mypatpool overload
RTA(config)#interface serial 0
RTA(config-if)#ip nat outside
RTA(config-if)#interface ethernet 0
RTA(config-if)#ip nat inside
```

The **ip nat pool** command creates the pool of addresses that are used for overloading. This pool, **mypatpool**, contains only 30 addresses. Using NAT overload, these 30 addresses can comfortably serve hundreds, or even thousands, of inside hosts. The **access-list** command creates the access list that is used to match addresses that are to be translated. The **ip nat inside source list 24** command configures the router to translate addresses that match access list 24 using inside global addresses from **mypatpool**.

You do not necessarily have to configure an address pool in order for NAT overload to work. If you don't have any available IP addresses, you can overload the address of the outside interface, as shown here:

Router(config)#**ip nat inside source list** *access-list-number* **interface** *interface-name* **overload**

Typically, home users receive only one IP address from their provider. Figure 11-11 shows how NAT overload can be configured using the outside interface.

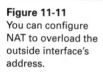

Figure 11-11
You can configure
NAT to overload the
outside interface's
address.

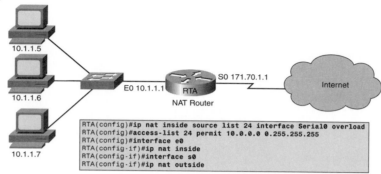

```
RTA(config)#ip nat inside source list 24 interface Serial0 overload
RTA(config)#access-list 24 permit 10.0.0.0 0.255.255.255
RTA(config)#interface e0
RTA(config-if)#ip nat inside
RTA(config-if)#interface s0
RTA(config-if)#ip nat outside
```

TCP Load Distribution

As an extension to static mapping, Cisco routers support *TCP load distribution*, a
powerful NAT feature that allows you to map one global address to multiple inside
addresses for the purpose of distributing conversations among multiple (usually mir-
rored) hosts. In Figure 11-12, the NAT router rotates conversations between two
inside Web servers at 10.1.1.6 and 10.1.1.7 when an outside host requests Web services at 171.70.2.10.

Figure 11-12
TCP load distribu-
tion assigns multiple
local addresses to a
single global
address.

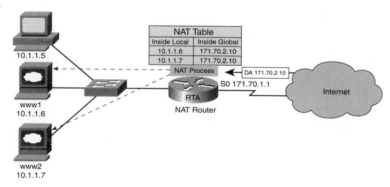

TCP load distribution can be used even if you are not translating between private
addresses and public addresses. The scenario depicted in Figure 11-13 shows that RTA
is configured to map both www1 (171.70.2.3/24) and www2 (171.70.2.4/24) to the
same inside global IP address (171.70.2.10/24). All three of these IP addresses are public addresses on the same subnet. In such configurations, the address 171.70.2.10 is
referred to as a *virtual host*.

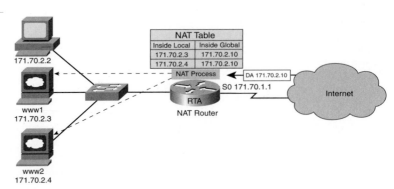

Figure 11-13
Traffic to the virtual host, 171.70.2.10, is distributed between www1 (171.70.2.3) and www2 (171.70.2.4).

The following are the steps for configuring a TCP load distribution:

1. Define a pool of addresses containing the addresses of the real hosts:

   ```
   Router(config)#ip nat pool name start-ip end-ip {netmask netmask |
     prefix-length prefix-length} type rotary
   ```

2. Define an access list permitting the address of the virtual host:

   ```
   Router(config)#access-list access-list-number permit source [source-wildcard]
   ```

3. Establish dynamic inside destination translation, identifying the access list defined in Step 2:

   ```
   Router(config)#ip nat inside destination list access-list-number pool name
   ```

4. Specify the inside interface:

   ```
   Router(config)#interface type number
   ```

5. Mark the interface as connected to the inside:

   ```
   Router(config-if)#ip nat inside
   ```

6. Specify the outside interface:

   ```
   Router(config-if)#interface type number
   ```

7. Mark the interface as connected to the outside:

   ```
   Router(config-if)#ip nat outside
   ```

Using the commands in these steps, RTA in Figure 11-13 is configured as shown in Example 11-7.

Example 11-7 Configuring TCP Load Distribution

```
RTA(config)#ip nat pool webservers 171.70.2.3 171.70.2.4 netmask 255.255.255.0
  type rotary
RTA(config)#access-list 46 permit host 171.70.2.10
RTA(config)#ip nat inside destination list 46 pool webservers
RTA(config)#interface e0
```

Example 11-7 Configuring TCP Load Distribution (Continued)

```
RTA(config-if)#ip nat inside
RTA(config-if)#interface s0
RTA(config)#ip nat outside
```

The keyword **rotary** is used so that the router rotates through the **webservers** pool when translating. Access list 46 is used to define the virtual host address.

RTA is configured to translate destination addresses that match 171.70.2.10 (access list 46), using the **webservers** pool. Because the **webservers** pool was defined using the **rotary** keyword, the first translation is to 171.70.2.3, the second is to 171.70.2.4, the third back to 171.70.2.3, and so on. In this way, the load is distributed among the Web servers.

Overlapping Networks

Overlapping networks result when you assign an IP address to a device on your network that is already legally owned and assigned to a different device on the Internet or outside network. Overlapping networks also result when two companies, both of whom use RFC 1918 IP addresses in their networks, merge. These two networks need to communicate, preferably without having to readdress all their devices.

Figure 11-14 illustrates an overlapping network scenario. The inside device, HostA, is addressed using the same IP subnet as the outside device, HostZ. HostA can't reach HostZ by using HostZ's IP address. If HostA pings 10.1.1.6, it will be pinging its local neighbor and not HostZ.

Figure 11-14
HostA wants to establish an IP connection with HostZ but cannot use HostZ's actual IP address (10.1.1.6).

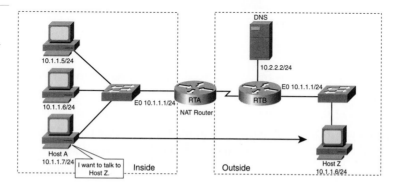

One way to allow HostA to communicate with HostZ is to use DNS and NAT. Instead of using HostZ's actual IP address, HostA can use HostZ's host name. For example, a user on HostA could issue the command **ping HostZ**, which would result in a name-to-address lookup using DNS (see Figure 11-15).

Figure 11-15
HostA's DNS request is translated by NAT.

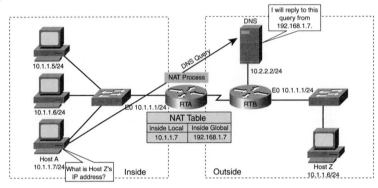

A NAT translation is for the DNS query sourced from 10.1.1.7. The query from 10.1.1.7 is translated by RTA so that it appears to be from the inside global address 192.168.1.7. The DNS server responds to this query, as shown in Figure 11-16.

Figure 11-16
In an overlapping networks scenario, DNS responses are translated by NAT.

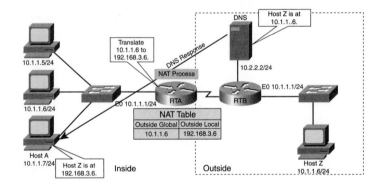

NOTE

NAT doesn't look at the payload of the DNS reply unless translation occurs on the IP header of the reply packet.

This DNS response is the key to making overlapping networks coexist. The DNS server responds with HostZ's actual IP address, 10.1.1.6; however, RTA translates the payload of the DNS response. Thus, Cisco's implementation of NAT actually alters the contents of a DNS packet, creating a simple table entry and mapping the outside global address, 10.1.1.6, to an outside local address, 192.168.3.6. In this way, HostA believes that HostZ is at 192.168.3.6 (presumably, a reachable IP network).

HostA can then begin a conversation with HostZ. When HostA sends a packet to HostZ, RTA creates an extended table entry, as shown in Figure 11-17. From HostA's point of view, this conversation is between 10.1.1.7 (HostA) and 192.168.3.6 (HostZ).

However, both the source and destination addresses are translated by RTA so that HostZ believes this same conversation is between 192.168.1.7 (HostA) and 10.1.1.6 (HostZ).

Figure 11-17
From HostA's point of view, the packet shown is sourced from 10.1.1.7, but after the translation, HostZ sees the same packet as sourced from 192.168.1.7.

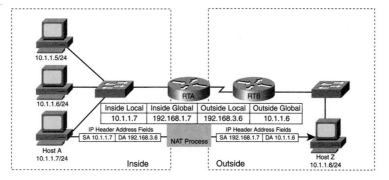

The configuration for RTA is shown in Example 11-8.

Example 11-8 Configuring NAT for Overlapping Networks

```
RTA(config)#ip nat pool inGlobal 192.168.1.1 192.168.1.254 prefix-length 24
RTA(config)#ip nat pool outLocal 192.168.3.1 192.168.3.254 prefix-length 24
RTA(config)#ip nat inside source list 2 pool inGlobal
RTA(config)#ip nat outside source list 2 pool outLocal
RTA(config)#access-list 2 permit 10.1.1.0 0.0.0.255
RTA(config)#interface e0
RTA(config-if)#ip nat inside
RTA(config-if)#interface s0
RTA(config)#ip nat outside
```

RTA uses the **inGlobal** address pool to translate HostA's address so that outside hosts can reach HostA. RTA uses the **outLocal** pool to translate outside hosts in the overlapping network so that HostA can reach those hosts. Example 11-9 provides the output of the **show ip nat translations** command after HostA has sent HostZ an IP packet.

Example 11-9 Output of show ip nat translations in an Overlapping Network Scenario

```
RTA#show ip nat translations
Pro Inside global      Inside local      Outside local      Outside global
--- 192.168.1.7        10.1.1.7          ---                ---
--- ---                ---               192.168.3.6        10.1.1.6
--- 192.168.1.7        10.1.1.7          192.168.3.6        10.1.1.6
```

The first entry was created when HostA sent a DNS query. The second entry was created when RTA translated the payload of the DNS reply. The third entry was created when the packet was exchanged between HostA and HostZ. The third entry is a summary of the first two entries and is used for more efficient translations.

Verifying NAT Configurations

You can display translation information and clear address translation entries from the NAT translation with the commands covered in this section.

The **show ip nat translations [verbose]** command can be used to verify the active translations, as shown in Examples 11-4 and 11-9. The **verbose** keyword can be used with this command to display more information, including the time remaining for a dynamic entry, as shown in Example 11-10.

Example 11-10 Using the show ip nat translations verbose Command

```
RTX#show ip nat translation verbose
Pro Inside global      Inside local      Outside local      Outside global
icmp 42.0.0.55:1536    192.168.0.21:1536 10.0.0.5:1536      10.0.0.5:1536
    create 00:00:09, use 00:00:06, left 00:00:53,
    flags:
extended, use_count: 0
```

You can use the **show ip nat statistics** command to see NAT statistics, as shown in Example 11-11.

Example 11-11 Using the show ip nat statistics Command

```
SanJose1#show ip nat statistics
Total active translations: 3 (3 static, 0 dynamic; 0 extended)
Outside interfaces:
  Serial0/0
Inside interfaces:
  FastEthernet0/0
Hits: 4  Misses: 0
Expired translations: 0
Dynamic mappings:
```

If you need to use a trace on NAT operation, you can use the **debug ip nat** command to display a line of output for each packet that gets translated. You can include the **detailed** keyword to output even more information. The output shown in Example 11-12 is a sample of a debug of address translation inside to outside.

Example 11-12 Using the debug ip nat Command

```
RTX#debug ip nat
IP NAT debugging is on
06:37:40: NAT:  s=192.168.0.21->42.0.0.55, d=10.0.0.5 [63]
06:37:40: NAT*: s=10.0.0.5, d=42.0.0.55->192.168.0.21 [63]
06:37:41: NAT*: s=192.168.0.21->42.0.0.55, d=10.0.0.5 [64]
06:37:41: NAT*: s=10.0.0.5, d=42.0.0.55->192.168.0.21 [64]
06:37:42: NAT*: s=192.168.0.21->42.0.0.55, d=10.0.0.5 [65]
06:37:42: NAT*: s=10.0.0.5, d=42.0.0.55->192.168.0.21 [65]
06:37:43: NAT*: s=192.168.0.21->42.0.0.55, d=10.0.0.5 [66]
06:37:43: NAT*: s=10.0.0.5, d=42.0.0.55->192.168.0.21 [66]
06:38:43: NAT: expiring 42.0.0.55 (192.168.0.21) icmp 1536 (1536)
```

You can decode the debug output in Example 11-12 by using the following key points:

- The asterisk next to **NAT** indicates that the translation is occurring in the fast path. The first packet in a conversation always goes through the slow path (process-switched). The remaining packets go through the fast path if a cache entry exists.
- s = a.b.c.d is the source address.
- d = a.b.c.d is the destination address.
- a.b.c.d -> w.x.y.z indicates that the address was translated.
- The value in brackets is the IP identification number. This information could be useful for debugging because it enables you to correlate with other packet traces from sniffers.

To clear all translated entries, use the **clear ip nat translation** *command.

You can clear a simple translation entry containing an inside translation, or both an inside and outside translation, by using the **clear ip nat translation inside** *global-ip local-ip* [**outside** *local-ip global-ip*] command.

You can clear a simple translation entry that contains an outside translation by using the **clear ip nat translation outside** *local-ip global-ip* command.

If you want to clear an extended entry (in its various forms), use the **clear ip nat trans-lation** *protocol* **inside** *global-ip global-port local-ip local-por*t [**outside** *local-ip local-port global-ip global-port*] command. Example 11-13 shows the use of this command.

Example 11-13 Using the clear ip nat translations Command

```
RTX#clear ip nat translations udp inside 192.168.2.2 1220 10.1.1.2 1220 outside
   171.69.2.132 53 171.69.2.132 53
```

If NAT is properly configured but translations are not occurring, clear the NAT translations and check to see if the translations occur.

NAT Considerations

NAT has several advantages, including the following:

- NAT conserves the legally registered addressing scheme by allowing the privatization of intranets, yet it allows legal addressing scheme pools to be set up to gain access to the Internet.

- NAT also reduces the instances in which addressing schemes overlap. If a scheme was originally set up within a private network, the network was connected to the public network (which might use the same addressing scheme). Without address translation, the potential for overlap exists globally.

- NAT increases the flexibility of connection to the public network. Multiple pools, backup pools, and load sharing/balancing pools can be implemented to help ensure reliable public network connections. Network design is also simplified because planners have more flexibility when creating an address plan.

- Deprivatization of a network requires the renumbering of the existing network; the costs can be associated with the number of hosts that require conversion to the new addressing scheme. NAT allows the existing scheme to remain, and it still supports the new assigned addressing scheme outside the private network.

NAT is not without drawbacks. The tradeoff for address translation is a loss of functionality, particularly with any protocol or application that involves sending IP address information outside the IP header. NAT disadvantages include the following:

- NAT increases delay. Switching path delays are introduced because of the translation of each IP address within the packet headers. Performance might be a consideration because NAT is currently accomplished by using process switching. The CPU must look at every packet to decide whether it has to translate it, and then alter the IP header—and possibly the TCP header. It is not likely that this process will be easily cacheable.

- One significant disadvantage when implementing and using NAT is the loss of end-to-end IP traceability. It becomes much more difficult to trace packets that undergo numerous packet-address changes over multiple NAT hops. This scenario does, however, lead to more secure links because hackers who want to determine the source of a packet will find it difficult, if not impossible, to trace or obtain the original source or destination address.

- NAT also forces some applications that use IP addressing to stop functioning because it hides end-to-end IP addresses. Applications that use physical addresses instead of a qualified domain name will not reach destinations that are translated across the NAT router. Sometimes, this problem can be avoided by implementing static NAT mappings.

The following traffic types are supported by Cisco IOS NAT:

- Any TCP/UDP traffic that does not carry source or destination IP addresses in the application data stream
- Hypertext Transfer Protocol (HTTP)
- Trivial File Transfer Protocol (TFTP)
- Telnet
- Archie
- Finger
- Network Timing Protocol (NTP)
- Network File System (NFS)
- rlogin, rsh, rcp

Although the following traffic types carry IP addresses in the application data stream, they are supported by Cisco IOS NAT:

- ICMP
- File Transfer Protocol (FTP) (including PORT and PASV commands)
- NetBIOS over TCP/IP (datagram, name, and session services)
- Progressive Networks' RealAudio
- White Pines' CuSeeMe
- Xing Technologies' Streamworks
- DNS "A" and "PTR" queries
- H.323/NetMeeting [12.0(1)/12.0(1)T and later]
- VDOLive [11.3(4)11.3(4)T and later]
- Vxtreme [11.3(4)11.3(4)T and later]
- IP multicast [12.0(1)T] (source address translation only)

The following traffic types are not supported by Cisco IOS NAT:

- Routing table updates
- DNS zone transfers
- BOOTP
- talk, ntalk
- Simple Network Management Protocol (SNMP)
- NetShow

Summary

In this chapter, you learned that NAT allows your network to scale without depleting your limited supply of global IP addresses. You learned how to configure static NAT, and you learned about dynamic NAT and NAT overload (PAT). You also saw how NAT can be used to provide connectivity in overlapping IP networks.

Review Questions

Use the following review questions to test your understanding of the concepts covered in this chapter. In some cases, there is more than one correct answer, so choose all that apply. Answers are listed in Appendix A, "Answers to Review Questions."

1. Which of the following are not RFC 1918 addresses?

    A. 1.1.1.1

    B. 172.31.255.221

    C. 192.168.192.192

    D. 172.168.0.1

2. Which of the following is true about static NAT?

    A. Static NAT translations timeout after 24 hours by default.

    B. Static NAT translations are assigned from an address pool.

    C. Static NAT maps one local address to one global address.

    D. Cisco routers use static NAT by default.

3. Which command correctly configures S0 as an outside interface?

    A. (config)#ip nat outside s0

    B. (config)#ip nat s0

    C. (config-if)#ip nat outside

    D. (config-if)#ip nat s0 out

4. Which of the following commands correctly configures NAT overload?

    A. (config)#ip nat inside source list 24 interface s0 overload

    B. (config)#ip nat inside source 24 pool mypool overload

    C. (config)#ip nat source 24 pool mypool overload

    D. (config)#ip nat source list 24 pool overload

5. For overlapping networks, which of the following is true about NAT:

    A. NAT can be used only in overlapping networks that use the same major network number, but not the same subnets.

    B. NAT translates the payload of DNS requests to facilitate name lookups between overlapping networks.

C. NAT cannot be used with overlapping networks.

D. NAT can modify only the IP header of a DNS query and response.

6. Which command modifies the timeout for dynamic NAT translations?

    A. (config-if)#ip nat timeout 1200

    B. (config)#ip nat timeout 120000

    C. (config-if)#ip nat translation timeout 1200000

    D. (config)#ip nat translation timeout 12000000

7. Which command can be used to clear all NAT translations?

    A. clear nat translations all

    B. clear ip nat translations all

    C. clear ip nat translations *

    D. clear nat translations *

8. What is one disadvantage of using NAT?

    A. Using NAT accelerates IP address depletion.

    B. NAT is not compatible with ICMP.

    C. NAT increases latency.

    D. NAT cannot support RFC 1918 outside global addresses.

9. Which of the following commands will output the NAT translations table?

    A. show ip nat translations table

    B. show ip nat translations

    C. show ip nat translations *

    D. show ip nat database

10. Which of the following commands configures TCP load distribution?

    A. RTA(config)#ip nat load-distribution

    B. RTA(config)#ip nat pool webservers 171.70.2.3 171.70.2.4 netmask 255.255.255.0 type overload

    C. RTA(config)#ip nat pool webservers overload

    D. RTA(config)#ip nat pool webservers 171.70.2.3 171.70.2.4 netmask 255.255.255.0 type rotary

Key Terms

Inside global address   In NAT, the IP address of an inside host as it appears to the outside network. The inside global address is the translated address. These addresses are typically allocated from a globally unique address space, typically provided by the Internet Service Provider (ISP) (if the enterprise is connected to the global Internet).

Inside local address   In NAT, the configured IP address assigned to a host on the inside network. The address might be globally unique, allocated out of the private address space defined in RFC 1918, or officially allocated to another organization.

NAT (Network Address Translation)   Mechanism for reducing the need for globally unique IP addresses. NAT allows an organization with addresses that are not globally unique to connect to the Internet by translating those addresses into globally routable address space.

Outside global address   In NAT, the configured IP address assigned to a host in the outside network.

Outside local address   In NAT, the IP address of an outside host as it appears to the inside network. These addresses can be allocated from the RFC 1918 space if desired.

Overlapping networks   Two or more networks using addresses from the same public or private IP address space.

Stub domain   A network that has a single connection to the outside world.

PAT (Port Address Translation)   A NAT process that maps multiple inside addresses to the same global address by using port numbers to keep track of the translations. This is sometimes called a many-to-one NAT, or *address overloading*.

Objectives

After completing this chapter, you will be able to perform tasks related to the following:

- AAA concepts
- Security protocols
- AAA authentication
- AAA authorization
- AAA accounting

Chapter 12

AAA

Introduction

Depending on the remote-access solutions you deploy, your network might allow access to remote users via public services such as plain ordinary telephone service (POTS), Integrated Services Digital Network Basic Rate Interface (ISDN BRI), or the Internet. Clearly, you must design your network to control who is allowed to connect to your network, and what they are allowed to do once they get connected. You might also want to configure an accounting system that tracks who logs in, when they log in, and what they do once they've logged in. *Authentication, authorization, and accounting (AAA)* security services provide a framework for these kinds of access control and accounting functions. AAA, also called Triple-A, stands for authentication (Who is it?), authorization (What are you allowed to do?), and accounting (What did you do?).

This chapter describes the access-control features included in AAA, and shows you how to configure these services on a Cisco router. This chapter also looks at Cisco Secure, which is a software solution that can be used to configure and monitor AAA.

AAA Overview

AAA is an architectural framework for configuring three different security features. By using a single framework, the three features—authentication, authorization, and accounting—can be configured consistently and cohesively.

What is meant by authentication, authorization, and accounting? Consider the following example.

If the user, flannery, dials into an access server configured with Challenge Handshake Authentication Protocol (CHAP), the access server prompts the user for a name and password. The process of supplying a username and password to gain access is called *authentication*. In other words, authentication asks the question, "Who are you?"

NOTE

In this chapter, the terms access server, and network access server (NAS), refer to a router connected to the edge of a network. This router allows outside users to access the network.

After flannery successfully authenticates to the access server, the user might be able to execute commands on that server. The server uses a process called *authorization* to determine which commands and resources should be made available to that particular user. Authorization asks the question, "What can you do?"

Finally, the number of login attempts, the specific commands entered, and other system events can be logged and time-stamped by the *accounting* process. Accounting can be used to trace a problem, such as a security breach, or it can be used to compile usage statistics or billing data. Accounting asks the question, "What did you do and when did you do it?"

Authentication can be configured without using AAA. In Chapter 2, "Modems and Asynchronous Connections," and Chapter 3, "PPP," you learned how to configure a local username and password database in conjunction with CHAP and Password Authentication Protocol (PAP). This same local database can be used to authenticate users starting an EXEC session with the router.

However, using AAA for authentication has several advantages.

First, AAA provides scalability. Typical AAA configurations rely on a server or group of servers to store usernames and passwords. This means that you don't have to build and update local databases on every router and access server in the network. The routers in your network become clients of these security servers. By centralizing the username/password database, you can enter and update information in one place.

Second, AAA supports standardized security protocols, namely Terminal Access Controller Access Control System Plus (TACACS+), Remote Authentication Dial-In User Service (RADIUS), and Kerberos. These protocols are discussed in the next section, "Security Protocols."

Third, AAA allows you to configure multiple backup systems. For example, you can configure an access server to consult a security server first, and a local database second. The second method is used if the first method returns an error.

Overall, these benefits mean that AAA gives you scalability, and an increased flexibility and control of access configuration.

Security Protocols

Access servers and other network hosts are often configured to use a security protocol. Hosts use a security protocol to communicate with a specialized security server. The security server maintains a password and username database, authorization configurations, and stores accounting information. The Cisco IOS supports three key security protocols: TACACS+, RADIUS, and Kerberos.

AAA is the means through which you configure your devices to use one of the following security protocols:

- *TACACS+*—A security application used with AAA that provides centralized validation of users attempting to gain access to a router or network access server. TACACS+ services are maintained in a database on a TACACS+ daemon running, typically, on a UNIX or Windows NT workstation. TACACS+ provides for separate and modular authentication, authorization, and accounting facilities.

- *RADIUS*—A distributed client/server system used with AAA that secures networks against unauthorized access. In the Cisco implementation, RADIUS clients run on Cisco routers and send authentication requests to a central RADIUS server that contains all user authentication and network service access information.

- *Kerberos*—A secret-key network authentication protocol used with AAA that uses the Data Encryption Standard (DES) cryptographic algorithm for encryption and authentication. Kerberos was designed to authenticate requests for network resources. Kerberos is based on the concept of a trusted third party that performs secure verification of users and services. The primary use of Kerberos is to verify that users and the network services they use are really who and what they claim to be. To accomplish this, a trusted Kerberos server issues tickets to users. These tickets, which have a limited lifespan, are stored in a user's credential cache and can be used in place of the standard username-and-password authentication mechanism.

Of the three protocols, TACACS+ and RADIUS offer the most comprehensive AAA support (see Figure 12-1). Kerberos provides a highly secure method of authentication, in which passwords are never sent over the wire. However, Kerberos does not support the authorization and accounting components of AAA and is, therefore, not covered in any more detail in this chapter.

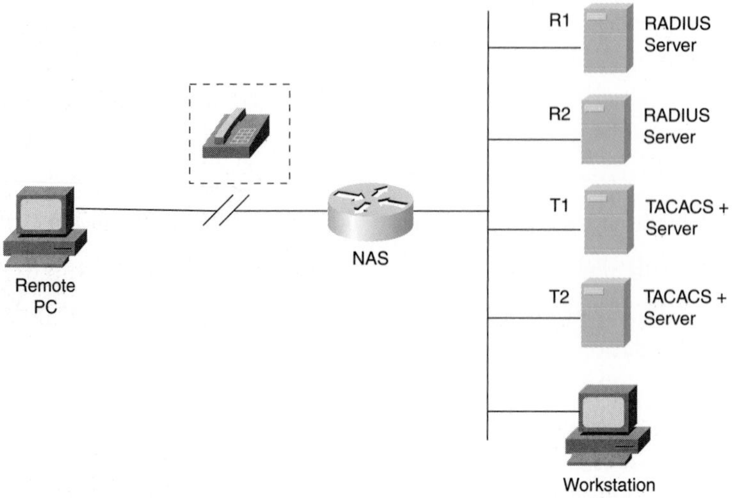

Figure 12-1
A network access server configured for AAA can authenticate and authorize remote users via TACACS+ or RADIUS.

TACACS+

TACACS+ provides the most comprehensive and flexible security configurations when using Cisco routers and switches. TACACS+ is derived from the TACACS and extended TACACS protocols. Both of these older protocols are considered deprecated protocols, which means they are no longer seen as viable solutions. A Cisco-proprietary protocol, TACACS+ is not compatible with TACACS or extended TACACS.

TACACS+ uses TCP to communicate between a TACACS+ server and a TACACS+ client. To take advantage of all of AAA's features, you must use TACACS+. Unlike RADIUS, TACACS+ separates the functions of authentication, authorization, and accounting.

RADIUS

Even though TACACS+ offers more flexible AAA configurations, RADIUS is a popular AAA solution because it is an open standard that typically uses fewer CPU cycles and is less memory intensive than TACACS+ (which is proprietary). The RADIUS protocol was developed by Livingston Enterprises as an access server authentication and accounting protocol. Unlike TACACS+, RADIUS uses UDP. Table 12-1 compares TACACS+ and RADIUS.

NOTE
RADIUS is specified in RFCs 2865, 2866, and 2868.

Table 12-1   **Comparison of TACACS+ and RADIUS**

TACACS+	RADIUS
Cisco-proprietary enhancement to TACACS.	Open standard developed by Livingston Enterprises.
Supports authentication, authorization, and accounting functions.	Supports authentication, authorization, and accounting functions.
Uses the AAA architecture, which separates authentication, authorization, and accounting.	Combines the functions of authentication and authorization.
Provides two ways to control the authorization of router commands: on a per-user or per-group basis.	Does not allow administrators to control which commands can be executed on a router.
Uses TCP.	Uses UDP.
Encrypts the entire body of the packet; more secure.	Encrypts only the password in the access-request packet; less secure.
Offers multiprotocol support.	Does not support ARA access, NetBIOS, NASI, and X.25 PAD connections.

Cisco Secure Access Control Server

The Cisco Secure Access Control Server (ACS) is specialized security software that runs on Windows NT/2000 and Unix. The software simplifies and centralizes control for all user authentication, authorization, and accounting. Cisco ACS employs a web-based graphical interface, and can distribute the AAA information to hundreds or even thousands of access points in a network.

The Cisco Secure ACS software uses either the TACACS+ or the RADIUS protocol to provide this network security and tracking.

Each of your network devices can be configured to communicate with an ACS. Service providers can use ACS to centralize control of dial-up access. With a Cisco Secure ACS, system administrators can use a variety of authentication methods that are aligned with a varying degree of authorization privileges. Centralizing control of network access simplifies access management and helps establish consistent provisioning and security policies.

Cisco Secure ACS also acts as a central repository for accounting information. Each user session that is granted by the ACS can be fully accounted for and stored in the server. This accounting information can be used for billing, capacity planning, and security audits.

Configuring AAA

Configuring AAA can be a complex process. It is imperative that you plan out your security policies before you begin to configure AAA.

To enable AAA, issue the following command in global configuration mode:

```
Router(config)#aaa new-model
```

The **aaa new-model** command enables the AAA feature so that you can enter other AAA commands. To disable AAA, use the **no aaa new-model** command.

The following sections describe how to configure the three elements of AAA using TACACS+, RADIUS, and local databases.

Configuring a TACACS+ Client

If you use a TACACS+ server or servers in conjunction with AAA, you must configure the router with the address(es) of the server(s) and the TACACS+ encryption key. The encryption key must be the same on both the TACACS+ server and its clients. Use the following syntax to configure the address of a TACACS+ server:

```
Router(config)#tacacs-server host ip-address
```

You can use multiple **tacacs-server host** commands to specify multiple hosts. The Cisco IOS software searches for the hosts in the order you specify them. The **tacacs-server key** command configures the encryption key, as shown here:

```
Router(config)#tacacs-server key word
```

Example 12-1 shows the commands that you use to configure a router to communicate with a TACACS+ server at 192.168.0.11, using the shared key **topsecret**.

Example 12-1 Configuring a TACACS+ Client

```
RTA(config)#tacacs-server host 192.168.0.11
RTA(config)#tacacs-server key topsecret
```

Figure 12-2 illustrates this configuration.

Figure 12-2
RTA can be configured to use the TACACS+ server (192.168.0.11) for AAA functions.

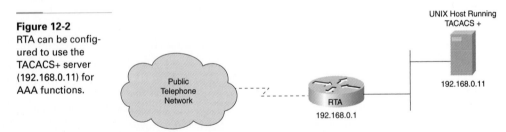

You can use the **show tacacs** command to verify your configuration and connection (see Example 12-2).

Example 12-2 Using the show tacacs Command

```
RTA#show tacacs
Server:192.168.0.11/49:opens=4 closes=4 aborts=0 errors=0
        packets in=6 packets out=6
        no connection
```

Configuring a RADIUS Client

You configure a router to use RADIUS, like TACACS+, by specifying a server address and shared key.

Use the **radius-server host** command to specify a server's IP address:

```
Router(config)#radius-server host ip-address
```

You can use multiple **radius-server host** commands to specify multiple hosts. The Cisco IOS Software searches for the hosts in the order you specify them. Use the **radius-server key** command to specify the encryption key:

```
Router(config)#radius-server key word
```

Example 12-3 shows the commands needed to configure a router to communicate with a RADIUS server at 192.168.0.22, using the shared key **topsecret**.

Example 12-3 Configuring a RADIUS Client

```
RTB(config)#radius-server host 192.168.0.22
RTB(config)#radius-server key topsecret
```

Figure 12-3 illustrates this configuration.

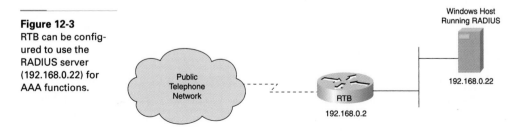

Figure 12-3
RTB can be configured to use the RADIUS server (192.168.0.22) for AAA functions.

Configuring AAA Authentication

Authentication provides the method of identifying users, including login and password dialog, challenge and response, and messaging support.

On a router, several different types of authentication exist. Typically, when you log in to a router through Telnet, you must authenticate. When you access privileged EXEC mode, you authenticate. When you establish a Point-to-Point Protocol (PPP) connection to the router, you authenticate. A username and password that successfully authenticates for one type may not work for another. AAA authentication can be used to configure all of these configuration types, including the following:

- Access to privileged EXEC mode (enable mode)
- Access to virtual terminals
- Access to the console
- CHAP and PAP authentication for PPP connections
- NetWare Asynchronous Services Interface (NASI) authentication
- AppleTalk Remote Access Protocol (ARAP) authentication

NOTE

This chapter does not cover NASI or ARAP configuration. For more information on these legacy dial-up protocols, refer to www,cisco.com/univercd.

You configure AAA authentication by issuing the **aaa authentication** command. When using this command, you must specify which type of authentication to configure (login, enable, PPP, etc.) Table 12-2 lists some of the keywords you use with the **aaa authentication** command.

Table 12-2   The aaa authentication Command Authentication Types

Keyword	Description
arap	Sets authentication method for ARAP.
enable	Sets authentication method for privileged EXEC mode.
login	Sets authentication method for logins on terminal lines, virtual terminal lines, and the console.
nasi	Sets authentication method for NASI.
ppp	Sets authentication method for any authentication protocol supported by PPP (CHAP, PAP, MS-CHAP).

After you specify an authentication type, you define either a default method list or a named method list. Named method lists must be applied to a specific interface before any of the defined authentication methods can be performed. The default method list is automatically applied to all interfaces if no other method list is defined.

These lists are called *method lists* because they list the types of authentication to be performed and the sequence in which they are performed. Authentication methods include the following:

- Using a password already configured on the router, such as the enable password or a line password
- Using the local username/password database
- Consulting a Kerberos server
- Consulting a RADIUS server, or group of RADIUS servers
- Consulting a TACACS+ server or group of TACACS+ servers

One of the advantages of AAA is that you can configure more than one of these methods to be tried in sequence. For example, you can configure the router to authenticate PPP users by first consulting a group of RADIUS servers. If the router fails to connect to a server, you can configure a backup method, such as using the local username/password database.

AAA commands can be confusing because so many syntax possibilities exist. When configuring AAA authentication, you follow a three-step process for each **aaa authentication** command, as shown in Figure 12-4:

1. Specify the authentication type (login, enable, PPP, etc.).

2. Specify the method list as default or give it a name.

3. List the authentication methods to be tried, in order.

NOTE

Using AAA, you can configure up to four methods in a method list. If all the defined methods return an error, the user is not authenticated.

Figure 12-4
Use the **aaa authentication** command to specify the authentication type, method list type, and authentication methods.

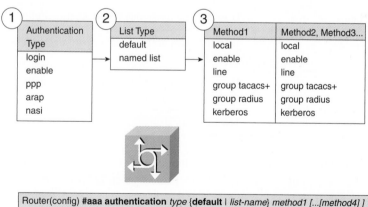

Router(config) #**aaa authentication** *type* {**default** | *list-name*} *method1* [...[*method4*]]

For example, the syntax for creating a method list to be used for PPP authentication is as follows:

```
Router(config)#aaa authentication ppp {default | list-name} method1 [...[method4]]
```

In the following sections, you look specifically at configuring three types of AAA authentication: login, enable, and PPP.

Configuring AAA Login Authentication

The **aaa authentication login** command enables AAA authentication for logins on terminal lines (TTYs), virtual terminal lines (VTYs), and the console (con 0). Using this command, you can create one or more lists that are tried at login:

```
Router(config)#aaa authentication login {default | list-name} method1 [...[method4]]
```

The default list is applied to all lines. If you configure a named list, you must apply the list to a specific line or group of lines using the **aaa login authentication** command.

Table 12-3 lists the keywords that are used to specify the authentication methods when using the **aaa authentication login** command.

Table 12-3   The aaa authentication login Method List Syntax

Keyword	Description
enable	Uses the enable password for authentication.
group radius	Uses a list of all RADIUS hosts defined by the **radius-server** command to authenticate users.
group tacacs+	Uses a list of all TACACS+ hosts defined by the **tacacs-server** command to authenticate users.
krb5	Uses Kerberos 5 for authentication.
line	Uses the line password for authentication.
local	Uses the local username/password database for authentication (not case sensitive).
local-case	Uses the local username/password database for authentication (case sensitive).
none	No authentication.

The additional methods of authentication are used only if the previous method returns an ERROR, not a FAIL. A FAIL response is significantly different from an ERROR. A FAIL means that the user has not met the criteria contained in the applicable authentication database to be successfully authenticated. Authentication ends with a FAIL response. An ERROR means that the security server has not responded to an authentication query. Because of this, no authentication has been attempted. Only when an ERROR is detected will AAA select the next authentication method defined in the authentication method list.

A typical ERROR is a failure to connect with a member of a server group due to link failure or a server-side problem.

To ensure that the user is granted access, even if all methods return an ERROR, specify **none** as the final method in the command line. If all defined methods end with an ERROR and **none** is not specified as the final method, the user will not be authenticated. If authentication is not specifically set for a line, the default is to deny access and no authentication is performed.

Depending on your network's security policy, you can always configure **none** as the final method, or you can decide that denying access when all other methods return an ERROR is the most secure course of action.

The commands in Example 12-4 create a default AAA authentication list.

Example 12-4 Configuring the Default Method List for AAA Login Authentication

```
RTA(config)#tacacs-server host 192.168.0.11
RTA(config)#tacacs-server host 192.168.1.12
RTA(config)#tacacs-server key topsecret
RTA(config)#aaa new-model
RTA(config)#aaa authentication login default group tacacs+ enable none
```

Because this authentication method list specifies TACACS+ as the first method, the **tacacs-server host** and **tacacs-server key** commands are used to configure RTA as a TACACS+ client. Two TACACS+ servers are specified (192.168.0.11 and 192.168.1.12). The server specified first, 192.168.0.11, is tried first.

The **aaa new-model** command enables the AAA feature. Finally, the **aaa authentication login** command defines the method list. The method list configures RTA to attempt to contact the TACACS+ servers first. If neither server is reached, this method returns an ERROR and AAA tries to use the second method, the **enable** password. If this attempt also returns an ERROR (because no **enable** password is configured on the router), the user is allowed access with no authentication.

The default list is applied to the console (con 0), all TTY lines (including the auxiliary line or AUX port), and all VTY lines. You can override the default method list by a named list to one or more of these lines. Example 12-5 shows how to configure a named list.

Example 12-5 Configuring a Named Method List for AAA Login Authentication

```
RTB(config)#radius-server host 192.168.0.22
RTB(config)#radius-server host 192.168.1.23
RTB(config)#radius-server key topsecret
```

continues

Example 12-5 Configuring a Named Method List for AAA Login Authentication (Continued)

```
RTB(config)#aaa new-model
RTB(config)#aaa authentication login default local
RTB(config)#aaa authentication login PASSPORT group radius local none
```

RTB is configured with the **radius-server host** and **radius-server key** commands because the named method list relies on RADIUS. The **aaa authentication login default local** command configures the default method as the local username/password database. This method is applied to all TTYs, VTYs, and the console by default.

The **aaa authentication login PASSPORT group radius local none** command creates a named method list called PASSPORT. The first method in this list is the group of RADIUS servers. If RTB cannot contact either RADIUS server, the local username/password database is tried. Finally, the **none** keyword ensures that, if no usernames exist in the local database, the user is granted access.

You apply named method lists for login authentication by using the **login authentication** command, as shown here:

```
Router(config-line)#login authentication listname
```

Example 12-6 shows the commands you need to apply the PASSPORT method list to all five VTYs.

Example 12-6 Applying Login Authentication Lists

```
RTB(config)#line vty 0 4
RTB(config-line)#login authentication PASSPORT
```

Enabling Password Protection at the Privileged Level

The **aaa authentication enable** command enables AAA authentication for privileged EXEC mode access. This authentication method is employed when a user issues the **enable** command in user EXEC mode:

```
Router(config)#aaa authentication enable default method1 [...[method4]]
```

Because authenticating for privileged EXEC mode is the same for all users on all lines, you cannot create a named list with the **aaa authentication enable** command. Only one privileged mode method list can exist: the default list.

Table 12-4 lists the keywords that are used to specify the authentication methods when using the **aaa authentication enable** command.

Table 12-4   **The aaa authentication enable Method List Syntax**

Keyword	Description
enable	Uses the enable password for authentication.
group radius	Uses a list of all RADIUS hosts defined by the **radius-server** command to authenticate users.
group tacacs+	Uses a list of all TACACS+ hosts defined by the **tacacs-server** command to authenticate users.
line	Uses the line password for authentication.
none	No authentication.

The commands shown in Example 12-7 create a method list that first tries to contact a TACACS+ server.

Example 12-7 Configuring Password Protection at the Privileged Level

```
RTA(config)#tacacs-server host 192.168.0.11
RTA(config)#tacacs-server host 192.168.1.12
RTA(config)#tacacs-server key topsecret
RTA(config)#aaa new-model
RTA(config)#aaa authentication enable default group tacacs+ enable none
```

If neither server can be contacted, AAA tries to use the **enable** password. If this attempt also returns an error (because no enable password is configured on RTA), the user is allowed access with no authentication.

Configuring PPP Authentication Using AAA

Many remote users access networks through a router using PPP over asynchronous dial-up or ISDN BRI. Such users bypass the router's command line interface entirely. Instead, PPP starts a packet session as soon as the connection is established.

Using the **aaa authentication ppp** command, you can configure AAA to authenticate these users by using any available PPP authentication method: CHAP, PAP or MS-CHAP. The syntax for this command is as follows:

```
Router(config)#aaa authentication ppp {default | list-name} method1 [...[method4]]
```

The additional methods of authentication are used only if the previous method returns an error, not if the user is unknown or denied access. Remember to specify **none** as the final method in the method list to have authentication succeed even if all methods return an error. Table 12-5 describes the method keywords available for the **aaa authentication ppp** command.

Table 12-5   The aaa authentication ppp Method List Syntax

Keyword	Description
group radius	Uses a list of all RADIUS hosts defined by the **radius-server** command to authenticate users.
group tacacs+	Uses a list of all TACACS+ hosts defined by the **tacacs-server** command to authenticate users.
if-needed	Does not authenticate if the user has already been authenticated on a TTY line.
krb5	Uses Kerberos 5 for authentication (can be used only for PAP authentication).
local	Uses the local username/password database for authentication (not case sensitive).
local-case	Uses the local username/password database for authentication (case sensitive).
none	No authentication.

Example 12-8 shows the commands you can use to apply a named AAA authentication list called **DIALIN** for PPP.

Example 12-8 Configuring AAA Authentication for PPP

```
RTA(config)#tacacs-server host 192.168.0.11
RTA(config)#tacacs-server host 192.168.1.12
RTA(config)#tacacs-server key topsecret
RTA(config)#aaa new-model
RTA(config)#aaa authentication ppp DIALIN group tacacs+ none
RTA(config)#interface bri0
RTA(config-if)#ppp authentication chap DIALIN
```

This authentication method list first tries to contact a TACACS+ server. If this action returns an error, the user is allowed access with no authentication.

The **ppp authentication** command is used to apply an AAA authentication method list for PPP. In Example 12-8, CHAP authentication uses the method list.

Configuring AAA Authorization

AAA authorization enables you to limit the services available to a user. When AAA authorization is enabled, the router uses information retrieved from the user's profile, which is located either in the local user database or on the security server, to configure the user's session. After this is done, the user is granted access to a requested service only if the information in the user profile allows it.

Cisco IOS Software supports five different types of authorization:

- **Authentication proxy services**—Applies specific security policies on a per-user basis.
- **Commands**—Applies to the EXEC mode commands a user issues. Command authorization attempts authorization for all EXEC mode commands, including global configuration commands, associated with a specific privilege level.
- **EXEC**—Applies to the attributes associated with a user EXEC terminal session.
- **Network services**—Applies to network connections. This can include a PPP, Serial Line Internet Protocol (SLIP), or ARAP connection.
- **Reverse Telnet access**—Applies to reverse Telnet sessions.
- **Configuration**—Applies to downloading configurations from the AAA server.
- **IP Mobile**—Applies to authorization for IP mobile services.

You configure AAA authorization by issuing the **aaa authorization** command. When using this command, you must specify which type of authorization to configure. Table 12-6 lists some of the keywords you use with the **aaa authorization** command.

Table 12-6   The aaa authorization Command Authorization Types

Keyword	Description
auth-proxy	Configures authorization for authentication proxy services.
commands	Configures authorization for EXEC commands.
config-commands	Configures authorization for configuration mode commands.
exec	Configures authorization for starting an EXEC session.
ipmobile	Configures authorization for Mobile IP services.
network	Configures authorization for network services.
reverse-access	Configures authorization for reverse Telnet connections.

After you specify an authorization type, you define either a *default method list* or a *named method list*. Named method lists must be applied to a specific interface before any of the defined authorization methods can be performed. The default method list is automatically applied to all lines and interfaces if no other method list is defined.

Table 12-7 lists authentication methods and their IOS keywords.

Table 12-7   AAA Authorization Method Keywords

Keyword	Description
group tacacs+	TACACS+ authorization defines specific rights for users by associating attribute-value pairs, which are stored in a database on the TACACS+ security server, with the appropriate user.
group radius	RADIUS authorization defines specific rights for users by associating attributes, which are stored in a database on the RADIUS server, with the appropriate user.
if-authenticated	The user is allowed to access the requested function, provided the user has been authenticated successfully.
none	The router does not request authorization information; authorization is not performed over this line/interface.
local	The router consults its local database, as defined by the **username** command, for example, to authorize specific rights for users. Only a limited set of functions can be controlled through the local database.

Before configuring AAA authorization, you must first perform the following tasks:

- Enable AAA using the **aaa new-model** command.
- Configure AAA authentication. Authorization generally takes place after authentication and relies on authentication to work properly.
- Configure the router as a TACACS+ or RADIUS client, if necessary.
- Configure the local username/password database, if necessary. Using the **username** command, you can define the rights associated with specific users.

The commands shown in Example 12-9 prepare a router for AAA authorization using TACACS+.

Example 12-9 Preparing to Configure AAA Authorization

```
RTA(config)#tacacs-server host 192.168.0.11
RTA(config)#tacacs-server host 192.168.1.12
RTA(config)#tacacs-server key topsecret
RTA(config)#aaa new-model
RTA(config)#aaa authentication login default group tacacs+ local enable
```

With TACACS+ and authentication configured, you can configure authorization by using the following syntax (see Figure 12-5):

```
Router(config)#aaa authorization type {default | list-name}
  [method1 [...[method4]]
```

Figure 12-5
Use the **aaa authorization** command to specify the authorization type, method list type, and authorization methods.

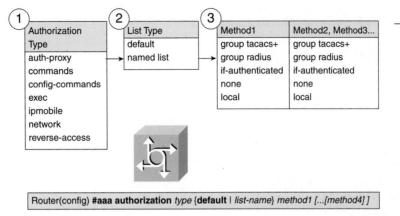

NOTE
Configuring a TACACS+ server or RADIUS server for authentication is beyond the scope of this book. If you are using Cisco Secure, consult Cisco's Web site for configuration information at www.cisco.com/univercd/cc/td/doc/product/access/acs_soft/index.htm.

The command in Example 12-10 configures authorization for reverse Telnet sessions.

Example 12-10 Configuring AAA Authorization for Reverse Telnet

```
RTA(config)#aaa authorization reverse-access default group tacacs+
```

Users attempting to reverse Telnet from the router must be authorized to issue the command first by a TACACS+ server.

Example 12-11 presents a sample EXEC authorization configuration. When configured with this command, the router contacts a TACACS+ server to determine if users are permitted to start an EXEC shell when they log in.

Example 12-11 Configuring AAA Authorization for EXEC Access

```
RTA(config)#aaa authorization exec default group tacacs+ local
```

Privilege Levels

You can use the **aaa authorization** command to control exactly which commands a user is allowed to enter on the router. Users can only enter commands at or beneath their privilege level. All IOS router commands are assigned a privilege level from 0–15. By default, three privilege levels are on the router:

- privilege level 1 = non-privileged (prompt is router>), the default level for login
- privilege level 15 = privileged (prompt is router#), the level after going into enable mode
- privilege level 0 = includes 5 commands: disable, enable, exit, help, and logout

When a user logs in to the router EXEC through the console or a VTY, the user can issue any command in privilege level 1 and/or privilege level 0 by default. Once the user authenticates using the **enable** command and enable password, that user has privilege level 15.

Levels 2-14 are not used in a default configuration, but commands that are normally at level 15 can be moved down to one of those levels, and commands that are normally at level 1 can be moved up to one of those levels. Obviously, this security model involves some administration on the router. To determine the privilege level as a logged in user, use the **show privilege** command.

NOTE

Instead of assigning privilege levels, command authorization can be done if the authentication server supports TACACS+. The RADIUS protocol does not support command authorization.

To determine what commands are available at a particular privilege level for the Cisco IOS Software Release you are using, enter a ? at the command line when logged in at that privilege level.

Configuring Command Authorization

You can configure precisely which commands belong to which privilege levels, including levels that you define. The commands shown in Example 12-12 move the **snmp-server** commands from privilege level 15 (the default) to privilege level 7. The **ping** command is moved up from privilege level 1 to privilege level 7.

Example 12-12 Configuring Privilege Levels

```
RTA(config)#privilege configure level 7 snmp-server host
RTA(config)#privilege configure level 7 snmp-server enable
RTA(config)#privilege configure level 7 snmp-server
RTA(config)#privilege exec level 7 ping
RTA(config)#privilege exec level 7 configure terminal
RTA(config)#privilege exec level 7 configure
```

You can use the **aaa authorization** command to grant access to commands by privilege level, as shown in Example 12-13.

Example 12-13 Configuring AAA Command Authorization

```
RTA(config)#aaa authorization commands 0 default group tacacs+ local
RTA(config)#aaa authorization commands 15 default group tacacs+ local
RTA(config)#aaa authorization commands 7 default group tacacs+ local
```

The user who logs in with level 7 privileges can **ping** and do **snmp-server** configuration in configuration mode. Other configuration commands are not available.

A user's privilege level can be determined by the security server or the local user-name/password database. To configure a local user for a specific privilege, use the following command:

`Router(config)#`**`username`** *`name`* **`privilege`** *`level`* **`password`** *`password`*

Example 12-14 shows the command you use to create a user named flannery with a privilege level of 7.

Example 12-14 Configuring User Privilege Levels

```
RTA(config)#username flannery privilege 7 password letmein
```

When this user logs in, she will only have access to commands in privilege level 7 and below.

Configuring AAA Accounting

Like authentication and authorization method lists, method lists for accounting define the way accounting is performed and the sequence in which these methods are performed.

Named accounting method lists enable you to designate a particular security protocol to be used on specific lines or interfaces for accounting services. The default method list is automatically applied to all interfaces except those that have a named method list explicitly defined. As with AAA authentication and authorization, a defined method list overrides the default method list.

Accounting method lists are specific to the type of accounting being requested. AAA supports six different types of accounting:

- **Network**—Provides information for all PPP, SLIP, or ARAP sessions, including packet and byte counts.
- **EXEC**—Provides information about user EXEC terminal sessions of the network access server.
- **Commands**—Provides information about the EXEC mode commands that a user issues. Command accounting generates accounting records for all EXEC mode commands, including global configuration commands, associated with a specific privilege level.
- **Connection**—Provides information about all outbound connections made from the network access server, such as Telnet, local-area transport (LAT), TN3270, packet assembler/disassembler (PAD), and rlogin.
- **System**—Provides information about system-level events.
- **Resource**—Provides start and stop records for calls that have passed user authentication, and provides stop records for calls that fail to authenticate.

You configure AAA accounting by issuing the **aaa accounting** command. When using this command, you must specify which type of accounting to configure. Table 12-8 lists some of the keywords you use with the **aaa accounting** command.

Table 12-8   The aaa accounting Command Accounting Types

Keyword	Description
commands	Configures AAA accounting for EXEC commands.
connection	Configures AAA accounting for outbound connections, such as Telnet and rlogin.
exec	Configures AAA accounting for starting an EXEC session.
nested	Configures AAA accounting to generate NETWORK records before the EXEC-STOP records. This keyword formats accounting logs so that start and stop events are kept together, which might be useful for billing purposes.
network	Configures AAA accounting for network services.
suppress	Configures AAA accounting to not generate accounting records for a specific type of user.
system	Configures AAA accounting for system events.
update	Enables periodic interim accounting records to be sent to the accounting server.

After you specify an accounting type, you must define either a default method list or a named method list. Named method lists must be applied to a specific interface before any of the defined authorization methods can be performed. The default method list is automatically applied to all lines and interfaces if no other method list is defined.

NOTE

System accounting does not support named method lists.

After specifying a named or default list, you must indicate the accounting record type. There are four accounting record types:

- none
- start-stop
- stop-only
- wait-start

For minimal accounting, use the **stop-only** keyword, which instructs the specified method (RADIUS or TACACS+) to send a stop record accounting notice at the end of the requested user process. For more accounting information, use the **start-stop** keyword to send a start accounting notice at the beginning of the requested event and a stop accounting notice at the end of the event. As in **start-stop, wait-start** sends both a start and a stop accounting record to the accounting server. However, if you use the **wait-start** keyword, the requested user service does not begin until the start accounting record is acknowledged. A stop accounting record is also sent.

To stop all accounting activities on this line or interface, use the **none** keyword.

Finally, after specifying the accounting type, and the accounting record type, configure the accounting method (see Figure 12-6). Accounting methods and their IOS keywords are listed in Table 12-9.

Figure 12-6
Use the **aaa account-ing** command to specify the account-ing type, method list type, accounting record type, and accounting methods.

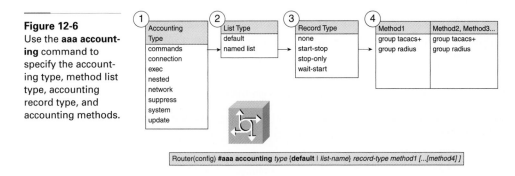

Table 12-9   AAA Accounting Method Keywords

Keyword	Description
group tacacs+	Accounting information is logged to a TACACS+ server.
group radius	Accounting information is logged to a RADIUS server.

Before configuring AAA accounting, you must first perform the following tasks:

- Enable AAA using the **aaa new-model** command.
- Configure the router as a TACACS+ or RADIUS client. This is required for AAA accounting. A server is needed to act as repository for the accounting data.

Example 12-15 shows a possible AAA accounting configuration:

Example 12-15 Possible AAA Accounting Configuration

```
RTA(config)#tacacs-server host 192.168.0.11
RTA(config)#tacacs-server host 192.168.1.12
RTA(config)#tacacs-server key topsecret
```

continues

Example 12-15 Possible AAA Accounting Configuration (Continued)

```
RTA(config)#aaa new-model
RTA(config)#aaa authentication login default group tacacs+ local enable
RTA(config)#aaa accounting network default start-stop group tacacs+
```

The **aaa accounting network** command enables accounting for network service, which includes information for all PPP, SLIP, or ARAP sessions, including packet and byte counts.

As configured in Example 12-15, RTA sends accounting information for PPP sessions to a TACACS+ server. The format of the output stored on the server varies depending on your TACACS+ or RADIUS implementation. Example 12-16 presents sample TACACS+ output from a UNIX TACACS+ daemon.

Example 12-16 AAA Accounting Output Logged via TACACS+

```
Wed Jun 27 04:02:19 2001 172.16.25.15    fgeorge   Async5  562/4327528
  starttask_id=35
service=ppp
Wed Jun 27 04:02:25 2001 172.16.25.15   fgeorge   Async5  562/4327528     update
task_id=35        service=ppp     protocol=ip     addr=10.1.1.2
Wed Jun 27 04:05:03 2001 172.16.25.15    fgeorge   Async5  562/4327528
  stoptask_id=35
service=ppp     protocol=ip     addr=10.1.1.2   bytes_in=3366   bytes_out=2149
paks_in=42      paks_out=28     elapsed_time=164
```

Summary

In this chapter, you learned how to configure AAA on a Cisco router. Specifically, you learned how to configure the router to act as a TACACS+ or RADIUS client, how to configure authentication, how to configure authorization, and finally, how to configure accounting.

Review Questions

Use the following review questions to test your understanding of the concepts covered in this chapter. In some cases, there is more than one correct answer, so choose all that apply. Answers are listed in Appendix A, "Answers to Review Questions."

1. Which of the following services is not part of AAA?

    A. Authentication

    B. Accounting

    C. Approval

    D. Authorization

2. Which of the following security protocols are used with AAA authentication?

    A. TACACS+

    B. RADIUS

    C. Secure Sockets Layer

    D. Kerberos

3. Which of the following security protocols are used with AAA authorization?

    A. TACACS+

    B. RADIUS

    C. Secure Sockets Layer

    D. Kerberos

4. Which command enables AAA on a Cisco router?

    A. (config)#aaa authentication enable

    B. (config)#aaa enable

    C. (config)#aaa new-model

    D. (config)#aaa new-model enable

5. Which of the following commands is used to configure a router as a TACACS+ client?

    A. (config)#tacacs+ ip 1.1.1.1

    B. (config)#tacacs-server ip 1.1.1.1

    C. (config)#tacacs-server 1.1.1.1

    D. (config)#tacacs-server host 1.1.1.1

6. Which of the following commands is used to configure the TACACS+ shared encryption key?

   A. (config)#**tacacs+ key** *key*

   B. (config)#**tacacs-server key** *key*

   C. (config)#**tacacs-server password** *password*

   D. (config)#**tacacs-server host-key** *key*

7. Which of the following commands correctly configures the default AAA login method list?

   A. RTA(config)#**aaa authentication login default enable**

   B. RTA(config)#**aaa authorization login default group tacacs+ enable none**

   C. RTA(config)#**aaa authentication default tacacs+ enable none**

   D. RTA(config)#**aaa authentication default login group tacacs+ enable none**

8. Which of the following commands correctly applies a named method list for AAA login authentication to a terminal line?

   A. RTB(config-line)#**ppp authentication PASSPORT**

   B. RTB(config-line)#**ppp authentication chap PASSPORT**

   C. RTB(config-line)#**login authentication PASSPORT**

   D. RTB(config-line)#**aaa authentication PASSPORT**

9. Which of the following commands correctly configures a default AAA authorization list for an EXEC session?

   A. RTA(config)#**aaa authorization default exec group tacacs+ local**

   B. RTA(config)#**aaa authorization exec default local**

   C. RTA(config)#**aaa authorization exec wait-start**

   D. RTA(config)#**aaa authorization exec group tacacs+ local**

10. If the **aaa authentication login A-LIST group tacacs+** command is applied to a terminal line, what will happen to users who attempt to authenticate and the TACACS+ server(s) return an error?

   A. The user will be authenticated.

   B. The user will be authenticated through a backup method.

   C. The user will not be authenticated.

   D. The user will be allowed to start an EXEC session.

Key Terms

AAA (authentication, authorization, and accounting)   An architectural framework for configuring security features.

Accounting   Method for tracking activity on a system or network.

Authentication   Method of identifying users, including login and password dialog, challenge and response, and messaging support.

Authorization   Method of prescribing the services available to a user.

Method list   In AAA, a list of methods that a router needs to use to perform authentication, authorization, or accounting.

Kerberos   A secret-key network authentication protocol used with AAA that uses the Data Encryption Standard (DES) cryptographic algorithm for encryption and authentication.

RADIUS (Remote Authentication Dial-In User Service)   A distributed client/server system used with AAA that secures networks against unauthorized access. In the Cisco implementation, RADIUS clients run on Cisco routers and send authentication requests to a central RADIUS server that contains all user authentication and network service access information.

TACACS+ (Terminal Access Controller Access Control System Plus)   Proprietary Cisco enhancement to TACACS. Provides centralized validation of users attempting to gain access to a router or network access server. Supports authorization and accounting functions, and authentication.

Answers to Review Questions

Chapter 1

1. A.
2. B.
3. C.
4. A.
5. D.
6. A and C.
7. A and B.
8. C.
9. C and D.
10. C.

Chapter 2

1. C.
2. B and C.
3. D.
4. A.
5. B.
6. C.
7. A.
8. D.
9. A and C.
10. A.

Chapter 3

1. C.
2. A.
3. C.
4. D.
5. B.
6. B and D.
7. A.
8. D.
9. B.
10. A, C, and D.

Chapter 4

1. A and D.
2. B.
3. C.
4. A.
5. A, B, C, and D.
6. A, C, and D.
7. D.
8. B.
9. D.
10. B.

Chapter 5

1. A.
2. A and D.
3. D.
4. C.
5. B.

6. C.

7. B.

8. D.

9. A.

10. B and D.

Chapter 6

1. A and D.

2. A.

3. A, B, and C.

4. C.

5. B.

6. A, B, and C.

7. C.

8. B.

9. A.

10. A.

Chapter 7

1. A.

2. C.

3. D.

4. C.

5. B.

6. C.

7. A.

8. C.

9. A.

10. C.

Chapter 8

1. C.
2. A.
3. B and C.
4. A.
5. C.
6. C.
7. D and C.
8. D.
9. A.
10. B.

Chapter 9

1. B and C.
2. B.
3. A.
4. B.
5. D.
6. C.
7. B.
8. D.
9. A and C.
10. C.

Chapter 10

1. D.
2. C.
3. A.
4. B.
5. A.

6. B.

7. D.

8. A.

9. D.

10. B.

Chapter 11

1. A and D.

2. C.

3. C.

4. A.

5. B.

6. D.

7. C.

8. C.

9. B.

10. D.

Chapter 12

1. C.

2. A, B, and D.

3. A and B.

4. C.

5. D.

6. B.

7. A.

8. C.

9. B.

10. C.

Emerging Remote-Access Technologies

Introduction

This appendix gives an overview of emerging remote-access technologies. Additionally, it discusses the advantages and disadvantages of accessing the Internet through cable modems, wireless connections, and digital subscriber lines (*x*DSL).

Cable Modems

Cable modems enable two-way, high-speed data transmissions by using the same coaxial lines that transmit cable television. Some cable service providers are promising data speeds up to 6.5 times that of T1 leased lines. This speed makes cable an attractive medium for transferring large amounts of digital information quickly, including video clips, audio files, and large chunks of data. Information that takes two minutes to download using Integrated Services Digital Network (ISDN) can be downloaded in two seconds through a cable-modem connection.

Cable-modem access provides speeds superior to leased lines, and with the added benefits of lower costs and simpler installation. When the cable infrastructure is in place, a firm can connect through installation of a modem or router. And because cable modems do not use the telephone system infrastructure, there are no local-loop charges. Products such as the Cisco uBR904 universal broadband router cable modem make cable access an even more attractive investment by integrating a fully functional Cisco IOS router, four-port hub, and cable modem into one unit (see Figure B-1). This combination allows businesses to replace combinations of routers, bridges, hubs, and single-port cable modems with one product.

Figure B-1
The Cisco uBR904 is
an IOS-based router
and integrated cable
modem.

Cable modems provide a full-time connection. As soon as users turn on their computers, they are connected to the Internet. This removes the time and effort of dialing in to establish a connection. The always-on cable connection also means that a company's information pipe is open at all times. The always-on nature of an end user's Internet connection increases the vulnerability of data to hackers and is a good reason to install firewalls and configure cable routers to maximize security. Fortunately, the industry is moving toward the standardization of cable modems, and the move is likely to address encryption needs. For example, new models of the Cisco uBR904 cable modem will provide IP Security (IPSec) and firewall capabilities. These features protect company local-area networks (LANs) and provide Virtual Private Network (VPN) tunneling, with options for authentication and encryption.

Because the connection is permanently established, cable modems cannot dial in to different networks or locations. Any network connection must take place through the Internet. For example, employees using a cable modem at home to surf the Web can connect to a company LAN only if the business connects its LAN to the Internet.

Availability could be the biggest barrier to cable-modem adoption by businesses because only a few office buildings have been outfitted for cable reception, compared to the almost 85 percent of households in North America that are wired for cable.

Some cable operators are in the process of replacing traditional one-way cable systems with the two-way architecture known as hybrid fiber coaxial (HFC). Because of the magnitude of this upgrade, and the need to expand networks to include businesses, the market penetration of cable modems is expected to lag behind that of DSLs.

How Cable Modems Work

Similar to telephone modems, cable modems modulate and demodulate data signals. However, cable modems incorporate more functionality designed for today's high-speed Internet services. In a cable network, data flowing from the network to the user is referred to as *downstream* and data flowing from the user to the network is referred to as *upstream*. From a user perspective, a cable modem is a 64/256 quadrature amplitude modulation (QAM) radio frequency (RF) receiver capable of delivering up to 30 to 40 megabits per second (Mbps) of data in one 6-megahertz (MHz) cable channel. This is almost 500 times faster than a 56-kilobit-per-second (Kbps) modem. The headend manages traffic flow from the user to the network, as shown in Figure B-2. Headends have facilities to do the following:

- Receive programming (for example, from NBC, CBS, and cable networks such as MTV and ESPN)

- Convert each channel to the channel frequency desired; scramble channels as needed (for the premium channels)

- Combine all the frequencies onto a single, broadband analog channel (frequency-division multiplexing [FDM])

- Broadcast the combined analog stream downstream to subscribers

Figure B-2
In a broadband cable provider's network, the headend manages traffic flow from the user to the network.

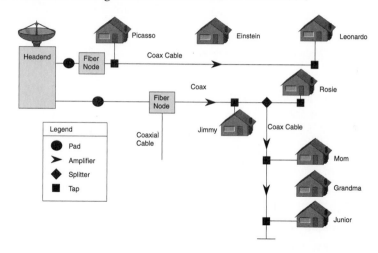

The data is modulated using a QPSK/16 QAM transmitter with data rates from 320 Kbps up to 10 Mbps. The upstream and downstream data rates can be configured to meet the needs of the subscribers. For example, business services can be programmed to both transmit and receive at relatively high rates. Residential users, on the other hand, can have their service configured to receive higher bandwidth access to the Internet, while limiting them to low-bandwidth transmission to the network.

A subscriber can continue to receive cable television service while simultaneously receiving data on a cable modem that is being delivered to a personal computer with the help of a simple one-to-two-way splitter (see Figure B-3). The data service offered by a cable modem can be shared by up to 16 users in a LAN configuration.

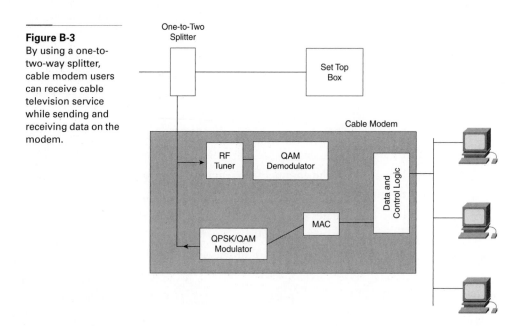

Figure B-3
By using a one-to-two-way splitter, cable modem users can receive cable television service while sending and receiving data on the modem.

Because some cable networks are suited for broadcast television services, cable modems can use either a standard telephone line or a QPSK/16 QAM modem over a two-way cable system to transmit data upstream from a user's location to the network. When a telephone line is used in conjunction with a one-way broadcast network, the cable data system is referred to as a *telephony return interface* (TRI) system. Telephone return means that the consumer (or the subscriber modem) makes a telephone call to a terminal server when the consumer requires return-path service. At the cable headend, data from individual users is filtered by telephone-return systems for further processing by a cable modem termination system (CMTS). The CMTS communicates with the cable modem to enforce the MAC protocol and RF control functions, such as frequency hopping and automatic gain control.

A CMTS provides data switching necessary to route data between the Internet and cable-modem users. Data from the network to a user group is sent to a 64/256 QAM modulator. The result is user-data modulated into one 6-MHz channel, which is the spectrum allocated for a cable television channel such as ABC, NBC, or TBS for broadcast to all users.

A cable headend combines the downstream data channels with the existing video, pay-per-view, audio, and local advertiser programs that are received by television subscribers. The combined signal is now ready to be transmitted throughout the cable distribution network. When the signal arrives at the user's site, the television signal is received by a converter box generally located on the top of a television, while user data is separately received by a cable modem or router and sent to a PC.

The CMTS, an important new element for support of data services, integrates upstream and downstream communication over a cable data network. The number of upstream and downstream channels in any particular CMTS can be designed and adjusted based on the size of the serving area, number of users, and data rates offered to each user.

Another important element in the operations and day-to-day management of a cable data system is an *element management system* (EMS). An EMS is an operations system designed specifically to configure and manage a CMTS and associated cable-modem subscribers. These operations include provisioning, day-to-day administration, monitoring, alarms, and testing of various components of a CMTS. From a central Network Operations Center (NOC), a single EMS can support many CMTS systems in a particular geographic region.

Beyond modulation and demodulation, a cable modem or router incorporates many features necessary to extend broadband communications to WANs. The Internet Protocol (IP) is used at the network layer to support Internet services such as e-mail, Hypertext Transfer Protocol (HTTP), and File Transfer Protocol (FTP). The data-link layer is comprised of sublayers, including the Logical Link Control (LLC) sublayer, link security sublayer conforming to the security requirements, and MAC sublayer suitable for cable-system operations. Cable systems use the Ethernet frame format for data-transmission channels. The downstream data channels and the associated upstream data channels on a cable network basically form an Ethernet WAN. As the number of subscribers increases, the cable operator can add more upstream and downstream data channels to meet the additional bandwidth requirements.

Cable Data Network Architecture

A CMTS provides an extended Ethernet network over a WAN with a geographic reach up to 100 miles. The cable data network could be fully managed by the local cable operations unit, or operations could be aggregated at a regional NOC for better scaling. A given geographic or metropolitan region could have a few cable television headend locations that are connected by fiber links. The day-to-day operations and management of a cable data network could be consolidated at a single location, such as a regional center, whereas other headend locations could be economically managed as local centers.

A basic distribution center is a minimal data network configuration that exists within a cable television headend. A typical headend is equipped with satellite receivers, fiber connections to other regional headend locations, and upstream RF receivers for pay-per-view and data services, as shown in Figure B-4. The minimal data network configuration includes a CMTS system capable of upstream and downstream data transport and an IP router to connect to the regional location.

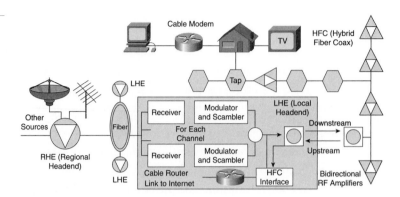

Figure B-4
The local headend connects to a regional headend using fiber connections.

A *regional center* is a cable headend location with additional temperature-controlled facilities to house a variety of computer servers, which are necessary to run cable data networks. The servers include file transfer, user authorization and accounting, log control (syslog), IP address assignment and administration (Dynamic Host Configuration Protocol [DHCP] servers), Domain Name System (DNS) servers, and Data-over-Cable Service Interface Specification (DOCSIS) control servers. In addition, a regional center could contain support and network management systems necessary for television and data network operations.

User data from local and regional locations is received at a regional data center for further aggregation and distribution throughout the network. A regional data center supports DHCP, DNS, and log control servers necessary for the cable data network administration. A regional data center provides connectivity to the Internet and the World Wide Web and contains the server farms necessary to support Internet services. These servers include e-mail, Web hosting, news, chat, proxy, caching, and streaming-media servers. Figure B-5 depicts the regional data center services.

Cable and the OSI Model
The cable data system comprises many different technologies and standards. For cable modems to be mainstreamed, modems from different vendors must be interoperable. The following sections look at cable network operation at the physical, data-link, network, transport, and application layers of the OSI reference model.

Figure B-5
The cable data network includes administration servers (NTP, DNS, and so on) and Internet support services (e-mail, caching servers, and so on).

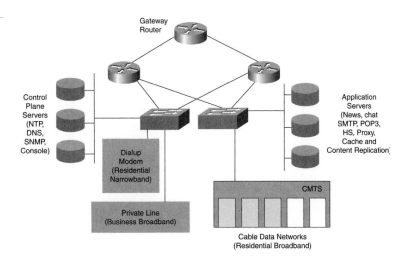

Physical Layer

At the physical layer, a downstream data channel is based on North American digital video specifications (specifically, International Telecommunication Union Telecommunication Standardization Sector [ITU-T] Recommendation J.83 Annex B) and includes the following features:

- 64 and 256 QAM
- 6 MHz-occupied spectrum that coexists with other signals in the cable plant
- Variable-length interleaving support, both latency-sensitive and latency-insensitive data services
- Contiguous serial bit stream with no implied framing, providing complete physical (PHY) and MAC-layer decoupling

The upstream data channel is a shared channel featuring the following:

- QPSK and 16 QAM formats
- Data rates from 320 Kbps to 10 Mbps
- Flexible and programmable cable modem under control of CMTS
- Time-division multiple access
- Support of both fixed-frame and variable-length protocol data units (PDUs)

Data-Link Layer

The data-link layer provides the general requirements for many cable-modem subscribers to share a single upstream data channel for transmission to the network. Among these requirements are collision detection and retransmission capability. The large geographic reach of a cable data network poses special problems as a result of the transmission delay between users close to headend versus users at a distance from cable headend. To compensate for cable losses and delay as a result of distance, the MAC layer performs ranging, by which each cable modem can assess time delay in transmitting to the headend. The MAC layer supports timing and synchronization, bandwidth allocation to cable modems at the control of CMTS, error detection, handling and error recovery, and procedures for registering new cable modems.

Network Layer

Cable data networks use IP for communication from the cable modem to the network. The Internet Engineering Task Force (IETF) DHCP typically forms the basis for IP address assignment and administration in the cable network.

Transport Layer

Cable data networks support both the TCP and the UDP at the transport layer.

Application Layer

All the Internet-related applications are supported here. These applications include HTTP, FTP, e-mail, Trivial File Transfer Protocol (TFTP), news, chat, and Simple Network Management Protocol (SNMP). The use of SNMP provides for management of the CMTS and cable data networks.

Cable Technology Summary

Many people are tuning into the Internet channel on their TV. Of all the high-speed Internet access solutions, cable TV systems are probably the most talked about. That's partly because they take advantage of existing broadband cable TV networks and partly because they promise to deliver high-speed access at an affordable price.

Internet access through cable is spreading rapidly. However, to reach the mainstream, cable operators face an uphill battle. Like phone companies offering ISDN service, cable operators must gain expertise in data communications if they're going to win and keep customers.

Technical hurdles abound: Although satellites are only one-way devices, cable modems can work in both directions if cable operators make their one-way networks into interactive HFC networks. When this is accomplished, the technology could offer the best price/performance combination of any Internet access method to date, delivering close to 10-Mbps speeds at less than $50 per month, which is significantly better than the cost/performance factor of ISDN access.

As discussed, making the cable-to-PC connection requires a cable modem to modulate and demodulate the cable signal into a stream of data. The similarity with analog modems ends there. Cable modems also incorporate a tuner (to separate the data signal from the rest of the broadcast stream); parts from network adapters, bridges, and routers (to connect to multiple computers); network-management software agents (so that the cable company can control and monitor its operations); and encryption devices.

Each cable modem has an Ethernet port that connects to the computer (or network) on one side and a port for the coaxial cable connection on the other. You install an Ethernet adapter in the PC and then connect it to the cable-modem Ethernet port with a standard Ethernet cable. As far as your PC is concerned, it's hooked directly to the Internet through an Ethernet cable. There are no phone numbers to dial and no limitations on serial-port throughput (as with ISDN modems). What you do get is high-speed throughput: downlinks vary from 500 Kbps to 30 Mbps, whereas uplinks can range from 96 Kbps to 10 Mbps.

Wireless Network Access

Tremendous strides have been made on wired networks. Copper and fiber networks dominate the Layer 1 space. The transmission capacity of wired networks is virtually limitless as carriers can arbitrarily add bandwidth as demand increases.

Despite the capacity of wired networks, wireless networks have the greatest success among consumers. Broadcast television, cellular telephone, paging, and direct broadcast satellite are all wireless services that have met with commercial success—even though wireless networks typically carry lower bit rates and higher costs than wired networking.

When installing cables underground, you might be forced to obtain permission from residents. Product managers who roll out wired services struggle with marketing and demographic studies to determine the best neighborhoods in which to introduce services.

Even if the right neighborhoods are identified, it is expensive and time-consuming to dig or install overhead cables. Furthermore, permits and easements must be obtained. To some observers, the fixed networks of wired systems look like vulnerable high-capital assets in a world of fast-changing technologies.

Numerous wireless access network technologies are intended by their proponents to serve the consumer market. These are direct broadcast satellite (DBS), Multichannel Multipoint Distribution Services (MMDS), and Local Multipoint Distribution Services (LMDS). Figure B-6 illustrates the network architecture of a typical wireless network. The return-path flows, if any, travel through wired networks or, in the case of LMDS, through wireless networks.

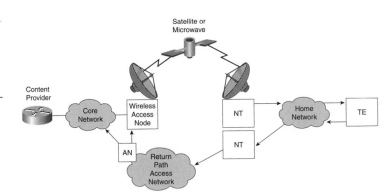

Figure B-6
The return path in a typical wireless network uses either the same network used for the forward transmission or another access network.

The content provider forwards content through the core network and to the wireless access node. This access node reformats data and modulates it for satellite or land-based microwave transmission. A receiving antenna at the home end forwards traffic through the home network to the terminal equipment, which is either a TV set-top box or a PC.

In the return path, the consumer uses either the same network used for the forward transmission or another access network. Another access network is needed when using DBS or MMDS services, which are one-way networks. The return-path network could be telephone return, xDSL, or another wireless service, such as digital personal communications services (PCS). PCS service includes wireless voice, a digital form of cellular telephony, and wireless data.

Because forward- and return-path traffic can use different physical media, traffic sources must be matched so that a single bidirectional session exists between the content provider and the terminal equipment. This matching can be performed by the wireless access node or by another switching/routing device inside the core network.

DBS

While cable operators were only *talking* about digital TV, DBS companies actually *achieved* it, taking the entire cable industry by surprise. Early entrants were Primestar, DirecTV, and United States Satellite Broadcasting (USSB), all of which launched in 1994.

In the United States, DBS is viewed as a commercial success. DBS signed a surprising five million customers in its first three years of operation. This response is particularly strong considering the fact that customers initially paid up to $800 for a home satellite dish and installation. Such a strong start has cable TV operators concerned. Even more troubling for U.S. cable operators is that the average DBS subscriber spends about 50 percent more per month than the average cable subscriber (about $52 versus $35 per month). This difference is partly because of sales of premium sports and movie packages.

Much of the success of DBS is because of imaginative programming packages. In particular, aggressive marketing of sports packages (including college basketball and professional football) has created varied content for which DBS has found an eager market.

Architecturally, DBS is a simple concept. DBS operators receive analog TV reception from the various networks at a single giant headend. The DirecTV headend, for example, is in Castle Rock, Colorado. The analog programming is encoded into Motion Picture Experts Group (MPEG) format for digital retransmission. A control function regulates the amount of bandwidth accorded to each MPEG stream and determines how the MPEG knobs (control parameters), such as the length of a group of pictures, are specified.

The settings of the knobs are closely guarded secrets of the DBS operators. ESPN, for example, tends to require more bandwidth than the Food Network. ESPN has a lot more motion; more importantly, it has a larger audience and greater advertising revenue. How much more would ESPN pay for access than the Food Network? How much extra bandwidth is ESPN getting, and for how much? What MPEG knobs should the carrier use, and what knobs does its competition use? This is not public information.

ESPN, the Food Network, and all other channels are encoded into MPEG transport streams, multiplexed together, and then converted to the uplink frequency. The DBS architecture is illustrated in Figure B-7.

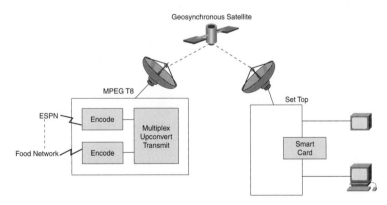

Figure B-7
Carrier's encode television network signals into MPEG transport streams that are multiplexed before sending the signal to a satellite.

The major North American geosynchronous satellites for DBS so far are placed at longitudes 85 degrees west (Primestar), 101 degrees west (DirecTV), and 119 degrees west (Echostar). The Primestar slot rests on the longitude that passes through the East Coast of the United States, the DirecTV longitude bisects the center of North America, and the Echostar longitude passes through the West Coast. From these orbits, each satellite can broadcast over the contiguous United States, southern Canada, and Mexico.

The satellite receives a signal and remodulates it to the designated spectrum for DBS. DBS occupies 500 MHz in the 12.2 Ku band. The Ku band occupies the frequency range from 10.7 GHz to 12.75 GHz. DBS satellites are allowed by regulation to broadcast at a higher power (120 W) than the larger C-band satellite dishes currently used by many households, to enable reception on small satellite dishes. This higher-powered transmission and smaller dish distinguish DBS from other forms of satellite reception.

The DBS uses quadrature phase shift keying (QPSK) modulation to encode digital data on the RF carriers. DirecTV encodes using MPEG-2 format to enable a density of up to 720 x 480 pixels on the user's television or monitor. Primestar uses a proprietary video compression system developed by General Instruments called DigiCipher-1. Echostar uses a transmission system based on the European Digital Video Broadcast (DVB) standard. DVB uses the MPEG-2 format and standardizes control elements of the total system, such as conditional access.

Although 720 x 480 is the maximum resolution offered today, DBS is capable of higher pixel resolution. In fact, DBS could be an early delivery vehicle for high-definition TV (HDTV) programming.

Data Service

DirecTV partnered with Microsoft to produce a push-mode data service over DBS. The service broadcasts approximately 200 popular Web sites, which are cached in the consumer's PC. Some content is cached at the service provider's site. Instead of having a point-to-point connection with the Internet, consumers access content on the hard drive or service-provider cache. In addition to Web sites, other data services, such as AgCast or stock quotes, can be offered, either by continuous feeds or by caching on the consumer's PC. The problem with this model is that you cannot access a Web site that is not part of the service because no point-to-point return-path connection exists.

One form of point-to-point data service, called DirectPC, can reach the Internet. DirectPC is jointly owned by DirecTV and Hughes Network Systems. DirectPC reserves 12 Mbps of downstream service and uses a telephone as a return path.

Because the footprint (the portion of Earth's surface covered by the signal from a communications satellite) is so large for geosynchronous satellites, it is possible that thousands of users might want to use the common 12 Mbps of service concurrently. The more concurrent users there are, the less bandwidth each user gets. To provide a balance between bit rate and the number of concurrent users, DirectPC offers approximately 400 Kbps of service to concurrent users.

MMDS

The success of DBS convinced telephone companies and other potential cable competitors that delivering digital video to consumers is a viable business. When these competitors analyzed the issues associated with DBS, they found that local content plays the greatest role in marketing a given service. Thus, some would-be competitors to DBS sought to improve on it by providing a wireless, multichannel broadband service with local channels called MMDS, referred to by the DAVIC (Digital Audio-Visual council) as Multipoint Video Distribution Systems (MVDS). MMDS provides local over-the-air stations and local advertisers access to digital delivery.

MMDS History

MMDS takes advantage of a microwave transmission technology known as *wireless cable*, which is a microwave technology used to deliver analog cable television service over the air to rural areas that cannot be served economically by wired cable.

The areas served by wireless cable were too sparsely populated to generate strong revenue as reflected in the lack of financial success for wireless cable operators. But the success of DBS and continued progress with digital technology (such as MPEG, digital modulation techniques, and advances in semiconductors) changed the perception of microwave from simply a rural delivery system to a system that could be used in urban areas. Telephone companies view microwave as a fast-start service to allow video distribution that can compete against cable and DBS.

In 1996, the FCC conducted spectrum auctions for MMDS. The FCC auctions offered 200 MHz in each of the nation's 493 *basic trading areas* (BTAs). A BTA represents a contiguous geographic market. BTA boundaries are drawn on county lines. The counties are aggregated by considering physical topography, population, newspaper circulation, economic activities, and transportation facilities (such as regional airports, rail hubs, and highways). The BTA concept was licensed by the FCC from Rand McNally.

MMDS uses 198 MHz of licensed spectrum, which could support 33 analog TV channels, in the range of 2.5 GHz.

MMDS Architecture

The key technical difference between MMDS and DBS is the use of ground-based, or terrestrial microwave, rather than geosynchronous satellites. The service difference is delivery of local content, which MMDS achieves by having local production facilities that can insert local over-the-air channels into the national feeds. Figure B-8 illustrates the MMDS service architecture.

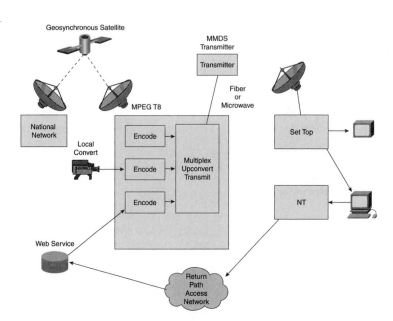

Figure B-8
MMDS networks include ground-based microwave transmission.

National television feeds are delivered by the programmer to a production facility. The feeds can come from geosynchronous satellite transmission or high-speed wired services, such as fiber-optic networks. There is little current movement to link MMDS with DBS, even though this appears to be a good technical fit. DBS could provide economic national distribution of programming for resale by MMDS.

Local content and advertising are acquired over the air, encoded into MPEG, and multiplexed with the national programming for local distribution to the viewers. MPEG enables digital multiplexing and thus is a key facilitator of MMDS. Data services might also be received from Web content providers. In this case, the information is in digital format but requires additional processing, such as encapsulation into MPEG and address resolution, before being transmitted.

After the programming mix is determined, composite programming is delivered by satellite or fiber to the MMDS broadcast tower. Generally, the MMDS headend and the MMDS broadcast tower are not co-located because the tower needs to be placed at a high elevation. At the receiving site, a small microwave receiving dish a little larger than a DBS dish is mounted outside the home to receive the signals. A decoder presents the TV images to the TV set. Other units are capable of decoding data for PC users. Return-path data is transmitted on another access network; telephone networks commonly are used for this purpose. For example, you could have an RJ-11 telephone jack on the set-top box. Consideration is also being given to other wireless networks, such as digital PCS and paging networks, for return-path purposes.

LMDS

A more aggressive strategy than MMDS is a delivery service called LMDS, also known in Canada as Local Multipoint Communication Service (LMCS). The major disadvantages of MMDS are the lack of an inband return path and the lack of sufficient bandwidth to surpass cable channel capacity (by offering superior interactive data services). A strong Internet access network must have two-way service and enough bandwidth to compete with data and cable.

LMDS is a two-way, high-bit-rate, wireless service under development by a variety of carriers to solve the return-path problem and vastly increase bandwidth. If significant technological hurdles can be overcome, LMDS offers the greatest two-way bit rate of any residential service, wired or wireless, at surprisingly low infrastructure costs.

No restrictions exist as to how carriers use their bandwidth, so bandwidth can be subdivided in any manner carriers see fit. If an LMDS carrier had 1150 MHz of bandwidth, for example, it would be possible to use 500 MHz for broadcast TV, 50 MHz for local broadcast, 300 MHz for forward data services, and 300 MHz for upstream data. Using only the relatively robust QPSK modulation, this bandwidth can provide the following:

- All the broadcast channels of DBS (500 MHz)
- All local over-the-air channels (50 MHz)
- Up to 1 Gb of full-duplex data service (600 MHz)

The potential exists to offer more TV than satellite and more data than cable. This frequency plan is just one example of how a carrier could choose to offer service. Other carriers might choose to segment their frequencies differently and would be permitted to do so under FCC rules.

For businesses in cities, LMDS is a cost-effective broadband wireless alternative to land-lines for multiple services. LMDS operates at higher frequencies where more spectrum is available (bandwidths currently range up to 155 Mbps) and smaller, cheaper antennas are possible.

LMDS is a small-cell technology, with each cell having about a 3- to-6-km radius. Small cells coupled with two-way transmission create a different set of architectural problems than MMDS.

Figure B-9 illustrates that LMDS headends function similarly to MMDS headends. National television feeds are delivered by the programmer to a production facility. In many cases, these national feeds come from DBS, but the feeds also can come from other geosynchronous satellite transmissions or high-speed wired services, such as fiber-optic networks.

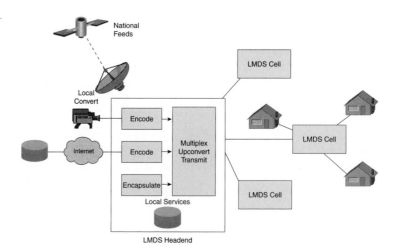

Figure B-9
Content acquisition at the LMDS head-end functions similarly to MMDS.

Local content and advertising are acquired over the air, encoded into MPEG, and multiplexed with the national programming for local distribution. As in the case of MMDS, MPEG is an important facilitator of LMDS because it enables digital multiplexing.

Data services received from Web content providers are already in digital format but would need additional processing, such as encapsulation into MPEG and address resolution, before being transmitted.

The program mix is delivered by satellite or fiber to the LMDS broadcast tower. Generally, the LMDS headend and the LMDS broadcast tower are not co-located because the headend production facilities are normally shared among several towers.

An LMDS transmitter tower is erected in the neighborhood, and traffic is broadcast to consumers using QPSK modulation with forward error correction (FEC). QAM modulation could be used, but QPSK is chosen because it is more robust than QAM 16 or QAM 64, and because bandwidth is so plentiful that spectral efficiency is not an issue.

As shown in Figure B-10, consumers receive the signal on a small dish about the size of a DBS dish or a flat-plate antenna. The dish is mounted outside the home and is connected by cable to a set-top converter, much the same way in which DBS connections are made. The signal is demodulated and fed to a decoder. Unlike DBS, LMDS is capable of two-way service, so both TV sets and PCs must be connected to the satellite dish. Furthermore, a two-way home networking capability must be supported instead of just the simple broadcast scheme of DBS.

In the return path, the customer transmits to the carrier using the same dish with QPSK modulation. A MAC protocol is required because the residences in the coverage area share the return spectrum.

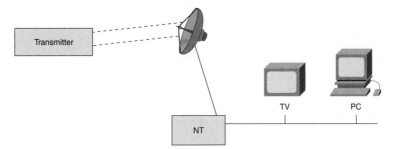

Figure B-10
LMDS customers receive the signal by using a dish or flat-plate antenna, which is mounted outside the home.

Wireless LAN

In the simplest of terms, a *wireless local-area network* (*WLAN*) does exactly what the name implies: it provides all the features and benefits of traditional LAN technologies, such as Ethernet and Token Ring, without the limitations of wires or cables. But to view a WLAN only in terms of the cables, it does not have is to miss the point: WLANs redefine the way LANs are viewed. Connectivity no longer implies attachment. With wireless bridging, local areas are measured not in feet or meters, but miles or kilometers. An infrastructure does not need to be buried in the ground or hidden behind the walls—an infrastructure can move and change at the speed of the organization. This technology has several immediate applications, including the following:

- IT professionals or business executives who want mobility within the enterprise, perhaps in addition to a traditional wired network
- Business owners or IT directors who need flexibility for frequent LAN wiring changes, either throughout the site or in selected areas
- Any company whose site is not conducive to LAN wiring because of building or budget limitations, such as older buildings, leased space, or temporary sites
- Any company that needs the flexibility and cost savings offered by a line-of-sight, building-to-building bridge to avoid expensive trenches, leased lines, or right-of-way issues

WLANs use a transmission medium, similar to wired LANs. Instead of using twisted-pair or fiber-optic cable, WLANs use either infrared (IR) light or RF. Of the two, RF is far more popular for its longer range, higher bandwidth, and wider coverage. Most wireless LANs today use the 2.4-gigahertz (GHz) frequency band, the only portion of the RF spectrum reserved around the world for unlicensed devices. The freedom and flexibility of wireless networking can be applied both within buildings and between buildings.

In-Building WLANs

WLAN technology can take the place of a traditional wired network or extend its reach and capabilities. Similar to their wired counterparts, in-building WLAN equipment consists of a PC Card, a Personal Computer Interface (PCI), Industry-Standard Architecture (ISA) client adapters, and access points, which perform functions similar to wired networking hubs (see Figure B-11). Similar to wired LANs for small or temporary installations, a WLAN can be arranged in a peer-to-peer or improvised topology using only client adapters. For added functionality and range, access points can be incorporated to act as the center of a star topology while simultaneously bridging with an Ethernet network.

Figure B-11
In a WLAN, PCs connect to wired networks through a wireless access point.

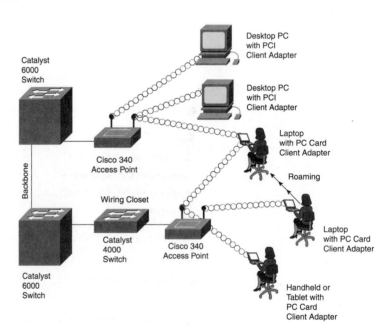

Building-to-Building WLANs

In much the same way that a commercial radio signal can be picked up in all sorts of weather, miles from its transmitter, WLAN technology applies the power of radio waves to truly redefine the local in LAN. With a wireless bridge, networks located in buildings miles from each other can be integrated into a single LAN. When bridging between buildings with traditional copper or fiber-optic cable, freeways, lakes, and even local governments can be impassible obstacles. A wireless bridge makes them irrelevant, transmitting data through the air and requiring no license or right of way.

Without a wireless alternative, organizations frequently resort to WAN technologies to link together separate LANs. Contracting with a local telephone provider for a leased line presents a variety of drawbacks. Installation is typically expensive and rarely immediate. Monthly fees are often high for bandwidth that, by LAN standards, is low. A wireless bridge can be purchased and then installed in an afternoon for a cost that is often comparable to a T1 installation charge alone. After the investment is made, there are no recurring charges. And today's wireless bridges provide the bandwidth you would expect from a technology rooted in data, rather than voice, communications.

The Wireless LAN Standard

In the wired world, Ethernet has grown to become the predominant LAN technology. Its evolution parallels, and indeed foreshadows, the development of the WLAN standard. Defined by the Institute of Electrical and Electronics Engineers (IEEE) with the 802.3 standard, Ethernet provides an evolving, high-speed, widely available, and interoperable networking standard. It has continued to evolve to keep pace with the data rate and throughput requirements of contemporary LANs. Originally providing for 10-Mbps transfer rates, the Ethernet standard evolved to include the 100-Mbps transfer rates required for network backbones and bandwidth-intensive applications. The IEEE 802.3 standard is open, decreasing barriers to market entry and resulting in a wide range of suppliers, products, and price points from which Ethernet users can choose. Perhaps most importantly, conformance to the Ethernet standard allows for interoperability, enabling users to select individual products from multiple vendors, while secure in the knowledge that they will all work together.

The first WLAN technologies were low-speed (1-2 Mbps) proprietary offerings. Despite these shortcomings, the freedom and flexibility of wireless allowed these early products to find a place in vertical markets such as retail and warehousing where mobile workers use hand-held devices for inventory management and data collection. Later, hospitals applied wireless technology to deliver patient information to the bedside. And as computers made their way into the classrooms, schools and universities began installing wireless networks to avoid cabling costs and to share Internet access. The pioneering wireless vendors soon realized that for the technology to gain broad market acceptance, an Ethernet-like standard was needed. The vendors joined together in 1991, first proposing, and then building, a standard based on contributed technologies. In June 1997, the IEEE released the 802.11 standard for WLAN.

Just as the 802.3 Ethernet standard allows for data transmission over twisted-pair and coaxial cable, the 802.11 WLAN standard allows for transmission over different media. Compliant media include IR light and two types of radio transmission within the unlicensed 2.4-GHz frequency band: frequency hopping spread spectrum (FHSS) and direct sequence spread spectrum (DSSS). Spread spectrum is a modulation technique developed in the 1940s that spreads a transmission signal over a broad band of radio frequencies. This technique is ideal for data communications because it is less susceptible to radio noise and creates little interference. FHSS is limited to a 2-Mbps data transfer rate and is only recommended for specific applications; for example, certain types of watercraft lend themselves to this technology. For all other WLAN applications, DSSS is the better choice. The recently released evolution of the IEEE standard, 802.11b, provides for a full Ethernet-like data rate of 11 Mbps over DSSS (as shown in Figure B-12, later in this appendix). FHSS does not support data rates greater than 2 Mbps.

Wireless LAN Security Issues

IEEE 802.11b standard 11-Mbps WLANs operate in the 2.4-GHz frequency band where there is room for increased bandwidth. Using an optional modulation technique within the 802.11b specification, it is possible to double the current data rate. Cisco already has 22 Mbps on the road map for the future. WLAN manufacturers migrated from the 900-MHz band to the 2.4-GHz band to improve data rate. This pattern promises to continue, with a broader frequency band capable of supporting higher bandwidth available at 5 GHz. The IEEE has already issued a specification (802.11a) for equipment operating at 5 GHz that supports up to a 54-Mbps data rate.

The wired equivalent privacy (WEP) option to the 802.11 standard is only the first step in addressing customer security concerns. Security is currently available today for wireless networking, offering up to 128-bit encryption and supporting both the encryption and authentication options of the 802.11 standard. The algorithm with a 40- or 128-bit key is specified in the standard. When WEP is enabled, each station (clients and access points) has up to four keys. The keys are used to encrypt the data before it is transmitted through the air. If a station receives a packet that is not encrypted with the appropriate key, the packet is discarded and never delivered to the host.

Although the 802.11 standard provides strong encryption services to secure the WLAN, the means by which the secure keys are granted, revoked, and refreshed are still undefined. Fortunately, several key administration architectures are available for use in the enterprise. The best approach for large networks is centralized key management, which uses centralized encryption key servers. A popular strategy includes the addition of encryption key servers to ensure that valuable data is protected. Encryption key servers provide for centralized creation of keys, distribution of keys, and ongoing key rotation. Key servers enable the network administrator to command the creation of Rivest-Shamir-Adleman (RSA) public/private key pairs at the client level that are required for client authentication. The key server also provides for the generation and distribution to clients and access points of the keys needed for packet encryption. This implementation eases administration and helps avoid compromising confidential keys.

Mobility Services

A primary advantage of WLANs is mobility, but no industry standard currently addresses the tracking or management of mobile devices in its Management Information Base (MIB). This omission prohibits users from roaming between wireless access points that cover a common area, such as a complete floor of a building. Individual companies such as Cisco have addressed this issue, providing their own versions of mobility algorithms that facilitate roaming within an IP domain (such as a floor) with an eye toward optimizing roaming across IP domains (such as an enterprise campus). Figure B-12 illustrates how Cisco wireless access points handle roaming and unauthorized access.

Figure B-12
Cisco's wireless access points can be configured to support roaming and encryption keys.

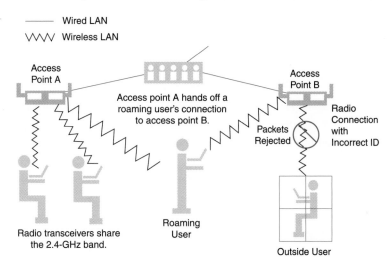

Wireless access points share the functions of both hubs and switches. Wireless clients associating with access points share the WLAN, similar to the way a hub functions, but the access point can additionally track movement of clients across its domain and permit or deny specific traffic or clients from communicating through it. For network managers to use these services to their advantage, it is necessary to instrument the access point like a hub and a switch.

The Cisco WLAN devices are manageable through common Telnet or SNMP (I or II) services and a Web browser interface to facilitate its monitoring and control. In addition to bridge statistics and counters, the access point also offers additional features that make it powerful and manageable, including mapping of wireless access points and their associated clients, and monitoring and reporting of client statistics. Access points can also control access and the flow of traffic through the WLAN through MAC and protocol-level access lists. Configuration parameters and code images for access points can be centrally configured and managed to facilitate consistency of WLAN network policy.

The Future of WLAN

Today, the WLAN has redefined what it means to be connected. It has stretched the boundaries of the LAN. It makes an infrastructure as dynamic as it needs to be. And it has only just begun: the standard is less than three years old, with the high-speed 802.11b yet to reach its first birthday. With standard and interoperable wireless products, LANs can reach scales unimaginable with a wired infrastructure. They can make high-speed interconnections for a fraction of the cost of traditional wide-area technologies. In a wireless world, users can roam not just within a campus but within a city, while maintaining a high-speed link to extranets, intranets, and the Internet.

Digital Subscriber Line

Digital subscriber line (*DSL*) technology is a modem technology that uses existing twisted-pair telephone lines to transport high-bandwidth data, such as multimedia and video, to service subscribers. The term xDSL covers numerous similar yet competing forms of DSL, including Asymmetric DSL (ADSL), Symmetric DSL (SDSL), high-data-rate DSL (HDSL), RADSL (Rate-adaptive DSL), and very-high-data-rate DSL (VDSL). xDSL is drawing significant attention from implementers and service providers because it promises to deliver high-bandwidth data rates to dispersed locations with relatively small changes to the existing telco infrastructure. xDSL services constitute dedicated, point-to-point, public network access over twisted-pair copper wire on the local loop (last mile) between a network service provider's (NSP's) central office and the customer site, or on local loops created either intra-building or intra-campus (see Figure B-13). Currently, the primary focus in xDSL is the development and deployment of ADSL and VDSL technologies and architectures. This section covers the characteristics and operations of ADSL and VDSL.

Figure B-13
DSL works over
copper local loops.

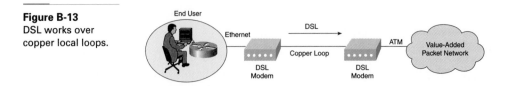

ADSL

ADSL technology is asymmetric. It allows more bandwidth downstream—from an NSP's central office to the customer site—than upstream from the subscriber to the central office (see Figure B-14). This asymmetry, combined with always-on access (which eliminates call setup), makes ADSL ideal for Internet/intranet surfing, video on demand, and remote LAN access. Users of these applications typically download much more information than they send.

Figure B-14
ADSL allows more bandwidth down-stream than upstream.

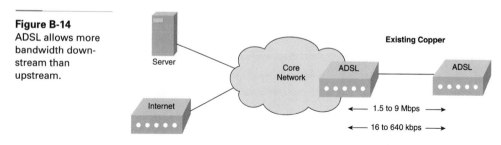

ADSL transmits more than 6 Mbps to a subscriber and as much as 640 Kbps more in both directions, as shown in Figure B-14. Such rates expand existing access capacity by a factor of 50 or more without new cabling. ADSL can literally transform the existing public information network from one limited to voice, text, and low-resolution graphics to a powerful, universal system capable of bringing multimedia, including full-motion video, to every home this decade.

ADSL will play a crucial role over the next decade or more as telephone companies enter new markets for delivering information in video and multimedia formats. New broadband cabling will take decades to reach all prospective subscribers. Success of these new services will depend on reaching as many subscribers as possible during the first few years. By bringing movies, television, video catalogs, remote CD-ROMs, corporate LANs, and the Internet into homes and small businesses, ADSL will make these markets viable and profitable for telephone companies and application vendors.

ADSL Services Architecture

Figure B-15 illustrates a typical end-to-end ADSL services architecture. It consists of customer premises equipment (CPE) and supporting equipment at the ADSL point of presence (POP). Network access providers (NAPs) manage Layer 2 network cores, whereas NSPs manage Layer 3 network cores. These roles are divided or shared among incumbent local exchange carrier (ILEC), competitive local exchange carrier (CLEC), and Tier 1 and Tier 2 Internet Service Provider (ISP) businesses. It is expected that over time, market forces will redefine current relationships between ADSL providers: some NAPs might add Layer 3 capabilities or extend service across the core.

CPE represents any combination of end-user PCs or workstations, remote ADSL terminating units (ATU-Rs), and routers. For example, a residential user might have a single PC with an integrated ADSL modem on a peripheral component interface card, or perhaps a PC with an Ethernet or universal serial bus (USB) interface to a standalone

ADSL modem (the ATU-R). In contrast, business users more often connect many end-user PCs to a router with an integrated ADSL modem or a router plus ATU-R pair.

Figure B-15
ADSL delivers high-speed Internet access to branch offices, residential customers, and small- to medium-size enterprises.

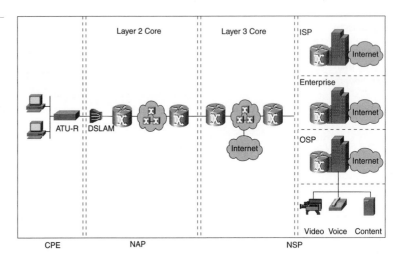

At the ADSL POP, the NAP deploys one or more DSL access multiplexers (DSLAMs) servicing the copper loops between the POP and CPE. In a process called *subtending*, DSLAMs can be chained together to enhance ATM pipe use. DSLAMs connect locally or through an inter-central office (CO) link to a local access concentrator (LAC) that provides ATM grooming, Point-to-Point Protocol (PPP) tunneling, and Layer 3 termination to local or cached content. A service selection gateway (SSG) might be co-located with the LAC, so that customers can dynamically select destinations. From the LAC/SSG, services extend over the ATM core to the NSP or IP network core.

Three different architectures are applicable to wholesale ADSL services:

- **ATM point to point**—Cross-connects subscribers to their ISP or enterprise destination with Permanent Virtual Circuits (PVCs) from the customer premise equipment (CPE) to the endpoint.

- **Aggregation**—Aggregates multiple subscriber virtual circuits (VCs) into trunk PVCs to reduce the number of VC connections across the network core; instead of one VC per subscriber, this uses one VC for many subscribers to the same destination.

- **SVC and MPLS**—Uses Switched Virtual Circuits (SVCs) to auto-provision connections from the CPE through the DSLAM to an edge label switch router (edge LSR), where it enters the Multiprotocol Label Switching (MPLS)-enabled network core.

Figure B-16 illustrates the end-to-end protocol stack used with xDSL.

Figure B-16
The ADSL protocol stack includes ATM at Layer 2.

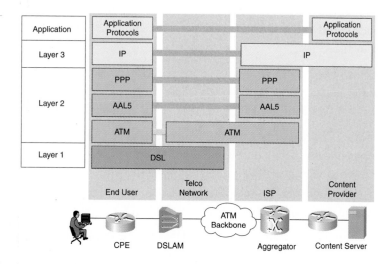

ADSL Capabilities

An ADSL circuit connects an ADSL modem on each end of a twisted-pair telephone line, creating three information channels—a high-speed downstream channel, a medium-speed full-duplex channel, and a basic telephone service channel (see Figure B-17). The basic telephone service channel is split off from the digital modem by filters, thus guaranteeing uninterrupted basic telephone service, even if ADSL fails. The high-speed channel ranges from 1.5 to 6.1 Mbps, and duplex rates range from 16 to 640 Kbps. Each channel can be submultiplexed to form multiple lower-rate channels.

Figure B-17
A key feature of ADSL is co-existence with POTS.

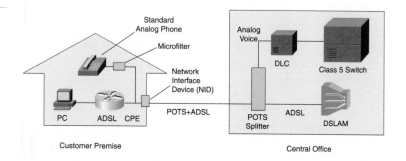

ADSL modems provide data rates consistent with North American T1 1.544-Mbps and European E1 2.048-Mbps digital hierarchies and can be purchased with various speed ranges and capabilities. The minimum configuration provides 1.5 or 2.0 Mbps downstream and a 16-Kbps duplex channel; others provide rates of 6.1 Mbps and 64-Kbps duplex. Products with downstream rates up to 8 Mbps and duplex rates up to 640

Kbps are also available today. ADSL modems accommodate Asynchronous Transfer Mode (ATM) transport with variable rates, compensation for ATM overhead and IP protocols.

Downstream data rates depend on many factors, including the length of the copper line, its wire gauge, presence of bridged taps, and cross-coupled interference. Line attenuation increases with line length and frequency and decreases as wire diameter increases.

Although the measure varies from telco to telco, ADSL can cover up to 95 percent of a loop plant, depending on the desired data rate. Customers beyond these distances can be reached with fiber-based digital loop carrier (DLC) systems. As these DLC systems become commercially available, telephone companies can offer virtually ubiquitous access in a relatively short time.

Many applications envisioned for ADSL involve digital compressed video. As a real-time signal, digital video cannot use link- or network-level error control procedures commonly found in data communications systems. ADSL modems, therefore, incorporate FEC that dramatically reduces errors caused by impulse noise. Error correction on a symbol-by-symbol basis also reduces errors caused by continuous noise coupled into a line.

ADSL Technology

ADSL depends on advanced digital signal processing and creative algorithms to squeeze so much information through twisted-pair telephone lines. In addition, many advances have been required in transformers, analog filters, and analog/digital (A/D) converters. Long telephone lines could attenuate signals at 1 MHz (the outer edge of the band used by ADSL) by as much as 90 decibels (dB), forcing analog sections of ADSL modems to work extremely hard to realize large dynamic ranges, separate channels, and maintain low noise figures. On the outside, ADSL looks simple—transparent synchronous data pipes at various data rates over ordinary telephone lines. The inside, where all the transistors work, is a miracle of modern technology.

To create multiple channels, ADSL modems divide the available bandwidth of a telephone line in one of two ways—FDM or echo cancellation. FDM assigns one band for upstream data and another band for downstream data. The downstream path is then divided by time-division multiplexing (TDM) into one or more high-speed channels and one or more low-speed channels. The upstream path is also multiplexed into corresponding low-speed channels. Echo cancellation assigns the upstream band to overlap the downstream, and separates the two by means of local echo cancellation, a technique well known in V.32 and V.34 modems. With either technique, ADSL splits off a 4-kHz region for basic telephone service at the DC end of the band.

An ADSL modem organizes the aggregate data stream created by multiplexing downstream channels, duplex channels, and maintenance channels together into blocks, and attaches an error correction code to each block. The receiver then corrects errors that occur during transmission up to the limits implied by the code and the block length. The unit could, at the user's option, also create superblocks by interleaving data within subblocks; this allows the receiver to correct any combination of errors within a specific span of bits. This in turn allows for effective transmission of both data and video signals.

ADSL Standards and Associations

The American National Standards Institute (ANSI) Working Group T1E1.4 recently approved an ADSL standard at rates up to 6.1 Mbps (ANSI Standard T1.414). The European Technical Standards Institute (ETSI) contributed an annex to T1.414 to reflect European requirements. T1.414 currently embodies a single terminal interface at the premises end. Issue II, now under study by T1E1.4, will expand the standard to include a multiplexed interface at the premises end, protocols for configuration and network management, and other improvements.

The ATM Forum and the DAVIC have both recognized ADSL as a physical-layer transmission protocol for unshielded twisted-pair (UTP) media.

The ADSL Forum was formed in December 1994 to promote the ADSL concept and to facilitate development of ADSL system architectures, protocols, and interfaces for major ADSL applications. The Forum has more than 200 members, representing service providers, equipment manufacturers, and semiconductor companies throughout the world. At present, the Forum's formal technical work is divided into the following six areas, each of which is dealt with in a separate working group within the technical committee:

- ATM over ADSL (including transport and end-to-end architecture aspects)
- Packet over ADSL (this working group recently completed its work)
- CPE/CO configurations and interfaces
- Operations
- Network management
- Testing and interoperability

VDSL

It is becoming increasingly clear that telephone companies around the world are making decisions to include existing twisted-pair loops in their next-generation broadband access networks. Hybrid fiber coaxial (HFC), a shared-access medium well suited to analog and digital broadcast, comes up somewhat short when used to carry voice telephony, interactive video, and high-speed data communications at the same time. Fiber all the way to the home (FTTH) is still prohibitively expensive in the marketplace. An attractive alternative, soon to be commercially viable, is a combination of fiber cables feeding neighborhood optical network units (ONUs) and last-leg-premises copper connections. This topology, which is often called fiber to the neighborhood (FTTN), encompasses fiber to the curb (FTTC) with short drops and fiber to the basement (FTTB), serving tall buildings with vertical drops.

One of the enabling technologies for FTTN is VDSL. In simple terms, VDSL transmits high-speed data over short reaches of twisted-pair copper telephone lines, with a range of speeds depending on actual line length. The maximum downstream rate under consideration is between 51 and 55 Mbps over lines up to 1000 feet (300 m) long. Downstream speeds as low as 14 Mbps over lengths beyond 4000 feet (1500 m) are also common. Upstream rates in early models will be asymmetric, similar to ADSL, at speeds from 1.6 to 2.3 Mbps. Both data channels will be separated in frequency from bands used for basic telephone service and ISDN, enabling service providers to overlay VDSL on existing services. At present, the two high-speed channels are also separated in frequency. As needs arise for higher-speed upstream channels or symmetric rates, VDSL systems might need to use echo cancellation.

VDSL Projected Capabilities

Although VDSL has not achieved the same degree of definition as ADSL, it has advanced far enough that realizable goals, beginning with data rate and range, can be discussed. Downstream rates derive from fractional multiples of the Synchronous Optical Network (SONET) and Synchronous Digital Hierarchy (SDH) canonical speed of 155.52 Mbps, namely 51.84 Mbps, 25.92 Mbps, and 12.96 Mbps. Each rate has a corresponding target range, as shown in Table B-1.

Table B-1   VDSL Projected Capabilities

Target Range (Mbps)	Distance (Feet)	Distance (Meters)
12.96–14.8	4500	1500
25.92–27.6	3000	1000
51.84–55.2	1000	300

Upstream rates under discussion fall into three general ranges:

- 1.6–2.3 Mbps
- 19.2 Mbps
- Equal to downstream

Early versions of VDSL will almost certainly incorporate the slower asymmetric rate. Higher upstream and symmetric configurations might be possible only for short lines. Like ADSL, VDSL must transmit compressed video, a real-time signal unsuited to error retransmission schemes used in data communications. To achieve error rates compatible with those of compressed video, VDSL will have to incorporate FEC with sufficient interleaving to correct all errors created by impulsive noise events of some specified duration. Interleaving introduces delay, such as 40 times the maximum-length correctable impulse.

Data in the downstream direction is broadcast to every CPE on the premises or transmitted to a logically separated hub that distributes data to addressed CPE based on cell or TDM within the data stream itself. Upstream multiplexing is more difficult. Systems using a passive NT must insert data onto a shared medium, either by a form of TDM access (TDMA) or a form of FDM. TDMA could use a species of token control called cell grants passed in the downstream direction from the ONU modem, or contention, or both (contention for unrecognized devices, cell grants for recognized devices). FDM gives each CPE its own channel, obviating a MAC protocol, but either limiting data rates available to any one CPE or requiring dynamic allocation of bandwidth and inverse multiplexing at each CPE. Systems using active NTs transfer the upstream collection problem to a logically separated hub that (typically) uses Ethernet or ATM upstream multiplexing.

Migration and inventory considerations dictate VDSL units that can operate at various (preferably all) speeds, with automatic recognition of a newly connected device to a line or to a change in speed. Passive network interfaces need to have hot insertion, whereas a new VDSL premises unit can be put on the line without interfering with the operation of other modems.

VDSL Technology
VDSL technology resembles ADSL to a large degree, although ADSL must face much larger dynamic ranges and is considerably more complex as a result. VDSL must be lower in cost and lower in power, and premises-VDSL units might have to implement a physical-layer MAC for multiplexing upstream data.

Four line codes have been proposed for VDSL:

- **Carrierless amplitude modulation/phase modulation (CAP)**—A version of suppressed carrier QAM. For passive NT configurations, CAP would use quadrature phase shift keying (QPSK) upstream and a type of TDMA for multiplexing (although CAP does not preclude an FDM approach to upstream multiplexing).

- **Discrete multitone (DMT)**—A multicarrier system using discrete fourier transforms to create and demodulate individual carriers. For passive NT configurations, DMT would use FDM for upstream multiplexing (although DMT does not preclude a TDMA multiplexing strategy).
- **Discrete wavelet multitone (DWMT)**—A multicarrier system using wavelet transforms to create and demodulate individual carriers. DWMT also uses FDM for upstream multiplexing, but also allows TDMA.
- **Simple line code (SLC)**—A version of four-level baseband signaling that filters the based band and restores it at the receiver. For passive NT configurations, SLC would most likely use TDMA for upstream multiplexing, although FDM is possible.

Early versions of VDSL will use FDM to separate downstream from upstream channels, and both of them from basic telephone service and ISDN. Echo cancellation might be required for later-generation systems featuring symmetric data rates. A rather substantial distance, in frequency, will be maintained between the lowest data channel and basic telephone service to enable simple and cost-effective basic telephone service splitters. Normal practice would locate the downstream channel above the upstream channel. However, the DAVIC specification reverses this order to enable premises distribution of VDSL signals over coaxial cable systems.

FEC will no doubt use a form of Reed Soloman coding and optional interleaving to correct bursts of errors caused by impulse noise. The structure will be similar to ADSL, as defined in T1.414. An outstanding question is whether FEC overhead (in the range of 8 percent) will be taken from the payload capacity or added as an out-of-band signal. The former reduces payload capacity but maintains nominal reach, whereas the latter retains the nominal payload but suffers a small reduction in reach. ADSL puts FEC overhead out of band.

If the premises VDSL unit comprises the network termination (an active NT), the means of multiplexing upstream cells or data channels from more than one CPE into a single upstream becomes the responsibility of the premises network. The VDSL unit simply presents raw data streams in both directions. As illustrated in Figure B-18, one type of premises network involves a star connecting each CPE to a switching or multiplexing hub; such a hub could be integral to the premises VDSL unit.

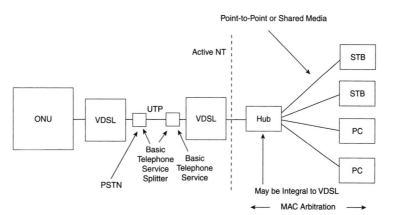

Figure B-18
In an active network termination, data channels from more than one CPE are multiplexed to a single VDSL unit.

In a passive NT configuration, each CPE has an associated VDSL unit (see Figure B-19). (A passive NT does not conceptually preclude multiple CPE per VDSL, but then the question of active versus passive NT becomes a matter of ownership, not a matter of wiring topology and multiplexing strategies.) Now, the upstream channels for each CPE must share a common wire.

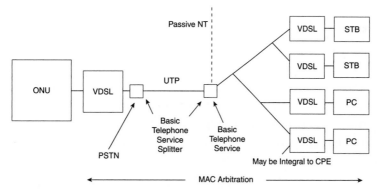

Figure B-19
In a passive network termination, each CPE connects to a VDSL unit.

Although a collision-detection system could be used, the desire for guaranteed bandwidth indicates one of two solutions. The first invokes a cell-grant protocol in which downstream frames generated at the ONU or farther up the network contain a few bits that grant access to specific CPE during a specified period subsequent to receiving a frame. A granted CPE can send one upstream cell during this period. The transmitter in the CPE must turn on, send a preamble to condition the ONU receiver, send the cell, and then turn itself off. The protocol must insert enough silence to let line ringing clear. One construction of this protocol uses 77 octet intervals to transmit a single 53-octet cell.

The second method divides the upstream channel into frequency bands and assigns one band to each CPE. This method has the advantage of avoiding any MAC with its associated overhead (although a multiplexer must be built into the ONU), but either restricts the data rate available to any one CPE or imposes a dynamic inverse multiplexing scheme that lets one CPE send more than its share for a period. The latter would look a great deal like a MAC protocol, but without the loss of bandwidth associated with carrier detect and clear for each cell.

VDSL Issues

VDSL is still in the definition stage; some preliminary products exist, but not enough is known yet about telephone line characteristics, radio frequency interface emissions and susceptibility, upstream multiplexing protocols, and information requirements to frame a set of definitive, standardizable properties. One large unknown is the maximum distance that VDSL can reliably realize for a given data rate. This is unknown because real line characteristics at the frequencies required for VDSL are speculative, and items such as short-bridged taps or unterminated extension lines in homes, which have no effect on telephony, ISDN, or ADSL, could have detrimental affects on VDSL in certain configurations. Furthermore, VDSL invades the frequency ranges of amateur radio, and every above-ground telephone wire is an antenna that both radiates and attracts energy in amateur radio bands. Balancing low signal levels to prevent emissions that interfere with amateur radio with higher signals needed to combat interference by amateur radio could be the dominant factor in determining line reach.

A second dimension of VDSL that is far from clear is the services environment. It can be assumed that VDSL will carry information in ATM cell format for video and asymmetric data communications, although optimum downstream and upstream data rates have not been ascertained. What is more difficult to assess is the need for VDSL to carry information in non-ATM formats (such as conventional Plesiochronous Digital Hierarchy [PDH] structures) and the need for symmetric channels at broadband rates (above T1/E1). VDSL will not be completely independent of upper-layer protocols, particularly in the upstream direction, where multiplexing data from more than one CPE might require knowledge of link-layer formats (that is, ATM or not).

A third difficult subject is premises distribution and the interface between the telephone network and CPE. Cost considerations favor a passive network interface with premises VDSL installed in CPE and upstream multiplexing handled similarly to LAN buses. System management, reliability, regulatory constraints, and migration favor an active network termination, similar to ADSL and ISDN, that can operate like a hub, with point-to-point or shared-media distribution to multiple CPE on-premises wiring that is independent and physically isolated from network wiring.

However, costs cannot be ignored. Small ONUs must spread common equipment costs, such as fiber links, interfaces, and equipment cabinets, over a small number of subscribers, as compared to HFC. VDSL, therefore, has a much lower cost target than ADSL because VDSL could connect directly from a wiring center or cable modems, which also have much lower common equipment costs per user. Furthermore, VDSL for passive NTs could be more expensive than VDSL for active NTs, but the elimination of any other premises-network electronics could make it the most cost-effective solution, and highly desired, despite the obvious benefits of an active NT.

VDSL Standards Status

At present, five standards organizations/forums have begun work on VDSL:

- **T1E1.4**—The U.S. ANSI standards group T1E1.4 has just begun a project for VDSL, making a first attack on system requirements that will evolve into a system and protocol definition.

- **ETSI**—The ETSI has a VDSL standards project, under the title High-Speed Metallic Access Systems, and has compiled a list of objectives, problems, and requirements. Among its preliminary findings are the need for an active NT and payloads in multiples of SDH virtual container VC-12, or 2.3 Mbps. ETSI works closely with T1E1.4 and the ADSL Forum, with significant overlapping attendees.

- **DAVIC**—DAVIC has taken the earliest position on VDSL. Its first specification, due to be finalized, will define a line code for downstream data, another for upstream data, and a MAC for upstream multiplexing based on TDMA over shared wiring. DAVIC is specifying VDSL only for a single downstream rate of 51.84 Mbps and a single upstream rate of 1.6 Mbps over 300m or less of copper. The proposal assumes, and is driven to a large extent by, a passive NT, and further assumes premises distribution from the NT over new coaxial cable or new copper wiring.

- **The ATM Forum**—The ATM Forum has defined a 51.84-Mbps interface for private-network User-Network Interfaces (UNIs) and a corresponding transmission technology. It has also addressed the question of CPE distribution and delivery of ATM all the way to premises over the various access technologies described previously.

- **The ADSL Forum**—The ADSL Forum has just begun consideration of VDSL. In keeping with its charter, the Forum will address network, protocol, and architectural aspects of VDSL for all prospective applications, leaving line code and transceiver protocols to T1E1.4 and ETSI and higher-layer protocols to organizations such as the ATM Forum and DAVIC.

Relationship of VDSL to ADSL

VDSL has an odd technical resemblance to ADSL. VDSL achieves data rates nearly ten times greater than those of ADSL, but ADSL is the more complex transmission technology, in large part because ADSL must contend with much larger dynamic ranges than VDSL. However, the two are essentially cut from the same cloth. ADSL employs advanced transmission techniques and FEC to realize data rates from 1.5 to 9 Mbps over twisted pair, ranging to 18,000 feet; VDSL employs the same advanced transmission techniques and FEC to realize data rates from 14 to 55 Mbps over twisted pair, ranging to 4500 feet. Indeed, the two can be considered a continuum, a set of transmission tools that delivers about as much data as theoretically possible over varying distances of existing telephone wiring.

VDSL is clearly a technology suitable for a full-service network (assuming that full service does not imply more than two HDTV channels over the highest-rate VDSL). It is equally clear that telephone companies cannot deploy ONUs overnight, even if all the technology were available. ADSL might not be a full-service network technology, but it has the singular advantage of offering service over lines that exist today, and ADSL products are more widely available than VDSL. Many new services being contemplated today—such as videoconferencing, Internet access, video on demand, and remote LAN access—can be delivered at speeds at or below T1/E1 rates. For such services, ADSL/VDSL provides an ideal combination for network evolution. On the longest lines, ADSL delivers a single channel. As line length shrinks, either from natural proximity to a central office or deployment of fiber-based access nodes, ADSL and VDSL simply offer more channels and capacity for services that require rates above T1/E1 (such as digital live television and virtual CD-ROM access).

Key Terms

ADSL (asymmetric digital subscriber line)   One of four DSL technologies. ADSL is designed to deliver more bandwidth downstream (from the central office to the customer site) than upstream. Downstream rates range from 1.5 to 9 Mbps, whereas upstream bandwidth ranges from 16 to 640 kbps. ADSL transmissions work at distances up to 18,000 feet (5488 meters) over a single copper twisted pair.

Cable modem   Modulator-demodulator device that is placed at subscriber locations to convey data communications on a cable television system.

DSL (digital subscriber line)   Public network technology that delivers high bandwidth over conventional copper wiring at limited distances. There are four types of DSL (collectively referred to as *x*DSL): ADSL, HDSL, SDSL, and VDSL. All are provisioned through modem pairs, with one modem located at a central office and the other at the customer site. Because most DSL technologies do not use the whole bandwidth of the twisted pair, there is room remaining for a voice channel.

DSLAM (digital subscriber line access multiplexer)   A device that connects many digital subscriber lines to a network by multiplexing the DSL traffic onto one or more network trunk lines.

HDSL (high-data-rate digital subscriber line)   One of four DSL technologies. HDSL delivers 1.544 Mbps of bandwidth each way over two copper twisted pairs. Because HDSL provides T1 speed, telephone companies have been using HDSL to provision local access to T1 services whenever possible. The operating range of HDSL is limited to 12,000 feet (3658.5 meters), so signal repeaters are installed to extend the service. HDSL requires two twisted pairs, so it is deployed primarily for PBX network connections, digital loop carrier systems, interexchange POPs, Internet servers, and private data networks.

Headend   End point of a broadband network. All stations transmit toward the headend; the headend then transmits toward the destination stations.

LMDS (Local Multipoint Distribution Service)   A relatively low-power license for broadcasting voice, video, and data.

MMDS (Multicast Multipoint Distribution Service)   MMDS is composed of as many as 33 discrete channels that are transmitted in a pseudo random order between the transmitters and the receivers.

MPEG (Motion Pictures Experts Group) Standard for compressing video. MPEG1 is a bit stream standard for compressed video and audio optimized to fit into a bandwidth of 1.5 Mbps. MPEG2 is intended for higher-quality video-on-demand applications and runs at data rates between 4 and 9 Mbps. MPEG4 is a low-bit-rate compression algorithm intended for 64-kbps connections.

SDSL (symmetric digital subscriber line) Also known as single-line digital subscriber line. One of four DSL technologies. SDSL delivers 1.544 Mbps both downstream and upstream over a single copper twisted pair. The use of a single twisted pair limits the operating range of SDSL to 10,000 feet (3048.8 meters).

VDSL (very-high-data-rate digital subscriber line) One of four DSL technologies. VDSL delivers 13 to 52 Mbps downstream and 1.5 to 2.3 Mbps upstream over a single twisted copper pair. The operating range of VDSL is limited to 1000 to 4500 feet (304.8 to 1372 meters).

WLAN (wireless local-area network) A WLAN is one in which a mobile user can connect to a local area network (LAN) through a wireless (radio) connection. A standard, IEEE 802.11, specifies the technologies for WLANs.

Configuring Cisco 700 Series Routers

This appendix introduces the following topics:

- Cisco 700 series routers
- Cisco 700 series software
- Cisco 700 series profiles
- Cisco 700 series user interface
- Configuring IP routing on a Cisco 700 series router

Introduction

Cisco offers several affordable remote-access solutions designed for home users and small offices. These products are described as small-office/home-office (SOHO) solutions. The Cisco 1000, 800, 700, and 600 series routers are SOHO routers that typically provide Integrated Services Digital Network Basic Rate Interface (ISDN BRI) access, although some models of the 800 and 1000 series can include a digital subscriber line (DSL), cable, or serial interface. (The 600 series are designed exclusively for DSL.) SOHO routers differ from branch access routers in several important ways:

- SOHO routers typically offer less performance (slower CPUs, less memory, slower switching architectures) but are more affordable than branch-office access routers.
- SOHO routers generally offer fixed interface configurations (usually a single WAN and single local-area network [LAN] interface), whereas today's branch-office routers are typically modular.
- Unlike many high-end routers, SOHO routers usually have a small chassis, designed for a shelf or desktop, and not a telecommunications equipment rack.

Configuring an 800 series or 1000 series router for remote access is accomplished using the commands and techniques shown in the chapters of this book. But the Cisco 700 is different. Routers in this series do not run Cisco IOS, which means the commands discussed in the earlier chapters do not necessarily work on a Cisco 700 series router.

Even though the 700 series routers support only ISDN BRI and do not run Cisco IOS, these routers continue to remain in service as a legacy technology. For some companies, ISDN BRI plays a significant role in their remote access strategy, and the 700 series is a viable and affordable option for providing ISDN BRI access to remote power users.

This appendix surveys the Cisco 700 series product line and describes how to configure 700 series routers for Point-to-Point Protocol (PPP) over ISDN BRI.

Overview of the Cisco 700 Series

NOTE

Earlier models of the Cisco 700 series had model numbers without the M suffix. The absence of the M suffix indicates that the routers have 1.5 MB of system RAM.

The Cisco 700 series product family includes the Cisco 761M, 775M, and 776M routers (see Figure C-1). These products offer two optional analog telephone interfaces to allow devices such as standard telephones, fax machines, and modems to share an ISDN BRI line, eliminating the need for multiple telephone lines or expensive ISDN telephones (see Figure C-2).

Figure C-1
The Cisco 776 is the latest model of 700 series routers
The Cisco uBR904 is an IOS-based router and integrated cable modem.

Although routers in this series don't run the IOS, they do support key internetworking features and protocols, including Internet Protocol (IP) and Internetwork Packet Exchange (IPX) routing of PPP. All PPP Link Control Protocol (LCP) options are supported, including Multilink PPP (MLP).

Cisco 700 series routers can function as Dynamic Host Configuration Protocol (DHCP) servers and be configured for Network Address Translation (NAT). By allowing for dynamic address assignment and NAT, the 700 series routers can be used to connect small LANs (typically five hosts or less) to the Internet or corporate network.

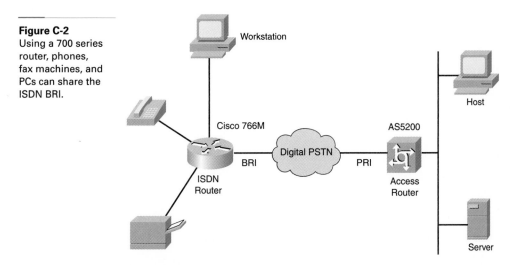

Figure C-2
Using a 700 series router, phones, fax machines, and PCs can share the ISDN BRI.

Cisco 700 Series Software

Cisco 700 series routers use specialized software, which is currently in Release 4.4. Although the concepts behind configuring an IOS-based router and a 700 series router are the same, the structure of the operating system and the command syntax is quite different. The following sections overview the key components of the 700 series operating system.

Profiles

A *profile* is a set of configuration parameters associated with ports on the router or WAN devices. There are two modes in which you can set parameters, the system mode and the profile mode. *System mode parameters* affect the configuration on a global level. Profiles are sets of local parameters. *Profile mode parameters* affect how the router handles the connection to a device.

You do not have to reconfigure the router every time you connect to a different device. Instead of using one set of configuration parameters for all devices, you can use different profiles to communicate with a variety of devices.

For example, you can create a user-defined profile called 2500 that contains the parameters to be used when communicating with a Cisco 2500 series router over the WAN.

You can customize your Cisco 700 series router to maintain up to 17 user-defined profiles. Profiles are saved in the Cisco 700 series router nonvolatile RAM (NVRAM).

In addition to user-defined profiles, there are three permanent profiles: Internal, LAN, and Standard. The Internal profile stores parameters used to communicate between the LAN and WAN ports on the Cisco 700 series router. The LAN profile stores parameters that configure the LAN port on the router. The Standard profile is the default profile.

Profiles and Connections

Profiles are either active or inactive. An active profile creates a *virtual connection* to the remote device associated with the profile. A virtual connection is a connection without physical channels. After creating a virtual connection, an on-demand call can be made to the associated remote device to establish a *physical connection*.

A physical connection is a dynamically created pipeline of packets from the Cisco 700 series router to an ISDN switch on the WAN. All connections are associated with the profile that defines the configuration of the connection.

Virtual and physical connections behave similarly; the difference is that physical connections forward packets to the WAN. Virtual connections monitor packet traffic on the LAN until a demand filter sees that a packet is destined for the WAN and initiates a call to the ISDN switch, opening the physical connection. After the call is established, the virtual connection becomes an active physical connection, and the packets move through the pipeline.

System and Profile Parameters

The system is composed of system mode parameters, user-defined profiles, and permanent profiles. System mode parameters can be changed only in system mode. The prompt indicates you are in system mode by displaying nothing or the router name, as shown here:

```
Router_name>
```

If you are in profile mode, the profile name appears on the prompt, separated from the system name by a colon (:), as shown here:

```
Router_name:Profile>
```

All profiles are based on the profile template and inherit the system-level values. When you create a new profile, its default values are taken from the profile template.

System Mode Parameter Set

System mode parameters affect the router as a system. Table C-1 lists the system parameters.

Table C-1   The Profile Mode Parameters

System Parameter Set Caller ID Parameters		
Date and time	Call waiting	PPP parameters
Directory number(s)	Country group	Screen length
Delay time	Address age time	Screen echo
Forwarding mode	Local and remote access	Simple Network Management Protocol (SNMP) parameters
Multidestination dialing	Phone 1 and 2	service profile identifiers (SPIDs)
Numbering plan	PPP client password	Switch type
Patterns	PPP client secret	System password
Passthru	Voice priority	Power Source 1 detect
PPP authentication	Compression	System name

Profile Mode Parameter Set

Changes made to profile mode parameters in system mode affect the profile template. When a profile is created, it inherits the matching system mode parameters from the profile template. Any changes to parameters in profile mode apply only to that profile. Changes made to profile parameters in system mode are stored in the profile template. When you use the **set user** command to create a user-defined profile, the default parameters for the new profile are taken from system mode.

Table C-2 lists the parameters that can be configured in a profile.

Table C-2   The Profile Mode Parameters

Profile Parameters		
Ringback number	Line speed	PPP authentication (outgoing)
Passthrough	Auto calling	All IP parameters, including filters
Learning	Demand	Password Authentication Protocol (PAP) password (client and host)

continues

Table C-2   The Profile Mode Parameters (Continued)

Profile Parameters		
Subnet mask	Timeout	All IPX parameters, including filters
Protocol	Called number	Challenge Handshake Authentication Protocol (CHAP) secret (client and host)
Loopback	Encapsulation	Bridging and Bridge filters (address, type, and user-defined)

Permanent Profiles

Cisco 700 series routers contain three permanent profiles. Permanent profiles can be modified, but they cannot be deleted. The permanent profiles are as follows:

- **LAN**—This profile determines how data is passed from the router to the LAN. It is used for routing and with the Ethernet connection.
- **Internal**—This profile determines how data is passed between the bridge engine and the IP/IPX router engine. Used when routing is enabled on LAN or USER profiles, it stores the parameters used to communicate between the LAN and WAN ports on the Cisco 700 series router.
- **Standard**—This profile is used for incoming ISDN connections that do not have a profile. If authentication is not required and the destination device that you are connecting to does not have a user-defined profile, the router uses the standard profile.

The decision to use the LAN or Internal profile involves some knowledge of your network design and whether you are bridging or routing to remote sites (or doing a combination of both). Use the LAN profile instead of the Internal profile to simplify the configuration. You can easily associate the LAN profile with the Ethernet interface and the user-defined profiles with the ISDN interface.

Sometimes, situations arise (infrequently) where you must route a protocol to one site and bridge the *same* protocol to another site. Simply leave the LAN profile as a bridging profile, and use the Internal profile for all routed protocol information.

Creating and Modifying Profiles

A new profile is created with the **set user** command. When you create a new profile, you automatically enter profile mode for that profile. The following example creates a user profile called tomd. Enter the **set user** command to create a profile using the profile template for the default values of the parameters, as follows:

```
Host> set user tomd
Host:tomd>
```

Notice that the profile mode is indicated by the prompt, which appears as the system name *and* the profile name, separated by a colon. Although this prompt is displayed, modifications to the parameters affect only the parameters in the profile. The changes do not affect system mode parameters or other profiles.

The **cd** command is used to change to system mode or to another profile. Following is an example of the **cd** command used to change to a permanent profile called LAN:

```
Router_name> cd LAN
Router_name:LAN>
```

Note that the prompt includes the name of the profile. You can now modify the LAN profile parameters.

Displaying Profile Configurations

The **show** commands display the values associated with a profile parameter in profile mode. The commands work in system mode to show the values associated with parameters in the profile template.

In profile mode, some **show** commands display only profile parameters. Parameter values that have been redefined in profile mode are indicated with a <*>. All other parameter values are inherited from the profile template.

Removing Profile-Based Values

You can remove any parameter value within a profile with the **unset** command. The parameter you removed inherits its value from the system mode.

In the following example, the profile parameter number is removed from the profile by using the **unset** command:

```
Host:Profile> unset number
```

Deleting Profiles

The **reset user** command deletes a user-defined profile from the router. The three permanent profiles (LAN, Internal, and Standard) cannot be deleted. This command also closes any connection associated with the profile.

In the following example, the **tomd** profile is removed from the system by using the **reset user** command:

```
Host:Profile> reset user tomd
```

Changing Profile Names

The **set profile user** command changes the name of an existing profile. Enter this command while in profile mode for the profile you want to affect. In the following example, the profile name is being changed from 2500 to 4500:

```
766:2500> set profile user 4500
766:4500>
```

Incoming Calls

When the router receives an incoming call, the router searches both active and inactive profiles for a profile with the same name as the calling device. If it finds a profile with the matching user ID, the router uses the configuration parameters of that profile while communicating with the remote device. If the profile is inactive, it is automatically activated for the duration of the connection.

When the call is finished, the physical link between the two devices is disconnected. However, the virtual connection to the remote router might be configured to remain active.

If the profile is configured to remain active after a link disconnects, a virtual connection remains. The virtual connection monitors the LAN traffic. If packets destined for the WAN are detected, the router opens up the physical connection and forwards the packets.

If the profile is configured to become inactive after a link disconnects, both the physical link and the virtual connection to the remote router are disconnected until another call is received from the same remote router.

Outgoing Calls

Outgoing calls require that the associated user-defined profiles are set to **active**, that the **set auto** command is on, and that a phone number to call is stored in the profile. If the profile is inactive, a number to dial is not available to the router.

Cisco 700 User Interface

The user interface has a UNIX-like directory structure, as shown in Figure C-3. Commands are set by entering **set** commands on the command-line interface. Also, to navigate from one profile to another, the **cd** (change directory) command is used.

Figure C-3
Profiles are part
of a hierarchical
structure, with the
system profile at
the top.

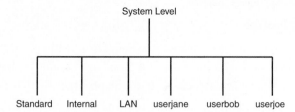

The **set** commands are automatically saved in NVRAM, and **reset** commands remove commands from NVRAM. To initialize the system, enter **set default**. The **set default** command is the same as the **erase start** command followed by the **reload** command in the Cisco IOS Software.

The **show** command displays information and parameters.

You can save **set** commands in a text file off line, and copy and paste them at the command-line prompt to configure the router.

Configuring the Cisco 700 Series

You must specify system level, LAN profile, and user profile parameters to prepare the Cisco 700 series router for operation in an ISDN environment.

- **System-level configuration**—Select the switch that matches the ISDN provider switch at the central office (CO). Set destination details, such as the directory numbers, and enter SPIDs, if required. System-level configuration also includes assigning a system name and setting MLP off if you are connecting to a Cisco IOS Software-based router running Release 11.0(3) or earlier.

- **LAN profile configuration**—Specify an IP address and subnet mask for the Ethernet interface. Specify the types of packets to be routed. In this case, turn IP routing on and set IP RIP update to periodic.

- **User profile configuration**—Specify the characteristics of each user that you plan to dial. Assign the user a name, set IP routing on, set the framing type, set the ISDN phone number you will dial, and set the static route.

Figure C-4

Configuring a Cisco 700 series router involves three main tasks: system-level configuration, LAN profile configuration, and user profile configuration.

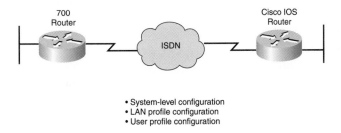

After these profiles are created, you can define optional features, including caller ID, authentication type, and timeout values for the ISDN connection.

System Level Configuration

Use the **set switch global** command to specify the ISDN switch to which the router connects. For ISDN BRI service, the switch type can be one of those listed in Table C-3.

Table C-3   ISDN Switch Types

Keyword	Switch Type
5Ess	5ESS
DMS	Northern Telecom DMS-100

continues

Table C-3   ISDN Switch Types (Continued)

Keyword	Switch Type
NI1	National ISDN-1
INS	Japan—NTT's Information Network System
VN3	France—ISDN BRI standard
NET3	Europe—ISDN BRI standard
1TR6	Germany—ISDN BRI standard
TPH	Australia
PERM64	Dedicated line service that enables the unit to use a single 64-kbps data stream connected to one port. With this option, Channel 1 runs at 64 kbps, and Channel 2 is not used. NTT's Super Digital service is an example of a leased line server. (Japan)
PERM128	Dedicated line service that enables the unit to use a single 128-kbps data stream connected to one port. With this option, Channels 1 and 2 are combined to run at 128 kbps. (An example is Japan NTT's HSD service.)
PERM2X64	Bundles the B channels even if they are not synchronized. (When the unit is set in PERM128 mode, only one PPP session runs at 128 kbps, and both B channels must be synchronized.)

Auto-detect of ISDN switch-type is available in later versions of the Cisco 700. Separate Cisco 700 images might require country-specific switches. The default if no switch is specified is 5ess. Several ISDN providers use ISDN switches that operate on dial-in numbers called SPIDs, which are used to authenticate that call requests are within contract specifications. These switches include National ISDN-1, DMS-100 ISDN switches, and the AT&T 5 Electronic Switching System (5ESS) switch. The local SPID number is supplied by the service provider.

The following command line shows the syntax for the first BRI 64-Kbps channel:

```
IOS-700>set 1 spid spid-number [ldn]
```

The system profile sets parameters that apply to all profiles on the selected router, unless overridden in the user profile. This is also called the *global configuration*.

LAN Profile Configuration

If you want to activate IP routing on the LAN profile, you need to enter the address and subnet mask commands on the Cisco 700. Also, you need to activate the routing with the **set ip routing on** command. Figure C-5 shows a sample LAN profile configuration.

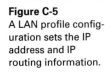

Figure C-5
A LAN profile config-
uration sets the IP
address and IP
routing information.

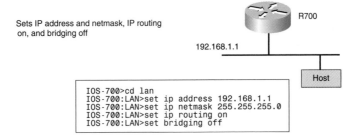

Sets IP address and netmask, IP routing
on, and bridging off

R700

192.168.1.1

Host

```
IOS-700>cd lan
IOS-700:LAN>set ip address 192.168.1.1
IOS-700:LAN>set ip netmask 255.255.255.0
IOS-700:LAN>set ip routing on
IOS-700:LAN>set bridging off
```

Different strategies are available for bridging and routing with a Cisco 700 series
router. Depending on the strategy, sometimes problems happen. For example, if IP
routing is activated on the LAN profile and IP routing is not turned on the standard
profile, as shown in Figure C-6, the IP traffic passes from the standard profile to the
bridge engine (labeled 1), passes to the LAN profile (labeled 2), and comes out on the
Ethernet interface/LAN profile (3). The difficulty arises with the return-trip packets
(4). The return traffic is routed from the LAN profile to the IP Routing Engine (5).
Having no access to the standard profile, the return traffic gets caught and stops in
the routing engine. The following is a typical misconfiguration:

```
cd lan
set bridging on
set ip routing on
set ip address 10.1.1.1
cd internal
set bridging on
cd standard
set bridging on
```

The solution is to turn off routing on the LAN interface and apply Layer 3 configuration to the internal profile.

If the IP routing is activated on the internal profile, as shown in Figure C-7, the IP traffic passes from standard profile to the bridge engine (labeled 1), passes to the LAN
profile (labeled 2), and comes out on the Ethernet interface LAN profile (3). The return
traffic then goes from the Ethernet segment to the LAN profile (4), goes to the bridging
engine (5), goes to the internal profile (6), goes to the IP routing engine (7), goes back
out to the internal profile (8), goes toward the bridge engine (9), and goes on to the
bridge engine that sends the packet out to the standard profile (10). The following is a
typical proper configuration when standard profile is involved:

```
cd lan
set bridging on
cd internal
set bridging on
set ip routing on
set ip address 10.1.1.1
cd standard
set bridging on
```

Figure C-6
IP routing is
configured on the
LAN profile but
not the standard
profile; this is a
misconfiguration.

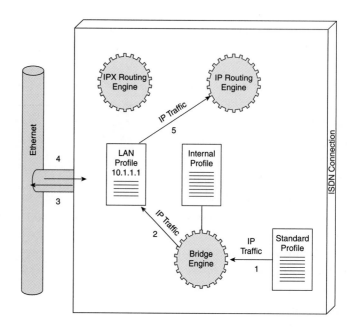

Figure C-7
IP routing is config-
ured on both the
internal profile and
the standard profile;
the LAN profile
is configured
for bridging.

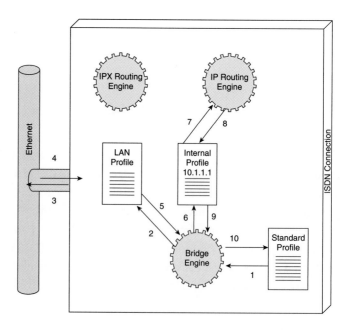

A similar solution can be implemented when using a user profile, as shown in Figure C-8. If both IP routing and bridging are turned on for the Chicago profile, all IP traffic flows to the IP routing engine (labeled 1). Not shown in Figure C-8 is that all other traffic (AppleTalk, NetBEUI, and IPX/Sequenced Packet Exchange [SPX]) flows to the bridge engine. The IP traffic flows from the IP routing engine to the internal profile (labeled 2) and then flows to the bridge engine (3). All traffic, whether IP or nonrouted traffic such as NetBEUI, flows to the LAN profile (4), and flows on to the Ethernet segment (5). The return trip traffic flows from the Ethernet segment into the LAN profile (6) and then flows to the bridge engine (7). The IP traffic flows to the internal profile (8) and then flows to the routing engine (9), followed by the Chicago profile (10). Traffic other than IP flows from the bridge engine to the Chicago profile (not shown in Figure C-8). The following is a typical correct configuration when a user profile is involved:

```
cd lan
set bridging on
cd internal
set bridging on
set ip routing on
set ip address 10.1.1.1
cd standard
set bridging off
set user Chicago
set bridging off
set ip routing on
set ip address 192.168.1.1
```

If you change an IP address of a profile, the IP routing is suspended, even if it still appears under the same profile when performing the **upload** command. To reactivate the IP routing process, you must either **reload** the router or type under the profile **set ip routing on**.

User Profile Configuration

Use the **set encapsulation ppp** command if you want PPP encapsulation for your ISDN interface and if you want any of the LCP options that PPP offers (for example, CHAP authentication). You must use PPP with PAP or CHAP if you will receive calls from more than one dialup source. This command must be entered if you are connecting to a Cisco IOS Software-based router.

Figure C-8
The user profile,
Chicago, and the
internal profile are
configured for
IP routing.

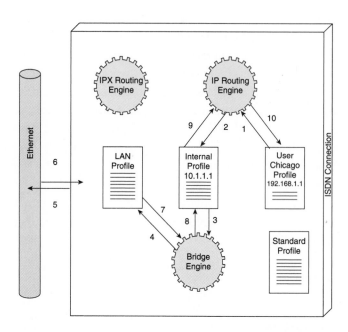

In addition to this command, each user profile must include the user's username (**set user** *username*), IP address (**set ip address** *ip address*), and subnet mask (**set ip netmask** *netmask*). You must also turn on IP routing using the **set ip routing on** command. If you do not include the subnet mask, the default mask for that class of address is assumed. As an example, if you are using the address 172.16.2.53 without configuring a network mask, the Cisco 700 assumes the mask to be 255.255.0.0, which is the default mask for a Class B address.

If you want to route IP with PPP, you must turn off Combinet Proprietary Protocol (CPP) by using the **set encapsulation ppp** command.

Routing IP using CPP is recommended only for connections between Cisco 700 products, not between a Cisco 700 series router and a Cisco IOS Software-based router. To route between non-CPP products, you must configure IP routing with PPP. With Version 4.1 and later of the Cisco IOS 700, encapsulation with PPP is the default.

The **set number** *number* command configures the phone number that is used to dial the Internet Service Provider (ISP) or remote router. This command is used in a user profile. The following is an example of this command:

```
IOS-700:User3>set number 14085551234
```

A *connection* is a dynamically created link to a remote site. Connections are closely related to profiles because all connections are associated with a profile that defines the configuration of the connection.

A *virtual connection* is a connection without any existing physical channels. An *active connection* is a connection with one or more existing physical channels. Profiles can be set to be either active or inactive. When a profile has been created, setting it to active creates a virtual connection to the associated remote device. After a call is made to the associated remote device, the connection becomes an active connection.

Virtual and active connections behave similarly. The only difference is that active connections are forwarding packets. Virtual connections exist to monitor packet traffic until a demand filter causes a call to be initiated. When this happens, the virtual connection becomes an active connection.

When the call is finished, the physical link between the two devices is disconnected. However, the virtual connection to the remote router might be configured to remain active.

If the profile is configured to remain active after a link disconnects, a virtual connection remains. The virtual connection monitors the LAN traffic. If packets destined for the WAN are detected, the router opens up the physical connection and forwards the packets.

If the remote user makes a call to you, the remote device is identified and associated with the virtual connection created by the user's profile. This causes the connection to become active.

When creating a profile, it can be set active or inactive by using the **set active profile-name** or the **set inactive profile-name** commands.

For the user profile specified, you can enter the default route and point it at a specific address, as follows:

`700:user>`**`set ip route destination 0.0.0.0/0 gateway 10.1.1.1`**

The address used (10.1.1.1) is the IP address of the BRI interface on the central-site router (see Figure C-9). All traffic for this user goes to the same IP address. To enable static routes, you must also set bridging off and make the user profile active.

Figure C-9
You can configure a
user profile with a
static default route.

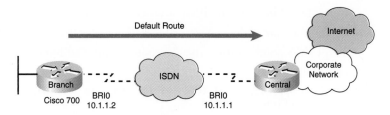

Branch:user>**set ip route destination 0.0.0.0/0 gateway 10.1.1.1**

As an example, consider Figure C-10. The Cisco 700 router (R700) has a static route to the (Cisco IOS) router central. Only the LAN and USER profiles are shown. You must also configure the system profile for the Cisco 700 router. The router-configuration information must be supplied by the ISP, and it depends on the configuration of the ISP and the switch type.

Figure C-10
The user profile on R700 includes a static default route to the central-site router.

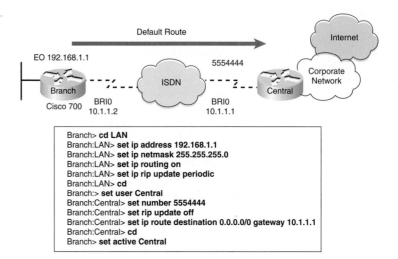

```
Branch> cd LAN
Branch:LAN> set ip address 192.168.1.1
Branch:LAN> set ip netmask 255.255.255.0
Branch:LAN> set ip routing on
Branch:LAN> set ip rip update periodic
Branch:LAN> cd
Branch:> set user Central
Branch:Central> set number 5554444
Branch:Central> set rip update off
Branch:Central> set ip route destination 0.0.0.0/0 gateway 10.1.1.1
Branch:Central> cd
Branch> set active Central
```

The PPP IP Control Protocol (IPCP) allows for the negotiation of certain parameters, such as an IP address and a specific compression protocol. Some points to remember when using IPCP negotiation on a Cisco 700 series router follow:

- A user profile is required to run PPP. IP routing must be turned on to receive an IPCP negotiated address.
- If a manually configured IP address exists on the internal profile, the IPCP address is assigned to the WAN (user) profile.
- If a manually configured IP address exists on the LAN profile, the IPCP address is assigned to the internal profile.
- If the LAN IP address is manually configured, the WAN interface must be unnumbered because the IPCP address is assigned to the internal profile.
- The remote-site router needs to be configured to hand off IPCP addresses. A sample IOS configuration for the central router to hand off an IPCP address is as follows:

```
Central(config)#ip local pool test 700 192.150.3.10 192.150.3.19
Central(config)#interface bri0
Central(config-if)#peer default ip address pool test
```

This configuration specifies the IP address to be used when the Cisco 700 dials into the central site.

Configuration Example

The sample configuration shown in Example C-1 statically routes IP between a 700 series router and a Cisco IOS router using PPP with CHAP authentication over ISDN, as shown in Figure C-11. Unnumbered IP is used on the ISDN segment to help conserve network address space. Dial-on-demand routing (DDR)ensures that with static routes between the two routers, there is no need for the routers to exchange routing updates and the ISDN line activates only when traffic demands.

Figure C-11
Boston is a Cisco 700 series router, configured with a static route.

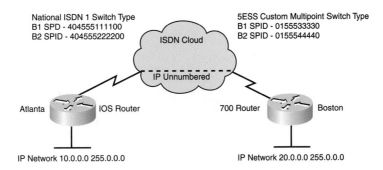

An alternative to DDR using static routes is DDR using a snapshot routing protocol. *Snapshot routing* allows routes to be automatically exchanged during a defined time interval instead of burdening a network administrator with the chore of manually maintaining static routes. Although the ISDN line must be activated to exchange snapshot routing updates, the duration and frequency of the snapshot interval can be configured so that any associated ISDN costs are relatively negligible compared with the benefits of simplified network administration.

Example C-1   Configuring a 700 Series Router for Static Routing

```
set systemname Boston
Boston> set switch 5ESS
Boston> set 1 spid 0155533330
Boston> set 2 spid 0155544440
Boston> set 1 directory 5553333
Boston> set 2 directory 5554444
Boston> cd lan
Boston:LAN> set bridging off
Boston:LAN> set ip routing on
```

continues

Example C-1   Configuring a 700 Series Router for Static Routing (Continued)

```
Boston:LAN> set ip address 20.1.1.1
Boston:LAN> set ip netmask 255.0.0.0
Boston:LAN> cd
Boston> set user Atlanta
Boston:Atlanta> set ppp clientname Boston
Boston:Atlanta> set ppp secret client
Enter new Password: gocisco1
Re-Type new Password: gocisco1
Boston:Atlanta> set ppp secret host
Enter new Password: gocisco1
Re-Type new Password: gocisco1
Boston:Atlanta> set bridging off
Boston:Atlanta> set ip routing on
Boston:Atlanta> set ip rip update off
Boston:Atlanta> set ip route destination 10.0.0.0/8 gateway 10.1.1.1
Boston:Atlanta> set 1 number 14045551111
Boston:Atlanta> set 2 number 14045552222
Boston:Atlanta> set ppp authentication outgoing chap
Boston:Atlanta> set timeout 300
Boston:Atlanta> set active
```

Atlanta's IOS configuration is shown in Example C-2.

Example C-2   Configuring an IOS Router to Accept Connections from a 700 Series Router

```
version 11.2
service udp-small-servers
service tcp-small-servers
!
hostname Atlanta
!
enable secret cisco
!
username Boston password gocisco1
ip subnet-zero
no ip domain-lookup
isdn switch-type basic-ni1
!
```

Example C-2   Configuring an IOS Router to Accept Connections from a 700 Series Router (Continued)

```
interface Ethernet0
 ip address 10.1.1.1 255.0.0.0
!
interface BRI0
 no ip address
 encapsulation ppp
 dialer rotary-group 0
 isdn spid1 014045551111000 5551111
 isdn spid2 014045552222000 5552222
 no fair-queue
 no cdp enable
!
interface Dialer0
 ip unnumbered Ethernet0
 encapsulation ppp
 dialer in-band
 dialer idle-timeout 300
 dialer map ip 20.1.1.1 name Boston 16175553333
 dialer map ip 20.1.1.1 name Boston 16175554444
 dialer hold-queue 10
 dialer load-threshold 200 either
 dialer-group 1
 no fair-queue
 no cdp enable
 ppp authentication chap
 ppp multilink
!
ip classless
ip route 20.0.0.0 255.0.0.0 Dialer0
ip http server
!
dialer-list 1 protocol ip permit
!
line con 0
 password console
 login
```

continues

Example C-2   Configuring an IOS Router to Accept Connections from a 700 Series Router (Continued)

```
line aux 0
line vty 0 4
 password telnet
 login
!
end
<*>
```

NOTE

Visit
www.cisco.com
for information on
configuration com-
mands specific to
these features.

Additional Configuration Parameters

You can add the interface functions desired or required by the particular ISDN situation, as follows:

- Filter inbound call setups with caller ID screening.
- Use callback with or without authorization.
- Implement MLP for better bandwidth use.
- Cisco 700 series routers implement MLP by default.

You must manually turn off the multilink capability if your router is connecting to a Cisco IOS Software-based router running Release 11.0(3) or earlier.

Glossary

A

AAA (Authentication, Authorization, and Accounting)   An architectural framework for configuring security features.

Access server   A router configured to accept dial-in calls over an ISDN or asynchronous interface.

Accounting   Method for tracking activity on a system or network.

Active period   In snapshot routing, the period of time during which a client and server exchange routing updates.

address overloading   *See* PAT.

ARAP (AppleTalk Remote Access Protocol)   Layer-2 protocol that provides Macintosh users direct access to information and resources at a remote AppleTalk site.

Asynchronous transmission   Method of data transmission in which each sent character is framed by start and stop bits. Because asynchronous transmissions use no clock or timing source to keep both the sender and the receiver synchronized, the sender must signal the start and stop of each character so that the receiver knows when to expect data.

Authentication   Method of identifying users, including login and password dialog, challenge and response, and messaging support.

Authorization   Method of prescribing the services available to a user.

B

B channel   An ISDN communication channel that bears or carries voice or data. The bearer channel is the fundamental component of ISDN interfaces. It carries 64,000 bits per seconds (64 kbps) in either direction.

Backup interface   An interface that remains in standby mode until the primary link goes down, or until the load on the primary link reaches (or exceeds) a predefined threshold.

BECN (Backward Explicit Congestion Notification)   Bit set by a Frame Relay network in frames traveling in the opposite direction of frames encountering a congested path. Data terminal equipment (DTE) receiving frames with the BECN bit set can request that higher-level protocols take flow control action as appropriate.

Branch office   A remote office that typically maintains at least one WAN connection to the central site, and might have several links to other remote sites. Generally, branch-office networks support fewer users than the central site, and therefore require less bandwidth.

Buffer   An area of memory shared by hardware devices or program processes that operate at different speeds or with different sets of priorities.

Bundle   Group of links being used together for MLP.

C

Callback   Dial-up feature wherein a remote client calls an access server, hangs up, and then receives a callback from the server. Used to consolidate toll charges and for restricting dial-up access.

Central site   Focal point of a company's network that houses enterprise services. Typically, all remote sites and users must connect to the central site to access information, either intermittently or continuously.

CHAP (Challenge Handshake Authentication Protocol)   Security feature supported on lines using PPP encapsulation that prevents unauthorized access. CHAP does not itself prevent unauthorized access; it merely identifies the remote end. The router or access server then determines whether that user is allowed access.

chat script   String of text that includes commands that can be sent to a device as an instruction to perform a specific task, such as dialing out or logging in.

CLID (Calling Line ID)   The ISDN number of the calling source. This is provided by the telco in the call setup messages. You can screen calls based on CLID for added security.

codec   Device used by telecommunications companies to encode analog waveforms into digital pulses and vice versa.

Committed Burst (Bc)   Negotiated tariff metric in Frame Relay network. The maximum amount of data (in bits) that a Frame Relay network is committed to accept and transmit at the CIR.

Compression   The running of a data set through an algorithm that reduces the space required to store or the bandwidth required to transmit the data set.

CQ (Custom queuing)   Queuing method in which bandwidth is allocated proportionally for each different class of traffic. CQ allows the configuration of the number of bytes or packets to be drawn from the queue, which is especially useful on slow interfaces.

CSU (channel service unit)   Digital interface device that connects end-user equipment to the local digital telephone loop. Often referred to together with DSU, as CSU/DSU. *See also* DSU.

D

D channel   An ISDN communication channel used for sending information between the ISDN equipment and the ISDN central-office switch. The delta channel carries the signaling and call progress messages.

DCE   Data communications equipment (EIA expansion) or data circuit-terminating equipment (ITU-T expansion). The devices and connections of a communications network that comprise the network end of the user-to-network interface. The DCE provides a physical connection to the network, forwards traffic, and provides a clocking signal used to synchronize data transmission between DCE and DTE devices. Modems and CSU/DSUs are examples of DCE. Compare with DTE.

DDR (dial-on-demand routing)   Technique whereby a Cisco router can automatically initiate and close a circuit-switched session as transmitting stations demand. The router spoofs keepalives so that end stations treat the session as active. DDR permits routing over ISDN or telephone lines using an external ISDN terminal adaptor or modem.

DE (Discard Eligible)   If the network is congested, DE traffic can be dropped to ensure the delivery of higher priority traffic.

Dedicated line   *See* leased line.

Dialer map class   Optional configuration that allows different characteristics for different types of calls to be assigned on a per-call-destination basis.

Dialer pool   A collection of physical interfaces that are grouped together to be used by a dialer profile.

DLCI (data-link connection identifier)   Value that specifies a PVC or an SVC in a Frame Relay network.

DNIC (Data Network Identification Code)   Part of an X.121 address. DNICs are divided into two parts: the first specifying the country in which the addressed PSN is located, and the second specifying the PSN itself.

DSU (data service unit)   Device used in digital transmission that adapts the physical interface on a DTE device to a transmission facility such as T1 or E1. The DSU is also responsible for such functions as signal timing. Often referred together with CSU, as CSU/DSU. *See also* CSU.

DTE (data terminal equipment)   Device at the user end of a user-network interface that serves as a data source, destination, or both. DTE connects to a data network through a DCE device (for example, a modem) and typically uses clocking signals generated by the DCE. DTE includes such devices as computers, protocol translators, and multiplexers. Compare with DCE.

E

EIA/TIA-232-C   Common physical layer interface standard, developed by EIA and TIA, that supports unbalanced circuits at signal speeds of up to 64 Kbps. Closely resembles the V.24 specification. Formerly known as RS-232.

Excess Burst (Be)   Negotiated tariff metric in Frame Relay internetworks. The number of bits that a Frame Relay internetwork attempts to transmit after Bc is accommodated. Be data, in general, is delivered with a lower probability than Bc data because Be data can be marked as DE by the network.

F

FECN (Forward Explicit Congestion Notification)   Bit set by a Frame Relay network to inform the DTE receiving the frame that congestion was experienced in the path from source to destination. DTE receiving frames with the FECN bit set can request that higher-level protocols take flow-control action as appropriate.

FIFO queuing (first-in, first-out queuing)   Queuing method that involves buffering and forwarding of packets in the order of arrival. FIFO embodies no concept of priority or classes of traffic. There is only one queue, and all packets are treated equally. Packets are sent out an interface in the order in which they arrive.

Floating static route   An administratively defined route that is assigned an administrative distance which is higher than an existing route. A floating static route is not installed in the routing table until the route with the lower administrative distance is flushed from the table.

FRAD (Frame Relay access device)   Any network device that provides a connection between a LAN and a Frame Relay WAN.

H

HSSI (High-Speed Serial Interface)   Network standard for high-speed (up to 52 Mbps) serial connections over WAN links.

Hunt group   A series of telephone lines that are programmed so that as incoming calls arrive, if the first line is busy the second line is tried, and then the third line is tried, and so on, until a free line is found.

I

Inside global address   In NAT, the IP address of an inside host as it appears to the outside network. The inside global address is the translated address. These addresses are typically allocated from a globally unique address space, typically provided by the Internet Service Provider (ISP) (if the enterprise is connected to the global Internet).

Inside local address   In NAT, the configured IP address assigned to a host on the inside network. Address can be globally unique, can be allocated out of the private address space defined in RFC 1918, or might be officially allocated to another organization.

Inverse ARP (Inverse Address Resolution Protocol)   Method of building dynamic routes in a network. Allows an access server to discover the network address of a device associated with a VC.

K

Kerberos   A secret-key network authentication protocol used with AAA that uses the Data Encryption Standard (DES) cryptographic algorithm for encryption and authentication.

L

LAPB (Link Access Procedure, Balanced)   Data-link layer protocol in the X.25 protocol stack. LAPB is derived from High-Level Data Link Control (HDLC).

LAPD (Link Access Protocol-D)   The data-link Layer-2 protocol that manages the exchange of information to the ISDN network. LAPD is defined in Q.921.

LCI (Logical Channel Identifier)   Number used to identify X.25 VCs. Also called Virtual Circuit Number (VCN).

LCP (Link Control Protocol)   PPP protocol that is responsible for negotiating, establishing, and maintaining a data link between end systems.

LDN (local directory number)   Used for call routing, the LDN is associated with a SPID (and therefore with North American BRI interfaces) and is necessary for receiving incoming calls on the second B channel.

LE (Local Exchange)   The ISDN central office (CO) that houses the ISDN switch. The LE implements the ISDN protocol and is part of the network.

Leased line   Transmission line reserved by a communications carrier for the private use of a customer. A leased line is a type of dedicated line. Also called a dedicated line.

Legacy DDR   Method of configuring DDR that restricts a physical dial interface to a single logical configuration.

Link compression   Method of compression that involves compressing both the header and payload sections of a data stream. Unlike header compression, link compression is protocol independent. Also known as per-interface compression.

LMI (Local Management Interface)   Set of enhancements to the basic Frame Relay specification. LMI includes support for a keepalive mechanism, which verifies that data is flowing; a multicast mechanism, which provides the network server with its local DLCI and the multicast DLCI; global addressing, which gives DLCIs global rather than local significance in Frame Relay networks; and a status mechanism, which provides an on-going status report on the DLCIs known to the switch.

Local access rate   The clock speed (port speed) of the connection (local loop) to the Frame Relay cloud. It is the rate at which data travels into or out of the network, regardless of other settings.

M

many-to-one NAT   *See* PAT.

Method list   In AAA, a list of methods that a router should use to perform authentication, authorization, or accounting.

MLP (Multilink PPP)   An LCP option that provides load balancing over multiple interfaces. MLP can improve throughput and reduce latency between systems by splitting Layer-3 packets and sending the fragments over parallel circuits.

MPPC (Microsoft Point-to-Point Compression)   A scheme used to compress PPP packets between Cisco routers and Microsoft client devices. The MPPC algorithm uses a Lempel-Ziv (LZ)-based algorithm with a continuous history buffer, called a dictionary.

Multiplexing   Scheme that allows multiple logical signals to be transmitted simultaneously across a single physical channel.

N

NAT (Network Address Translation)   Mechanism for reducing the need for globally unique IP addresses. NAT allows an organization with addresses that are not globally unique to connect to the Internet by translating those addresses into globally routable address space.

NBMA (Non-broadcast multiaccess)   Term describing a multiaccess network that does not support broadcasting (such as X.25), or one in which broadcasting is not feasible.

NCP (Network Control Protocol)   PPP protocol that is responsible for establishing network-layer communication (such as IP) between end systems.

NTN (National Terminal Number)   Part of an X.121 address. Used to identify the specific DTE on the PSN.

Null modem cable   Cable used to join DTE devices directly, rather than over a network.

O

Outside global address   In NAT, the configured IP address assigned to a host in the outside network.

Outside local address   In NAT, the IP address of an outside host as it appears to the inside network. These addresses can be allocated from the RFC 1918 space if desired.

Overlapping networks   Two or more networks using addresses from the same public or private IP address space.

Oversubscription   When the sum of the CIRs on all the VCs coming in to a device exceeds the access line speed. Oversubscription can also occur when the access line can support the sum of CIRs purchased, but not of the CIRs plus the bursting capacities of the VCs.

P

PAD (Packet assembler/disassembler)   Device used to connect simple devices (like character-mode terminals) that do not support the full functionality of a particular protocol to a network. PADs buffer data and assemble and disassemble packets sent to such end devices.

PAP (Password Authentication Protocol)   Authentication protocol that allows PPP peers to authenticate one another. The remote router attempting to connect to the local router is required to send an authentication request. Unlike CHAP, PAP passes the password and host name or username in the clear (unencrypted). PAP does not itself prevent unauthorized access, but merely identifies the remote end. The router or access server then determines if that user is allowed access. PAP is supported only on PPP lines.

Passive interface   An interface that listens for routing updates, but does not send them.

PAT (Port Address Translation)   A NAT process that maps multiple inside addresses to the same global address by using port numbers to keep track of the translations. This is sometimes called a many-to-one NAT, or address overloading.

Payload compression   Method of compression that involves compressing only the data portion (including the Layer-3 and Layer-4 headers) of the data stream. The frame header is left untouched. Also known as per-virtual-circuit compression.

PCM (pulse code modulation)   Transmission of analog information in digital form through sampling and encoding the samples with a fixed number of bits.

PDN (Public Data Network)   Network operated either by a government (as in Europe) or by a private concern to provide computer communications to the public, usually for a fee.

per-interface compression   *See* link compression.

per-virtual-circuit compression   *See* payload compression.

PLP (Packet-Layer Protocol)   Network layer protocol in the X.25 protocol stack.

POTS (plain old telephone service)   General term referring to the variety of analog telephone networks and services in place worldwide.

PQ (priority queuing)   Queuing method in which packets belonging to one priority class of traffic are sent before all lower priority traffic to ensure timely delivery of those packets.

Predictor   Compression algorithm that determines whether the data is already compressed. If so, the data is just sent—no time is wasted trying to compress already compressed data.

Primary link   A WAN link, such as a leased line or PVC, that is assigned a backup interface.

PSDN (Packet-switched data network)   *See* PSN.

PSE (Packet switching exchange) Typically, a switch in an X.25 PSN.

PSN (Packet-switched network) Network that uses packet-switching technology for data transfer. Sometimes called a packet-switched data network (PSDN).

PSTN (Public Switched Telephone Network) General term referring to the variety of telephone networks and services in place worldwide. Sometimes called plain old telephone service (POTS).

PVC (Permanent virtual circuit) *See* VC.

Q

Q.921 Also referred to as LAPD. Specifies the data-link protocol used over ISDN's D channel.

Q.931 ITU-T specification for signaling to establish, maintain, and clear ISDN network connections.

Quiet period In snapshot routing, the period of time during which no routing updates are exchanged, and routing table entries are frozen.

R

RADIUS (Remote Authentication Dial-In User Service) A distributed client/server system used with AAA that secures networks against unauthorized access. In the Cisco implementation, RADIUS clients run on Cisco routers and send authentication requests to a central RADIUS server that contains all user authentication and network service access information.

Redistribution The process of importing static, connected, or dynamically learned routes into a routing protocol.

Reverse Telnet Outgoing Telnet session that passes from the access server to an attached device over an asynchronous serial connection. Used to configure attached modems, routers, and terminals.

RS-232 *See* EIA/TIA-232-C.

S

SAPI (Service Access Point Identifier) An address used at Layer 2 to manage different data types for the same individual device connecting to the ISDN network. The SAPI and TEI together form the Layer-2 address.

Secondary link   A backup WAN link that is activated once the primary link fails, or once the primary link reaches (or exceeds) a predefined load threshold.

SLIP (Serial Line Internet Protocol)   Standard protocol for point-to-point serial connections using TCP/IP. Predecessor of PPP.

Smoothing   *See* traffic shaping.

Snapshot routing   Method of gathering routing information during an *active time,* taking a snapshot of the information, and using that routing information for a configured length of time (referred to as the *quiet time*).

Split horizon   Routing technique in which information about routes is prevented from exiting the router interface through which that information was received.

SS7 (Signaling System 7)   On the PSTN, SS7 is a system that puts the information required to set up and manage telephone calls in a separate network rather than within the same network that the telephone call is made on.

Stacker   A Lempel-Ziv (LZ)-based compression algorithm that looks at the data, and sends each data type only once with information about where the type occurs within the data stream. The receiving side uses this information to reassemble the data stream.

Standby mode   On a backup interface, an interface state wherein the interface is shut down and awaiting primary link failure, or primary link overload.

Statistical multiplexing   Technique whereby information from multiple logical channels can be transmitted across a single physical channel. Statistical multiplexing dynamically allocates bandwidth only to active input channels, making better use of available bandwidth and allowing more devices to be connected than with other multiplexing techniques. Packet switching networks typically employ statistical multiplexing.

Stub domain   Network that has a single connection to the outside world.

Stub network   Network that has only one entry/exit point.

Subinterfaces   One of a number of virtual interfaces on a single physical interface.

SVC (Switched virtual circuit)   *See* VC.

Synchronous transmission   Method of data transmission in which a common timing signal is used between hosts. A clock signal is either embedded in the data stream or is sent separately to the interfaces.

T

TACACS+ (Terminal Access Controller Access Control System Plus)   Proprietary Cisco enhancement to TACACS. Provides centralized validation of users attempting to gain access to a router or network access server. Supports authorization, accounting functions, and authentication.

TCP header compression   Also known as Van Jacobsen (VJ) compression. This type of compression is used to compress TCP headers.

TDM (time-division multiplexing)   Technique in which information from multiple channels can be allocated bandwidth on a single wire based on preassigned time slots. Bandwidth is allocated to each channel regardless of whether the station has data to transmit.

TEI (terminal endpoint identifier)   An address used at Layer 2 to manage individual devices connecting to the ISDN network. The TEI is typically dynamically negotiated with the ISDN switch.

Telecommuter site   Home office that connects to the central site or branch office as needed.

Traffic shaping   Configuration that limits surges that can congest a network. Data is buffered and then sent into the network in regulated amounts to ensure that the traffic fits within the promised parameters. Also called smoothing.

U

UART (Universal Asynchronous Receiver/Transmitter   A UART is a specialized microchip designed to control a computer's interface to its attached serial devices (such as an external modem or a mouse).

V

V.35   ITU-T standard describing a synchronous, physical layer protocol used for communications between a network access device and a packet network.

Van Jacobsen (VJ) compression   *See* TCP header compression.

VC (Virtual circuit)   Logical circuit created to ensure reliable communication between two network devices. A VC is defined by some kind of identifier, such as a DLCI or VPI/VCI pair. A VC can be either permanent (PVC) or switched (SVC).

Virtual Circuit Number (VCN)   *See* LCI.

Virtual circuit   Logical circuit created to ensure reliable communication between two network devices. A virtual circuit can be either permanent (a PVC) or switched (a SVC, covered in Chapter 6, "X.25"). Virtual circuits are used in Frame Relay and in X.25. In ATM, a virtual circuit is called a virtual channel. Sometimes abbreviated VC.

VoIP (Voice over Internet Protocol)   The capability to carry normal telephony-style voice over an IP-based Internet with POTS-like functionality, reliability, and voice quality.

VPN (Virtual Private Network)   Use of encryption and tunneling protocols to create a private data network over the public Internet.

W

WFQ (weighted fair queuing)   Congestion management algorithm that identifies conversations (in the form of traffic streams), separates packets that belong to each conversation, and ensures that capacity is shared fairly between these individual conversations. WFQ is an automatic way of stabilizing network behavior during congestion and results in increased performance and reduced retransmission.

Index